THE SUICIDAL CHILD

THE
SUICIDAL
CHILD

CYNTHIA R. PFEFFER, MD

Cornell University Medical College and
The New York Hospital — Westchester Division

FOREWORD BY MELVIN LEWIS, MD

THE GUILFORD PRESS
New York   London

© 1986 The Guilford Press
A Division of Guilford Publications, Inc.
200 Park Avenue South, New York, N.Y. 10003

Printed in the United States of America

Second printing, September 1986

LIBRARY OF CONGRESS CATALOGING IN PUBLICATION DATA

Pfeffer, Cynthia R.
   The suicidal child.

   Bibliography: p.
   Includes indexes.
   1. Youth—United States—Suicidal behavior.
2. Children—United States—Suicidal behavior.
3. Suicide—United States—Prevention.   I. Title.
[DNLM: 1. Suicide—in infancy & childhood.
HV 6546 P524s]
HV6546.P44   1986   618.92′858445071   85-31710
ISBN 0-89862-664-1

To My Family

ACKNOWLEDGMENTS

I am indebted most of all to my patients, whose misfortunes aroused my interest and guided me to understand them. Without their willingness to cooperate in my research, the knowledge that has accrued would not have been possible.

Numerous colleagues have been helpful to me in designing the research and in gathering the data. Robert Plutchik, PhD, Professor of Psychiatry at the Albert Einstein College of Medicine, and Joseph Richman, PhD, Clinical Associate Professor of Psychiatry at Albert Einstein College of Medicine, have been colleagues of mine for many years. They have joined me in efforts to understand suicidal children and in reviewing and constructively commenting on the manuscript. In addition to their assistance with this book, I am very appreciative to H. Robert Blank, MD, Clinical Associate Professor of Psychiatry at Cornell University Medical College, for his valuable comments on this text.

Gratitude in helping to conduct this research is extended to other colleagues, granting agencies, and the hospitals in which I have worked. I wish to thank Hope Conte, PhD, for her help in the beginning phases of this project; Mark S. Mizruchi, PhD, for his work in data analysis; Susan Zuckerman, PhD, Robert Lipkins, MA, and Marsha Mintz for their research assistance in interviewing patients and coordinating aspects of this project; Robert Michels, MD, Chairman of the Department of Psychiatry at Cornell University Medical College, and Otto Kernberg, MD, Medical Director of The New York Hospital—Westchester Division, for their administrative support; Paulina Kernberg, MD, who has been the Division Chief of Child and Adolescent Psychiatry at The New York Hospital—Westchester Division and the Albert Einstein College of Medicine; Ms. Emily Marallo and Ms. Sue Murphy for help in data tabulation; and Ms. Fran Magrino, Ms. Adrienne Ferretti, and Mr. James Duffy for their essential assistance in coordinating the typing of the manuscript. I am extremely appreciative for the funding received from The New York Hospital—Westchester Division Research Committee, the Herman Goldman Foundation, the National Institute of Mental Health Small Grant Division, and the Gralnick Foundation. Finally, I wish to thank collectively the other psychiatrists, neurologists, pediatricians, psychologists, social workers, nurses, child psychiatry fellows, and school administrators for participating in phases of this research.

Appreciation is expressed for permission to reprint excerpts from the following previously published material:

The Dollmaker by Harriette Arnow. Copyright 1954 by Harriette Simpson Arnow. Published in 1954 by Avon Books, Macmillan Publishing Company.

"The Concept of Developmental Lines" by Anna Freud. Published in *The Psychoanalytic Study of the Child*. Reprinted by permission of International Universities Press.

The Ego and the Mechanisms of Defense by Anna Freud. Reprinted by permission of International Universities Press.

Collected Papers, Vol. II, by Sigmund Freud. Authorized translation under the supervision of Joan Riviere. Published by Basic Books, Inc., by arrangement with The Hogarth Press, Ltd., and The Institute of Psycho-Analysis, London. Reprinted by permission.

The Standard Edition of the Complete Psychological Works of Sigmund Freud by Sigmund Freud. Translated and edited by James Strachey. Reprinted by permission of Sigmund Freud Copyrights, Ltd., The Institute of Psycho-Analysis, and The Hogarth Press.

The Counterfeiters by André Gide. Translated by Dorothy Bussy. Copyright 1927, 1951, 1955 (renewed) by Alfred A. Knopf, Inc. Vintage Books edition published in 1973 by Random House, Inc.

"The Poor Boy in the Grave" by The Brothers Grimm. Copyright 1952 by W. H. Auden. Published in *Tales of Grimm and Andersen* in 1952 by the Modern Library—Random House, Inc.

Jude the Obscure by Thomas Hardy. Copyright 1961 by The American Library of World Literature, Inc. Published in 1961 by New American Library.

"Some Thoughts about the Role of Verbalization in Early Childhood" by A. Katan. Published in *The Psychoanalytic Study of the Child*. Reprinted by permission of International Universities Press.

"Baa, Baa, Black Sheep" by Rudyard Kipling. Published in *Wee Willie Winkie: City of Dreadful Night: American Notes*.

Vivienne: The Life and Suicide of an Adolescent Girl by John E. Mack and Holly Hickler. Published in 1981 by Little, Brown and Company.

"From A Very Little Sphinx" by Edna St. Vincent Millay. Copyright 1929, 1956 by Edna St. Vincent Millay and Norma Millay Ellis. Published in *Collected Poems* in 1956 by Harper & Row.

Voices of Death by Edwin S. Shneidman. Copyright 1980 by Edwin S. Shneidman. Published in 1980 by Harper & Row and in 1982 by Bantam Books, Inc.

The Adventures of Tom Sawyer by Mark Twain. Published in 1980 by New American Library.

FOREWORD

Suicide among the young (15- to 24-year-olds) is now the third most common form of death, following accidents and homicides. More than 5000 adolescents and young adults die every year from suicide, giving a mortality rate for suicide in this age group of 12.3 per 100,000, and accounting for 18.8% of all deaths in this age group. Depression, failure of emotional support from the family, despair, and hopelessness are powerful factors influencing the dramatic rise in adolescent suicide in the past decade. Predictions have been made that by the year 2000 there will be a 94% increase in suicide rates in the 15- to 19-year-old age group, notwithstanding the very recent trend toward a slightly lower rate for all ages. Suicidal attempts and suicidal behavior, it must be remembered, are even more common than completed suicide.

What do we know about suicidal behavior in children and adolescents? What are the causes? How can the children be treated? How can suicide be prevented? Cynthia Pfeffer addresses these questions and more in a straightforward and thorough way, drawing on the available research (to which she herself has contributed) and her rich clinical experience.

This book is, in fact, an informative gold mine about suicide in children and adolescents. Cynthia Pfeffer provides us with a synthesis of clinical experience and knowledge to give us a large, well-documented picture of the phenomenon of suicide in the young. The causes of suicide and attempted suicide are examined closely, and all the risk factors are carefully described. Dr. Pfeffer explores the contributions from psychoanalysis, including psychoanalytic theories of depression, as well as more recent findings from research in child psychiatry. She outlines for us some of the current methods used in research, including the use of structured interviews. Most refreshingly and importantly, Dr. Pfeffer throughout brings us back to clinical examples. In fact, a pleasing and distinguishing feature of this book is the richness of its case illustrations. The families of depressed and suicidal children too are not neglected. On the contrary, they are described in compelling and dynamic detail.

In addition, Dr. Pfeffer brings to bear a developmental perspective that enables her to take a fresh look at suicide and attempted suicide in the preadolescent (ages 6–12 years) child. This age group is an important one to study, and has hitherto received less attention than the adolescent age group. Dr. Pfeffer's emphasis on this group is therefore an especially useful contribution.

Dr. Pfeffer has succeeded in maintaining a balance between psychoanalysis as a foundation for her understanding of the children and their families and current research data, including epidemiologic findings. She is willing to explore in depth the child's experience of being depressed and suicidal, and does so with great sensitivity.

Readers will appreciate the many levels of this book. There is something in it for everyone: Researcher and clinician alike will find much useful and practical information that will help them understand, treat, and, we hope, prevent this tragic phenomenon of suicide and attempted suicide in children and adolescents.

Melvin Lewis, MD

PREFACE

I know a hundred ways to die.
I've often thought I'd try one:
Lie down beneath a motor truck
Some day when standing by one.

Or throw myself from off a bridge—
Except such things must be
So hard upon the scavengers
And men that clean the sea.

I know some poison I would drink.
I've often thought I'd taste it.
But mother bought it for the sink,
And drinking it would waste it.

—Edna St. Vincent Millay, "From A Very Little Sphinx"

Until recently, suicidal behavior among children and adolescents was not considered a problem of great concern. However, recent newspaper reports about youth suicide have made the general public aware of and alarmed about the occurrence of suicide in children and adolescents. For example, on February 16, 1984 *The New York Times* reported:

> **Boy, 14, Is Found Hanged on Tree**—A 14-year-old boy was found dead, an apparent suicide by hanging from a tree a few miles from where another boy hanged himself 10 days earlier, the police said today.

Another *New York Times* article, on November 20, 1984, noted:

> **Boy, 8, Found Hanged After Theft Accusation**—An eight-year-old boy, said to be depressed over accusations that he stole four dollars at school, was on a hospital life support system today after being found hanging by his belt from his bunk bed, police officials said.

On March 8, 1985 *The New York Times* reported:

> Psychiatrists and counselors from a suicide–prevention group met privately with 350 students at a vocational high school today after a student shot himself in the head in a class. The 17-year-old student was in critical condition.

Reports such as these have sensitized the public to ask questions about how to recognize, treat, and prevent suicidal behavior in youngsters. However, there is still a great deal of disbelief that suicidal behavior in children under 12 years of age actually occurs.

I, too, was not aware of the significance of the problem of suicidal behavior in young people until I became the director of a child psychiatry emergency service in a large New York municipal hospital. I was surprised by the large number of preadolescent suicidal patients that I evaluated. These children enacted dangerous, life-threatening behaviors. Among the outstanding cases was a 9-year-old girl who believed that she had something bad in her stomach that was telling her to hurt other people. Frightened by this, she tried to stab herself in the stomach in her attempt to kill the bad thing inside of her. I remember a 9-year-old boy who jumped out a sixth-floor window because he wanted to die. He landed in bushes, and as a result, he miraculously escaped death. However, he sustained several fractured vertebrae and broke his legs.

Wishing to learn more about the phenomenon of preadolescent suicidal behavior, I searched the child and adolescent psychiatric literature to find answers to my many questions. However, there appeared to be a paucity of information, and some of the concepts described in the literature did not agree with my own clinical impressions. Therefore, I decided to explore suicidal behavior in preadolescents by means of systematic research.

This book is derived, in large measure, from the information obtained in my research as well as from the clinical and research work of others. It focuses primarily on preadolescent suicidal behavior and provides a comprehensive overview of current knowledge about suicidal behavior in this age group. In addition to the research findings, numerous clinical illustrations are provided throughout the book in order to acquaint clinicians with how these children appear. (In the interest of protecting the privacy of the patients, all names and identifying details have been altered.)

The first section of the book contains four chapters. The early scientific literature about childhood suicidal behavior is reviewed in Chapter 1. In Chapter 2, a definition of suicidal behavior in children is offered, and difficulties in arriving at this definition are discussed. In addition, a classification of suicidal behavior in children is delineated. The incidence of completed suicide, the prevalence of nonfatal suicidal behavior in the young, and research on factors affecting the changing suicide rates in children and adolescents are reviewed in Chapter 3. Chapter 4 encompasses detailed clinical descriptions of and hypotheses about the development of suicidal episodes in children.

The second section discusses key factors that enhance risk of childhood suicidal behavior. Two chapters focus on the affects associated with suicidal behavior and extensively discuss characteristics of childhood depression. Another chapter discusses the development of normal children's concepts of death and compares these to the unique death concepts found in suicidal children. Two chapters are devoted to family characteristics and psychodynamics of suicidal children and suicidal parents. Finally, characteristics of ego mechanisms are discussed in relation to risk for suicidal behavior in children. A hypothesis about the process of change in ego functioning leading to suicidal behavior is offered. Whenever pertinent, comparisons of these issues are made for children, adolescents, and adults.

The third section of the book is devoted to techniques useful for evaluating suicidal risk in children. Clinical interview methods, the unique characteristics of play of suicidal children, and the special value of play observation in diagnosing childhood suicidal behavior are described. The Appendix of the book includes the Child Suicide Potential Scales, which were developed for my research and used for clinical work in evaluating suicidal risk in preadolescents.

The fourth section of the book discusses therapeutic interventions. This section begins with an overview of how to plan treatment and when to decide upon psychiatric outpatient or inpatient treatment. Chapter 14 is devoted to individual outpatient psychotherapy, and Chapter 15 includes psychiatric hospital treatment. Adjunctive treatments such as family intervention and use of medication are described in the last chapter.

The epilogue of the book summarizes some general concepts about childhood suicidal behavior as they have been extensively detailed in earlier sections of the book and ends on an optimistic note. It points out that we have learned a great deal about the phenomenon; that we have had considerable success in treating childhood suicidal behavior and some success in preventing it. It stresses the importance of a network of supportive and concerned people who provide emotional maintenance and foster the emotional growth of the child. Finally, it points out that this book has defined and characterized suicidal behavior within the developmental period of preadolescence and that more is to be learned about this phenomenon and its relation to suicidal behavior of individuals in other stages of the life cycle.

CONTENTS

CLINICAL DESCRIPTIONS AND EPIDEMIOLOGY OF CHILDHOOD SUICIDAL BEHAVIOR

CHAPTER ONE

A HISTORICAL OVERVIEW OF SUICIDAL BEHAVIOR IN CHILDREN

> But he suddenly recognized the pistol: Boris had just raised it to his temple. La Perouse understood and immediately turned icy cold as if the blood were freezing in his veins. He tried to rise and run towards Boris—stop him—call to him. . . . A kind of hoarse rattle came from his throat; he remained rooted to the spot, paralytic, shaken by a violent trembling.
> —André Gide, *The Counterfeiters*

Suicidal tendencies in children and adolescents were described by authors, poets, and composers long before descriptions appeared in psychiatric and medical journals. Shakespeare's Romeo and Juliet, Goethe's Young Werther, Thomas Hardy's Jude the Obscure, Salinger's Teddy, and Kipling's Punch are but a few fictional characters who exhibited suicidal tendencies. However, clinicians have only minimally made use of these descriptions to understand suicidal motives in their patients.

An exception was Editha Sterba, who utilized psychoanalytic theory in her revealing analysis (1951) of a schoolboy's suicide described in André Gide's novel *The Counterfeiters*. Boris, the 13-year-old boy, was the son of a Russian piano virtuoso mother and a French father who died when Boris was quite young. Boris, while living with his mother, developed a severe mental disturbance that was treated by a Polish female physician. Her treatment consisted of letting him talk, the equivalent to modern psychoanalysis. Sterba described the complications of Boris's life, his loneliness, his intense guilt over masturbation wishes, his poignant and uniquely meaningful relationship to a girlfriend, and his misery about being sent to boarding school. Sterba defined the essential motives of Boris's suicide as his intense guilt over masturbation, the recurrence of magical beliefs that he had killed his father, his need for self-punishment, and his unconscious death wishes against himself. When he learned of the death of his girlfriend, Boris was thrown into intense despair that was magnified by his inability to make friends at school. He was eventually befriended by a group of schoolmates who developed a plot to torment him. However, Boris was so in need of gaining their esteem that he was willing unquestioningly to participate in their plan, which eventually resulted in his suicide.

This example is relevant to understanding contemporary suicidal children and adolescents. The complexities of intrapsychic functioning and social pressures defined in this fictional account encompass some of the themes observed in suicidal children.

The following is a clinical example that highlights these issues.

Child I: Donald was 12 years old when he was admitted to a child psychiatry inpatient unit after he overdosed on a large number of his mother's tranquilizers. On many occasions, Donald expressed the desire to die. His mother was very worried because whenever Donald was angry he threatened to throw himself out a window. Three months before hospitalization, Donald overdosed . on a few tranquilizers that he obtained from the family medicine cabinet. His mother discovered this a day later, but she did not seek psychiatric evaluation for her son.

Donald acknowledged that he took the overdoses because he felt sad and angry about being teased by children at school. Donald had not had lasting friendships. Instead, he was often ridiculed by other children at school. Donald stated, "I am very lonely. Why don't the others like me?" He acknowledged becoming involved in fights in which he was beaten up by his peers. Often he felt despondent and wished that he "would be accepted by friends."

Like Boris, Donald's difficulties were reflected in conflicts with peers. He felt that he was an outcast and disliked. Intense stress from peer problems and hopelessness provoked this child's suicidal behavior. His distress was heeded by his family only after he made a second suicide attempt.

EARLY PSYCHIATRIC REPORTS OF SUICIDAL CHILDREN

The history of the scientific study of suicidal children begins in the 19th century when the first psychiatric descriptions of suicidal children appeared in French and German journals. In 1885 Durand-Fardel published 21 case histories of children under 14 years of age who committed suicide; Morselli, in 1881, reported on the suicides of children in Austria, Denmark, England, France, Germany, Italy, and Sweden; Emminghaus, in 1887, reported on completed suicides in children. Persier (1899), Siegert (1893), and Baer (1901) discussed childhood suicide in papers published near the end of the 19th century. Some of the conclusions of these studies were that the incidence of suicide increased with age and that completed suicides were more common in towns and cities than in rural environments.

PSYCHOANALYTIC FORMULATIONS OF
SUICIDAL BEHAVIOR IN CHILDREN

Most of the early theoretical analyses of childhood suicidal behavior were presented by psychoanalysts. Therefore, many hypotheses about childhood suicidal impulses have been formulated on the basis of psychoanalytic theory.

In 1910 the Vienna Psychoanalytic Society devoted a scientific meeting to discussion of Dr. Baer's publication *Suicide in Childhood*. Among the psychoanalysts attending the meeting were Drs. Adler, Federn, Freud, Rank, Steckel, Tausk, and Wittels. Dr. Oppenheim (1910), the main speaker, emphasized that suicide in children represented a highly abnormal condition with a particular kind of causation that is unique to this age group. He based his ideas on the statistical facts that completed suicide rates for young children are low, that they increase only after age 15 years, and that increases over time of suicide rates among children are not as rapid as the increase of suicide rates in adults. Oppenheim noted, however, that from the statistical data no inferences could be made about children's motives for suicide. He outlined several key issues relevant to suicidal motives of children: the death of family members, the child's conflicts with family members, the impact of suggestion stimulated by the suicide of an emotionally important person, and stories of suicide appearing in the press. Other influences were the role of school and its disciplinary system, methods of teaching, and school examinations.

Dr. Sadger, who was attending the meeting, remarked that the role of sexuality or hope for love should not be overlooked. He noted that a precipitating factor for suicide in almost all cases seemed to be a lack of love. Sigmund Freud agreed that from an analysis of customary statistics no judgment could be made about suicidal motives. Freud indicated that careful study of individual cases of children who attempt suicide would provide insights about the dynamics of childhood suicide. Freud believed that the most significant influence on suicide was conflict with loved persons. He also noted that incest may be a precipitating factor.

This discussion raised questions that are remarkably similar to many of the issues about childhood suicidal behavior currently being debated. However, in more recent times there are more empirically and systematically derived data from which to draw conclusions. For example, the following children depict clinical features associated with modern-day suicidal behavior. These examples represent children who are stressed by family disruption, parental abuse, and academic failure.

Child II: Martin was 11 years old when he was psychiatrically hospitalized after he ingested six Valium stolen from his mother. He had become increasingly

unhappy, showed a marked decline in school performance, and was less obe-
dient with his parents. These changes became evident after his parents divorced.

He regretted the loss of his father and vented hostilities toward his mother.
His suicide attempt occurred 6 months after the divorce, at a time that his
mother, feeling she could not manage Martin, requested that Martin go to live
with his father.

Initially, Martin seemed to enjoy his new school and life with his father.
However, Martin missed his old friends and became severely depressed. The
day before the suicide attempt, Martin told his father that he was not worthy
of his father, saying "Why don't you turn away from me?" The following day
Martin ingested the Valium.

The family disruption caused by the parental discord, and breakup
of the home, increased Martin's unhappiness. He devalued himself and
was overcome by strong hostile feelings directed primarily toward his
mother. His suicide attempt alerted his family to seek immediate intervention.

Child III: Leonard was 9 years old when he was admitted to a child psychiatry
inpatient unit after he jumped out of a second-floor window at a residential
treatment center. He had been placed in the residential treatment center 2
months before his suicide attempt. He had a long history of unmanageable
behavior problems that included assaultive behavior, running away, stealing,
truancy, and school failure. Outpatient therapy was unsuccessful in diminishing
these problems, which began when he was 6 years old and at the time his father
abandoned the family.

Two years before his hospitalization, his mother's boyfriend moved in with
the family. However, Leonard argued repeatedly with him. Arguments escalated to such an extent that the man severely beat Leonard. Eventually, Leonard's school guidance counselor notified the Bureau of Child Welfare, after
Leonard arrived one day with bruises on his face, arms, and back. He had been
beaten by his mother's boyfriend. Leonard was removed from his home and
placed in a residential treatment center.

Leonard was unable to adjust to his new environment. He attempted to
run away on several occasions. His mother noted that this was one of Leonard's
main problems, saying: "Whenever he cannot endure something, he will sim-
ply run away. Usually, he runs away when he gets into trouble with authority
or with me. Following rules does not seem to make sense to him. He thinks
everything is stupid."

Leonard's mother noticed that he was "withdrawn and depressed since
he entered the residential center. He phones me saying he is going crazy. He
told me that he does not belong. He wishes he were not born and wants to
die. He told me he often thinks about killing himself and will do it unless he

is returned home. He told me that he is not afraid to die. This all scares me and I worry about whether he is being helped at the residential center."

Leonard's suicide attempt occurred after he had a fight with two boys at the center. He was sent to his room to calm down. However, he was so enraged, unhappy, and confused that he decided to kill himself by jumping out the second-floor window.

Intrapsychic and environmental turmoil experienced by many children is dramatically represented by this example. The relation between depression and conduct problems in conjunction with family separations and violence is an important feature that characterizes many suicidal children.

Child IV: Sarah, a 7-year-old child with learning disabilities, was admitted to a child psychiatry day treatment program after she expressed repeated ideas of wishing to kill herself. She said that she wanted to drown herself, take pills, or strangle herself. Three months before, she was evaluated at school because she appeared to have difficulty concentrating in class and was unable to read or to do math. She was a shy child who was liked by many children.

Her parents noted that since Sarah started the second grade, she more easily cried, had trouble falling asleep, and complained of nightmares. She reported a repetitive dream of a woman on a horse coming to take her away. She told her mother: "Sometimes at school I hear a voice calling me and telling me to run away. It scares me because I think that I will be killed. I wish I did not have to go to school."

Sarah was admitted to the child psychiatry day treatment program so that her depression and learning problems could be managed. This treatment plan was possible because her family was cooperative and able to care for her at home.

This example depicts the special problems encountered by some learning-disabled children when they feel excessively stressed by the demands of school. This shy, compliant child felt sad, hopeless, and bad about not being able to keep up in school. She wanted to withdraw and wished she did not have to stay in class, but did not want to disobey her parents or teachers. The stress overwhelmed her and a severe depression became evident. A psychiatric day program provided the appropriate interventions to stabilize this child's compromised state.

Another historical dimension of childhood suicide was highlighted by Zilboorg (1936, 1937), a psychoanalyst, who proposed a cultural–ethnological model. Zilboorg hypothesized that those people at highest risk for suicidal behavior are the ones who unconsciously identify with a dead person. Such individuals are impelled to join the dead person. Zilboorg believed that it was not the actual loss of the dead person that created the suicidal impulse; it was the fantasies about the sequellae of the loss that increased suicidal risk.

Zilboorg pointed out that the act of mourning represents a ritualized and sublimated form of identifying with a dead person. The actively suicidal person cannot sublimate this need to identify with the dead; instead the person acts out a primitive pattern of mourning. The following example illustrates the complexity of these dynamics in a young child.

Child V: Andrea was a 6-year-old child whose suicidal behavior was motivated by her wishes to join her dead father in heaven. Andrea was hospitalized in a child psychiatry inpatient unit after she ran into the street in front of a moving truck. This behavior followed an increasing series of accidents in which she sustained minor burns. Andrea admitted that she ran into the street so that she would be hit by a car. She wanted to die because, she said, "I miss my Daddy."

Andrea's father died when she was 4 years old. His death was caused by a car accident. Andrea's mother had been severely depressed since her husband's death and at times found it difficult to care for Andrea. Her mother had frequent suicidal wishes and bouts of crying spells. Often she would become angry at Andrea's demands and severely discipline her daughter. In the weeks before Andrea was hospitalized her mother had become particularly depressed. She consulted a psychiatrist, who began treating her with psychotherapy and antidepressants. However, Andrea's behavior worsened and eventually she attempted to kill herself.

This example illustrates the complex relationships between parental death, parental depression and suicidal ideation, and childhood suicidal behavior. Andrea's mother was prone to severe depression and had not adjusted to her husband's death. Andrea seemed to be responding to her mother's deteriorating psychological state and acted out suicidal impulses also expressed by her mother. The suicidal method of being hit by a car was a dramatization of the cause of her father's death. Andrea missed him and wanted to be with him.

In 1937 Bender and Schilder studied suicidal preoccupations and attempts in children. They presented brief clinical vignettes of children who attempted suicide and were hospitalized in the psychiatric units of Bellevue Hospital in New York City. The children ranged in age from 7 to 15 years. Bender and Schilder reported that in a 2½-year time period there were 2000 admissions to the children's service of the Bellevue Psychiatric Hospital but that only 18 suicidal children were under 13 years of age. These children had a conscious motive to escape from an intolerable situation. Bender and Schilder formulated the idea that suicidal behavior was a result of a child's wish to escape from an unbearable situation that involved a deprivation of love. Deprivation fostered aggressive reactions that were primarily directed against those who denied love. Resulting guilt feelings caused the aggressive impulses to be turned back upon the self. This formulation is still considered to be one of the classic dynamics for childhood as well as adult suicide.

The following child illustrates the dynamic of escape from intolerable circumstances.

Child VI: Andrew was 10 years old when he was psychiatrically hospitalized after he threatened to jump out the third-floor window of his apartment. This suicidal threat occurred during a fight with his mother when she reprimanded him for not going to school. Andrew wanted to die because he had "too many problems."

For the past 4 years, Andrew had experienced many stresses. Initially, he started having problems when he entered the first grade. He had problems learning and refused to go to school, fought with other students, and destroyed school property. He responded to feelings of isolation with episodes of crying, instability, and headaches. He did not want to go to school and cried frequently, requesting that he not be sent there. Because of these problems he was admitted to a special education class.

Another stress resulted when Andrew was 8 years old and his father abandoned the family. Andrew missed his father and often wandered in the neighborhood in search of his dad. He recalled intense arguments between his parents, and he blamed himself for driving his father away. Andrew was enraged when his mother limited his excursions in the neighborhood.

When Andrew was 9 years old, his mother developed a relationship with another man. Andrew resented this and provoked arguments with his mother. Her attempts to discipline Andrew caused him to run away from home. Eventually, when Andrew was almost 10 years old, his mother's boyfriend attempted to control Andrew's behavior and began to physically abuse Andrew. Andrew's thoughts about his father intensified. He stayed away from the home for many hours in an effort to locate his father. He spoke about wanting to commit suicide. The suicidal threat resulted from the culmination of his intolerable family and school situation.

This child illustrates the extreme degree of stresses that are endured by children, often over a long time period. Although Andrew exhibited clear signs of emotional difficulties for a long time, his family did not seek psychiatric treatment for him. Thus, the stresses continued until his behavior became extreme.

For many years after Bender and Schilder's report, little was specifically reported about suicidal behavior in children. However, in the middle 1960s there was an increase in the number of psychiatric reports about suicidal behavior in children. These reports seemed to parallel the increase in suicide rates in younger age groups. Clinicians systematically began to investigate the descriptive, etiological, and outcome variables related to suicidal behavior in young children. These studies and findings are discussed in subsequent chapters of this book.

CHAPTER TWO

DEFINITION AND CLASSIFICATION OF SUICIDAL BEHAVIOR IN CHILDREN

> He became aware of the misfortune too late; there was no repairing it. "Ah," cried he, "now all is over with me! The wicked man did not threaten me for nothing; if he comes back and sees what I have done, he will kill me. Rather than that I will take my own life." —The Brothers Grimm, "The Poor Boy in the Grave"

Many clinicians have questioned whether children can be suicidal. These doubts have arisen primarily because many clinicians cannot comprehend the fact that young children have conscious intentions to kill themselves and that children understand concepts of death sufficiently to want to take their own lives. Yet, clinical evidence shows that preadolescents exhibit a variety of dramatic life-threatening behaviors that have clear self-harm intentions. The following brief vignettes illustrate this.

Child I: Louis was attending a child psychiatric day hospital program, when at the age of 9 years he appeared depressed, told the staff he wanted to die, and had an increasing series of serious accidents. Louis was in the day treatment program because of unmanageability at school and academic failure. His mother did not appreciate the seriousness of her son's sadness and suicidal ideas. Because she left him home alone and he had more accidents and intense preoccupation with dying, psychiatric hospitalization was recommended.

Child II: Patrick was 12 years old when he was referred for outpatient psychiatric evaluation. He had become excessively withdrawn, could not concentrate on school work, and thought about killing himself. These symptoms developed shortly after his parents told him that they were planning to be divorced. Patrick was depressed about this and felt hopeless about his future. He wanted to kill himself so that he would not have to experience the breakup of his family.

Child III: Arlene was psychiatrically hospitalized when she was 11 years old, after she attempted to cut her wrists with a knife on two occasions. The first episode occurred in the morning when she awoke feeling angry and frustrated at herself. She scratched her right wrist with a kitchen knife. Her parents took her to a hospital emergency room where she was thought not to be suicidal and sent home. The day before her hospital admission, she again cut herself on the left wrist on the spur of the moment because she thought her mother was angry at her. Arlene wanted to die because she thought that no one loved her. She thought she was bad and deserved to die.

Arlene claimed to be unhappy most of her life, "ever since I can remember." Her sadness became more noticeable 3 months before her hospitalization. Arlene worried about many things and she wanted the house to be perfectly ordered and neat. She displayed hand-washing rituals and arranged her books and school supplies in special order. She constantly competed for her mother's attention and affection, and bitterly complained that it was not enough. Arlene complained that no one cared about her. She viewed herself as demanding, easily irritated, and a bad girl who was difficult to live with. She saw no reason at all for being loved by her parents and she wanted to die.

Child IV: Walter was psychiatrically hospitalized when he was 8 years old and climbed on the roof of his house with the intent to kill himself by jumping off the roof. Walter had frequent intense arguments with his father, who severely disciplined him. On many occasions Walter was hit with a belt and locked in his room. His suicidal threat on the roof occurred after his father disciplined him. Walter ran to the roof thinking only of killing himself. However, he did not jump only because his mother pleaded with him and told him how much she loved him and that she would see to it that his father did not discipline him in the same way again. Psychiatric hospitalization was indicated to evaluate the child's suicidal propensities and the family interactions.

Although these examples are illustrative of childhood suicidal behavior, there are a number of problems in defining suicidal behavior in children. One problem concerns the many types of self-destructive behaviors that occur and whether they should be considered suicidal. For example, statistical data about suicide in young children do not exist. Although recent studies confirm the fact that children as young as 5 years have expressed suicidal tendencies, the National Center for Health Statistics tends not to classify completed suicide as a cause of death in children under 10 years of age. The rationale for this is the assumption that one cannot classify children as suicidal because, based on developmental theory, it is proposed that children do not understand the finality of death until approximately 10 years of age (Fredrick, 1978). Thus, it may be that many deaths that could be considered suicidal may be classified in other categories. For example, it is clear that accidents are a common cause of death in children and it may be that many deaths classified as accidental may have been suicides. Furthermore, to make appropriate judgments about whether self-destructive behaviors such as hair pulling, head banging, self-mutilation of body parts, anorexia, self-biting, wrist cutting, jumping from heights, and ingestion of toxic substances are suicidal, it is necessary to clarify the underlying cause of the behavior, the meanings the child ascribes to the behavior, and the resultant degree of damage caused by the behavior.

There is a wide variety of etiologies of self-destructive behaviors that include developmental, metabolic, and psychological factors. For example, many self-injurious behaviors have a developmental etiology and therefore should not be considered suicidal. Shintoub and Soulairac (1961) observed that about 15% of all normal toddlers, who are 9 to 18 months old, engage in some form of self-injurious behavior. In addition, they observed that the percentages of self-injurious behaviors usually decrease with age and disappear by 5 years of age. However, these observations do not preclude the fact that some children under 5 years of age may demonstrate behavior that can be considered suicidal. For example, newly acquired data provided by Rosenthal and Rosenthal (1984) have demonstrated that children as young as 2½ or 3 years old exhibit suicidal tendencies. Such young children talk about wanting to kill themselves and have attempted to jump from high places, ingest poisons, and hang themselves. These data support the conclusion that suicidal behavior can be expressed at any age or developmental level.

Genetic and metabolic factors may be important in the etiology of self-injurious behaviors. Picker, Poling, and Parker (1979) gave the examples of the Cornelia De Lang and Lesch–Nyhan syndromes to illustrate these genetic and metabolic etiologies. Self-mutilation observed in the Cornelia De Lange syndrome, a rare disorder that includes impaired mental and motor development, consists of repeated eye picking, hitting the face with one's fist, or self-biting. In the Lesch–Nyhan syndrome, which is due to an inherited deficiency in the enzyme hypoxanthine guanine ribosyltransferase, the self-mutilation includes severe lip biting and other forms of severe self-biting. Additional features of this syndrome include mental retardation, chorioathetosis, and hyperuricemia. These self-injurious behaviors should not be considered suicidal behaviors, especially since these children do not have a conscious intent to kill themselves.

Many other self-injurious behaviors result in serious injury or death, but they lack a clear psychological motive to kill, destroy, or anihilate oneself. For example, a child with anorexia nervosa may not wish to kill herself but may wish to alter her body image and self-concept. It can be concluded from this that when attempting to define a self-destructive behavior as suicidal, it is essential to evaluate the meaning that the child ascribes to the behavior, the child's intent to kill himself or herself, or the child's wish to die. This intent or wish to die is a basic component in defining suicidal behavior in children.

Shneidman (1975) offered a definition of suicidal behavior in adults that can also be applied to children. He defined suicide as "the human act of self inflicted, self intended cessation," and added that this act includes a "multitude of conscious and unconscious motivational states" (p. 1774). He noted that a person may have "chronic, pervasive, habitual, characterological orientations towards suicide as an integral part of his total psychological makeup, affecting his philosophy of life, need systems, aspirations, identification, and unconscious beliefs. Every person is capable of having acute, relatively short lived exacerbated, clinically sudden shifts of cessation orientation" (p. 1778).

Not feeling that this definition adequately conveyed the essence of suicide, Shneidman (1985) updated his concepts and proposed the following definition: "Currently in the Western world, suicide is a conscious act of self-induced annihilation, best understood as a multidimensional malaise in a needful individual who defines an issue for which the suicide is perceived as the best solution" (p. 203). This definition emphasizes the contextual, psychological, and intense needful state of the individual who effects a solution to his or her intolerably painful state by stopping consciousness.

Although such a definition has applicability to children, some people believe that one cannot say a child is suicidal unless the child appreciates the finality of death. Recent systematic studies by Pfeffer, Conte, Plutchik, and Jerrett (1979) and by Orbach and Glaubman (1978), however, have challenged this belief. Their studies revealed that very young children exhibit suicidal behaviors. These children have distinct ideas about death, but they do not always believe that death is final. In other words, if a child thinks of jumping out the window because he or she wishes to die, it is the goal of achieving death the defines this child as suicidal. Death has a specific meaning to the child, and this meaning is associated with a solution to the child's perception of overwhelming distress. Therefore, it does not matter what the child realistically understands about death. It is not the child's knowledge about the finality of death that is important in defining childhood suicidal behavior but rather, it is essential that the child have some type of concept of death.

It can be concluded that the definition of suicidal behavior for children is similar to that for adults. A modification in the definition should incorporate the idea that it is not necessary for a child to have an understanding of the finality of death but it *is* necessary to have a concept of death, regardless of how idiosyncratic it may be. Therefore, suicidal behavior in children can be defined as any self-destructive behavior that has an intent to seriously damage oneself or cause death.

CLINICAL PROBLEMS IN DIAGNOSING
CHILDHOOD SUICIDAL BEHAVIOR

Besides the theoretical issues of whether children can be considered suicidal, there are a number of problems that make it difficult to diagnose a child's condition as suicidal. One clinical problem that arises is that it is frequently difficult to elicit directly from the child the intentions to kill himself or herself. This difficulty is caused by the child's anxiety, denial, secrecy, or inability to verbalize sufficiently these feelings and ideas. Therefore, when evaluating a child for suicidal behavior, it is preferable to focus on the observed behavior and subsequently attempt to determine the child's intention of causing death. Furthermore, because self-destructive behavior has such a potentially grave outcome, it is preferable to consider any self-destructive behavior as suicidal until there is proof to the contrary.

Information that may help determine a child's suicidal intention can be obtained from interviews with the child and with people who know the child. However, often it is impossible to obtain historical information from family members because the family may keep secret the fact that a child had intentions to kill himself or herself. This secrecy arises from parents' guilt over their role in the child's behavior or because of a fear of social stigma associated with suicidal behavior. Many parents minimize the purposeful life-threatening goals of their children. Some parents say that a child's injuries were accidental. One example is a family whose 11-year-old son committed suicide by hanging. The child was found hanging from a chinning bar in his bedroom. The family notified all the relatives about the death but said that the child had died in a sporting accident. This distortion of reality is one example of survivors' difficulties in coping with suicidal behaviors, especially of young children.

Another factor that has hampered the understanding and development of a definition of suicidal behavior in children has been the frequent lack of clinicians' detailed descriptions of suicidal thoughts and actions in children. Often clinicians do not search out and acquire a full picture of the suicidal tendencies of their child patients. The anxiety generated by discovering that a child may harm himself or herself frequently sets up conscious and unconscious defenses in the clinician, who may then minimize the suicidal tendencies in the child. In fact, many clinicians do not ask all the questions necessary for a complete assessment of suicidal risk in their child patients. As a result, many suicidal children are not discovered during clinical assessment.

One example is provided by a psychiatrist who did not carefully and systematically evaluate his patient. Another clinician who interviewed the same child obtained a detailed account of the child's frequent thoughts of wanting to kill himself. Such information was obtained, not because of the difference in circumstances at the time of each psychiatric assessment, but because the second psychiatrist spent time in questioning the child about suicidal tendencies. The first psychiatrist did not have an appreciation of the seriousness of the child's self-destructive tendencies. The second psychiatrist was more sensitive in evaluating the child's feelings and wishes, his discontents, and his varied healthy and maladaptive methods of coping with stress.

All of these issues—the social, the personal, and the psychiatric—have made it difficult to define, diagnose, and describe suicidal tendencies in children. The next section focuses on one of the most difficult diagnostic problems, which is making the distinction between accidental and suicidal death in children.

ACCIDENTAL VERSUS SUICIDAL DEATH IN CHILDREN

It is often difficult to determine whether a child's death was an accident or a suicide. Social stigma, religious taboos, psychological stress, and economic sequellae of a suicidal death are but a few factors that influence whether there will be an acknowledgment of suicidal intent or tendency. A vivid example of lack of acknowledgment is a family whose 9-year-old boy stabbed himself when his parents were out of the house. His parents told others that the boy's death was an accident that occurred during his play activities. Another case is a wealthy family whose 10-year-old daughter killed herself by ingesting pills. The parents, very influential in the town, convinced the medical examiner to document the cause of death as an accidental aspiration caused by a bronchial illness. A third example is a very disturbed boy who jumped out of an apartment window and died. The family, for years, told everyone that he fell out the window because he was dizzy from medication. In many families, reality is distorted about suicidal deaths as a way of preserving dignity, relieving guilt, and diminishing memories of painful family interactions.

Often the circumstances surrounding the death make it seem as if the death was an accident, especially if the death occurred in isolation and away from witnesses. This issue was clearly depicted in a report by Eth, Pynoos, and Carlson (1984) of the self-inflicted death of a 10-year-old boy by gunshot. Although the police and coroner classified the death as an accidental one, the possibility of suicide was not directly addressed. The events became clarified only after another child, Jimmy, who witnessed the shooting, described the fatal circumstances to his mother. Sean, who shot himself, begged Jimmy to show him his father's gun. Jimmy emptied the gun of bullets before giving it to Sean. Jimmy left the room to go to the bathroom but upon his return, Sean reloaded the gun and placed it to his head. Sean pulled the trigger but the gun did not fire. Jimmy shouted "Stop," but Sean pulled the trigger again and the gun fired. Jimmy's account of these events suggested that the gunshot wound to the left temple of Sean's head was self-intended and premeditated. This report illustrates that young children can plan and carry out fatal self-inflicted injuries. It emphasizes that attention needs to be given to evaluating the possibility of suicidal motives in cases of seemingly accidental childhood fatalities.

S. Freud (1901) pointed out that many apparent accidental injuries that happen to such patients are really instances of self-intended injury: "What happens is that an impulse to self-punishment, which is constantly on the watch and which normally finds expression in self-reproach or contributes to the formation of a symptom, takes ingenious advantage of an external situation that chance happens to offer, or lends assistance to that situation until the desired injurious effect is brought about. Such occurrences are by no means uncommon in cases even of moderate severity, and they betray the part which the unconscious intention plays by a number of special features" (p. 179). Besides the theoretical issues of whether children can be considered suicidal, there are a number of problems that make it difficult to diagnose a child's condition as suicidal.

Freud (1901) described this phenomenon when he pointed out the complexity of defining suicidal behavior and of understanding a person's intentions to die. He stated that

> anyone who believes in the occurrence of half-intentional self-injury will be prepared also to assume that in addition to consciously intentional suicide there is such a thing as half-intentional self destruction (self destruction with an unconscious intention), capable of making skillful use of a threat to life and of disguising it as a chance mishap. There is no need to think such self destruction rare. For the trend to self destruction is present to a certain degree in very many more human beings than those in whom it is carried out; self injuries are as a rule a compromise between this instinct and the forces that are working against it, and even where suicide actually results, the inclination to suicide will have been present for a long time before in lesser strength or in the form of an unconscious and suppressed trend.
> . . . Even a conscious intention of committing suicide choses its time, means, and opportunity; and it is quite in keeping with this that an unconscious intention should wait for a precipitating occasion which can take over a part of a causation and, by engaging the subject's defensive forces, can liberate the intentions from their pressure. (pp. 180–181)

Thus, Freud's theory depicted the psychological and situational complexities involved in accidental suicidal behavior. There are, however, few empirical studies that investigate the differences between suicidal and accidental behavior, especially in children.

Tabachnick and associates (1966) demonstrated distinctions between accidental and suicidal deaths in adults. Thirty adult subjects in their study were chosen from the Los Angeles coroner's death list. For every accident victim, a suicide victim was matched for age. The suicidal deaths were restricted to self-inflicted gunshot wounds, and the accidental deaths were restricted to one-car automobile fatalities in which the driver was the victim. Interviews were conducted with people who knew the deceased. The distinguishing features between the accident and the suicide victims were that those who died by accident had encountered no clear traumatic situations prior to their deaths. Two-thirds of the accident victims had contemplated moving or had moved to situations of greater responsibility in the year before the accident. However, the people who died by suicide had encountered the loss of an important person, or had experienced feelings of failure or being unloved prior to their deaths. There have been no studies like this one in children to evaluate whether there are determinable characteristic differences between children who die by accident and those who die by suicide.

There have been a few studies, however, that evaluate other features of suicidal versus accidental deaths in children. Shaffer (1974) reviewed the coroner's reports of children under the age of 15 years who were certified as having died from the same causes as children who were reported to have committed suicide in the same year. The survey revealed that most verdicts of accidental death occurred in the infant and toddler age groups. Shaffer concluded that it was reasonable to assume that these were not suicidal deaths. Furthermore, there were very few accidental deaths in the 10- to 14-year age group. Since this study is the only study of completed suicide in children under the age of 15 years, replication studies are needed to validate these findings in different populations of children.

McIntire and Angle (1970), in another study, looked at the classification of self-poisoning in children. It was a 1-year cooperative study carried out at 50 poison control centers; 46 in the United States, 2 in Canada, 1 in Scotland, and 1 in New Zealand. It was the first attempt on an international basis to investigate the dynamics of self-poisoning in children. One of the most important findings occurred in the analysis of the Edinburgh population, where it was discovered that only 13% of the poisonings in children over 6 years old were due to accident. Self-destructive intent were evident in three-fourths of the children in the Edinburgh population. The study concluded that self-poisoning in children over 6 years of age is rarely accidental.

In 1968, in an attempt to improve the international statistical recording of the cause of death in children, a category called "undetermined death" was added to the classification of death. This category included any unnatural deaths that may have been either accidental or purposely inflicted but lacked the degree of clarity needed to make this diagnosis easily. In 1974 Shaffer (1974) reviewed the coroner's records in the United Kingdom of all children up to age 14 where this category appeared. He estimated that a number of such undetermined death verdicts were incorrectly diagnosed and that it seemed likely that most of the cases were suicidal. However, even if all of these cases were recategorized as suicidal deaths, he concluded that although the rate of suicide per 100,000 per year in children would increase, the phenomenon would still be a rare event.

THE RANGE OF SUICIDAL BEHAVIORS IN CHILDREN

Studies have pointed out that children can be diagnosed as being suicidal. Studies also suggest that suicidal behavior in children, as in adults, can be classified according to the degree of lethality. Lethality is a complex concept, especially with regard to children. It refers to the probability that the effects of an agent or action may cause death.

Shneidman (1975) defined lethality as the probability of a person killing himself or herself in the immediate future. Shneidman ranked a person's lethality into four levels: (1) high when the individual definitely wishes to die and anticipates that actions taken will result in death; (2) medium when the individual's ambivalence plays a partial, covert, or unconscious role to decrease the desire to die or impede the implementation of an action that will definitely cause death; (3) low when the individual plays some small but not insignificant role to prevent death; and (4) absent when intention to die does not exist. This definition of lethality is based upon the individual's desire to die and his or her manifest actions. The greater the likelihood that an action will cause death, the higher the rating of lethality. Ingestion of rat poison or cyanide pills, for example, would be rated as having a high degree of lethality. Ingestion of two aspirin pills would be rated as having a low degree of lethality. Similarly, a superficial cut on the wrist would have a low lethality rating, but a deep cut in the same location may have a high degree of lethality.

The concept of lethality involves the actual outcome of an action as well as the individual's understanding of the effect of the behavior. The assessment of lethality in children is often difficult to make based on these two factors. Therefore, in the clinical assessment of a suicidal child, it is important to determine if the rating of lethality is the same when rated by a suicidal child and when rated by an independent observer. For example, a suicidal child may believe that a jump off a high bridge would not cause death when, in fact, this action would be rated as highly lethal by an independent judge. Similarly, ingestion of a few aspirin pills may be considered by the child to be able to cause death, but this action would not be considered lethal when judged by an independent observer.

There may be several reasons for this type of discrepancy. The child may lack knowledge of the effects of certain agents and their lethal potential. Certainly, adults may misjudge an agent's lethality too. However, children are particularly vulnerable to an unrealistic assessment of lethality because of immaturity of their developmental level with respect to cognition, judgment, concepts of cause and effect, and perceptual skills. Although the actual level of lethality of a drug is low, its ingestion may be considered highly lethal by the child.

Another issue that may create confusion in the determination of lethality involves shifts in states of ego functioning commonly observed in suicidal individuals. Shneidman (1980) pointed out that during an acute suicidal phase, a person may undergo impairments in judgment, attention, cognitive capacities, impulse control, memory, and perceptual skills. A person who has these impairments may not be able to evaluate objectively the potential lethality of an action. This may be particularly true for children, whose sense of judgment, impulse control, and cognitive abilities are not fully mature.

Children are not able fully to realize the implications of the seriousness of an agent's ability to cause death. Therefore, for children, lethality should be considered less important when categorizing childhood suicidal behavior. Instead, suicidal impulses in children should be considered serious and potentially lethal. This suggestion is even more pertinent if one considers that children are not always able to verbalize their thoughts about the dangerousness of their actions.

Because a child's understanding of lethality is difficult to diagnose, the classification of suicidal behavior in children should be based on the manifest behavior of the child. Thus, classification of suicidal behavior in children can be done by assessing the degree of action taken to actualize suicidal impulses. Suicidal tendencies in children may be conceptualized broadly to include suicidal ideas or actions. Pfeffer and associates (1979) described a spectrum of suicidal behavior for children that includes nonsuicidal impulses, suicidal ideas, suicidal threats, suicidal attempts, and suicide. Each category of suicidal tendency has been defined and is based primarily upon the observable degree of self-injurious action taken.

Nonsuicidal behavior is defined as no evidence of any self-destructive thoughts or actions. Suicidal ideation is defined as thoughts or verbalizations of causing serious injury or death to oneself. Examples would be a child stating "I want to kill myself" and a child's reporting an auditory hallucination of instruction to kill himself or herself. A suicidal threat is defined as a verbalization of impending self-destructive suicidal action and/or a precursor action which, if fully carried out, could lead to serious harm or to death. One example might be a child who states "I am going to run in front of a car" while standing at the curb of the street. Another may be a child who puts a knife under his or her pillow or a child who stands near an open window and says "I will jump out."

Suicidal attempts are divided into the categories of mild attempts and serious attempts. A mild attempt is an actual self-destructive action that realistically would not have endangered life and did not necessitate medical attention. A child who ingests a few pills of low lethality would be an example. A serious attempt is an actual self-destruction action that realistically could have led to the child's death and may have necessitated intensive medical care. An example of this would be a child who jumped out the fourth-floor window and sustained several fractures. Suicide is any self-destructive action that caused the death of the child.

This spectrum of childhood suicidal behavior is based primarily on observable behavior. In all cases, children are considered suicidal if they intended to cause self-harm. The value of this spectrum of suicidal behavior is that it provides a useful schema for estimating seriousness of suicidal behavior for the clinician as well as for the researcher. This spectrum suggests that there is a continuity to the severity of suicidal behavior in children. For example, children who have suicidal behavior that includes attempts will have expressed either suicidal ideas or threats. In addition, this spectrum provides a way of estimating changes in the level of suicidal severity. If a child reports suicidal ideas and then exhibits a suicidal threat, it is evident that his or her suicidal severity has increased. Finally, this spectrum is based on defined criteria to estimate suicidal severity.

SUMMARY

This chapter has discussed the problems that hamper development of a conclusive definition of childhood suicidal behavior. It is often difficult to know whether a behavior is accidental or suicidal. This distinction is particularly difficult to estimate in children. Despite these problems, a definition of suicidal behavior in children has been reached that is close to the definition used for adult suicidal behavior. This definition is as follows: Suicidal behavior in children is any self-destructive behavior that has the intent to hurt oneself seriously or to cause death.

A spectrum of severity of suicidal behavior has been outlined that includes nonsuicidal behavior, suicidal ideas, suicidal threats, mild suicidal attempts, serious suicidal attempts, and suicide. This spectrum is based on defined criteria to estimate the seriousness of the suicidal behavior and changes in suicidal severity. A child who shows more serious suicidal behavior on this spectrum will have also experienced less serious suicidal behavior on this spectrum.

THE EPIDEMIOLOGY OF CHILDHOOD SUICIDAL BEHAVIOR

> The doctor says there are such boys springing up amongst us—boys of a sort unknown in the last generation—the outcome of new visions of life. They seem to see all its terrors before they are old enough to have staying power to resist them. He says it is the beginning of the coming universal wish not to live. —Thomas Hardy, *Jude the Obscure*

Some have said that suicide is an increasing event among children and adolescents in our society. Another concern is whether young children commit suicide and if this is a serious problem. In order to draw conclusions about these issues, it is essential to look at the statistics of suicide among youth. Therefore, this chapter contains statistical information about the incidence and prevalence of suicidal behavior. The chapter takes account predominantly of statistics for children and adolescents. Also, it includes data about adults in order to provide a developmental perspective on the phenomenon of suicidal behavior.

THE INCIDENCE OF SUICIDE IN CHILDREN

Accidents, homicides, and suicides are, in that order, the three most common causes of death for 15- to 24-year-olds. Table 3-1 shows the 10 leading causes of death in 5- to 14-year-olds, 15- to 24-year-olds, and those of all ages in 1981 (*U.S. Monthly Vital Statistics*, 1982). It must be remembered that data for child suicide are for children 10 years and older since the National Center for Health Statistics tends not to classify suicide as a cause of death for children younger than 10 years of age.

Although suicide is one of the 10 leading causes of death in each of these three age groups, suicide is among the three most common causes of death only in the 15- to 24-year-old age group. This fact suggests that there may be specific factors influential during adolescence and young adulthood that are associated with the higher incidence of suicide in these age groups.

23

TABLE 3-1

The 10 leading causes of death in the United States in 1981

Age 5–14 years	Age 15–24 years	All ages
1. Accidents	1. Accidents	1. Heart disease
2. Malignant neoplasms	2. Homicide	2. Malignant neoplasms
3. Congenital anomalies	3. Suicide	3. Cerebrovascular disease
4. Homicide	4. Malignant neoplasms	4. Accidents
5. Heart disease	5. Heart disease	5. Chronic pulmonary disease
6. Influenza and pneumonia	6. Congenital anomalies	6. Influenza and pneumonia
7. Suicide	7. Cerebrovascular disease	7. Diabetes mellitus
8. Chronic pulmonary disease	8. Influenza and pneumonia	8. Cirrhosis of liver
9. Cerebrovascular disease	9. Chronic pulmonary disease	9. Arteriosclerosis
10. Septicemia	10. Nephritis and nephrosis	10. Suicide

Note. From U.S. Monthly Vital Statistics (1982).

This trend is more explicitly revealed when the number of suicidal deaths is reviewed over time. Table 3-2 shows the number of suicidal deaths from 1968 to 1982 for age groups 5 to 14 years, 15 to 24 years, and all ages (U.S. Monthly Vital Statistics, 1984). The peak year for suicides in the total population and among 15- to 24-year-olds was 1977. There was a slight decrease in the total number of suicides in 1978, 1979, and 1980 and another gradual increase in 1981 and 1982. The number of suicides among 15- to 24-year-olds gradually decreased from 1978 to 1982. However, while the number of suicides for 5- to 14-year-olds decreased in 1978 through 1980, it increased in 1981 and 1982.

Table 3-2 also shows that the total number of suicides generally has increased in all of these age groups in the last decade, but the greatest increase is in the 15- to 24-year age group. The least increase was in the 5- to 14-year-old age group, where in the last 10 years the number of suicides was very low and relatively constant. This trend suggests that there may be specific factors that protect preadolescents from a high incidence of suicide. Hypotheses about these factors are presented later in this section. Furthermore, studies of factors that are associated with changes in the number of suicidal deaths over time are discussed later in this section. Although these data point out that the number of suicides in all age groups has increased, they do not provide information about how the numbers of suicide are related to the number of people in each age period categorized. To evaluate this question, it is necessary to review age-specific mortality rates, which describe the incidence of suicide in a given age group of people.

In 1982, 200 children between 5 and 14 years old committed suicide in the United States (*U.S. Monthly Vital Statistics*, 1984). This represents an age-specific mortality rate for suicide of 0.6 per 100,000. This accounts for 2.1% of all deaths in this age group and 0.5% of all suicides in all age groups. With regard to adolescents, there were 5,025 suicides among youngsters who were ages 15 to 24 years old in 1982. This is an age-specific mortality rate for suicide of 12 per 100,000 and accounts for 12% of all deaths in this age group. This information indicates that adolescents and young adults have a significantly higher rate of suicide than preadolescents and a significantly greater percentage of deaths within their respective age groups.

Furthermore, there has been a significant change in suicide rates during the last several decades, especially in the child and adolescent age groups. Figure 3-1 shows the age-specific suicide rates by 5-year age groups for 1955, 1965, and 1978 (*U.S. Monthly Vital Statistics*, 1980).

In 1955 there was a steady increase in suicide rate with age. In 1965 the suicide rate for adolescents, 15 to 19 years old, was higher than in 1955. In 1978 the youth suicide rate drastically increased, beginning in

TABLE 3-2

Number of deaths from suicide in the United States from 1968 to 1982

Year (in reverse order)	Total all ages	Age 5–14 years	Age 15–24 years
1982	28,242	200	5025
1981	27,596	167	5161
1980	26,869	142	5239
1979	27,206	152	5246
1978	27,294	153	5115
1977	28,681	182	5565
1976	26,832	163	4647
1975	26,832	170	4736
1974	25,683	188	4285
1973	25,118	157	4098
1972	25,004	120	3858
1971	24,092	141	3479
1970	23,480	132	3128
1969	22,364	136	2731
1968	21,372	118	2357

Note. From *U.S. Monthly Vital Statistics* (1984).

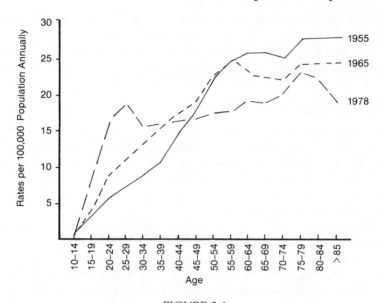

FIGURE 3-1

Age-specific suicide rates by 5-year age groups: 1955, 1965, 1978. (From *U.S. Monthly Vital Statistics*, 1980.)

the 10- to 14-year age group and reaching a peak in the 25- to 29-year age group. Thereafter, the suicide rates decreased, then gradually increased, and reached another peak in the elderly age group. Thus, since 1978 a bimodal distribution of suicide rates has evolved, with peaks during adolescence and old age.

The dramatic increases in suicide rates for adolescents and young adults are also evident when one looks at the data on the percentage of increases in suicide rates in these age groups. Table 3-3 shows the percentage increase in suicide rates for children and adolescents from 1955 to 1978.

These data suggest that over time there has been a general increase of child and adolescent suicides, with the greatest increase taking place

TABLE 3-3

Percentage increase in youth suicide rates from 1955 to 1978

Age group (years)	Rate in 1955	Rate in 1978	Percentage increase
10–14	0.3	0.8	166
15–19	2.6	8.0	208
20–24	5.6	15.9	202

among adolescents and young adults. However, this information does not provide insights into how these changes in suicide rates are related to changes in the population of a given age group of people. Studies evaluating the issue of population changes and suicide rates are presented in the next section of this chapter.

FACTORS AFFECTING SUICIDE RATES IN CHILDREN AND ADOLESCENTS

The suicide rates for 10- to 14-year-olds have gradually increased over time, but the number of suicides in this age group remains relatively low. Although there have been some research reports about younger children, below age 14 years, who commit suicide (Jan-Tausch, 1964; Amir, 1973; Sathyavathi, 1975), these reports include preadolescents with adolescents.

The most comprehensive investigation of suicides in children under 14 years of age was carried out by Shaffer (1974). He studied 30 children who committed suicide in England and Wales from 1962 to 1968. These were the only documented cases of suicide in children under age 14 years during this time period. Shaffer reviewed the coroner's records, educational reports, medical and psychiatric records, and social service reports. He found that none of the children was under 12 years old and that the ratio of boys to girls was 2.3 to 1. There were 21 boys and 9 girls in the sample.

Shaffer was interested in understanding why there is a relatively low suicide rate in preadolescents and young adolescents (Shaffer, 1974; Shaffer & Fisher, 1981). He utilized statistical methods to study factors that seem to protect young children from suicide. Three ideas were offered as an explanation. The first concerns the association between affective illness and suicide. Although depression occurs in children, Shaffer presented evidence that the prevalence of depression is lower than among adults. The second idea is the possibility that the family network protects children from suicidal behavior by its inherent reduction of isolation and by offering emotional support. Evidence to support this was derived from studies of adults showing that single adults who live alone have higher suicide rates. A third idea is that a degree of psychological maturity is required before a child can succumb to despair and hopelessness. This develops with the evolution of abstract thinking in the adolescent period.

Shaffer's ideas correctly focus on three of the major factors that affect suicide risk in children and adolescents. These include the role of affective illness, family factors, and developmental variables. Such issues also were discussed by Corder and Haizlip (1984) in their report on three preadolescents who committed suicide. Unlike Shaffer (1974), who obtained information by record review, these clinicians acquired information by means of personal interviews with the families, friends, and teachers of these children. Although the sample of children was smaller than that in Shaffer's study, Corder and Haizlip determined that there were several similarities in the family backgrounds and personality characteristics of the two 9-year-old boys who shot themselves and the 7-year-old boy who died by self-poisoning. These three children seemed to be enmeshed in intense family interactions, and the children were considered to have special precocious skills by their families. The family's sense of self-esteem was maintained by the recognition of the child's achievements by others. Furthermore, there appeared to be no specific or dramatic psychological or environmental stress during the immediate period preceding the suicides. Instead, there was a discernible increase of stress over a long time that seemed to erode the child's coping mechanisms and diminish the family's sense of self-esteem. The suicides occurred at a time when mounting stresses resulted in a serious sense of loss of self-esteem for the children and families.

This study derived its information about youngsters who committed suicide from retrospective accounts of people who knew the children. This method of information gathering, known as the psychological autopsy, is one of the most valuable techniques for studying individuals who have committed suicide.

Shafii, Carrigan, Whittinghill, and Derrick (1985) also utilized a psychological autopsy approach in their study of 20 children and adolescents, aged 12 to 19 years, who committed suicide. These researchers interviewed families, friends and significant other people as soon as possible after they learned of the suicide from the local coroner's office or newspaper obituary reports. In many cases, initial contact was made with the family by telephone and the first meeting often took place during visiting hours in the funeral home. Follow-up contacts with the families took place for a three year period. In addition, matched pairs of youngsters served as a comparison and were similar with regard to sex, race, education, religious background, family income, and father's level of education. The results pointed out that family suicidal behavior, parental absence, parental psychopathology, parental abuse, previous suicidal behavior of the youngster, drug and alcohol abuse, and antisocial behaviors were significantly more common among the suicide victims than the comparison group. This study, one of the first systematic prospective studies of its kind, provided important information for suicide prevention by pointing out the significant relationship between earlier suicidal behavior and suicide among children and adults. An important implication is that once suicidal behavior in a child or an adolescent is recognized, effective methods be employed to prevent a future suicide.

Currently, Shaffer, too, is using the psychological autopsy method to study a large number of adolescents who committed suicide. However, since this study is now in process, results of the investigation are not yet available.

The dramatic rise in adolescent suicide has stimulated epidemiological analyses of factors that increase the rate of suicide. A number of studies have tried to explore the relationship between suicide and population changes. For example, Hellon and Solomon (1980) examined the changing relationship between age and suicide in Alberta, Canada, which had the second highest suicide rate in Canada in 1976. The time period of investigation was the census years from 1951 through 1977. Age-specific suicide rates were calculated by averaging the rates for the 5 years surrounding each census year. To determine changes in rate over time, age-specific rates for each age group were expressed as 100 for the base year of 1951 and subsequent rates were plotted for each census year in relation to 1951 rates. Finally, to assess the extent to which suicide in young persons contributed to the overall increase in suicide rates, deaths by suicide among persons 15 to 29 years old were expressed as a percentage of all suicides in the population. These percentages were compared to the corresponding age structure of the population of Alberta.

The findings revealed that in 1951 the suicide rates increased directly with age until ages 50 to 54 years for men and increased until 40 to 54 years for women. There was a decline in suicide rates in both sexes among the elderly. The 1951 age profile was consistent with the tradition of higher rates among older in contrast to younger people. While the 1956 profile was similar to the 1951 profile, the suicide rates for 1951 onward increased primarily in the younger age group of 15 to 24 years of age. In 1976, for example, there were two peaks in suicide rate; one peak occurred in the 20- to 24-year-old males and the other peak in the 50- to 54-year-old males. With regard to age-specific change in rates, the rates for the younger age groups increased faster than the rates among older people. For example, for the 15- to 19-year-olds, the rate in 1951 was 1.6 per 100,000; the rate increased 12.5 times in 1976 to a rate of 20.0 per 100,000.

This study found the following relationships: The older the age group, the less the increase in suicide rates. The number of deaths from suicide expressed as the percentage of all suicides showed a definite trend toward a higher percentage of suicide by persons 15 to 29 years old than other age groups. This trend for percentage of suicide was not primarily related to any change in the age structure of the Alberta population. This study illustrated that there is something unique about suicide in adolescents that is accounting for the increase in suicide rates over time; but it did not discern what factors may be accounting for these trends.

In another study, Solomon and Hellon (1980) amplified on previous findings and explored the question of whether suicide rates increased as a specific cohort or group of people aged. All 4313 suicides in Alberta, Canada, between 1951 and 1977 were examined. The first cohort was 15 to 19 years old in 1951. As that group aged, its suicide rates were calculated for age periods: 20–24 years old, 25–29 years old, 30–34 years old, 35–39 years old, and 40–44 years old. A second cohort of 15- to 19-year-olds, in 1956, were also evaluated for suicide rates as this group aged. The suicide rates when these people reached ages of 20–24 years, 25–29 years, 30–34 years, and 35–39 years were calculated. Similar analyses were carried out for those cohorts of people who were 15 to 19 years old in the years 1961, 1966, 1971, and 1976.

The analyses revealed that within each cohort of people, the suicide rates increased directly with age. The rates for each successive cohort of people were higher than for any previous cohort. Therefore, each cohort of people had its own specific suicide risk which has been increasing over time. Conclusions from these findings are that suicide rates increase with age and that suicide risk is cohort specific.

These findings are important in providing epidemiological insights into suicide. Other studies that validate these results are of value. Such an attempt to replicate and explore the analyses of Solomon and Hellon was undertaken by Murphy and Wetzel (1980). They used the data from the vital statistics records of the United States. The purpose of their replication was to use a wider data base and to evaluate a new population in order to control for any effects of social change. Six cohorts of people and six age intervals were used; these were analyzed for 1930 to 1934, 1935 to 1939, 1940 to 1944, 1945 to 1949, 1950 to 1954, and 1955 to 1959. The results showed trends similar to those reported in the study of Solomon and Hellon (1980), although the rates were not as high. It was determined that the rate for each successive 5-year cohort was higher than that of the preceding 5-year cohort at the same age. These findings are significant since the United States did not undergo the same social changes that occurred in Alberta; thus, these trends may be independent of certain social changes. Finally, a third cohort analysis of suicide rates was carried out in Australia (Goldney & Katsikitis, 1983). The time period ranged from 1951 to 1979. The results confirmed most findings of the two previous analyses. Thus, these three studies, using analyses of large populations from different cultural backgrounds, showed that suicide rates increase over time, are age specific, and are independent of social changes. However, these studies did not uncover whether other factors also accounted for the cohort-specific increases in suicide rates.

An implication of these analyses, which showed an increasing rate of suicide over time and with age, is that it may be expected that the increase of suicide rates in youngsters may continue. In fact, some projections of unpublished data from the National Center for Health Statistics (*U.S. Monthly Vital Statistics*, 1979) indicate that by the year 2000 the suicide rates will be even higher. The projected suicide rates in the year 2000 are shown in Table 3-4. However, these statistics are based on the assumption that the population will remain relatively similar in year 2000 to what it was in 1978. The projection does not account for other types of population changes such as changes in the number of people in a given age or racial/ethnic group.

Another analysis of youth suicide was provided by Holinger and Offer (1982). This analysis did consider changes in the population over time. Specifically, it related the changes in the proportion of adolescents in the total population to the adolescent suicide rate in the United States during the 20th century. These researchers hoped to be able to formulate a model that would predict future trends in adolescent suicide rates. The study utilized statistics from all suicides of 15- to 19-year-olds in the United States from 1933 to 1975. This study showed that there was a significant positive correlation between adolescent suicide rates, changes in the adolescent population, and changes in the proportion of adolescents in the total United States population. In other words, increases or decreases in the number of 15- to 19-year-olds in the total population are related to corresponding increases and decreases in adolescent suicide rates. Therefore, according to these authors, it would be expected that since the population of children and adolescents decreased from the late 1950s through the 1970s, the trends for suicide for 15- to 19-year-olds would decrease in the late 1970s and 1980s.

Based on this model, it could be predicted that the suicide rates would decrease. This expectation differs from the prediction presented by the National Center for Health Statistics in which it was predicted that by 2000 there would be an increase of 94% in suicide rates for 15- to 19-year-olds. Validation of each of these predictions is needed.

Other factors, such as sex and racial/ethnic variables, are important features that are associated with different suicide rates. Table 3-5

TABLE 3-4
Projected increase in suicide rates by the year 2000

Age group (years)	Rate in 1978	Rate in 2000	Percentage increase
10–14	0.8	15	13
15–19	8.0	15.5	94
20–24	15.9	36.3	114
All ages	12.5	17.6	41

TABLE 3-5

Suicide rates per 100,000 for sex and racial/ethnic groups in 1982

Variable	Total	Men	Women
All ages and all racial/ethnic groups	11.6	18.3	5.4
Whites	12.4	19.4	5.8
Other racial/ethnic groups	6.4	10.8	2.6

Note. From *U.S. Monthly Vital Statistics* (1984).

shows the suicide rates for all ages with respect to sex and racial/ethnic groups in 1982 (*U.S. Monthly Vital Statistics*, 1984). Three features are evident: The suicide rates for men are higher than for women of all racial/ethnic groups; the suicide rates are higher in whites than non-whites; the suicide rate for white men is higher than any other group. With regard to adolescents, the rates for whites were higher than for nonwhites during the period 1961 to 1975 (Holinger, 1978). However, among the 20- to 24-year-old group, the rates for whites and nonwhites were equal. Additional research that relates age groups, racial/ethnic factors, and suicide rates is needed.

PREVALENCE OF SUICIDAL IDEAS AND NONFATAL ACTS IN CHILDREN

Whether there are similarities between individuals who contemplate, attempt, or commit suicide requires extensive study. Support for the notion that there is a continuous spectrum that ranges from suicidal ideas, threats, attempts, and suicide has been put forth for children and adults (Pfeffer, Conte, Plutchik, & Jerrett, 1979, 1980; Pfeffer, Solomon, Plutchik, Mizruchi, & Weiner, 1982; Pfeffer, Zuckerman, Plutchik, & Mizruchi, 1984; Paykel, Myers, Lindenthal, & Tanner, 1974). For example, Paykel and associates (1974) interviewed 720 subjects from the general population to determine the frequency and severity of suicidal feelings. They asked the following questions that evaluated severity of suicidal ideas and actions: (1) Have you ever felt that life was not worth living? (2) Have you ever wished you were dead? (3) Have you ever thought of taking your life even if you would not really do it? (4) Have you ever reached the point where you seriously considered taking your life or perhaps made plans how you would go about doing it? (5) Have you ever made an attempt to take your life? A total of 8.9% reported suicidal feelings of some degree in the past year. Of these. 3.5% reporting feelings that life is not worth living and 0.6% reported a suicide attempt. The responses were on a continuum so that the subjects reporting more intense feelings also reported less intense feelings. Those with suicidal feelings resembled other published descriptions of completed suicides with respect to presence of depression, social isolation, and stress. This study is important in suggesting that a continuum of suicidal behavior exists and includes suicidal ideas, suicidal threats, suicidal attempts, and completed suicide. The findings of this study serve to highlight the worthwhileness of studying nonfatal suicidal behavior as a way of further understanding completed suicide.

A number of studies have attempted to determine the frequency of attempted suicide compared to suicide. For example, it has been estimated that the ratio of suicidal attempts to suicide in youngsters, ages 8 to 19 years old, ranges from 50 : 1 to 100 : 1 (Jacobziner, 1960, 1965). This estimate was based on studies of children and adolescents reported to poison control centers in New York City and, therefore, must be viewed as very tentative. Study of other populations that include psychiatric patients are needed to clarify such estimates. Nevertheless, it appears that nonfatal suicidal behaviors outnumber suicides. This fact suggests that it may be difficult to predict from among all youngsters who think about or attempt suicide, which ones will eventually commit suicide.

Dorpat and Ripley (1967) studied the relationship between attempted suicide and suicide in adults. They reviewed 15 published follow-up studies of attempted suicides to obtain information on the incidence of suicide. The incidence of suicide among the attempted suicides ranged from 0.03% in one short-term study to 22.0% in the longest follow-up study. Dorpat and Ripley also reviewed nine published studies of suicide. Among the people who committed suicide, the incidence of prior suicidal attempts varied from 8.6% to 62.0%. In both analyses, it was determined that the incidence of prior attempts was higher among the suicide completers than in the general population and that the incidence of suicide was higher among the attempters than in the general population. This information suggests that studies of nonfatal suicidal behavior are valuable in developing a better understanding of risk for suicide.

Unlike the relatively low number of children who commit suicide, there has been an increase in the documented number of children who contemplate or attempt suicide. For example, in 1937 Bender and Schilder (1937) noted that there were 18 suicidal children under 13 years old out of 2000 admissions to Bellevue Hospital in New York City. Previous estimates of suicidal children seen in outpatient psychiatric clinics ranged from 1% to 10% (Shaffer, 1974). Recent estimates of childhood suicidal ideas, threats, or attempts are higher than previously reported. Pfeffer and colleagues (1979) determined, in a sample of 58 children consecutively admitted to a municipal hospital child psychiatric inpatient service, that 72% of the children had suicidal ideas, threats, or attempts. The racial/ethnic distribution of that population of children was 10% white, 41% black, and 49% Hispanic. Furthermore, among all the children referred for admission to this child psychiatric inpatient unit, 33% of the children had suicidal ideas, threats, or attempts. The prevalence of suicidal behavior of these inpatients was compared with children consecutively admitted to the same municipal hospital's child psychiatric outpatient clinic (in 1980). Among 39 children studied in the outpatient clinic, 33% displayed suicidal ideas, threats, or attempts. The racial/ethnic distribution of these psychiatric outpatients was 47% white, 37% black, and 16% Hispanic. These studies indicated that a relatively high number of children seeking psychiatric care are at risk for suicidal behavior.

These studies were in a municipal hospital psychiatric inpatient and outpatient setting where all the children admitted to the inpatient unit were from low-social-status backgrounds and the majority of children in the psychiatric outpatient clinic were from low-middle to low-social-status backgrounds. In another investigation, Pfeffer and associates (1982) attempted to determine the prevalence of suicidal behavior in children from different social status backgrounds and racial/ethnic groups. They studied all admissions to a voluntary hospital child psychiatric inpatient unit which had a racial/ethnic distribution of 73.8% white and 26.2% black or Hispanic. The social status distribution was predominantly upper-middle social status. Therefore, the racial/ethnic and social status distributions of this voluntary hospital inpatient sample and the municipal hospital inpatient sample of children were significantly different. Among the 65 inpatient children consecutively admitted to the voluntary hospital unit, 78.5% had suicidal ideas, threats, or attempts; a finding that was similar to the 72% of suicidal children in the municipal hospital inpatient population. Therefore, these studies showed that the racial/ethnic or social status distributions were not the prominent factors in determining the prevalence of suicidal behavior in children. Furthermore, these studies point out that suicidal behavior was very common among children requiring psychiatric hospitalization regardless of demographic factors.

To further test these conclusions, Pfeffer, Plutchik, Mizruchi, and Lipkins (1986) studied consecutive admissions to a voluntary hospital child psychiatric outpatient clinic. This clinic has a racial/ethnic and social status distribution similar to that of the voluntary hospital child psychiatric inpatient unit. The demographic factors differed from the municipal hospital's child psychiatric outpatient clinic. Among 101 children admitted to the child psychiatric outpatient clinic, 24.8% showed suicidal ideas, threats, or attempts. These findings also suggest that neither racial/ethnic nor social status distributions were major factors affecting the prevalence of suicidal behavior among children requiring inpatient or outpatient psychiatric care. The findings strengthen the conclusion that all children seeking psychiatric intervention should be comprehensively evaluated for suicidal risk.

Additional corroborating evidence for a frequent prevalence of suicidal tendencies among children who are in intensive psychiatric care was presented by Cohen-Sandler, Berman, and King (1982a) for a sample of child psychiatric inpatients. The racial/ethnic distribution of the children was evenly represented by white and nonwhite children. This study focused on only those children who exhibited suicidal action. Among 76 children consecutively admitted to a psychiatric inpatient unit, 26% of the children had threatened or attempted suicide. These findings do not include children with suicidal ideas. These findings support observations by Pfeffer's group that suicidal behavior is common in children seeking intensive psychiatric care.

All of these reports focused on populations of children with acknowledged psychiatric disturbances. Pfeffer and colleagues (1984) also studied the prevalence of suicidal tendencies in schoolchildren who have no history of psychiatric symptomatology. All children attending special education classes for emotionally disturbed or neurologically impaired children were excluded from the study. The study was conducted in a metropolitan community of over 100,000 people. Children were randomly selected from a school roster of all the 1565 preadolescents in the community. Among the 101 children interviewed, 11.9% had suicidal ideas, threats, or attempts. This percentage was lower than that reported for suicidal children attending psychiatric outpatient clinics or those admitted to psychiatric inpatient units.

These studies provided new information about the prevalence and spectrum of suicidal tendencies in children in psychiatric and nonpsychiatric settings. Table 3-6 shows the spectrum of suicidal behavior determined in Pfeffer *et al.*'s studies of children in the municipal hospital psychiatric inpatient and outpatient populations, the voluntary hospital inpatient and outpatient populations, and the school population of children. It can be seen that there were significantly more children with suicidal threats and attempts in the two psychiatric inpatient populations than in the psychiatric outpatient groups and the school population group. Suicidal ideas were the prominent mode of expressing suicidal tendencies in the two psychiatric outpatient populations as well as in the school population. These findings indicate that children with the most severe degrees of suicidal behavior tend to be treated in the most intensive psychiatric settings. However, this does not mean that children with less severe degrees of suicidal tendencies, such as suicidal ideas, do not need intensive psychiatric treatment. For exam-

TABLE 3-6
The spectrum of suicidal behavior of children

Psychiatric unit	Nonsuicidal		Suicidal ideation		Suicidal threats		Mild suicidal attempts		Serious suicidal attempts		Total	
	n	%	n	%	n	%	n	%	n	%	n	%
Municipal hospital inpatient unit	16	28.0	11	19.0	15	26.0	8	13.5	8	13.5	58	100
Voluntary hospital inpatient unit	22	20.8	27	25.5	21	19.8	29	27.4	7	6.6	106	100
Municipal hospital outpatient unit	26	66.7	5	12.9	3	7.6	3	7.6	2	5.2	39	100
Voluntary hospital outpatient unit	76	75.2	16	15.9	8	7.9	0	0.0	1	1.0	101	100
School population	89	88.1	9	8.9	2	2.0	1	1.0	0	0.0	101	100

Note. From Pfeffer et al. (1979, 1980, 1986).

ple, there was a high percentage of children with suicidal ideas admitted to the psychiatric inpatient unit. These children were considered to be at high risk for future serious suicidal behaviors. It should be emphasized that children with any type of suicidal impulses must be evaluated for their degree of suicidal risk.

There is a prevalence of more boys than girls under 12 years of age with suicidal behavior (Jacobziner, 1960; Pfeffer *et al.*, 1980, 1982). However, Pfeffer *et al.*'s studies demonstrated that the degree of severity of suicidal behavior along the spectrum of suicidal ideas, threats, or attempts is not different for boys and girls. In other words, while boys under 12 years are at greater risk to develop suicidal behavior than girls of this age, there is no difference in degree of severity of suicidal tendencies between boys and girls who express suicidal impulses. This finding is different than for adolescents. Among adolescents, boys commit suicide more frequently than girls, but girls attempt suicide more frequently than boys. Adolescent boys express more serious suicidal behavior than adolescent girls.

SUMMARY

Although suicide is relatively rare in children under 12 years of age, suicidal ideas, suicidal threats, and attempts are relatively common. Furthermore, suicide in adolescents is among the three most common causes of death, and this is related to changes in number of adolescents in the population and year of birth.

Children from every type of social status background may be vulnerable to suicidal behavior. In children under 12 years of age, boys demonstrate suicidal behavior more frequently than girls, but the severity of suicidal behaviors is not different for boys and girls. However, adolescent boys show more serious suicidal behavior than adolescent girls. Of those who commit suicide, a high percentage have exhibited previous suicidal behavior.

CHAPTER FOUR

THE SUICIDAL EPISODES OF CHILDREN

> At the back of the door were fixed two hooks for hanging garments, and from these the forms of the two youngest children were suspended, by a piece of box cord around each of their necks, while from a nail a few yards off the body of little Jude was hanging in a similar manner. An overturned chair was near the elder boy, and his glazed eyes were slanted into the room; but those of the girl and the baby boy were closed. —Thomas Hardy, *Jude the Obscure*

The literature on suicidal behavior is devoid of comprehensive descriptive reports about the actual suicidal episodes of children. For example, Lukianowicz (1968) only minimally described the details of children's suicidal episodes. Among some of his examples were: Albie, age 9 years, who ran into the street and threw himself in front of an oncoming vehicle because his father forced him to go to school; Harold, age 8 years, who thought of killing himself by throwing himself under a moving vehicle or by jumping into the sea and drowning because he would not endure his unbearable family life; and Carol, age 12 years, who attempted to jump off a bridge because of violent fights with her parents. Because of the dearth of more comprehensive accounts of children's suicidal episodes, this chapter includes detailed accounts of situations leading to the suicidal episodes of children. Discussion focuses on developmental factors that contribute either to a child's sense of self-preservation or to his or her vulnerability to a suicidal episode. This discussion is integrated with descriptions of social and intrapsychic factors that affect the onset and outcome of the suicidal episode.

COMPONENTS OF THE SUICIDAL EPISODE

Many clinicians believe that suicidal behavior in children is an impulsive event that is prompted by inability to control and contain distressing feelings. Such an assumption minimizes the specificity of such underlying factors as early developmental experiences, affects, ego functioning, and personal relationships that are the main components responsible for the expression of the suicidal episode. For the purposes of this discussion, the suicidal episode is defined as the circumstance just before and at the time the child shows suicidal tendencies.

The drama of a child's suicidal episode is profoundly moving. The suicidal episode has conscious and unconscious components, a time of development, and a duration of expression and resolution. It contains elements of ego organization and disorganization that are determined by the meaning the child consciously and unconsciously ascribes to the current situation and by the child's capacity to cope with the stress he or she feels.

Figure 4-1 depicts the relationship between four main types of factors that interact in specific ways to create the suicidal episode. The outer circle shows the dynamic equilibrium between the conscious and

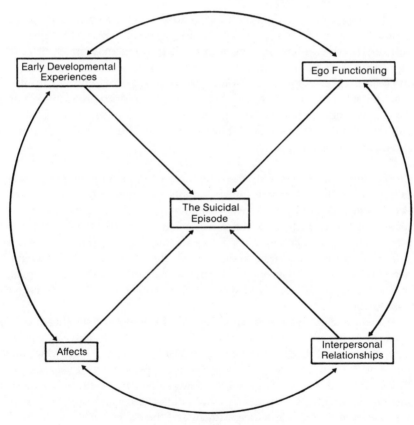

FIGURE 4-1
Classification of factors that promote the suicidal episode.

unconscious effects of a child's early developmental experiences, affects, ego functioning, and interpersonal relationships. Throughout life, this dynamic equilibrium exists so that each category of factors interacts with the other categories of factors. For example, the conscious and unconscious memory traces of early developmental experiences are continually aroused by the child's current life experiences. An example of this is a boy who was severely abused as a toddler and at the age of 9 years provokes others to be angry and want to hit him. These early conscious and unconscious memories of affects and thoughts influence the child's current perceptions, emotions, and behaviors. In similar fashion, for example, the child's current state of affect expression may affect the child's ego functioning and the quality of his or her interpersonal experiences. Illustrations of this would be a child who is enraged and cannot control her wishes to hit a friend, and a child who is so depressed that he believes he is the worst person in the world and the cause of others' problems.

The suicidal episode develops because there are conflicting forces: those that promote self-preservation and opposing forces that press for self-destructive behavior. These opposing forces exist in an unstable equilibrium. A point in time occurs when there is an abrupt change in the balance of these forces, resulting in what appears to be an impulsive suicidal act. This is why suicidal episodes in children are transient and hard to predict. When the current situation becomes increasingly stressful, the likelihood of a suicidal act increases. The following examples illustrate these points.

Child I: June was 9 years old when she threatened to jump out of a window of her fourth-floor apartment. June's parents were divorced and her mother, a quiet and depressed woman, was planning to remarry. June hated her father for leaving and was angry about her mother's future marriage. June was overly attached to her mother and refused to be without her. She frequently refused to go to school and was afraid to sleep alone. She cried and screamed so much at night that the neighbors often called the police. June was excessively envious of her mother's relationship with a boyfriend and told her mother, "You should only love me."

June's suicidal episode occurred within the context of significant family changes. A maternal aunt, who allowed June's mother to move in with her after the parental divorce and who was essential in June's caretaking, died. June and her mother lived with this aunt for approximately 1 year and continued to live in her house for many months after the death. June's mother met her boyfriend after the death. Four months after meeting her boyfriend, June's mother found her own apartment and the boyfriend joined them. Because of the move to a new residence, June transferred to a different school. She missed her old friends and felt sad because she had difficulty making new friends. She was extremely upset and angry about this, was afraid to sleep alone, and refused to go to school.

The move also meant a change in her mother's daily routine. June's mother left for work at a much earlier hour, and as a result, June had to go to school by herself. June did not cooperate with this. In the morning, June ran out when her mother left for work and tried to hang onto the car or cling to her mother so as not to let her go.

June's suicidal episode occurred one morning when June was particularly upset about going to school. The day before, she not only did poorly on a test but had an argument with another girl at school. She was afraid that other children would begin to tease her at school. When June awakened, she was excessively infantile and refused to eat breakfast. She said that the milk in her cereal was sour. Her mother insisted that June quickly finish breakfast so that she could go to work. June screamed uncontrollably that her mother ''did not care'' about her feelings and was only concerned about herself and her boyfriend. June yelled, ''If you don't have enough to give, I come first.'' June sobbed and stamped her feet. She yelled at her mother, ''If you leave me alone today, I will jump out the window.''

June's mother was startled and very frightened. In shock, she stared at June, who continued to scream and stamp her feet. June looked at her mother, stood up, and screamed that she was ''going to jump out the window.'' June ran to a window. Jarred by June's rapid movement, her mother quickly grabbed June and prevented her from injuring herself. June fell sobbing into her mother's arms. June's mother did not go to work that day. Instead, she called a nearby child psychiatric clinic and arranged for an emergency psychiatric consultation.

June's suicidal episode evolved as a climax to the intense stress she felt from her changed environmental circumstances. Not only did the composition of her family change, but her actual home and school settings changed too. As a result, June was excessively stressed by intense feelings of anger, anxiety, and depression. These mushrooming unpleasant affects eventually overwhelmed her to the point of suicidal desperation.

Child II: This example is of a much younger child, Adam. He was 6 years old when he threatened to jump out of a moving car. He lived with his parents and 3-year-old brother. For several months preceding Adam's suicidal episode, Adam's mother was very anxious and preoccupied with the terminal cardiac illness of her mother. She spent many hours at the hospital visiting her mother and made special arrangements to take Adam's brother with her while Adam was in school. During this time, Adam's father complained about his wife's unavailability. He had angry outbursts, a characteristic that Adam also shared.

Adam acknowledged having chronic difficulty getting along with his brother. In fact, because of this, Adam considered himself crazy. Adam's mother had been worried for a long time about Adam's out-of-control behaviors and was specifically worried about how she would take care of him when summer vacation began. She felt overwhelmed by the needs of her sick mother, her volatile, demanding husband, and her two boys. She was concerned that Adam had become increasingly aggressive in school and toward his younger brother. Adam hit his brother with toys, took toys away from his brother, and dictatorially ordered his brother to carry out his wishes. In addition, as the school semester was coming to an end, Adam became increasingly disobedient with his mother and alarmingly out of control at home. In one temper outburst, Adam cracked the apartment windows when he threw his brother's toys against them.

Adam's suicidal episode occurred on a weekend morning while his mother was driving the children to a relative who would babysit for them. Adam questioned his mother about why he could not go with her to see his grandmother in the hospital. He suggested that she leave his brother with the relative, saying "Take me to the hospital with you." His mother tried to convince Adam to stay with the relative. She told him that she could not take care of everyone all the time and now she had to take care of her mother. When Adam heard this, he became furious; he yelled at his mother and reminded her that she always took his brother to the hospital and not him. While screaming that he wanted to go to the hospital, he opened the car door as the car was moving fast and attempted to jump out. Adam's mother rapidly pulled him onto the seat next to her. She was trembling when she thought that her son could have been killed or seriously injured. She immediately detoured and drove to the hospital specifically to see a psychiatrist about Adam.

Adam's suicidal episode occurred as the culmination of a longstanding feeling of being deprived of his mother's love. These feelings became intensely unmanageable for him at the time his mother was preoccupied with the illness of her mother. Adam felt jealous that his mother gave more attention to his brother than to him. Adam's earlier attempts to express these concerns, by uncontrolled aggressive outbursts, did not change his feelings or circumstance. His suicidal episode was the event that shifted his mother's attention away from others and entirely onto him.

Child III: This example of suicidal action evolved less rapidly. Benjamin was an exceptionally intelligent 11-year-old when he seriously attempted suicide by ingesting 20 aspirins. He was the only child of parents who expected high academic achievement from their son. Benjamin's father, a successful businessman, never completed college. He hoped that his son would not only finish college but join him in the family business as soon as Benjamin completed additional postgraduate training at business school. Benjamin's mother idealized her husband and shared his fantasies.

Benjamin was more troubled in school during the year of his suicide attempt. He worried about finishing grammar school and going into a new junior high school. In addition, he realized that he would be expected to maintain his current academic and athletic interests. Benjamin tried to talk with his parents about his worries. However, he felt that they were not able to understand his feelings. His parents, in their attempts to relax and reassure their son, minimized his complaints and told him that they had faith that he was very competent to work things out. Benjamin felt desperately alone with no alternatives for expressing his worries.

The suicidal episode occurred on Sunday afternoon when his school band was to play at a special city concert. Benjamin was preoccupied about having two school tests on Monday and worried about having enough time to study. Rehearsing most of Saturday aggravated this fear. He woke up early Sunday morning and tried to study. Within an hour, he became very despondent and did not want to awaken his parents. He wished he were dead. He thought of killing himself. He tried to study but could not concentrate. He went to the bathroom to wash his face, hoping that he might feel better. He thought again of going to his parents but believed that they would be annoyed and disappointed in him, especially on this special day when he was to be in a city band concert. He recalled that they had been talking about this event for several weeks. He looked at himself in the mirror and suddenly thought of taking pills to kill himself. He found a bottle of aspirin in the medicine cabinet, took out a handful of aspirins, and swallowed them.

Benjamin returned to his desk to wait for the effects of the aspirin. Within a few minutes his mother came into his room to say good morning, but she found him sobbing. She was especially surprised because she expected that he would be enthusiastic about the special concert. He told her that he did not want to play in the concert and preferred to remain home. She was startled but listened to him. Realizing that she was listening to what he was saying, he felt comforted. Eventually, he told her that he felt so unhappy that he wished he were dead. He told her that he had taken the aspirins.

Benjamin was a child who, for a long time, wanted to gain affection from his parents by gratifying their wishes and fantasies about him with high academic and extracurricular school achievements. However, Benjamin felt that he could not continue to satisfy his parents' high expectations. He believed that his parents did not fully understand him and that they were unaware of his intensifying distress. His suicide attempt provoked a family crisis which allowed his parents to take note of their son's worries. This suicidal crisis led to improved communication between the child and his parents.

These examples depict the dynamic elements underlying children's suicidal episodes. They illustrate the chronic problems experienced by these children who eventually respond to a current stressful situation by exhibiting suicidal behavior. Thus, suicidal action is a symptom determined, in part, by conscious and unconscious elements that are derived from early developmental experiences and are reexperienced in current situations. In fact, suicidal behavior, itself helps to defend against inordinately painful affects such as anxiety, sadness, and anger by removing the child from a current stressful situation. In most cases, similar distressing affects had been experienced by the child during an earlier period of his or her life.

S. Freud (1914), in his paper "Remembering, Repeating, and Working Through," spoke about the reawakening of past feelings in present situations. He proposed that "the patient does not *remember* anything of what he has forgotten and repressed, but *acts* it out. He reproduces it not as a memory but as an action; he *repeats* it, without, of course, knowing that he is repeating it" (p. 150). Freud's remarks are relevant to understanding the occurrence of children's suicidal episodes. Suicidal action can be influenced, in part, by intensification of feelings that are derived from memories of past experiences. However, in most cases suicidal behavior occurs in a context of major current stress.

One example that explicitly conveys the thesis that the suicidal episode is a way of remembering and acting out past unconscious elements is presented here. This example describes a child who had a psychotic mother. His memories of her reactions to him helped influence the onset of his suicidal behavior.

Child IV: Jeffrey, 6 years old, was psychiatrically hospitalized after he attempted to kill himself with a belt around his throat. Jeffrey was found by his grandmother while he was sitting alone on his bed with his eyes bulging and his face blue.

Jeffrey's suicidal episode had several specific unconscious determinants involving a series of previous parental rejections. Just after his birth, his parents separated and he was cared for by his grandmother. His mother relinquished custody of him to his father when Jeffrey was 3 years old because she was pregnant. Two years before the suicidal episode, Jeffrey's father remarried. Jeffrey's stepmother's subsequent pregnancy shocked Jeffrey, who worried that his father and stepmother would give him away when the new baby was born. This fear was related to his past, when his natural parents gave him to his grandmother. These two experiences form, in part, the basis for the suicidal episode and his method of suicidal action.

Many memories of his earlier experiences influenced his suicidal behavior. When Jeffrey was cared for by his psychotic mother, she frequently strapped him to his bed when she disciplined him. When his mother was angry at Jeffrey, she told him that she was sorry that he had not died at birth. She told him that he was born with "a cord around his neck" and that it was only because of the doctor's efforts that he was saved. A final element that promoted the suicidal episode was Jeffrey's renewed belief that he had driven his mother away because of his behavior. These thoughts were reawakened because of his current worries that in the last year his stepmother found it more difficult to tolerate his behavior. Jeffrey was very sad; he worried that he was not loved by anyone. He feared that when the new baby was born, he would be abandoned. During one of his moments of intense despair, he attempted suicide.

Jeffrey's suicidal attempt by putting a belt around his neck was a reaction to a highly unpleasant life situation plus the painful memories of the statements his mother had made repeatedly. He had been scolded by his mother, who reminded him that she wished him dead. His suicidal method was the best way to act out what he remembered of his mother's wishes; that is, to tie "a cord around his neck." His guilt for his bad behavior was intense. He believed he would be rejected by his father and stepmother because of his behavior and that he deserved punishment. Memories of his disturbed relations with his mother were evoked by Jeffrey's current difficulties with his stepmother. Jeffrey attempted suicide when he was alone and felt hopelessly rejected.

DEVELOPMENT OF A SENSE OF SELF-PRESERVATION IN CHILDREN

The wish to destroy oneself involves a response to immediate social and environmental stresses and also specific personality vulnerabilities. Personality vulnerabilities that promote suicidal behavior in children evolve as a result of an interaction between developmental processes, early life experiences, and constitutional factors.

Psychoanalysts have suggested hypotheses about how children develop an appropriate sense of protecting themselves from self-destructive impulses. They agree that a child's ability to maintain and preserve the intactness of his or her body evolves through the child's interactions with important people in the child's environment. The analytic position suggests that the environment should provide specific elements in order to promote the healthy development of a child's sense of self-preservation. Some of these factors are as follows:

1. Protection of the child from injury
2. A structure so that the child knows what to expect in situations
3. An opportunity to play and explore
4. Freedom to express emotions without being punished

Winnicott (1944) emphasized the important role of the mother in creating an environment that is conducive to the child's development. He proposed that it is a maternal function to supply an environment that will gradually allow the child to take over the care of his or her bodily well-being. Winnicott's emphasis was on the important reciprocal interaction between the mother and child.

A. Freud (1963) elaborated upon the process of the child's development of self-preservation. She observed that it is a very "slow and gradual manner in which children assume responsibility for the care of their own body and its protection against harm" (p. 255). In the same paper, "The Concept Of Developmental Lines," she described the maturation of ego functions needed to promote self-preservation. These ego functions include, among others, an increased orientation to the external world, an understanding of cause and effect, and the ability to control dangerous wishes.

A. Freud (1936), speaking about young children, also explicated the important role of the environment during a child's early years. She said:

> The greater the importance of the outside world as a source of pleasure and interest, the more opportunity is there to experience "pain" from that quarter. . . . During this period the individual is still too weak to oppose the outside world actively, to defend himself against it by means of physical force or to modify it in accordance with his own will; as a rule the child is too helpless physically to take to flight and his understanding is as yet too limited for him to see the inevitable in the light of reason and submit to it. . . . In this period of immaturity and dependence the ego, besides making efforts to master instinctual stimuli, endeavors in all kinds of ways to defend itself against the objective "pain" and dangers which menace it. (p. 74)

In their recent paper, "Self-Preservation and Care of the Self," Khantzian and Mack (1983) also stressed a developmental perspective and elaborated on the critical role of early nurturing patterns and the protective functions of parents that are internalized and integrated into the development of adequate structures and ego functions that insure children's self-preservation. It was proposed that self-destructiveness is a result of failures and impairments in the development of these functions. These deficiencies offset the character structure of the child and leave him or her vulnerable to self-destructive behavior. These authors proposed that "such people are not so much compelled or driven in their behavior as they are impaired or deficient in self-care functions that are otherwise present in the mature ego" (p. 210).

Khantzian and Mack proposed that the following functions need to be developed for adequate self-preservation: (1) sufficient positive self-esteem to feel oneself to be worth protecting, (2) capacity to anticipate situations of risk, (3) ability to control impulses, (4) pleasure in mastering situations of risk, (5) knowledge about the outside world and oneself sufficient for survival in it, (6) ability to be self-assertive to protect oneself, and (7) ability to choose others who will enhance one's protection and not jeopardize one's existence. In fact, failure of these functions provides a basis for understanding the development of suicidal tendencies in children. Suicidal children succumb to intense stress because their ego functioning is overwhelmed and unable to defend against painful emotions, experiences, and fantasies. Some specific features of ego functioning observed during the suicidal episode are described in the next section.

EGO FUNCTIONING DURING
THE SUICIDAL EPISODE

The suicidal episode develops as a result of a crisis of ego functioning. This crisis arises from stress in the environment and the ego's incapacity to defend against unpleasant affects, fantasies, and memories. During this crisis, ego functions become reorganized in response to intense stress. A more extensive discussion of the specific processes of ego reorganization that lead to suicidal behavior is presented in Chapter 10.

An almost universal feature of ego functioning of suicidal individuals was described in Shneidman (1980), who observed that during the moments of the suicidal episode there evolves a massive narrowing of ego functioning that he termed "psychic constriction." He gave an example of such psychic constriction in the case of a woman who leaped over a balcony but miraculously survived. Her words offer a convincing account of psychic constriction: "The only way to lose consciousness, I thought, was to jump off something good and high. . . . I just walked around until I found this open staircase. As soon as I saw it, I just made a beeline right up to it. And then I got to the fifth floor and everything just got very dark all of a sudden, and all I could see was this balcony. Everything around it just blacked out. It was just like a circle. That was all I could see, just the balcony . . . and I went over it" (p. 16). This suicidal person was in an extreme state of cognitive impairment resulting from severe emotional distress.

Similar phenomena of ego constriction have been observed for children. Drastic changes develop in such ego mechanisms as cognitive skills, affect regulation, impulse control, reality testing, and fantasy expression. During the suicidal episode, unconscious impulses may be expressed, affects may become painful, fantasies may become intensified, identifications magnified, and ability to use appropriate judgment may be impaired. An acutely suicidal child may function at a regressed level so that the expressions of primitive impulses become acted out. The following example illustrates ego constriction in a child.

Child V: Lawrence, age 10 years, jumped out the bedroom window of his second-floor apartment. He had an argument with his father, who was loud and verbally abusive. Lawrence closed the door of his room and stood by his open window thinking about how helpless he felt in making his father understand him. He felt that there was no use in trying anymore. He felt extremely angry and thought about many past arguments with his father. Suddenly, he leaned out the window and tumbled down. He did not remember leaning out the window or falling. It was only after he hit the ground and felt the intense pain of his broken leg that he was aware of the argument with his father, standing in the room alone, and walking to the window with an idea of wanting to harm himself. Lawrence's ego constriction made it possible for him to fall out the window.

Other examples of ego constriction in children during suicidal episodes are children who repetitively take pills one after another in an automatic fashion, children who attempt to drown by swimming out as far as they can, and children who suddenly run into traffic. These children are in an intense state of ego constriction and do not have an objective awareness of their immediate situation and responses. It is this phenomenon of ego constriction that makes it impossible for the suicidal child to assess his or her situation objectively, and as a result the child's suicidal behavior often looks sudden and impulsive.

SELF-DESTRUCTIVE METHODS USED DURING THE SUICIDAL EPISODE

The examples in the previous sections show the variety of methods used by children to carry out their suicidal impulses. The suicidal methods used by today's youth are quite varied. Holinger (1978) reported that the most common suicidal methods for 10- to 14-year-olds in the United States include firearms and explosives, hanging, poisoning by liquids and solids, and poisoning by gas. The trends for this age group agree with the findings of Shaffer (1974) in his study of youngsters who committed suicide in England and Wales. Shaffer found that carbon monoxide gas, hanging, drug overdose, and firearms were the most frequent suicidal methods. He noted that girls took more drug overdoses and boys tended to hang themselves.

Studies of 6- to 12-year-old children who threatened or attempted suicide indicate that the methods utilized were varied but similar to those used by children who commit suicide. Children who contemplate, threaten, or attempt suicide use jumping from heights, ingesting poisons, hanging, stabbing, drowning, running into traffic, burning, and so forth (Pfeffer, 1981b; Pfeffer *et al.*, 1979, 1980, 1982). Children use jumping from heights as the most common suicidal method but rarely use firearms.

Many explanations have been offered as to how a particular method is chosen during the suicidal episode. Bender and Schilder (1937) believe that when there are strong aggressive motives, cutting, stabbing, and more violent methods are utilized. Others believe that the choice of method depends predominantly upon the degree of access to a lethal object or the skill in utilizing a particular instrument for self-destruction. Others hold strongly to the psychodynamic explanation of choice of method, where it is believed that unconscious factors influence the method utilized. Most probably the choice of method is determined by a combination of these factors.

SINGLE VERSUS REPETITIVE SUICIDAL EPISODES

An important issue is whether an in-depth analysis of a child's suicidal episode can enhance one's ability to predict and ameliorate future suicidal action. Shaffer (1974) noted, in a retrospective record review of children who committed suicide in England and Wales, that a high percentage (46%) of the 30 children who committed suicide had previously discussed, threatened, or attempted suicide. These findings suggest either that the remaining 54% of the children in this study had no previous suicidal behavior or that the historical data on their suicidal behavior were not available in the records that were reviewed. Nevertheless, it may be that a careful analysis of one suicidal episode may help predict when the child will be susceptible to repeated suicidal episodes, and in this way help to prevent subsequent suicidal behavior.

There are many ways a suicidal episode can affect the future behavior of a child. One common effect is that a single suicidal episode may be an organizer for a better life. In most children, the suicidal episode is a precipitant that alerts the family to the child's deep distress and, therefore, serves as a stimulant to seek appropriate intervention. In fact, the outcome of most suicidal preadolescents is good if appropriate interventions are carried out. The following example illustrates this.

Child VI: Eleven-year-old Joanne seriously attempted suicide by ingesting her stepmother's tranquilizers. Her suicidal episode was the culmination of severe stresses generated by her divorced parents' continued arguments, her inability to live in her mother's home, and her fear of living with her father, who became abusive if Joanne did not obey his instructions. On the day she received her report card, Joanne was acutely anxious. She worried that her father would be terribly angry because she did not make the honor roll. She paced around the house until she could no longer control her emotions. Joanne rushed into the bathroom and found some tranquilizers. She took 30 pills; 4 hours later she was discovered by her father in a semicomatose state. Joanne was rushed to a hospital where a psychiatrist recommended that Joanne be transferred to a psychiatric hospital for additional evaluation. After diagnostic assessments and short-term treatment on the psychiatric unit, Joanne was referred to a residential treatment center because her family life was far too tumultuous for her.

Five years have passed since this suicidal episode. Joanne has not shown other suicidal behaviors. Joanne remembers her hospital care with gratefulness. She feels that she does not wish to die and believes that she has learned to cope with life's stresses.

This child's suicidal episode and subsequent psychiatric treatment were determining forces that deterred her from subsequent suicidal behavior. This example is typical of the types of positive outcome that can be expected of many suicidal preadolescents if they follow a prescribed treatment program. In this example, the treatment decreased the child's intrapsychic distress in addition to providing a 24-hour therapeutic environment away from the turmoil of her current family pressures.

A different outcome of a suicidal episode is repetitive suicidal behavior. This is frequently seen if the child is not engaged in an intervention program that suits the child's specific needs. The following example illustrates this.

Child VII: Jerry, age 7 years, was admitted to a psychiatric hospital after he attempted to knife himself in the chest. Extensive hospital psychiatric treatment helped to resolve his suicidal tendencies sufficiently so that plans were made to place him in a residential treatment center. However, within 2 months after entering the treatment center, Jerry threatened to jump out a window. He felt unaccepted by his peers and wanted to go home. Frightened by his serious suicidal tendencies, the staff of the residential treatment center recommended that Jerry be rehospitalized. In the hospital, it was necessary to help him work on developing better peer interactions before he was able to reenter the residential treatment center. In this case, the child's suicidal threats were repetitive mechanisms to cope with intense stress of problems with peers.

Some children's repeated suicidal episodes occur as single events. In other children, suicidal behaviors may appear as multiple minievents within one major suicidal episode. Multiple minievents of suicidal behavior occur primarily when a child's initial suicidal messages are not heeded. The following example depicts the phenomenon of repeated minisuicidal episodes.

Child VIII: Joshua, age 9 years, attempted to jump off a school balcony, fell off the playground climbing bars, and attempted to burn his hair. Joshua was living in a foster home at the time of his suicidal actions because his parents could not care for him. The mother was an alcoholic and his father was unable to manage Joshua's hyperactive behavior. His suicidal behavior occurred when another foster child was about to leave the foster home and be reunited with his family. Joshua wanted to leave too; he wished he could return to his father. This wish was unattainable. Joshua preferred to die rather than to remain in the foster home. When Joshua burned his hair, he was taken to see a psychiatrist. His earlier suicidal behaviors were rationalized as accidental events caused by his hyperactivity. Joshua is an excellent illustration that children repeat suicidal efforts as long as intrapsychic and environmental stability does not exist.

Another effect of a suicidal episode is that an initial suicidal episode may increase a child's vulnerability to more serious suicidal behaviors in the future. Nine-year-old Karen was an example of how earlier suicidal tendencies escalate in degree of seriousness.

Child IX: Karen was overcome by loneliness, poor academic abilities, and feelings that children made fun of her. She made threats to kill herself. One year after her first episode of suicidal ideas, she ingested aspirin because she did not want to go to school. This behavior occurred after the family moved to a different neighborhood. This move produced a change in schools for Karen. The stress of having to make new friends, adjust to new teachers, and complete more difficult school work prompted Karen's suicidal action.

These clinical vignettes point out the variety of ways in which suicidal episodes are expressed by preadolescents. However, systematic empirical studies that follow such children prospectively over long periods of time are needed to evaluate the specific factors that are instrumental in promoting a positive outcome. Knowledge of these factors can be incorporated into programs geared to prevent suicidal behavior.

SOCIAL FACTORS INVOLVED IN THE SUICIDAL EPISODE

The emergence of suicidal episodes in children is influenced also by social variables that influence how children cope with stress. When the pain of a child's circumstances is unbearable, a child may respond by expressing suicidal impulses. This dynamic is illustrated in the next example.

Child X: Daniel, age 7 years, was unable to cope with a situation that he found intolerably confusing and very frightening. He believed that he needed psychiatric hospitalization because he fought with everyone in his family. He felt that he was to blame for the family's problems, and because of this he thought that he should die. Hospitalization occurred immediately after he climbed onto the roof of the family home and screamed to his mother that he was going to jump. His father pleaded and repeatedly assured him of love. Finally, he acquiesced to come off the roof.

Several months before Daniel's suicide threat, he showed a marked increase in destructive behaviors. He broke objects in the home but could not communicate why he was so angry. His mother entered psychotherapy because of severe depression. She had become overwhelmed by problems in the marriage. She was considering separating from Daniel's father, but this issue had not been directly spoken about to Daniel and his sisters. Daniel seemed to have incorporated his mother's depression. His escalated destructive behavior was a response to the impending destruction of the family unit. His leave-taking via his suicidal threat was the dramatization of his parents' separation. Daniel's behavior was a signal, among many indicators, that something was seriously wrong in the family.

Many children's suicidal episodes occurred within the context of disciplinary measures by the parents. Shaffer (1974), in reviewing reports of 30 children who committed suicide, discovered that the most common immediate precipitating event for the children's suicidal episodes was a "disciplinary crisis." The children were both expecting and receiving punishment from school or their parents. One example was Jody's mother, who attributed his suicide threat to the home situation which had gotten out of control.

Child XI: Jody, age 10 years, no longer listened to his mother's attempts to limit his behavior. His mother felt that a battle for control would invariably arise, with Jody either physically hurting her or threatening to harm himself. Jody's mother was concerned about the severity of fights between Jody and his sister. Also, she was concerned about Jody's school refusal. His suicide attempt occurred one morning when he refused to go to school. His mother attempted to force him to go by saying that he would not be allowed to watch TV that evening if he stayed home. Jody, upon hearing this, ran to the open apartment window, saying that he would jump out. His mother was able to restrain him and then arranged for a neighbor to help her bring him to the hospital emergency room. Jody was hospitalized on a child psychiatry inpatient unit for evaluation of this suicidal episode and his school refusal.

For many suicidal individuals it is not easy to determine whether a suicidal episode resulted from a person's attempts to manipulate the environment or attempts to cope with severe despondency, or both. Attempts to produce a change in the environment by means of suicidal behavior may imply that the individual has some degree of hope of a positive outcome. Sometimes if a suicidal episode occurs in a public setting, when a child knows that rescue is possible, there is hope of a positive outcome. However, many other episodes occur without hope, and many take place in situations when rescue is less likely. Albert is an excellent example of a child who both felt despair and wished to effect a drastic change in his environment.

Child XII: This 11-year-old boy was discharged from a psychiatric inpatient unit 3 weeks before his suicidal episode. He became anxious about relating to other children, especially because he feared that they would tease him. He begged his outpatient therapist to send him back to the hospital where he felt comfortable and wanted. His therapist tried to help Albert adjust to his new situation. However, one morning Albert fought with another boy at school. After the fight, Albert was brought to see his therapist. He was still in an agitated, angry state and demanded that he be immediately sent to the hospital. Without waiting for a response from his therapist, he walked to the window and yelled that he would jump out. However, he had enough self-control to hear his therapist say that perhaps it was too difficult for him and that he might do better in the hospital.

This child's suicide threat was his desperate effort to change his frightening situation. The child believed that a change would be possible, and he even demanded what he wanted. Thus, he negotiated effecting this wish by threatening suicide.

The outcome of a child's suicidal episode, as the previous example illustrates, often is affected by the social forces operative in the immediate circumstance when the suicidal episode develops. Stengel (1962) stated that in only a minority of suicidal acts is nothing left to chance. He believed that among the factors determining the outcome, the reaction of the environment is often decisive. He observed that the behavior of the majority of suicidal persons serves to give the environment an opportunity to intervene. The presence of another person during a suicidal episode may help account for why many suicidal children do not kill themselves. However, there are no empirical studies to determine whether children's suicidal episodes take place predominantly in isolation or in the presence of others. The next child is an example of children who make suicide attempts when they are alone.

Child XIII: Sam, age 11 years, was hospitalized after he swallowed many of his mother's tranquilizers. He had become increasingly sullen, angry, and depressed during the 2 months before his suicide attempt. He had difficulty falling asleep and cried in bed for several hours. One evening his mother found him sitting in the bathroom in a very drowsy state. She tried to arouse him but finding it very difficult, she called her doctor, who advised that she bring Sam to the hospital. After Sam's admission to the pediatric unit, he spoke openly about his suicide attempt. He attributed his suicidal behavior to family problems. He disliked his mother's boyfriend and said, "this man is taking my father's place." Sam cried when he saw this man "hug and kiss" his mother. He felt his mother no longer loved him. He said that killing himself would end his crying.

Unlike Sam, Kathleen was a child who appeared to initially act out her suicidal tendencies alone but subsequently involved another person in her suicidal episode.

Child XIV: Kathleen, age 9 years, was at the extreme of despair, feeling that no one loved her. She was abandoned by both parents and was being raised by an alcoholic aunt. One day, while at school, she left her classroom and went to the balcony of the school auditorium with the plan of jumping off the balcony. She wanted to die in order to relieve her intensely sad feelings. She waited until the teacher came in to see what she was doing. Suddenly she ran toward the balcony edge, crying "I want to kill myself." The teacher raced to her rescue. She collapsed into the teacher's arms, sobbing, but grateful that someone cared to find her and offer help.

An important issue to study is: What was different about Sam and Kathleen with respect to their suicidal episodes? Why did Sam not plan to be found but Kathleen did? Each child was deeply depressed, yet they orchestrated their suicidal episodes in a different manner. Kathleen explicitly waited until someone appeared before she carried out her suicide plan, but Sam's suicidal episode was devoid of involvement with others. His rescue occurred purely by chance. A few hypotheses may be offered to answer these questions. First, there may be differences in children's intent to die which may be greatly influenced by the intensity of depression and hopelessness experienced by the child. Second, the child who carries out suicidal behaviors in isolation may have been intensely preoccupied with death over a long period of time and have carefully thought out a plan of suicidal behavior. In contrast, the child who demonstrates suicidal behavior in a more public setting may not have as intense preoccupations with death. Third, the degree of impulsiveness of a child in response to stress may determine how he or she executes the suicidal intent. It may be that suicidal events that are orchestrated in isolation are more carefully planned while suicidal episodes that occur without regard to the social context of the situation are due to more impulsive responses of the child.

The suicidal episodes of children are influenced not only by involvements with adults but also by interactions with peers. Some children threaten or attempt to kill themselves because they feel devalued or rejected by their peers. The next child is an example of this type of peer relationship.

Child XV: Delores was 10 years old when she was hospitalized for repeatedly running away from home. On a child inpatient unit, she was teased and verbally abused by her peers. Whenever she was teased, she thought of killing herself. She felt so isolated and unloved that she wanted to escape. Her most promising remedy was thoughts of planning her suicide.

Another precipitant of suicidal behavior is learning about the suicidal behavior of a peer. This phenomenon usually occurs among adolescents and is relatively infrequent among preadolescents. It may be due to developmental differences between preadolescents and adolescents that are manifested by adolescent tendencies to form stronger peer group cohesiveness and identifications than are seen among preadolescents. This phenomenon may be accounted for by the fact that an adolescent may frequently identify with a friend who carries out suicidal actions.

The following example illustrates how interactions of preadolescents with adults were significant in deterring suicidal behavior and in influencing the development of a peer support network that was helpful in preventing a peer's suicidal behavior.

Child XVI: Jonathan was 9 years old when he threatened to stab himself at a residential treatment center. The preadolescents in his bunk were influenced by the staff's leadership and attempts to limit their friend's suicidal behavior. The peers in his bunk were so shocked at his threats that they got together to watch him and to prevent his self-harm. No other child in that group expressed suicidal tendencies. The youngsters identified with the adult standards rather than their friend's suicidal behavior.

This example illustrates that developmental issues, especially with regard to peer relationships and interactions with adults, are important in shaping the evolution of children's suicidal episodes. It also illustrates an approach of suicide prevention that incorporates developing an alliance of peers to help protect other friends and not collude with suicidal intentions.

SUMMARY

The drama of children's suicidal episodes is repeated every time a child attempts to take his or her own life. The episode is a complex event that evolves out of the interactions of a number of factors that affect the child's ego functioning. The suicidal episode is an event that arises from desperation.

Variables that affect the child's ego functioning during the suicidal episode include the child's previous life experiences, immediate environmental stresses, and the child's current state of affect regulation. Additional research is needed to analyze the immediate factors that help deter suicidal behavior. Nevertheless, research has determined that there are specific factors such as depression, preoccupations with death, and types of family situations that increase risk of childhood suicidal behavior. These risk factors are described extensively in the next several chapters.

RISK FACTORS FOR CHILDHOOD SUICIDAL BEHAVIOR

CHAPTER FIVE

AFFECTIVE DISORDERS AND SUICIDAL BEHAVIOR IN CHILDREN AND ADULTS

The boy's face expressed the whole tale of their situation. On that little shape had conveyed all the inauspiciousness and shadow which had darkened the first union of Jude, and all the accidents, mistakes, fears, errors of the last. He was their nodal point, their focus, their expression in a single term. For the rashness of those parents he had groaned, for their ill assortment he had quaked, and for the misfortunes of these he had died.
—Thomas Hardy, *Jude the Obscure*

A variety of studies have shown that the presence of an affective disorder is one of the most important factors that promoted risk for suicidal behavior in adults and children. This chapter includes descriptions of research on psychological, diagnostic, and biological variables that confirm the findings of a significant relationship between affective disorders and suicidal behavior. Studies of the relationship between affective disorders and suicidal behavior are more comprehensive for adults than for children. In view of this, many studies of adults are discussed in this chapter because they offer insights into hypotheses that may be tested with children. Investigations of physiological components of affective disorders, as they relate to suicidal behavior in adults and children, are also presented. As a result, the present chapter encompasses a perspective on psychobiological features linking affective disorders to suicidal behavior.

RESEARCH WITH ADULTS

The fact that a greater number of adults than children exhibit suicidal behavior makes it easier to develop studies using adults to investigate the relationship between affective disorders and suicidal behavior. Many of the studies described in this section point out findings for adults that also have been documented in children. These studies highlight a developmental continuum for children, adolescents and adults with regard to affective disorders and suicidal behavior.

Several studies have documented a relationship between completed suicide and affective disorders. Guze and Robins (1970) reviewed 17 follow-up reports which showed that affective disorders were associated with very high suicide rates. Among adults with primary affective disorders, completed suicide is 30 times more prevalent than in the general population. Dorpat and Ripley (1960) studied 114 consecutive suicides in King's County, Washington, in 1957 and 1958 and reported that in every case, symptoms of depression were obvious. Marked psychomotor retardation, severe insomnia, and anorexia were frequently reported. Tsuang (1978) reviewed follow-up hospital records of 525 adult psychiatric patients. Thirty suicides were identified. The percentage of death for each diagnostic group was: schizophrenia, 10.1%; depression, 9.3%; and controls, 1.9%—findings emphasizing that suicide was a significant factor in the long-term outcome of both schizophrenia and primary affective disorders. In an extensive study, 134 suicide victims were documented in St. Louis, Missouri, in 1956 and 1957 (Robins, Murphy, Wilkinson, Gassner, & Kayes, 1959). Interviews were carried out with close friends and relatives within a few weeks to months after the suicide. In this study, Robins and colleagues (1959) found that 94% of the suicide victims were psychiatrically ill, with 68% of the total group suffering from either manic–depressive disorder or chronic alcoholism. However, only 2% of the subjects in this sample were schizophrenic. The diagnosis of manic–depressive disease in this study included the diagnosis of involutional melancholia and psychotic depressive reaction. Those individuals with manic–depressive disease were in the depressive phase shortly before death. Sixty-eight percent of the manic–depressives and 77% of the alcoholics communicated their suicidal intentions prior to their suicides. Sixty-two percent of the manic–depressives and alcoholics had medical and psychiatric care within 1 year of their deaths.

Depression is also common among suicide attempters. Weissman (1974) reported that retrospective studies revealed that depression is the most common diagnosis, accounting for 35% to 79% of all suicide attempters. This study did not define the frequency of other diagnostic categories among suicide attempters. In addition, this study pointed out that suicidal risk is directly associated with severity of depressive symptoms.

Other studies also estimate that as many as 80% of suicide attempters are depressed at the time of the attempt. Silver, Bohnert, Beck, and Marcus (1971) found that of 45 patients admitted to Philadelphia General Hospital after making a suicide attempt, 47% had a primary diagnosis of affective disorder such as manic–depressive depression, involutional melancholia, psychotic depressive reaction, or depressive neurosis. Of the remaining subjects, 18% were alcoholics, 16% had personality disorders, and 9% were schizophrenic. All patients were seen within 1 day following admission to the hospital so that they were evaluated as soon as possible after their suicide attempt. Objective ratings of depression, carried out without knowledge of the patient's suicidal status, were significantly higher for the suicide attempters than for a group of 394 nonsuicidal psychiatric inpatients. Eighty percent of the suicidal patients were clinically depressed, with 49% being severely depressed and 31% being moderately depressed. Thus, the major finding of this study was that the suicidal patient is likely to be chronically depressed at the time of the suicide attempt. It must also be realized, however, that some suicide attempters have other psychiatric disorders that include alcoholism, personality disorders, and schizophrenia.

Depression has been correlated also with suicidal ideation. In an attempt to compare degree of depression in individuals with suicidal ideation and those who made suicide attempts, Lester and Beck (1977) studied 121 suicidal psychiatric inpatients. The Beck Depression Inventory (Table 5-1), a scale that measures the intensity of depression, was administered to each patient without the interviewer knowing the suicidal status of the patient. The results showed that symptoms and severity of depression were similar for individuals with suicidal ideation and suicide attempts. This study indicated that there is a continuum of severity and types of symptoms of depression in people with varying degrees of suicidal status.

Another area of investigation which has helped clarify the relation between affective disorders and suicidal behavior is the classification of suicidal behavior. Beck and his colleagues pointed out that it is an oversimplification to evaluate suicidal intent as a single dimension (Beck, Beck, & Kovacs, 1975; Beck, Weissman, Lester, & Trexler, 1976). They developed an objective rating scale to measure suicidal intent. This scale has been used extensively both in clinical evaluations and in systematic research of suicidal people. This Suicide Intent Scale, presented in Table 5-2, evaluates a suicidal person's behavior before, during, and after the suicidal act.

The scale has two main parts. The first part includes items on the objective circumstances of the suicidal attempt such as preparation and manner of expression of the attempt, the setting, and prior clues given by the person that could enhance or hamper intervention. The second part provides information from the suicidal person's self-report on his or her concept of the method's lethality, the extent of premeditation and intention, the purpose of the attempt, and expectations of rescue. As a modification of this scale, an additional part, concerned with risk and outcome, was added later (Pierce, 1977).

Utilizing this scale, Beck and his associates showed that when a per-

TABLE 5-1
Beck Depression Inventory

In each category, circle which statement applies to you in the past week.
1. 0 I do not feel sad.
    1 I feel sad.
    2 I am sad all the time and I can't snap out of it.
    3 I am so sad or unhappy that I can't stand it.
2. 0 I am not particularly discouraged about the future.
    1 I feel discouraged about the future.
    2 I feel I have nothing to look forward to.
    3 I feel that the future is hopeless and that things cannot improve.
3. 0 I do not feel like a failure.
    1 I feel I have failed more than the average person.
    2 As I look back on my life, all I can see is a lot of failures.
    3 I feel I am a complete failure as a person.
4. 0 I get as much satisfaction out of things as I used to.
    1 I don't enjoy things the way I used to.
    2 I don't get real satisfaction out of anything anymore.
    3 I am dissatisfied or bored with everything.
5. 0 I don't feel particularly guilty.
    1 I feel guilty a good part of the time.
    2 I feel quite guilty most of the time.
    3 I feel guilty all of the time.
6. 0 I don't feel I am being punished.
    1 I feel I may be punished.
    2 I expect to be punished.
    3 I feel I am being punished.
7. 0 I don't feel disappointed in myself.
    1 I am disappointed in myself.
    2 I am disgusted with myself.
    3 I hate myself.
8. 0 I don't feel I am any worse than anybody else.
    1 I am critical of myself for my weaknesses or mistakes.
    2 I blame myself all the time for my faults.
    3 I blame myself for everything bad that happens.
9. 0 I don't have any thoughts of killing myself.
    1 I have thoughts of killing myself, but I would not carry them out.
    2 I would like to kill myself.
    3 I would kill myself if I had the chance.
10. 0 I don't cry any more than usual.
    1 I cry more than I used to.
    2 I cry all the time now.
    3 I used to be able to cry, but now I can't cry even though I want to.
11. 0 I am not more irritated now than I ever am.
    1 I get annoyed or irritated more easily than I used to.
    2 I feel irritated all the time now.
    3 I don't get irritated at all by the things that used to irritate me.
12. 0 I have not lost interest in other people.
    1 I am less interested in other people than I used to be.
    2 I have lost most of my interest in other people.
    3 I have lost all my interest in other people.

(continued)

TABLE 5-1
(Continued)

13. 0 I make decisions about as well as I ever could.
    1 I put off making decisions more than I used to.
    2 I have greater difficulty in making decisions than before.
    3 I can't make decisions at all anymore.
14. 0 I don't feel I look any worse than I used to.
    1 I am worried that I am looking old or unattractive.
    2 I feel that there are permanent changes in my appearance that make me look unattractive.
    3 I believe that I look ugly.
15. 0 I can work about as well as before.
    1 It takes an extra effort to get started at doing something.
    2 I have to push myself very hard to do anything.
    3 I can't do any work at all.
16. 0 I can sleep as well as usual.
    1 I don't sleep as well as I used to.
    2 I wake up 1–2 hours earlier than usual and find it hard to get back to sleep.
    3 I wake up several hours earlier than I used to and cannot get back to sleep.
17. 0 I don't get more tired than usual.
    1 I get tired more easily than I used to.
    2 I get tired from doing almost anything.
    3 I am too tired to do anything.
18. 0 My appetite is no worse than usual.
    1 My appetite is not as good as it used to be.
    2 My appetite is much worse now.
    3 I have no appetite at all anymore.
19. 0 I haven't lost much weight, if any, lately.
    1 I have lost more than 5 pounds.
    2 I have lost more than 10 pounds.
    3 I have lost more than 15 pounds.
    I am purposely trying to lose weight by eating less. Yes _____ No _____
20. 0 I am no more worried about my health than usual.
    1 I am worried about physical problems such as aches and pains; or upset stomach; or constipation.
    2 I am very worried about physical problems and it's hard to think of much else.
    3 I am so worried about my physical problems that I cannot think about anything else.
21. 0 I have not noticed any recent change in my interest in sex.
    1 I am less interested in sex than I used to be.
    2 I am much less interested in sex now.
    3 I have lost interest in sex completely.

TABLE 5-2
Suicide Intent Scale

In each category, circle the statement that best applies.

Circumstances related to suicidal attempt

1. *Isolation*
   0 Somebody present
   1 Somebody nearby or in contact (as by phone)
   2 No one nearby or in contact
2. *Timing*
   0 Timed so that intervention is probable
   1 Timed so that intervention is not likely
   2 Timed so that intervention is highly likely
3. *Precautions against discovery and/or intervention*
   0 No precautions
   1 Passive precautions, for example, avoiding others but doing to prevent their intervention (alone in room, door unlocked)
   2 Active precautions, such as locking doors
4. *Acting to gain help during or after the attempt*
   0 Notified potential helper regarding attempt
   1 Contacted but did not specifically notify potential helper regarding the attempt
   2 Did not contact or notify potential helper
5. *Final acts in anticipation of death*
   0 None
   1 Partial preparation or ideation
   2 Definite plans made (e.g., changes in a will, taking out insurance)
6. *Suicide note*
   0 Absence of note
   1 Note written but torn up
   2 Presence of note

Self-report

1. *Patient's statement of lethality*
   0 Thought that what he had done would not kill him
   1 Unsure whether what he had done would kill him
   2 Believed that what he had done would kill him
2. *Stated intent*
   0 Did not want to die
   1 Uncertain or did not care if he lived or died
   2 Did want to die
3. *Premeditation*
   0 Impulsive, no premeditation
   1 Considered act for less than 1 hour
   2 Considered act for less than 1 day
   3 Considered act for more than 1 day
4. *Reaction to the act*
   0 Patient glad he has recovered
   1 Patient uncertain whether he is glad or sorry
   2 Patient sorry he has recovered

(continued)

TABLE 5-2
(*Continued*)

Risk

1. *Predictable outcome in terms of circumstances known to him*
   0 Survival certain
   1 Death unlikely
   2 Death likely or certain
2. *Would death have occurred without medical treatment?*
   0 No
   1 Uncertain
   2 Yes

Note. Copyright © 1978 by Aaron T. Beck, MD. Further information about this scale and/or permission to use and reproduce it may be obtained from the Center for Cognitive Therapy, Room 602, 133 South 36th St., Philadelphia, PA 19104.

son has an accurate concept of the lethality of his or her suicidal act, the degree of damage to the person's life is proportional to the suicidal intent. Therefore, a person with a high suicidal intent and an accurate concept of lethality would be at highest suicidal risk while a person with low suicidal intent and accurate concept of lethality would be of lowest risk.

Silver and colleagues (1971) utilized the Beck Suicide Intent Scale in a study of 45 suicidal inpatients. They found that the degree of suicidal intent was significantly related to the degree of the patient's depression. Thus, patients who had high scores on depression also had the highest suicide intent scores. This study concluded that the degree of depression in adults was directly related to the degree of suicidal intent.

Hopelessness is an important component of depressed symptomatology. However, hopelessness is apparent in patients with other psychiatric disorders besides depression. Since patients who are not depressed become suicidal, it is important to determine what the interactive effects of hopelessness and depression are in suicidal behavior. Beck, Weissman, Lester, and Trexler (1974) designed a scale to measure hopelessness. This scale, depicted in Table 5-3, provides a systematic estimate of hopelessness that could be used in research with suicidal individuals to determine the relationship between hopelessness and depression. The scale has a 20-item true–false format, and the degree of hopelessness can be estimated by the score on this scale.

Wetzel (1976) studied the relationship between hopelessness, depression, and suicide intent. He utilized 154 hospitalized psychiatric patients who were not diagnosed as schizophrenic but who had either

TABLE 5-3
Beck Hopelessness Scale

	True	False
1. I look forward to the future with hope and enthusiasm.	___	___
2. I might as well give up because I cannot make things better for myself.	___	___
3. When things are going badly, I am helped by knowing they cannot stay that way forever.	___	___
4. I cannot imagine what my life would be like in 10 years.	___	___
5. I have enough time to accomplish the things I most want to do.	___	___
6. In the future, I expect to succeed in what concerns me most.	___	___
7. My future seems dark to me.	___	___
8. I expect to get more of the good things in life than the average person.	___	___
9. I just don't get the breaks, there is no reason to believe I will in the future.	___	___
10. My past experiences prepared me well for my future.	___	___
11. All I can see ahead of me is unpleasantness rather than pleasantness.	___	___
12. I don't expect to get what I really want.	___	___
13. When I look ahead to the future, I expect that I will be happier than I am now.	___	___
14. Things just won't work out the way I want them to.	___	___
15. I have great faith in the future.	___	___
16. I never get what I want so it's foolish to want anything.	___	___
17. It is very unlikely that I will get any real satisfaction in the future.	___	___
18. The future seems vague and uncertain to me.	___	___
19. I can look forward to more good times than bad times.	___	___
20. There is no use in really trying to get something I want because I probably won't get it.	___	___

Note. Copyright © 1978 by Aaron T. Beck, MD. Further information about the scale and/or permission to use and reproduce it may be obtained from the Center for Cognitive Therapy, Room 602, 133 South 36th St., Philadelphia, PA 19104.

an intentional self-inflicted injury or repeated suicidal thoughts within 1 week of interview, or who had no suicidal preoccupations. He used the Beck Suicide Intent Scale, the Beck Hopelessness Scale, and the Zung Self-Rating Depression Scale (Zung, 1965) to rate the patients. He found that the severity of suicidal intent was significantly related to depression scores. Furthermore, hopelessness was highly correlated with suicidal behavior. Hopelessness scores differentiated between suicidal and nonsuicidal subjects and between highly suicidal and less suicidal subjects. One of the most important findings of this study was that hopelessness correlated higher with suicide intent or suicidal behavior than depression did in all cases. In the analysis of the data it was determined that when the effect of hopelessness was controlled statistically, depression no longer correlated with suicide intent. However, when the effect of depression was controlled statistically, hopelessness remained significantly correlated with suicide intent. Therefore, the data supported the hypothesis that although depression is related to suicide intent, hopelessness is more crucial to suicidal risk than depression.

Evidence of an important relation between hopelessness and suicide was offered in a recent 5- to 10-year follow-up study of 207 patients previously hospitalized because of suicidal ideation but not for suicide attempts. In this study, Beck, Steer, Kovacs, and Garrison (1985) utilized the Beck Depression Inventory, the Hopelessness Scale, and the Scale for Suicide Ideation, which were administered to each patient during the time of his or her hospitalization. The Scale for Suicide Ideation includes 19 items that quantify the frequency and duration of suicidal thoughts and the patient's attitudes toward them. Of the 107 patients 34 (16.4%) died from all causes and 14 (6.9%) committed suicide. The Hopelessness Scale scores were the only scores that significantly differentiated between the patients who committed suicide and those who did not. This study suggested that the degree of present hopelessness has an important role in predicting future suicide in individuals with suicidal ideation. Furthermore, the findings suggested that when scores of hopelessness were statistically controlled, severity of depression did not differentiate between suicide victims who had previous suicidal ideation from those patients who did not commit suicide. This study supports Wetzel's (1976) previous study regarding hopelessness as a significant factor in suicidal behavior.

Although many studies indicate that there is a strong relationship between depression and suicidal behavior, it is not entirely clear what differences exist between depressed people who are suicidal and those who are not. In order to consider this question, Stallone, Dunner, Ahearn, and Fieve (1980) looked at the distinguishing factors between suicidal and nonsuicidal depressed people. All 205 patients met criteria for primary affective disorder and were categorized into three groups: suicide attempters who made at least one suicide attempt, suicide contemplators who thought about but never attempted suicide, and nonsuicidal patients who never thought about or attempted suicide. Of the patients studied 35.1% were attempters, 36% contemplators, and 28.8% nonsuicidal individuals.

The affective disorders were classified as a bipolar I group, with all the members having a history of severe mania requiring hospitalization; a bipolar II group which had members with a history of hypomania never requiring hospitalization but with a history of severe depression requiring hospitalization; a "bipolar other" group which had a history of mild highs and lows never requiring hospitalization; and a unipolar group which had a history of depression but no history of mania or hypomania.

The bipolar II group had the highest percentage of suicide attempters (45.3%), the bipolar other group had the highest percentage of contemplators (59.4%), and the bipolar I group had the highest percentage of nonsuicidal individuals (38.9%). Females had twice as many attempters as males, but contemplators were evenly represented by males and females. Positive family history of suicidal behavior was twice as prevalent among attempters and contemplators than among the nonsuicidal individuals. The attempters and contemplators were more socially isolated than the nonsuicidal people. Thus, the attempters and contemplators were more similar to each other than either was to the nonsuicidal group on variables of social isolation and family history of suicidal behavior but differed with respect to type of affective disorder and sex.

In summary, this section has pointed out several conclusions about the relationship between affective disorders and suicidal behavior in adults. Studies have shown that there is a significant relationship between affective disorders and suicide, suicide attempts, and suicidal ideation. In adults who have an accurate concept of the lethality of a suicidal act, the degree of damage to life is proportional to the degree of suicidal intent and the degree of depression. Furthermore, the degree of hopelessness appears to be a more critical factor for suicidal risk than the degree of depression. Studies to evaluate whether similar relationships exist for children are needed in order to assess if there is a continuity of suicidal risk factors in different developmental periods of life. The next section highlights studies of children with regard to these issues.

RESEARCH WITH CHILDREN

It has been determined that a significant relationship exists between depression and suicidal behavior in children. For example, Shaffer (1974) observed that approximately 42% of 30 children who committed suicide showed signs of depressed mood and tearfulness. Furthermore, in studies of child psychiatric inpatients and outpatients carried out by Pfeffer and associates (1979, 1980, 1982), depression significantly correlated with a spectrum of suicidal behavior that included suicidal ideas, suicidal threats, and suicidal attempts. Pfeffer and coworkers (1984) also found, in a sample of 100 normal schoolchildren, that depression was significantly more severe among the suicidal children than among the nonsuicidal children. Finally, Mattsson, Seese, and Hawkins (1969) found that among suicidal children referred for psychiatric emergency care, 40% had signs of depression for at least 1 month before being seen.

Carlson and Cantwell (1982) systematically assessed the relationship between severity of depression and the degree of suicidal ideas and attempts in children and adolescents. One hundred and two children and adolescents who were psychiatric inpatients and psychiatric outpatients were interviewed. Forty-five children had no suicidal ideas, 45 had occasional thoughts of suicide, and 12 seriously felt like killing themselves. In addition, 22 children of the total group made a suicide attempt. The average degree of depression for the children with occasional suicidal ideas was greater than for the children without suicidal ideas and less than for the children with severe suicidal ideation. Thirty-three percent of the children with occasional suicidal thoughts met the diagnostic criteria for major affective disorder. The children with serious suicidal ideation were rated as severely depressed. Eighty-three percent of this group were diagnosed as having a major affective disorder.

The children with serious suicidal ideation felt more hopeless than the children with little or no suicidal ideation. In addition, the children with depressive disorders were twice as likely to feel hopeless than children with other psychiatric diagnoses. Among all the depressed children in this population, 30% made a suicide attempt, in contrast to 18% nondepressed children who attempted suicide. Thirty-eight percent of the nonattempters and 50% of the attempters felt hopeless.

This study concluded that there was a direct relation between feeling depressed and being suicidal. However, not all children who were suicidal were depressed. There was a clearer relation between children with depression and suicidal ideation than between suicide attempters and depression.

Additional investigation of the relation between depression and suicidal behavior was carried out by Robbins and Alessi (1985a) in their study of 64 adolescent psychiatric inpatients. The purpose of the study was to evaluate associations between psychiatric symptoms that were assessed during structured interviews and suicidal behavior. The structured interviews followed the format of the Schedule for Affective Disorders and Schizophrenia (SADS), a well-known procedure to diagnose severe psychopathology in adolescents and adults (Spitzer & Endicott, 1977). The SADS evaluates aspects of suicidal tendencies that include the intent to die, the number of previous suicide attempts, and the lethality of the most recent suicide attempt. Statistical analysis that reflected correlations between these suicide items and each of 38 SADS psychiatric symptoms was undertaken.

Among the 64 adolescents, 31 made no suicide attempts, 15 made two or more attempts, and six made very serious attempts. Five of the six patients who made very serious suicide attempts had diagnoses of major depressive disorder. The other patient had a dysthymic disorder. Furthermore, the medical seriousness of the suicidal behavior was associated with conscious intent to die and with the number of previous nonlethal suicide attempts. Symptoms associated with suicidal behavior included depressed mood, negative self-evaluation, anhedonia, insomnia, poor concentration, indecisiveness, lack of reactivity of mood, psychomotor disturbance, and alcohol and drug abuse. These findings strongly suggest that symptoms of depressive disorders are significantly related to suicidal risk in adolescents. Furthermore, similar research methodology can be used to evaluate whether these findings would occur in preadolescents.

Another study, carried out by Cohen-Sandler and colleagues (1982a), of 76 psychiatrically hospitalized inpatient children who were 5 to 14 years old attempted to distinguish between suicidal children, depressed nonsuicidal children, and children with other psychiatric disorders. The children were considered suicidal when the child "engaged in overt, potentially self-destructive behavior and verbalized either intent to inflict lethal self-harm or a wish to kill himself or herself" (p. 179). The group of depressed, nonsuicidal children fulfilled criteria for depression by having both dysphoric mood and self-depreciatory ideation, and four or more of the following symptoms: sleep disturbance, change in school performance, diminished socialization, change in attitude toward school, somatic complaints, loss of energy, and changes in appetite and weight. The children with other psychiatric disorders included all children who were not in either the suicidal or depressed groups. The suicidal children were found to have experienced increasingly greater amounts of stress as they matured than the other children in the study. This stress included primarily disruptive family events such as losses and separations from important people. This study, therefore, provided important information about some distinguishing characteristics of depressed suicidal and depressed nonsuicidal children.

Kazdin, French, Unis, Esveldt-Dawson, and Sherick (1983b) used a modification of the Beck Hopelessness Scale in a study of the relationship between depression, suicidal status, and hopelessness in children. Sixty-six psychiatrically hospitalized children, ages 8 to 13 years, were evaluated. The children who scored high on the hopelessness scale showed significantly more depression and lower self-esteem than the children who scored low on the scale. The suicidal children showed more hopelessness than the children who were not suicidal. As was found in studies of adults, the most important finding of this study was that suicidal risk was correlated more with hopelessness than with depression. Thus, this study supported the hypothesis that the relationship among suicidal behavior, depression, and hopelessness is the same for children and adults.

Although depression has been clearly associated with suicidal behavior in children, the relation between suicidal behavior and other affect states such as aggression has been not well studied in children. Shaffer (1974) found that among 30 children who committed suicide, 17% of the children had only antisocial symptoms that included aggressive behavior; 13% of the children had only affective symptoms of depression, 57% of the children had mixed antisocial affective symptoms, and 13% had neither antisocial nor affective symptoms. Furthermore, in an attempt to further evaluate the relationships between nonfatal suicidal behavior, depression, and aggression in children, Pfeffer and colleagues (1982) evaluated 102 children, 6 to 12 years old, seen in a municipal hospital psychiatric inpatient unit and outpatient clinic. Four groups of children with suicidal and/or assaultive behaviors were defined. The first group, called *nonassaultive–nonsuicidal*, was made up of children with no assaultive ideas, threats, or attempts; and no suicidal ideas, threats, or attempts. The second group, called *suicidal-only*, consisted of children with no assaultive ideas, threats, or attempts; and with either suicidal ideas, threats, or attempts. The third group, called *assaultive-only*, included children with either assaultive ideas, threats, or attempts; but no suicidal ideas, threats, or attempts. The fourth group, called *assaultive–suicidal*, included children with suicidal ideas, threats, or attempts, and assaultive ideas, threats, or attempts. Among all the children, 16.7% were nonassaultive–nonsuicidal, 10.8% were suicidal-only, 25.5% were assaultive-only, and 47.0% were assaultive-suicidal. The distribution of these four groups of suicidal and/or assaultive children was remarkably similar to the distribution noted by Shaffer (1974) for children who committed suicide.

Other findings of this study were that dysthymic disorder and major depressive disorder were the most common diagnoses among the suicidal-only children. Aggression was significantly greater for both the assaultive–suicidal children and the assaultive-only children than for either the nonassaultive–nonsuicidal children or the suicidal-only children. The assaultive-only children and the assaultive–suicidal children experienced significantly more parental violence than the other children. The parents of the assaultive–suicidal children and suicidal-only children had significantly more suicidal behavior than the parents of the other children.

The findings of this study delineated two types of suicidal children. One type, the suicidal-only, is composed of children with relatively stable ego functioning, including good reality testing, who decompensate and become overtly depressed only under the influence of extreme environmental stress. The other group of suicidal children, the assaultive–suicidal, have distinct ego deficits and are prone to identify with parental acting out of suicidal tendencies. These suicidal children are subject to a variety of parental symptomatic behaviors, predominantly including rage episodes and serious assaultive tendencies. Thus, although some suicidal children show intense depression, other suicidal children exhibit relatively less depression but show high intensity of aggression. This study provides clear evidence that there are subgroups of suicidal children with distinct clinical characteristics and that both depression and aggression are important affects in determining risk for suicidal behavior.

In summary, many studies similar to those carried out in adults to evaluate the relationships between affective disorders and suicidal behavior have been completed for children. Essentially, these studies of children show that there are similarities between children and adults for many psychological factors associated with affective disorders and risk for suicidal behavior.

Studies specifically have shown that depression is associated with suicidal behavior in children and that as the degree of depression increases, risk for suicidal behavior increases. In addition, risk for childhood suicidal behavior is more influenced by the degree of hopelessness than by the degree of depression. Finally, there are at least two types of suicidal children. One type includes children with stable ego functioning and severe depression. The other type includes children with deficits in ego functioning and extreme parental psychopathology. These children appear to be less depressed but more aggressive.

Further studies are needed to compare risk factors for suicidal behavior in children with those in adults. An especially important area for investigation is the relationship between suicidal behavior and biological variables. More studies involving biological factors and suicidal behavior have been undertaken for adults than for children. A variety of such studies are highlighted in the next section.

THE BIOLOGY OF AFFECTIVE DISORDERS AND SUICIDAL BEHAVIOR

A frontier of psychiatric research involves the measurement of biochemical and physiological parameters of affective disorders and suicidal behavior. Such research has great promise not only in defining biological markers that help us understand the pathophysiology of affective disorders and suicidal behavior but also in serving to identify warning signs of suicidal behavior.

An emerging area of diagnostic importance is the use of the dexamethasone suppression test to diagnose major depression. This test has been used extensively and for a long time to diagnose endocrinopathies related to abnormalities in the hormone cortisol. Carroll and his associates (1981) described the standardization, validation, and clinical utility of this test. They studied 368 adult patients who were psychiatric inpatients and outpatients with a variety of disorders that included major depression, schizophrenia, personality disorders, and neurosis. In addition, a group of 70 normal subjects were included in the study.

The procedure for the dexamethasone suppression test follows: On the first day of the test, blood samples of cortisol are obtained at 8:00 A.M., 4:00 P.M., and 11:00 P.M. At 11:00 P.M., 1 mg of dexamethasone is administered orally to the patient. The next day, blood cortisol levels are obtained at 8:00 A.M., 4:00 P.M., and 11:00 P.M. A plasma cortisol level of 5 μg/dl or above in any of the three blood samples obtained on the second day is associated with the diagnosis of major depression. It has been noted that 98% of the positive results are detected when the results of the postdexamethasone blood samples at 4:00 P.M. and 11:00 P.M. are combined. The diagnostic confidence for major depressive disorder associated with a plasma cortisol concentration above 5 μg/dl is 95%. However, approximately 4% of normal subjects have been found to have positive dexamethasone suppression test results. The reason for this is not known. In addition, the dexamethasone suppression test in identifying patients with major affective disorder has a sensitivity of 67% and a specificity of 96%. Sensitivity is the percentage of subjects who actually have the disorder who are positively identified with the dexamethasone suppression test. Specificity is the percentage of subjects who do not have the disorder and who do not have false-positive dexamethasone test results.

Carroll and associates (1981) believed that age of adult subjects, sex, and recent use of psychotropic drugs have no effect on the dexamethasone suppression test results. However, more recent studies have shown that the dexamethasone suppression test results can be influenced by a number of other factors. For example, nonsuppression of cortisol during the dexamethasone suppression test has been found to occur in patients with such psychiatric disorders as dysthymic disorders, obsessive–compulsive disorders, schizophrenia, manic disorders, dementia, and eating disorders (Arana, Barreira, Cohen, Lipinski, & Fogelson, 1983; Insel & Goodwin, 1983). Because other diagnoses have been found to be associated with nonsuppression of cortisol during the dexamethasone suppression test, the value of this test in discriminating between major affective disorders and these other psychiatric disorders is more limited than Carroll and associates' reports initially indicated. Additional investigations are needed to decipher more fully the potential usefulness of the dexamethasone suppression test as a diagnostic procedure.

Nevertheless, Carroll *et al.* suggested that the dexamethasone suppression test may be applied also to preadolescents and adolescents. There are a few investigations that have studied this issue. One study, carried out by Poznanski, Carroll, Banegas, Cook, and Grossman (1982), of 18 dysphoric child outpatients who were 6 to 12 years old used 0.5 mg of dexamethasone. Only one blood sample after administration of dexamethasone was drawn, at 4:00 P.M. Among the 18 patients, eight were diagnosed as having a major depressive disorder. The remaining children who were not depressed were diagnosed as having a conduct disorder (two children), attention deficit disorder (two children), no psychiatric diagnosis (one child), labile personality (one child), academic underachievement (one child), histronic personality (one child), and separation anxiety disorder (one child). Out of the nine children with major depressive disorder, five had abnormal dexamethasone tests. The sensitivity of the test for major depressive disorder was at least 56%. Only one child with a nondepressed diagnosis had an abnormal test. There was a specificity of 89%; findings that were similar for adult depressed patients.

Targum (1981) was also one of the earliest investigators who evaluated the dexamethasone suppression test in children. He studied 19 prepubertal psychiatric inpatients who were 9 to 13 years old and all of whom were diagnosed as having a conduct disorder. No child had a major depressive disorder. Each child received 1 mg of dexamethasone administered at 11:30 P.M. Two children out of 19 showed an abnormal dexamethasone response. The majority of patients in this study showed normal dexamethasone test results; findings that support its usefulness in diagnosing major depression. The author, puzzled by the two children with abnormal dexamethasone tests, hypothesized that perhaps these children may represent a spectrum of affective disorders and that they may subsequently develop symptoms consistent with major depressive disorder.

Obviously, additional research is necessary to evaluate the dexamethasone suppression test in children. For example, as with adult patients, Geller, Rogol, and Knitter (1983) questioned the value of the dexamethasone suppression test in diagnosing major depressive disorder in children. They studied 14 children who were all outpatients and diagnosed as having a major depressive disorder. Each child received 20 μg/kg of dexamethasone orally at 11:30 P.M. The next day plasma cortisol was measured at 4:00 P.M. Only two children had elevated plasma cortisol levels. These findings differed from those of Poznanski and associates (1982), who observed that 56% of children with major affective disorder had elevated plasma cortisol. However, the doses of dexamethasone were different in these studies. In addition, these studies used small numbers of children. Therefore, the findings of these reports must be considered tentative.

Recent studies have provided additional information about the role of the dexamethasone suppression test in diagnosing severe depression in children. Klee and Garfinkel (1984) administered 1 mg of dexamethasone to 33 child and adolescent psychiatric inpatients and found the test to have 40% sensitivity and 92% specificity. The lower sensitivity and higher specificity in this study may be related, in part, to the 1-mg dose of dexamethasone used. Higher sensitivities were reported by Weller, Weller, Fristad, and Preskorn (1984) and by Petty, Asarnow, Carlson, and Lesser (1985) who used 0.5 mg of dexamethasone to evaluate child psychiatric inpatients. Sensitivities of 70% and 87% were obtained in these studies, respectively. However, Petty and associates (1985) were concerned about the low specificity (53%) in their study. The reason for this low specificity was not clear and these researchers suggested that further studies are needed to evaluate this finding.

There appears to be a relation between the dexamethasone suppression test and completed suicide in adults. In one study, carried out by Coryell and Schlesser (1981), 243 adult psychiatric inpatients who were depressed were given the dexamethasone suppression test. Four of these patients who later committed suicide were among the 96 patients who had abnormal dexamethasone suppression tests. Since the sample size of individuals who committed suicide was so small, additional studies are needed to validate these findings. If these findings are validated, the dexamethasone suppression test may be shown to be a useful diagnostic test to predict suicidal risk.

Evaluation of the relation between the dexamethasone suppression test and suicidal behavior in adolescent inpatients was carried out by Robbins and Alessi (1985b). Of the 45 inpatients evaluated, 23 attempted suicide. All six patients who showed nonsuppression of plasma cortisol in response to 1 mg of dexamethasone attempted suicide. However, 17 of the 22 patients with normal dexamethasone suppression tests attempted suicide. Of those who attempted suicide, four of the six nonsuppressors made medically lethal attempts and none of the 17 suppressors made severe suicide attempts. Thus there was a highly significant association of dexamethasone nonsuppression with potentially lethal suicidal behavior. Because this sample is relatively small, the findings should be considered preliminary. Nevertheless, this study suggests that the dexamethasone suppression test may be a useful diagnostic tool for assessing suicidal risk.

Another focus of research with suicide victims involves disturbances of circadian rhythmicity. Circadian rhythms involve physiological and hormonal variables known to vary in a well-defined cyclical fashion in normal individuals. Rockwell, Winget, Rosenblatt, Higgins, and Hetherington (1978) evaluated the heart rate; body temperature; and urinary levels of creatinine, 17 hydroxyketogenic steroids, epinephrine, norepinephrine, sodium, and potassium in 15 male adults. One subject committed suicide 2 weeks after the study. This suicidal subject demonstrated a desynchronization of urinary metabolites that was significantly different from the other subjects. The significance of this study is that it points out another direction to search for possible biological indicators for suicide.

A different avenue of research has shown that alterations in the neurotransmitter serotonin, associated with depression, have been found in individuals who committed suicide. Among 68 subjects studied by Asberg, Traskman, and Thoren (1976), two committed suicide. These two subjects had low levels of 5-hydroxyindoleacetic acid in their spinal fluid. In an enlarged study, the same investigators measured the concentrations of the monoamine metabolites 5-hydroxyindoleacetic acid, homovanillic acid, and 3-methoxy-4-hydroxyphenylglycol in spinal fluid (Traskman, Asberg, Bertilsson, & Sjostrand, 1981). The subjects of the study included 30 psychiatric patients who attempted suicide and 45 healthy volunteers. The suicide attempters, especially those with more violent suicidal methods, had significantly lower 5-hydroxyindoleacetic acid than the controls. A follow-up of these patients within 1 year showed that among those patients with a low 5-hydroxyindoleacetic acid level, there was a 20% mortality by suicide.

Other studies have supported these findings. Agren (1980) found low levels of 5-hydroxyindoleacetic acid in the cerebrospinal fluid to be related to suicidal behavior in depressed patients; Brown and associates (1982) noted an association between aggression, suicidal behavior, and low levels of 5-hydroxyindoleacetic acid in patients with personality disorders without affective disorder; and Ninan and colleagues (1984) found that suicidal schizophrenic patients had lower levels of 5-hydroxyindoleacetic acid than nonsuicidal schizophrenic patients.

These studies are worthy of further pursuit especially because they indicate that levels of 5-hydroxyindoleacetic acid may be a biological marker of suicide. In addition, the studies more clearly point out that there is an important relationship between intensity of aggression and suicide. Thus, in addition to depression, other affects such as aggression may be important factors for suicidal behavior.

Another associated pioneering area of research involves analysis of brains of suicidal and nonsuicidal subjects. Stanley, Virgilio, and Gershon (1982) measured the binding sites of imipramine, a drug used to treat depression, in the frontal cortex of the brain. Nine subjects who committed suicide and nine deceased nonsuicidal subjects were studied. The binding affinity of imipramine was no different in the suicidal and nonsuicidal subjects, but the suicidal subjects had 44% fewer binding sites than the nonsuicidal subjects. Since imipramine binding may be associated with neuronal uptake of serotonin, a decrease in the number of imipramine binding sites in the brain may indicate a functional decrease in serotonergic neuronal activity. In order to evaluate this, a study would have to be done to see if changes in concentrations of serotonin and 5-hydroxyindoleacetic acid in the spinal fluid occur in the same patients with decreased imipramine binding sites.

In summary, there is a growing body of information that links suicidal behavior in adults to abnormalities of neurophysiological functioning. However, studies of such biological markers for suicidal behavior in children have not been done. Neuroendocrine abnormalities of cortisol secretion found with the dexamethasone suppression test in depressed adult patients have been shown to provide tentative clues for those adults who later committed suicide. Abnormalities in the functioning of the serotonin neurotransmitter system have been found in adult suicidal individuals. These findings open up avenues for research investigations of other neurophysiological pathways. These findings suggest the existence of a biological basis for some groups of people with suicidal behavior.

Although studies of biological markers for childhood suicidal behavior are nonexistent, the search to define biological markers for affective disorders in children has remarkably paralleled physiological investigations in adults. Cytryn, McKnew, Logue, and Desai (1974) were among the first to look at biological variables in childhood depression. They found that changes in such urinary metabolites as 3-methoxy-4-hydroxyphenylglycol occur in depressed children, but there were no differences for urinary norepinephrine and for 4-hydroxy-3-methoxy-mandelic acid between depressed and normal children (McKnew & Cytryn, 1979).

Puig-Antich and his associates (Puig-Antich, 1980; Puig-Antich, Novacenko, Goetz, Corser, Davies, & Ryan, 1984) have conducted the most extensive investigations of physiological correlates of childhood affective disorders. Among their studies, they documented plasma cortisol hypersecretion in some children with major depressive disorder. This hypersecretory pattern is similar to that found in some adults with major affective disorders. Preliminary findings indicated that approximately one-fifth of children diagnosed as having major affective disorder hypersecrete cortisol during periods of illness. In addition, Puig-Antich *et al.* studied growth hormone response to insulin-induced hypoglycemia in groups of children with major affective disorder, other depressed children, and nondepressed children. The results indicated that there was a hyposecretion of growth hormone among children with major affective disorder. Ninety percent of the major affective disorder group had a peak growth hormone response below 4 ng/ml in the first hour. Fifty percent of the other depressed children and 0% of the nondepressed children had peak values above 4 ng/ml. These findings are similar to those for adults with major affective disorders.

Another area of investigation has been the nature of sleep disturbances and rapid-eye-movement (REM) sleep measures in children with major affective disorders. Puig-Antich and colleagues (1982) initially studied 54 children diagnosed with major affective disorder, 25 children with other emotional disorders, and 11 normal children. The three groups of children did not differ on measurements of sleep. These findings are different than for adults. Adult depressed individuals have different sleep patterns than nondepressed individuals. The investigators offered two possible explanations for these findings. One explanation is that children with major affective disorders suffer from a different depressive disorder than adults. A second explanation is that lack of distinctive sleep findings in depressed children is due to maturational factors so that certain features of the affective disorder are not present until the individual reaches adulthood. Thus, the sleep findings in adult depressives would be due to an interactive effect between age and depression.

In a second study, Puig-Antich and his group (Puig-Antich, Goetz, Hanlon, Tabrizi, Davis, & Weitzman, 1983) documented a distinguishing pattern of sleep measures in children who recovered from a major affective illness. In this study of 28 fully recovered children who had a major affective disorder, it was determined that these children had significantly shorter first rapid-eye-movement-period (REMP) latencies than nondepressed and normal children. REMPs are specific features of sleep that occur several times throughout a given night. REMP latencies are the phases of sleep just before the onset of REMP. In addition, Puig-Antich and associates' study showed that the children who recovered from a major affective disorder had a higher number of REMPs compared with themselves when these children were in maximum phase of depression and also compared with nondepressed and normal children. These investigators suggested that a short first REMP latency may be a marker of a past depressive episode or a trait in childhood major depressive disorder. This finding suggests that some physiologic correlates of major affective disorder are different for children and adults. However, these sleep measurements have not been studied with respect to suicidal tendencies in children.

SUMMARY

This chapter has pointed out some of the significant associations between affective disorders and suicidal behavior in adults and children. Findings revealed that severity of depression and degree of hopelessness are significantly related to suicidal behavior in children and adults. Although investigations of biological markers for suicide and depression are more numerous and extensive for adults, several similarities in findings exist between adults and children. Dexamethasone suppression test response, cortisol hypersecretion, and hyposecretion of growth hormone in insulin-induced hypoglycemia have been documented for children and adults with major affective disorders. Physiological indicators of sleep disturbances, however, seem to differ among depressed children and adults.

The importance of these findings is that these factors can be used to diagnose risk for depression. Since depression is associated with suicidal behavior, these biological variables may be important clues for suicidal risk. These findings also suggest that there is a valid neurophysiological basis for affective disorders and that there may be a biological basis for suicidal behavior in some individuals. Additional research is needed to uncover the possibility of other biological factors in suicidal behavior.

In view of the strongly documented association between depressive disorders and suicidal behavior, the phenomenology of childhood depression is reviewed in the next chapter. The criteria used to diagnose childhood depression, a specific risk factor for childhood suicidal behavior, are highlighted in that discussion.

CHAPTER SIX

DEPRESSIVE DISORDERS IN CHILDREN

> When a matured man discovers that he has been deserted by Providence, deprived of his God, and cast without help, comfort, or sympathy, upon a world which is new and strange to him, his despair, which may find expression in evil-living, the writing of his experiences, or the more satisfactory diversion of suicide, is generally supposed to be impressive. A child, under exactly similar circumstances as far as its knowledge goes, cannot very well curse God and die. It howls till its nose is red, its eyes are sore, and its head aches. —Rudyard Kipling, "Baa, Baa, Black Sheep"

The previous chapter supplies evidence for the association of affective disorders and suicidal behavior in children and adults. Furthermore, studies have shown that depression is a specific risk factor for suicidal behavior in children (Pfeffer *et al.*, 1979, 1980, 1982, 1984; Carlson & Cantwell, 1982). In view of this fact, it is necessary to have comprehensive knowledge about childhood depression in order to understand the phenomenon of childhood suicidal behavior. Therefore, several features of depression in children that are not reviewed in Chapter 5 are discussed here. In this chapter, a historical perspective on depression in children is provided by exploring the past controversies about whether depressive disorders exist in children. Clinical criteria used to diagnose depression in children are discussed. Cases of depressed children illustrate the varied clinical pictures seen in these affective disorders. Furthermore, data about the prevalence of depression in children are provided.

PSYCHOANALYTIC THEORIES: A HISTORICAL PERSPECTIVE

Early theories of depression were developed primarily by psychoanalysts. S. Freud, K. Abraham, and S. Rado were among the most important contributors to these theories. They attempted to differentiate between the normal processes of mourning and the pathological state of severe depression. Psychoanalytic theory has been and still is one of the most important foundations for understanding the psychodynamic aspects of depression.

S. Freud (1917b), in "Mourning and Melancholia," said:

> Mourning is regularly the reaction to the loss of a loved person, or to the loss of some abstraction which has taken the place of one such as one's country, liberty, an ideal, and so on. . . . The distinguishing mental features of melancholia are a profoundly painful dejection, cessation of interest in the outside world, loss of the capacity to love, inhibition of all activity, and a lowering of the self-regarding feelings to a degree that finds utterance in self-reproaches and self-revilings, and culminates in delusional expectation of punishment. This picture becomes a little more intelligible when we consider that, with one exception, the same traits are met with in mourning. The disturbance of self-regard is absent in mourning; but otherwise the features are the same. (pp. 243–244)

Freud derived these remarks from his analyses of adult patients. However, the cardinal symptoms of depression as he described them have been shown, in empirical studies, to be the same for adults and children.

Freud (1917b) stated:

> Melancholia is in some way related to an object-loss which is withdrawn from consciousness in contradistinction to mourning in which there is nothing about the loss that is unconscious. . . . In mourning, it is the world which has become poor and empty; in melancholia it is the ego itself. (p. 246)

Thus, Freud was very careful in distinguishing features of mourning responses to a real loss from the features of the unconscious reactions to fantasied loss that are evident in melancholia. His theory, therefore, suggests that qualities of conscious and unconscious functioning coupled with experiences of loss are the essential components of depressive reactions.

One of the earliest clinicians to describe depressive disorders in children was Rene Spitz (1945, 1946), who developed the concept of "anaclitic depression." His work focused primarily on infants and toddlers. Spitz (1945) noted that "there is a point under which the mother–child relations cannot be restricted during the child's first year without inflicting irreparable damage" (p. 70). In one study (1946), a group of children were raised away from their mothers in a nursery setting which provided multiple mother substitutes. These children developed a pathological syndrome of weepiness and withdrawal. This syndrome occurred during the child's second half of the first year of life and persisted for 2 to 3 months. Many of these children lost weight, developed insecurities and susceptibility to infection, and showed a decline in developmental abilities. Spitz called this syndrome "anaclitic depression.'' He realized that this syndrome was remarkably similar to Freud's (1917b) descriptions of melancholia, especially since Spitz proposed that the most significant etiological factor for anaclitic depression was loss of the presence of consistent mothering. Anaclitic depression is the infant's affective response to an actual environmental experience of loss of adequate nurturing. Spitz observed that if the mother was returned to the child within 3 months after the onset of anaclitic depression, the child recovered from the condition. If the mother is not reunited with the child, a life-threatening outcome may occur.

Another group of 164 infants studied by Spitz (1945) were raised without mothering in a foundling home. These children showed, from the third month after birth, an extreme susceptibility to infection. Forty percent of the children living in the institution died during a measles epidemic, in comparison to 0.5% mortality of children living in the community. Unlike the children in the community, the children in this institution showed general irreversible retardation in emotional, cognitive, and motoric functions. Spitz considered this syndrome of ''hospitalism'' to be the manifestation of a catastrophic depression. However, there have been many debates about the validity of findings of this specific study. The study was conducted in a Mexican village institution, and these findings may be related partly to the general level of nutrition of the children, the sanitary conditions of the institution, and the quality of care the children received. Nevertheless, Spitz's studies emphasize that loss of a consistent mothering caretaker in the early periods of an infant's life causes depressive symptomatology and potentially life-endangering consequences.

Numerous controversies exist about the psychoanalytic theories concerning affective disorders in children. One often debated controversy focuses on Melanie Klein's developmental theories (Klein, 1948). She hypothesized that every child goes through a stage of development called the ''depressive position.'' This phase is assumed to begin when the child is approximately 6 months old. During this developmental phase the infant experiences both frustrating and pleasurable experiences involving interaction with the mother. Klein postulated that the child perceives loss of good mothering as a frustration. She assumed that the child interprets this frustration as being caused by his or her own destructive urges. These feelings, she believed, are internalized by the child and expressed as sadness.

Klein's theories are considered unique and not typical of other psychoanalytic theories of child development. A major criticism of Klein's theories is that she postulates that the infant has attained higher levels of psychological functioning than are clinically demonstrable. Other researchers and clinicians do not believe that infants have developed the complex psychological functioning described by Klein.

Another focus of controversy involves Klein's postulate that intense depressive affect is a normal developmental phenomenon. Other researchers and clinicians consider depression in infants to be a pathological state.

Other theories have been based on observations of normal children's affective states, mourning responses, and experiences of loss and separation from mother. For example, Bowlby (1973a, 1973b) defined three stages of a child's responses to separation from mother as protest, despair, and detachment. The protest phase includes the initial and painful frustrations due to the loss of the mother and the child's adaptive attempts by means of temper tantrums and anger to restitute or prevent the loss. In this phase there is still a hope that the mother will return, and the child wishes to search for her. The child's anger is focused on those people held responsible for the loss and aroused by the frustrations in not finding the mother. These observations are invaluable and provide a model for understanding the similar but more extreme responses exhibited by suicidal children. For example, this type of protest is also seen in many suicidal children who exhibit intense rage as a result of their attempts to restitute the loss of an emotionally important nurturing person.

Bowlby's phase of despair includes feelings of hopelessness, sadness, and wishes about reuniting with the lost parent. The longing for the mother continues, but the hope that she will return begins to diminish. The child ceases to be demanding and becomes apathetic and withdrawn. The characteristics of this phase are important because many suicidal children express wishes to reunite with a lost person. Such children feel abandoned, despairing, and hopeless. Bowlby proposed that this phase of despair is followed by the next phase of detachment.

Bowlby postuated that in this phase of detachment, a state of recovery begins as the child abandons the wish to reunite with the mother and lessens his or her feelings and thoughts of her. He considered this phase to be a transitional phase in which the child begins to seek new relationships. The process of developing new lasting relationships ends the child's process of mourning. This transitional stage is an important element for resolving a child's suicidal tendencies. The resolution of suicidal impulses can be promoted by fostering new and supportive attachments to other people.

During the 1960s intensification of research on childhood depression occurred. These studies were based on direct and extensive observation of children. For example, Sandler and Joffe (1965) described a group of 100 children treated psychoanalytically at the Hampstead Child Therapy Clinic, London, and noted that a large number of children of all ages showed a depressive reaction to a variety of internal and external precipitating circumstances. Sandler and Joffe stated:

> The depressive reaction, considered as a basic affective state can, like anxiety, be of long or short duration, of low or high intensity, and can occur in a wide variety of personality types and clinical conditions. . . . and at any developmental stage. (p. 90)

These descriptions were among the first to define depression in children as a basic affect that occurs in a variety of clinical conditions. However, other clinicians challenged the observation that children could be depressed.

Controversy, therefore, became focused into three lines of thought: (1) Depression as a clinical syndrome similar to that seen in adults does not exist in children; (2) childhood depression does exist, but it consists of symptoms that mask the overt depression; and (3) depression in children has unique characteristics in addition to those that are seen in adult depression. Rochlin (1965) and Rie (1966) believed that children cannot develop depression in the same way as adults because children do not have a fully developed superego and, as a result, cannot experience the kind of guilt that promotes self-punishment and self-destructive actions. Toolan (1962) and Glaser (1967) argued that other symptoms such as delinquency, school phobia, learning disabilities, enuresis, and psychophysiologic reactions hide or mask underlying depressive features. Cytryn and McKnew (1972) attempted to classify childhood depression into three subtypes: acute depression, chronic depression, and masked depression. However, they (Cytryn, McKnew, & Bunney, 1980) later refuted the idea of masked depression by stating:

> Almost all who have studied depressed children find that severe depression is often associated with aggressive and somatic symptoms. If the acting-out behavior predominates and the depression seems secondary and of lesser magnitude in the clinical picture, the child should be diagnosed as having a conduct disturbance with depressive features. . . . If the child fits the established criteria for a depressive disorder, that should be the primary diagnosis, with other diagnostic features stated as ancillary. (p. 23)

The most important outcome of these controversies was the beginning recognition of childhood depression and of the need for systematic research on this condition.

Other postulates linked depression in children to psychodynamic and developmental schemas. These hypotheses provide additional viewpoints about the processes leading to the evolution of depression in children. For example, Malmquist (1971) hypothesized the existence of unique manifestations of childhood depression that paralleled the child's level of development and experiences. He classified depression in children in relation to such factors as age of the child, deprivation, organic diseases, and difficulties with separation and loss. These ideas emphasized the roles of a child's experiences as the main factors that promote depressive symptoms.

Another developmentally oriented theory was proposed by E. J. Anthony (1975), who considered that children's depression arises in response to the reactivation of earlier problems in development. He categorized childhood depression into a preoedipal type and an oedipal type. The preoedipal type involves an early history of separation threats, fears of abandonment, loss of impulse control, shame, and anger. In his current life situation, the child who experienced these threats in the past is more vulnerable to these types of threats and responds to them by becoming depressed. Anthony considered that the oedipal type of depression involves aspects of self-esteem that involve feelings of disappointment, failure, and hopelessness. Such children become depressed when they are unable to fulfill tasks and as a result feel worthless and unlovable. This type of depression is linked to the child's abilities to master and carry out tasks.

EMPIRICAL RESEARCH: A HISTORICAL PERSPECTIVE

During the 1970s and beginning of the 1980s diagnostic criteria for childhood depression were developed and systematically evaluated. Research moved away from psychoanalytic hypotheses and toward developed schemas of classifying the signs and symptoms of depression in children. Extensive empirical investigations were begun. Poznanski and Zrull (1970) were among the first to provide systematic studies revealing that childhood depression can be diagnosed in children.

Other studies during this period of time used diverse methodologies and diagnostic criteria. Therefore, this was an important period of research on childhood depression when appropriate methodological instruments and diagnostic criteria were developed. For example, Weinberg, Rutman, Sullivan, Penick, and Dietz (1973) used a broad range of criteria to diagnose childhood depression. These criteria (Table 6-1) are still among the most widely used in studies of depressed children. Further validation of these criteria is necessary. For example, some investigators have questioned the necessity for aggressive behavior as one of the criteria for depression.

Other studies tried to clarify which specific criteria are most important for diagnosing childhood depression. Kuperman and Stewart (1979) applied criteria designed for adults to a group of 372 children who were psychiatric inpatients and outpatients. Twenty-two children met the criteria for depression. An analysis was carried out to determine the relative frequencies of 11 criterion symptoms used to diagnose depression. Among the 22 depressed children, an average of seven criterion symptoms was documented for each patient. The percentage of chil-

TABLE 6-1
Weinberg Criteria for Childhood Depression

I. Dysphoric mood:
   Sadness, loneliness, hopelessness, cries easily, moodiness
II. Self-depreciatory ideation:
   Worthless, guilty, suicidal ideas and attempts, persecutory ideas
III. Plus two or more of the following:
   1. Aggressive behavior: belligerent, hostile, quarrelsome, fighting
   2. Sleep disturbance: initial or terminal insomnia, difficulty awakening in morning.
   3. Change in school performance: daydreaming, poor concentration, poor memory, loss of interest
   4. Diminished socialization: withdrawn, loss of interest
   5. Change in attitude toward school: lack of enjoyment, school refusal
   6. Somatic complaints: headaches, stomachaches, muscleaches, other complaints
   7. Loss of usual energy: fatigue, loss of motivation
   8. Unusual change in appetite and weight

Note. From "Depression in Children Referred to an Educational Diagnostic Center: Diagnosis and Treatment" by W. A. Weinberg, J. Rutman, L. Sullivan, E. C. Penick, and S. G. Dietz (1973), *Journal of Pediatrics*, 83: 1065–1072. Reprinted by permission.

dren with a positive response for each item was: frequency of crying, 70%; recent social withdrawal, 70%; irritability or short temper, 64%; sleep disturbance, 60%; somatic complaints, 60%; low energy, 60%; talk of or actual suicide attempt, 46%; recent decline in school work, 37%. This study documented that the most frequent symptoms of depression in children were crying, social withdrawal, irritability, sleep disturbance, somatic complaints, and loss of energy. Suicidal thoughts and actions occurred in less than 50% of the children. Thus, this study pointed out that many depressed children are not suicidal. In addition, it supported the Weinberg criteria as a valid way to diagnose depression in children. However, this type of study needs to be replicated, especially since this study used a retrospective research design to gather data and a relatively small sample of depressed children.

An advance in research methodology occurred with the development of rating scales that could be used to diagnose childhood depression. Kazdin (1981) provided an overview and analysis of the varied research instruments currently used in studies of childhood depression. He noted that there is agreement among researchers that many of the current research scales provide similar information. Furthermore, there are two main types of research scales used to evaluate depression in children. One type is the self-report scale and the other type is based on interviewer or observer ratings.

Self-report scales explore a child's subjective evaluations of his or her feelings and experiences. One of the most widely used self-report scales is the Children's Depression Inventory that was developed by Kovacs and Beck (1977). This scale was derived from the Beck Depression Inventory for adults. The Children's Depression Inventory consists of 27 factors that can be responded to on a 3-point scale of frequency or severity of symptomatology. It can be used for youngsters who are 8 to 17 years old. The child is asked to select which sentences describe his or her feelings and ideas in the past 2 weeks. Some sample questions from the Children's Depression Inventory are presented in Table 6-2.

The psychometric properties of this scale were tested on a variety of samples of children including psychiatric and pediatric outpatients and schoolchildren. The scale has acceptable test–retest reliability and concurrent validity (Kovacs, 1983). However, its internal consistency and factorial structure vary in different populations. The Children's Depression Inventory discriminates children with major depressive or dysthymic disorders from children with other psychiatric diagnoses or normal children. Furthermore, the test provides a measure of severity of depression as well as an assessment of changes in depression over time. The scores on this scale can range from 0 to 54. It has been suggested that a score of 13 or above distinguishes depressed from nondepressed children. A score of 9 is the average score in nonpsychiatric samples of children.

TABLE 6-2

Sample items from the Children's Depression Inventory

Remember, pick out the sentences that describe your feelings and ideas in the PAST TWO WEEKS.

1. ____ I am sad once in a while.
   ____ I am sad many times.
   ____ I am sad all the time.
2. ____ Nothing will ever work out for me.
   ____ I am not sure if things will work out for me.
   ____ Things will work out for me okay.
3. ____ I do most things okay.
   ____ I do many things wrong.
   ____ I do everything wrong.
4. ____ I do not think about killing myself.
   ____ I think about killing myself but I would not do it.
   ____ I want to kill myself.
5. ____ I feel like crying everyday.
   ____ I feel like crying many days.
   ____ I feel like crying once in a while.

Note. Reprinted by permission from Maria Kovacs, PhD.

Most children feel comfortable in answering the questions on this inventory. However, shortcomings in any self-report instrument that is used for children are that some children avoid answering questions because of their poor attention, immature cognitive abilities, or disturbing responses to inner affective states.

Another diagnostic format is the semistructured interview method, which not only allows the child to report on his or her own perceptions but also allows the clinician to make objective observations and draw conclusions about the child's emotional state. The advantage of this semistructured interview is that the clinician's ratings are based on the information derived from the child's own report and information known to the clinician from other sources such as the child's parents. However, since the clinician must make the final ratings, shortcomings of this procedure may stem from possible biases of the clinician. Knowledge of certain background factors may bias the clinician's judgments. For example, if the child is attractive or is cooperative, the clinician's scores may be different than for a child with a congenital disfigurement or an uncooperative child.

One of the most widely used semistructured interview instruments for the study of depressed children is the Schedule for Affective Disorders and Schizophrenia for School-Age Children—Present Episode (Kiddie-SADS-P) developed by Chambers, Puig-Antich, and their associates (Chambers, Puig-Antich, & Tabrizi, 1978). This scale can be used for children who are 6 to 16 years old. It is derived from the adult version of the Schedule for Affective Disorders and Schizophrenia. The Kiddie-SADS-P provides scores that are based on information derived from an interview with the parents and a separate interview with the child. This interview instrument is designed to gather information about the child's functioning and symptoms. Scores for symptoms relevant to affective disorders, schizophrenia, conduct disorders, and other emotional disorders are obtained. Each symptom can be rated along a spectrum of severity. This interview instrument is very detailed, contains a very large number of questions, and takes almost 2 hours to complete.

The criteria items and scores of these criteria items that are used to make a given diagnosis on the Kiddie-SADS-P interview are based on research diagnostic criteria established in studies of depressed adults. Assessment of the reliability and validity of this instrument is currently underway.

The elaborateness and sensitivity of this instrument is illustrated in an example of one item and the types of questions and scores to be considered. The item "Negative Self-Image" is defined as "feelings of inadequacy, inferiority, failure, and worthlessness, self-depreciation, self-belittling." The types of questions used to evaluate this item are shown in Table 6-3.

TABLE 6-3
Kiddie-SADS-P Item: "Negative Self-Image"

Questions
1. How do you feel about yourself?
2. Are you down on yourself?
3. Do you like yourself as a person? Why? Describe yourself.
4. Do you ever think of yourself as ugly? Why?
5. Do you often think like that?
6. Do you think you are better or worse than you are?
7. Is anyone of your friends worse than you are?
8. What things are you good at? Any others?
9. What things are you bad at?
10. How often do you feel this way about yourself?
11. What would you like to change about you?

Scores
0 No information.
1 Not at all.
2 Slight: Occasional feelings of inadequacy.
3 Mild: often feels somewhat inadequate or would like to change looks or brains or personality.
4 Moderate: often feels like a failure, or would like to change two of the above.
5 Severe: frequent feelings of worthlessness, or would like to change all three.
6 Extreme: pervasive feelings of being worthless or a failure or he/she says he/she hates himself/herself.

Note. Reprinted by permission from Joaquim Puig-Antich, MD.

Many applications of the Kiddie-SADS technique have been utilized in systematic studies. For example, Chambers, Puig-Antich, Tabrizi, and Davies (1982) attempted to determine if children with major depression reported symptoms of psychosis and if psychotic symptoms were similar to those of adult depressives. Fifty-eight children who were 6 to 12 years of age and who fulfilled research diagnostic criteria for major depression were studied. Forty-eight percent of the sample reported hallucinations at some time. Thirty-six percent of the children reported auditory hallucinations that consisted of one or more words other than their names. Among the types of auditory hallucinations were commands that were thematically consistent with depressed mood. Almost all of the command hallucinations involved suicidal commands such as "kill yourself," "stab yourself," or "jump out a window." Sixteen percent of the children reported visual or tactile hallucinations. Four children were rated as having delusional ideas. It was reported that in all cases, the onset of hallucinations and delusions was simultaneous with or subsequent to the onset of the major depression. The conclusions of this study were that hallucinations and delusions in depressed children had the same characteristics as those found in psychotic depressive conditions of adults. Implications of this study suggest that hallucinations and delusions are symptoms of a variety of psychotic conditions that include schizophrenic disorders as well as severe affective disorders. Therefore, other criteria besides hallucinations and delusions are needed to categorize the type of psychotic disorder of a given child.

While the above study documented the existence of psychotic symptoms in seriously depressed children, Freeman, Poznanski, Grossman, Buchsbaum, and Banegas (1985) added to this information by evaluating the clinical characteristics and longitudinal course of six children who were depressed and had psychotic thinking. These six children were among a group of 33 children who were diagnosed, using the Kiddie-SADS semistructured interview format, as having a major depressive disorder. The symptoms of depression were found to be more severe for the six children than for the others. Four of the six children were considered to have a schizoaffective disorder because they had nonaffective types of hallucinations and psychotic symptoms before the depressive episode was evident. These psychotic features were of one or more voices speaking to the child, visual hallucinations that were persistent over time, or persecutory, guilty, or grandiose delusions that were fixed over time. The family histories of all six children showed a high frequency of family members with such depressive spectrum disorders as alcoholism, sociopathy, and depression. Four of the five children tested has positive dexamethasone suppression tests. These four children diagnosed as having a schizoaffective disorder showed varied longitudinal courses with regard to manifestation of depression and psychotic thinking. Although these findings are based on a small number of children, they suggest that there is a subgroup of severely depressed children who have psychotic features and a different longitudinal course from that of nonpsychotic depressed children.

Another study, carried out by Orvaschel, Puig-Antich, Chambers, Tabrizi, and Johnson (1982), was an attempt to assess whether interviews that gather retrospective information from the parent and child are reliable means of determining the type and degree of child psychopathology. Since the Kiddie-SADS-P is used for the present episode only, a modification of the Kiddie-SADS-P was developed to ascertain both past and current episodes of psychopathology in the same population. The modified version is called the Kiddie-SADS-E and rates the presence or absence of symptomatology by means of retrospective reports from the child and parents. Seventeen children, previously assessed with the Kiddie-SADS-P, were selected, and follow-up interviews were done using the Kiddie-SADS-E 6 months to 2 years later. Initially, the children were 6 to 11 years old, and at follow-up they were 8 to 13 years old. All but one child were given the same diagnosis during both the initial and follow-up interviews. A consistent trend was a tendency to underreport past psychopathology by both the parents and the child during the second interview. However, the results of this study confirmed that retrospective history is a reliable means of gathering information. Therefore, this instrument, the Kiddie-SADS-E, can be very helpful in studying the course of childhood depression by obtaining retrospective information about the child.

Other frequently used interview instruments are the Interview Schedule for Children developed by Kovacs, the Diagnostic Interview for Children and Adolescents developed by Herjanic, the Bellevue Index of Depression developed by Petti, the Children's Depression Rating Scale developed by Poznanski, and the Children's Affective Rating Scale developed by McKnew and Cytryn (Herjanic, Herjanic, Brown, & Wheatt, 1975; Kazdin, 1981).

Like the Kiddie-SADS-P, which provides scores that can make a diagnosis, the Interview Schedule for Children (ISC) can be used for children who are 8 to 13 years old (Kovacs, Feinberg, Crouse-Novak, Paulauskas, & Finkelstein, 1984). Information is obtained during a semistructured interview with the parent and the child. The responses can be scored for symptoms that are pertinent to depression. Other symptoms that conform to psychiatric disorders other than depression can be rated with this scale. Assessments of reliability and validity are in progress.

This scale is too lengthy to be included in this text. However, a sample of the interview for one symptom, "loss of pleasure or interest," is given in Table 6-4. This scale differs from the Kiddie-SADS-P because the criterion items are not derived from research diagnostic criteria of adults. Instead, these criteria include a wide variety of symptoms found in children with different psychiatric disorders.

Another structured interview schedule that encompasses factors that provide information about a broad range of psychopathology is the Diagnostic Interview for Children and Adolescents (DICA). This interview was designed to permit a "yes" or "no" response (Herjanic *et al.*, 1975; Herjanic & Campbell, 1977; Herjanic & Reich, 1982). Questions are asked of the parent and the child. The content of the interview covers the following areas: factual information such as demographic data, description of the child's behaviors, psychiatric symptoms, mental status assessment, and developmental history. The time required for administering this interview is approximately 1½ hours.

This scale differs from the Kiddie-SADS-P and the ISC in the manner in which questions are asked. Each question is specifically rated as "yes" or "no"; the other two interviews are conducted by asking several questions about an issue and then making a global score. Some sample DICA questions about depression are presented in Table 6-5.

TABLE 6-4
Interview Schedule for Children (ISC): "Loss of Pleasure or Interest"

Questions
Tell me about things you like to do: sports/games/hobbies, going out with friends.
Are they fun?
Is it easy for you to have fun? Did you today? Yesterday?
Are there things you used to like to do but you don't anymore? What?
What did you do for fun when you were feeling better? Why not anymore? Since
you don't, what do you do instead?
Have you been feeling like you don't want to play? Like nothing is fun? Every-
day? Many days? Once in a while? Does the feeling stay all day? Part of the
day? A short while? Can anything make the feeling go away?
Is it hard to be interested in things? Do you have to push yourself to do activities?
If your friends come around does that feeling go away? All the time? Most of
the time? Once in a while?

Scores
0   None; not at all.
1-2 Minimal; infrequent/occasional reduction in pleasure; transient boredom but
     not marked; not a problem.
3-4 Mild; more frequent reduction in pleasure; notable/of concern to others; less
     interested than before in at least 2 spheres of activity; enjoyment/involve-
     ment requires some effort.
5-6 Moderate; considerable reduction in pleasurable activities; anhedonic more
     often than not or periods of pronounced anhedonia; loss of interest in sev-
     eral spheres; disrupts social functioning.
7-8 Severe; complete/almost complete loss of interest/pleasure; prolonged
     periods on anhedonia; can't be cheered up/aroused; pronounced impairment
     in social functioning.
9   Not assessed; inadequate data.

Note. Reprinted by permission from Maria Kovacs, PhD.

These questions are only a partial list of the factors inquired about in
relation to assessing depression.

The following three interview scales focus specifically on symptoms
of depression. They have the widest use in studies that attempt to
assess a child's degree of depression.

The criteria used to make the diagnosis of depression differ in these
three scales. (Of the previously discussed interview instruments, the
Kiddie-SADS-P and the ISC use Research Diagnostic Criteria for adults
and DSM-III criteria, respectively; and the DICA uses criteria defined
by Feighner [Feighner, Robins, Guze, Woodruff, Winokur, & Muñoz,
1972], which were developed by the research group at Washington
University in St. Louis, Missouri, in their work with adults.) Nevertheless, each of these three interview schedules provides comprehensive data about a child's depression and other types of psychiatric
diagnoses.

The Bellevue Index of Depression (BID) can be used for children who are 6 to 12 years old. The BID consists of two subscales. One subscale measures the intensity of symptoms and the other subscale measures the duration of the problem. This interview procedure is based on the Weinberg criteria for depression. There are 40 items that require a response from the child and the parent. Some sample questions from the BID are presented in Table 6-6.

The Children's Depression Rating Scale (CDRS) can be used for 6- to 12-year-old children (Poznanski, Cook, & Carroll, 1979; Poznanski, Grossman, Buchsbaum, Banegas, Freeman, & Gibbons, 1984). It is based on the Hamilton Depression Rating Scale for Adults and consists of 16 items to be rated. This scale can be used to rate severity of depression (Poznanski *et al.*, 1979). Information is derived from the child, the parents, and others who know the child. Several items from this scale are given in Table 6-7.

The Children's Affective Rating Scale (CARS) can be used for 5- to 15-year-old youngsters (McKnew, Cytryn, Efron, Geishon, & Bunney, 1979). This scale measures the child's depressed mood, behavior, and the child's verbal expression and fantasy associated with depression. This scale is presented in Table 6-8.

It is becoming evident that these instruments can measure depression. Their use is primarily for research purposes and choice is deter-

TABLE 6-5

Sample questions about depression from the Diagnostic Interview for Children and Adolescents (DICA)

Each question is answered by a "yes" or "no" response.

1. Have you ever felt really down in the dumps, sad or had such a bad feeling inside that you felt like crying a whole lot more than usual?
2. Have you ever been through a period of time when you just couldn't seem to have fun, and the things you usually liked to do no longer seemed to be fun?
3. Have you ever been through a period when you felt really down on yourself, and thought you would be better off dead or you thought about killing yourself?
4. Have you even been through a period when you didn't want to be with your friends or family and you didn't care any longer what happened to you?
5. Have you been feeling that way in the past week?
6. A. When you felt sad and down, did that feeling sometimes start one day and come back the next day?
   B. Did these low or sad feelings ever come and go for a whole week?
   C. Did you ever have a time when they came and went for 2 weeks or longer?
   D. What is the longest period of time you can remember when you had sad or low feelings that came and went off and on quite frequently?

Note. Reprinted by permission from Barbara Herjanic, MD, and the Washington University School of Medicine.

TABLE 6-6
Some questions on the Bellevue Index of Depression (BID)

Each question is scored using two 4-point scales that determine the intensity and duration of time of the symptoms. Clinicians circle the scores that best describe the intensity and duration in response to each question.

Intensity	Duration
1 = Not at all	1 = Less than 1 month
2 = A little	2 = 1 to 2 months
3 = Quite a bit	3 = 6 months to years
4 = Very much	4 = Always

1. (a) How often do you look sad, lonely, or unhappy? Is this a problem?
   (b) How often do you feel sort of sad, lonely, unhappy, or feel that nothing is going to turn out right? Do you get those thoughts?
2. How often do you find you go from feeling happy or feeling pretty good to feeling mad or bad or sad for no reason? Does that happen to you?
3. Do you find sometimes that you get really irritated and annoyed?
4. (a) Do you find that you're really sensitive about things, or that you're very touchy about things?
   (b) Do you find you cry easily or cry a lot?
5. (a) Are you the kind of guy, when people ask you to do things, whether it's your mom or teacher, you always say, O.K., sure, I'll do it right away, or are you the kind of guy that says no! no! no!?
   (b) Are you an easy person to please or a hard person to please?
6. How often do you feel worthless or useless or dumb, ugly, or guilty?
7. Do you think people are out to get you or hurt you?
8. Do things ever get so bad that you get so irritated and annoyed that you wished that you were dead?
9. Do you think about ways of making yourself die?
10. Have you ever tried to make yourself die?

Note. Reprinted by permission from Theodore A. Petti, MD, MPH.

mined by practical issues such as time needed to administer the instrument, the specific methodology of the study, and the population to be evaluated. They all require further empirical study to see if they are actually comparable in their assessment of depression in different populations of children. Furthermore, they have an important role in clinical practice as an aid to diagnosing depression in children and for assessing the degree of change in depressive symptoms.

CLINICAL DIAGNOSTIC CRITERIA FOR AFFECTIVE DISORDERS IN CHILDREN

There is now a consensus among clinicians and researchers that depression in childhood exists as a psychiatric disorder and that there are specific criteria for making such a diagnosis. The agreed upon criteria

TABLE 6-7
Some items on the Children's Depression Rating Scale (CDRS)

Irritability
What things make you get grouchy or mad?
How mad do you get?
Do you ever feel in a mood where everything bothers you? How long do these moods last? How often do these moods occur?

Ratings
1 Rare.
2 Occasional.
3 Several times a week for short periods.
4
5 Several times a week for longer periods.
6
7 Constant.

Suicidal ideation
Do you know what the word "suicide" means?
Have you ever thought of doing it? When? (If yes) How have you thought of doing it?
Have you ever said you would like to kill yourself even if you didn't mean it? Describe.
(If appropriate) Have you ever tried to kill yourself?

Ratings
1 Understands the word "suicide" but does not apply term to self.
2 Sharp denial of suicidal thoughts.
3 Has thoughts about suicide, usually when angry.
4
5 Has recurrent thoughts of suicide. If moderately depressed, strongly denies thinking about suicide.
6
7 Has made suicide attempt within the last month or is actively suicidal.

Guilt
Do you ever feel like it's your fault or blame yourself if something bad happens?
Do you ever feel bad or sorry about certain things you have done or wished you had done? What are they? (Note act and whether guilt is proportional to deed.)
Do you know what the word "guilty" means? Do certain things make you feel guilty?

Ratings
1 Does not express any undue feeling of guilt. Appears appropriate to precipitating event.
2
3 Exaggerates guilt and/or shame out of proportion to the event described.
4
5 Feels guilty over things not under his or her control. Guilt is definitely pathological.
6
7 Severe delusions or guilt.

(continued)

TABLE 6-7
(*Continued*)

Self-esteem

Do you like the way you look? Can you describe yourself? (With a young child, ask about hair, eyes, face, clothes, etc.) Would you want to change the way you look? What way?

Do think smart or stupid?

Do you think you are better or worse from other kids?

Do most kids like you? Do any not like you? Why?

Do you get called names? What are they? Do other kids put you down?

What things are you good at? Not so good at? What?

Do you ever feel down on yourself?

Would you like to change anything about yourself?

Ratings

1 Describes self in primarily positive terms.

2

3 Describes self with one important area where the child feels deficit.

4

5 Describes self in preponderance of negative terms or gives bland answers to questions.

6

7 Refers to self in derogatory terms. Reports that other children refer to him/her frequently by using derogatory nicknames and child puts self down.

Note. Reprinted by permission from Elva O. Poznanski, MD, and Hartmut B. Mokros, PhD.

are the same as used to diagnose depression in adults and are clearly described in the third edition of the American Psychiatric Association's *Diagnostic and Statistical Manual of Mental Disorders* (DSM-III) (1980).

According to the DSM-III, the essential feature of affective disorders is a "disturbance of mood, accompanied by a full or partial manic or depressive syndrome, that is not due to any other physical or mental disorder" (p. 205). The most frequently diagnosed affective disorders in preadolescents are major affective disorder, dysthymic disorder, and adjustment disorder with depressive features. The major affective disorders include bipolar disorder and major depression. Bipolar disorder includes disorders in which there is a manic episode. This type of disorder is so rare in children under 12 years old that it is not focused on in this description. Major depression may be classified as a single episode or recurrent episodes. The symptoms of dysthymic disorder are essentially similar to those of major depression but are not as severe and are of different duration from a major depressive episode. The adjustment disorder with depressive features is a maladjusted reaction to an identifiable psychosocial stress that begins within 3 months of the onset of the stress. This psychiatric disorder will remit after the stress ceases.

Table 6-9 details the specific DSM-III criteria for major depressive disorder and dysthymic disorder. It can be seen in Table 6-9 that the criteria for major depressive disorder and dysthymic disorder are quite similar. Exceptions are that major depression can exist with melancholia. The criteria used to diagnose melancholia are listed in Table 6-10. In dysthymic disorder, there is an absence of psychotic features such as delusions, hallucinations, or incoherence or loosening of associations.

CLINICAL EXAMPLES OF DEPRESSED CHILDREN

The following clinical examples illustrate the signs and symptoms of childhood affective disorders within the context of the child's psychosocial background.

Child I: Major Depression with Recurrent Episodes. Sampson was 10 years old when he was admitted to a psychiatric inpatient unit because of serious self-destructive action and suicidal ideas. This was his second psychiatric hospitalization. Since the death of his mother, 6 months before his hospitalization, Sampson was increasingly tearful, unable to concentrate in class, and belligerent with his peers. He lived with his father and paternal grandparents after his mother died.

TABLE 6-8
Children's Affective Rating Scale (CARS)

Item: Mood and behavior
Low: Dejected, some hesitancy in social contact.
Moderate: Dejected, occasionally tearful, voice monotonous.
High: Extremely sad posture and facial expression, occasional crying, slow speech, monotonous voice. Difficult to contact or relate to, stays to himself; lacks responsiveness to environment. Serious disturbances of appetite and sleep.

Item: Verbal expression
Low: Talks of being disappointed, thwarted, excluded, blamed, criticized.
Moderate: Talks of being unloved, worthless, unattractive, lost, ridiculed, rejected, sad, crying.
High: Talks or suicide, being killed, abandoned, hopeless.

Item: Fantasy
Low: Disappointed, thwarted, mistreated, excluded, blamed, criticized.
Moderate: Mild physical injury, loss of material possession, being lost, ridiculed, rejected.
High: Suicide, being killed, mutilation, loss of significant person.

Note. Reprinted by permission from Leon Cytryn, MD.

TABLE 6-9
Comparison of major depressive and dysthymic disorders (DSM-III)

	Major depressive disorder	Dysthymic disorder
Duration	Less than 1 year	1 year or more
Intensity of symptoms	Severe	Mild to moderate
Depressed mood	+	+
Loss of interest	+	+
Number of the following items to make diagnosis:	4	3
Excessive anger	−	+
Poor or increased appetite	+	+
Weight loss or gain	+	+
Insomnia or hypersomnia	+	+
Psychomotor agitation or retardation	+	+
Fatigue	+	+
Worthlessness	+	+
Excessive guilt	+	+
Poor concentration	+	+
Death preoccupations	+	+
Suicidal ideation or attempts	+	+
Social withdrawal	+	+
Hopelessness	+	+

Note. The presence or absence of a symptom is indicated by + or −.

Hospitalization was recommended because Sampson began to stuff thumb tacks into his mouth and talk about wanting to kill himself. He hated himself and provoked punishment from his teachers because he talked out of turn in class. He started fights with other children. During his initial period in the hospital, Sampson was regularly tearful, had a very poor appetite, and had difficulty falling asleep. He was awakened during the night by nightmares of

TABLE 6-10
Criteria to diagnose melancholia (DSM-III)

A. Loss of pleasure in all or almost all activities and
B. Lack of reactivity to usual pleasurable stimuli and
C. At least three of the following:
    Distinct quality of depressed mood
    Depression is regularly worse in the morning
    Early morning awakening of at least 2 hours before usual time of awakening
    Marked psychomotor retardation or agitation
    Significant anorexia or weight loss
    Excessive or inappropriate guilt

ghosts and monsters who threatened to kill him with a gun. In the hospital unit, Sampson was unable to stay in class for the total required time. He was sent out of class because of fighting with other children.

Sampson had a long history of developmental symptoms and severe depression. As a toddler, he had eating problems until he was 3 to 4 years old. He had phobias of grass and water. Toilet training was slow, beginning at 2½ years and finishing when Sampson was 4 years old. He had separation anxiety which became evident by his refusal to begin kindergarten. In fact, his mother, an ineffectual, depressed woman, kept him home all year rather than begin kindergarten. Sampson's mother suffered from bouts of depression, low self-esteem, and an intense sense of helplessness. As a result, she was often not involved with him and sent him to babysitters for care.

Sampson was hospitalized for the first time on a child psychiatry unit when he was 8 years old because of profound depression, delusional thinking that he was the devil, thoughts that he was to blame for his mother's sadness, and suicidal ideas of jumping out a window. He remained in the hospital for 6 months until he was transferred to a child psychiatric day hospital treatment program. After the death of his mother from a heart attack and stroke, Sampson's behavior became bizarre and dangerous. He acted as if he were a dog, ate paper and erasers, and stuffed thumb tacks into his mouth. He wanted to die and reported nightmares of an unidentified person chasing him.

Sampson represented a child with recurrent major depression that included mood-congruent psychotic delusions of guilt and thoughts that he deserved punishment. In addition Sampson experienced separation anxiety at the time he entered kindergarten. This association of separation anxiety and major depressive disorder in children has been noted in the studies of Geller, Chestnut, Miller, Price, and Yates (1985).

Child II: Major Depression with Melancholia. Henry was 11 years old when he was psychiatrically hospitalized. When asked why he thought he was coming to the hospital, he responded: "I don't know. My grandmother thinks I should be here." Henry's grandmother provided a history indicating that in the 2 months before hospital admission, Henry became increasingly disturbed, complaining of hearing voices telling him to kill himself. Henry had trouble sleeping. He had difficulty falling asleep and awoke at 4:30 every morning. He banged his head against the wall when he heard voices telling him to kill himself. His grandmother reported that Henry demanded money from her and that if she did not give it to him, he threatened to kill himself by jumping out the window. He appeared bored, had a short attention span, and was afraid to sleep in his room by himself. He showed difficulty with his school work to the extent that he was referred to a special remedial education program. The school reported not only that Henry showed a deterioration in his academic potential but that he seemed more anxious and agitated, was unable to sit still in class, made bizarre facial expressions and odd noises, and seemed preoccupied with imaginary thoughts.

Henry had a very tragic life. His parents separated after he was born; his mother became so severely depressed that she killed herself. Henry had been taken care of by his maternal grandmother since the time of his mother's death. During his second year, his father was tragically killed in an automobile accident.

Henry was an amicable, active toddler whose development progressed appropriately. He had special interests in automobiles and played for hours with his toy cars. He showed almost no interest in other toys. He knew that his parents were dead and that his father died in a car accident. The cause of his mother's death was confusing. He was not told that she had committed suicide. Henry became upset by change and preferred sameness in the environment.

His depressive episode was precipitated by his grandmother's increased disability due to arthritis and by his responses to his 15-year-old sister's rebellious behavior. Henry reacted to this family turmoil initially with intense anxiety and fears of doom. The symptoms of this child were very severe and included mood-congruent hallucinations and signs of melancholia.

The onset and evolution of childhood depression is important to document especially because of the implications for treatment. There are some children whose symptoms first signify a behavior disorder with temper tantrums, violation of rules, destructiveness, and aggressive behavior; but in whom clear symptoms of depression later become evident. In contrast, there are other children who first appear to be depressed and then develop symptoms of a conduct disorder. Puig-Antich (1982) described the relationship between major depression and conduct disorder in 43 children who met diagnostic criteria for major depression. Thirty-seven percent of these children were diagnosed as having a conduct disorder. The onset of major depression was found to precede the onset of conduct disorder in 87% of the cases. The most frequent items found in the diagnosis of conduct disorder in these children were: chronic violation of rules at home and/or school (87%), persistent physical fighting (75%), pathological lying (50%), stealing (44%), fire setting (31%), school expulsion (31%), and truancy (31%). The following child illustrates this phenomenon.

Child III: Major Depression and Conduct Disorder. Frank represents a child who initially presented with clear depressive symptomatology but within a relatively short time showed less obvious depressive symptomatology. Violent, uncontrollable behavior, appearing like that found in conduct disorders, became evident.

Frank, age 10 years, became increasingly tearful and did not want to go to school. He told his mother that at school he learned about how to commit suicide. In disbelief, his mother spoke with his teachers and found that there had never been a lesson about suicide. Frank continued to allude repeatedly to suicidal preoccupations and to withdraw from his usual activities. He could not sleep well at night. His mother tried to speak with him and coax him to participate in school. Frank's mother sought psychiatric consultation for him because she was afraid that he wanted to kill himself. Frank began to see a psychiatrist on an outpatient basis and soon showed signs of anger, frustration, and destruction of his belongings. When his therapist confronted him about this, Frank said that he was angry that his mother did not take care of him and he wished he could have a new mother. Frank told his therapist that he was angry because his mother was planning to remarry. This was not true. His mother, a divorcee, was pursuing her career and had no imminent marriage plans.

Referral for psychiatric hospitalization occurred after Frank came home and told his mother that he was almost hit by a car. Frank's behavior had become increasingly problematic. He was truant from school and often stole money from his mother. Frightened that Frank was becoming increasingly unmanageable and potentially dangerous to himself, his mother brought him for hospital admission.

This example represents one important kind of difficulty that clinicians have in diagnosing childhood depression. Had Frank been seen only after symptoms of anger, truancy, stealing, and lying, a clinician may have considered him to have a conduct disorder with a history of acute suicidal preoccupations. However, in this case, the initial occurrence of depressive symptoms that included withdrawal from activities, dysphoric mood, suicidal ideas, change in energy level, and problems sleeping was documented clearly. This example points out the importance of taking a detailed history of the timing of expression of the child's symptoms. It points out that severe depression may lead to the development of additional symptoms that subsequently appear to be the predominant form of psychiatric problems.

Child IV: Dysthymic Disorder. Steven was an 11-year-old child who showed signs of change in his behavior and feelings for at least one year before being seen by a psychiatrist. A psychiatric referral was made because of Steven's recurrent thoughts that he wished he were dead and his plans to kill himself by either jumping off a roof or by hanging himself. He had withdrawn increasingly from friends and complained about being teased by his peers. Steven wished that he did not have to attend school and had been observed on several occasions to be crying in school. His academic work deteriorated from his previous outstanding performance to an average level of school achievement. Steven felt inadequate in his scholastic work and described feeling tired when he tried to complete homework. He had trouble falling asleep because he had dreadful thoughts of the next year when he would enter a different junior high school.

There were no significant changes within the family except that his father had become more preoccupied with financial worries; he was not home as early as before because he had to attend professional meetings. Steven's mother was worried about her son and husband. She tried to compensate for her husband's absence by spending more time with Steven. She had long discussions with Steven about his father and tried to encourage Steven in his school work and with friends. However, Steven became more anxious as the next school year approached, and he repeatedly talked of wishing to end his life. His mother arranged a consultation for him with a psychiatrist.

Steven represents the type of child that is commonly seen in child psychiatry settings. Children with dysthymic disorders are at serious risk for suicidal behavior and require careful intensive evaluation of their suicidal risk.

Child V: Adjustment Disorder with Depressive Features. Anthony, age 9 years, began to show sadness, crying spells, and difficulty sleeping within 6 weeks after his father announced that he was moving out of the house. On many occasions, Anthony refused to go to school unless his father took him there. Anthony's symptoms abated to some degree when his parents began to plan with Anthony how the family would remain in communication with each other. Anthony felt comforted to know that although his parents no longer planned to live together, they could work together in taking care of him. Brief intervention with a psychiatrist helped Anthony to understand that his parents both loved him and planned to take good care of him. His symptoms remitted within several weeks after beginning brief psychotherapy.

PREVALENCE OF DEPRESSION IN CHILDREN

The vignettes presented in the previous section can be used as clinical models for evaluating affective disorders in children. They illustrate the relationship of depressive symptoms to stressful circumstances. However, severe depression in children is not a common disorder in the general population, although signs of severe depressive disorders are common in specific groups of children. This section presents information about the prevalence of severe depressive disorders in children.

Kashani, Husain, Shekim, Hodges, Cytryn, and McKnew (1981b) warn that "the reported prevalence of depression varies greatly depending on the population studied and the diagnostic criteria" (p. 145). In their survey of the literature, they noted that there are great differences in prevalence of depression reported in different studies. These differences may be due to different criteria used to diagnose depression and the varied populations with regard to age, developmental level of the children, and the specific setting from which the children were selected.

As more uniform criteria such as those outlined in the DSM-III are used to diagnose childhood depression, data from different studies will become more comparable. Table 6-11 lists the prevalences of childhood depression determined in investigations using DSM-III diagnostic criteria for depression.

The prevalence of depression is lowest in the general population and highest among child psychiatric inpatients and children with cancer and orthopedic problems. It is also evident that these prevalences were reproducible in different studies. For example, the prevalences of depression in the three samples of children from the general population are about the same, and the prevalences of depression for child psychiatric inpatients in two of the three different studies are essentially the same. The major conclusions from these data are that major depressive disorder in children is relatively rare in the general population and that, among children with serious life-threatening illness or severe psychopathology, major affective disorder is relatively common. These findings suggest that these children may be at greatest risk for suicidal behavior.

FOLLOW-UP OF DEPRESSED CHILDREN

The studies of prevalence of depression in different populations of children do not provide information about the duration of the depressive disorders, the potential for recurrence of depression, or the long-term outcome of depressed children. Other types of systematic prospective studies are needed to address these issues.

To date, the number of follow-up studies of depressed children has been minimal, and such studies are just beginning to be developed. Poznanski, Krahenbuhl, and Zrull (1976) evaluated 10 children initially diagnosed as having a major depressive disorder. This study reassessed the children 6½ years after the initial evaluation and found that 50% were clinically depressed. As this group of depressed children reached adulthood, the children resembled adult depressives. Dependency appeared prominent and overt aggression was considerably reduced at follow-up. Job performance and productivity were uniformly low. This study supported the idea that childhood depression and adult depression are the same disorder, which can begin in childhood and continue into adult life.

In another study of 133 children in the New York Longitudinal Study, Chess, Thomas, and Hassibe (1983) found that two children had recurrent major depression, three children had a dysthymic disorder, and one child had an adjustment disorder with depressed mood. All children were diagnosed using DSM-III criteria. One child, initially diagnosed as having a major depressive disorder at age 8 years, reported repeated episodes at 15, 17, 18, and 19 years of age. Each episode

TABLE 6-11

Prevalence of depression in children diagnosed by DSM-III criteria

Investigators	Population	Number of children	Mean age (years)	Percentage with major depressive disorder
Kashani and Simonds (1979)	General population	103	9.7	1.9
Kuperman and Stewart (1979)	Psychiatric inpatients and out-patients	175	12.4	8.0
Carlson and Cantwell (1980)	Psychiatric inpatients and out-patients	210	11.6	13.3
Kashani, Barbero, and Bolander (1981a)	Pediatric inpatients	100	9.5	7.0
Kashani and Hakami (1982)	Pediatric oncology patients	35	11.8	17.0
Pfeffer, Solomon, Plutchik, Mizruchi, and Weiner (1982)	Psychiatric inpatients	65	10.1	20.0
Pfeffer, Zuckerman, Plutchik, and Mizruchi (1984)	General population	101	9.7	0.0
Kazdin, French, Unis, Esveldt-Dawson, and Sherick (1983b)	Psychiatric inpatients	66	10.5	18.1
Kashani, Venzke, and Millar (1981c)	Orthopedic inpatients	100	10.0	23.0
Kashani, Cantwell, Shekim, and Reid (1982)	Psychiatric inpatients	100	11.9	13.0
Kashani et al. (1983)	General population	641	9.0	1.8

lasted months and was treated with medication. The second child was initially diagnosed as having a major depressive disorder at age 12 years but did not come to clinical attention until age 21 years. A third depressive episode occurred in this person at age 25 years. A third child had behavior problems at age 5 years and was diagnosed as having a dysthymic disorder at 10 years. The fourth child had a behavior disorder at 30 months of age and the first appearance of a dysthymic disorder at 17 years of age. A fifth child with a dysthymic disorder had the first appearance of a behavior disorder at 13 years of age and the onset of a dysthymic disorder at 16 years of age.

The conclusions of this study corroborate the idea that childhood depression and adult depression are similar entities. Second, there were both qualitative and quantitative differences in the children with major depression and dysthymic disorder. The children with major depressive disorder had strong family histories of depressive illness and no external precipitants for the depression. In contrast, the children with dysthymic disorder had no family history of affective disorder and marked chronic chaotic situational experiences.

Kovacs and her associates (1984) have undertaken one of the most comprehensive systematic follow-up studies of depressed children. It is a 5-year prospective study in which four evaluations are done in the first year and two evaluations occur in each subsequent year. The children, who were initially 8 to 13 years old, were divided into a depressed group of 65 children and a comparison group of 49 psychiatric outpatients. The 65 depressed children, diagnosed using DSM-III criteria, had either major depressive disorder, a dysthymic disorder, or an adjustment disorder with depressive features. There were more girls than boys among the depressed children but there were three times as many boys as girls in the comparison group of psychiatric outpatients. The major depressive disorders had an onset at a later age (10.1 years) than the dysthymic disorder (8.5 years) or adjustment disorder (9.6 years). The average length of episodes was greatest for the dysthymic disorder (68 weeks), in contrast to the length of episode for the major depressive disorder (32 weeks) and adjustment disorder with depressive features (25 weeks).

Dysthymic disorder was found to lead to vulnerability to having a major depressive disorder. In 4½ years after the onset of a dysthymic disorder, 70% of the children developed a major depressive disorder. There is no difference in this incidence among boys and girls.

The findings revealed that the younger the child who develops a major depressive disorder or dysthymic disorder, the longer it will take to recover. The cumulative recovery rates for dysthymic disorder increase linearly with time. In the first year after the diagnosis is made, only 5% recover, but by 3½ years after onset, 67% recovered. It took

more than 6 years to reach a maximal rate of recovery of 89%. The cumulative recovery rate for major depressive disorder indicates that it
will remit satisfactorily on its own. In 6 months, the probability of
recovery is 25%; in 1 year, the probability of recovery is 55%; and in
2 years, the probability of recovery is 93%. However, there is a high
probability of developing a second episode of major depressive disorder. The probability of a recurrent major depressive disorder in 4–6
months after recovery is 13%; in 10–12 months the probability that
another episode will occur is 31%; and 2 years after recovery, the probability of a new episode is 44%. Furthermore, the presence of a dysthymic disorder in a child with a major depressive disorder increases
the chances of a second episode of a major depressive disorder. The
probability of getting a second episode of major depressive disorder
in these children within 1 year of recovery from the first episode is 63%.
The probability of recovery from an adjustment disorder with depressed
mood is quite high. By 9 months after onset of this disorder, it can be
expected that 90% of the children will recover from this disorder.

   This study indicates that children with initial episodes of depressive
disorders will have recurrent and chronic depressive symptomatology.
Furthermore, the presence of a dysthymic disorder increases risk for
a major depressive disorder. It should be noted that these children are
chronically at high risk for suicidal behavior.

   Early diagnosis and treatment of the depressed child cannot be
overemphasized, especially since a variety of other long-lasting problems have been found to be associated with serious depressive disorders in children. For example, Puig-Antich, Lukens, Davies, Goetz,
Brennan-Quattrock, and Todak (1985a, 1985b) examined the psychosocial functioning of severely depressed children during and after recovery from the depressive episode. The children evaluated in the first
study (1985a) were 52 children with a current diagnosis of major depression, 23 nondepressed children with a neurotic disorder, and 40 normal children. Using the Psychosocial Schedule for School-Age Children
(Lukens, Puig-Antich, Behn, Goetz, Tabrizi, & Davies, 1983), a semistructured interview guide, data were obtained about the child's symptoms, developmental history, demographic factors, and psychosocial
variables. Psychosocial relationships were significantly impaired for the
depressed and neurotic children but these impairments were worse for
the depressed children. In addition, certain impairments that were
specific to the children with a current major depressive disorder were
poor communication, lack of warmth, high irritability, tension and
hostility between mother and child and between father and child, as
well as being severely teased by peers and having unsatisfactory sibling relationships.

   The second study (1985b) evaluated 21 children during an episode of major depressive disorder and again after these children achieved a sustained period of recovery from the affective disorder for at least 4 months. The results suggested that recovery from a major depressive disorder is not accompanied by full improvement of all aspects of psychosocial functioning. School functioning improved after recovery and was not different from that of the normal control group of children. In contrast, the mother–child and father–child relationships only partially improved. Although peer relationships improved considerably, sibling relationships remained disturbed. In general, this study revealed that the most impaired areas of psychosocial functioning of the depressed children take longer to recover or only partially recover. The data suggest that attention must be directed to evaluating psychosocial functioning in depressed children and that children who recover from a depressive episode may require additional psychotherapeutic interventions aimed at ameliorating or diminishing the residual psychosocial aspects of dysfunction. Thus serious childhood depressions are encompassing disorders that are not only associated with life-threatening behaviors but also with long-term social incapacities.

SUMMARY

The earliest endeavors to understand depression in children and adults focused on psychoanalytic theory which provided a psychodynamic exploration of depressive disorders. Loss of a real person or loss of a sense of well-being was reported to be the major contributing factor to depression.

In the last few years it has been conclusively shown that affective disorders can be diagnosed in children and that there may be subgroups of severely depressed children. Depression in children can be classified into major depressive disorder, dysthymic disorder, and adjustment disorder with depressive features. Children with these depressive disorders are at high risk for suicidal behavior.

Although major depressive disorder among children is rare in the general population, it is relatively common among child psychiatric patients and children with serious medical problems. Furthermore, children with a dysthymic disorder are at high risk for developing a major depressive disorder. In addition, it can be expected that depressed children would have recurrent and chronic depressive symptomatology. Therefore these children would be at high risk for recurrent suicidal behavior.

CHAPTER SEVEN

CHILDREN'S CONCEPTS OF DEATH

"I do not know," said he, "folks say death is bitter, but it tastes very sweet to me. It is no wonder that the farmer's wife has so often longed for death." He seated himself in a little chair, and was prepared to die. —The Brothers Grimm, "The Poor Boy in the Grave"

Endeavors to understand childhood suicidal behavior have involved questions about children's understanding of death. Koocher (1973) emphasized that the inevitability of death exerts a profound influence on all human beings and that ideas about death are found in everyone. For a long time it was believed that children could not be considered suicidal because they do not comprehend the finality of death. However, Pfeffer and associates (1979, 1980, 1982, 1984) suggested that intense fantasies about death are early warning signs of suicidal risk in children.

In this chapter a comparison is made between the development of normal children's concepts about death and the ideas about death found in children who are at risk for suicidal behavior. The first part of the chapter focuses on normal children's concepts about death in order to show that children's fantasies, feelings, and concepts about death evolve through a developmental process that begins when the child is very young. The second part of the chapter highlights death concepts in suicidal children. In addition, normal and suicidal children's verbatim statements about death are provided to demonstrate that children are capable of clearly explaining their thoughts about death.

NORMAL DEVELOPMENT OF DEATH CONCEPTS

Thoughts about death begin when children are very young. In fact, children as young as 2 years old have been observed to express their thoughts about death. Such young children exhibit very concrete, egocentric explanations of life events and solutions to stressful situations and feelings. For example, Von Hug-Hellmuth (1965) described an account of a 10-year-old boy who wished to free himself from his mother's prohibitions, and because of this wish, the child wanted his mother to "be shot dead." Brent (1977) offered another report that illustrated that very young children have concrete ideas about death. In this report a 2-year-old boy made statements about death that related to his father's car. This example illustrated that young children do not differentiate between animate and inanimate objects with regard to processes of life and death. The boy, in this case, equated his filled bottle of milk with gasoline. He thought that when a car runs out of gasoline, the car dies. Similarly, the child believed that if he does not have food, he will die. This report showed that very young children have clear concepts about death but that their understanding of death is very immature, given their limited cognitive capacities.

Empirical studies of children who are less than 4 years old, with regard to death concepts, have not been carried out. Most information about such young children's ideas about death stems from ancedotal reports. Children as young as 2 years old have been observed to ask questions about how people die. Young children fear that a separation from mother may indicate that she is dead. Clinicians have noted that fears about death in young children may arise in relation to a child's feelings of frustration, anger, and helplessness (S. Anthony, 1940; Chadwick, 1929), as well as a child's fears about punishment, retribution, and injury (Caprio, 1950). Thus, death concepts of children are influenced by the child's experiences and are expressions of the child's observations about his or her interactions in the environment, which are especially influenced by the child's relationships with the parents.

Empirical studies about children's concepts of death have essentially involved preadolescents and adolescents. One of the earliest empirical investigations of children's beliefs about death was carried out by Nagy (1948), who utilized written compositions, drawings, and discussions with 378 children who were 3 to 10 years old. Several questions were asked: What is death? Why do people die? How can you recognize death? The children were also asked to discuss a dream about death. Essentially, Nagy's study grouped children by age and evaluated concepts of death in different age groups of children. She found that children who were younger than 5 years did not recognize death as irreversible. Children who were 5 to 9 years old personified death as a separate person. Children older than 9 years recognized that death is a process that takes place according to biological processes. In short, the study showed that children of different age periods conceptualize death differently and that as children grow older, they gradually understand that death is an irreversible event.

Most studies of children's concepts of death approach this issue from a developmental perspective. Age and degree of cognitive development have been factors used to group children in these studies. In fact, Melear (1973) showed that age alone is not the main factor in determining children's concepts of death. He interviewed 41 children, 3 to 12 years old, and showed that children within the same age groups may have different ideas about death. For example, some children in his study who were 5 years old viewed death as temporary while other 5-year-olds thought that death was final. His study suggested that other factors, such as cognitive level, personal experience, and emotional state of the child, may be important in influencing a child's concepts about death.

Empirical studies show that most children can be grouped into defined periods of age and cognitive levels with regard to their understanding of death (Koocher, 1973). Table 7-1 illustrates a developmental grouping of children's concepts of death. The ages represent mean ages although there are many children within a given age group who have different ideas about death than do the other children in the same age group. Furthermore, as children become older and achieve higher levels of cognitive functioning, their concepts of death are more mature (Koocher, 1973; Safier, 1964; Wass & Scott, 1978).

NORMAL CHILDREN'S STATEMENTS ABOUT DEATH

Koocher (1974) pointed out that "children seemed very interested in making their ideas about death known and were quite willing to elaborate on them in detail" (p. 406). Furthermore, children show "no adverse reaction to being interviewed on this topic" (p. 406). My studies also indicate that children are very willing to express their ideas about death.

The following histories and verbatim statements of normal children illustrate how children specifically conceptualize death and show that they are able to give detailed accounts of their ideas. These illustrations

TABLE 7-1
A developmental grouping of children's concepts of death

Mean age (years)	Cognitive level (after Piaget)	Concepts of death
7.4	Preoperational	Everything is alive and vulnerable to death. Death is temporary.
10.4	Concrete operational	An outside agent causes death. Death is personified and temporary.
13.3	Formal operational	Internal biological processes cause death. Death is final.

were taken from children who participated in my research. The children were asked about their preoccupations with death. The questions included thoughts of their own death, the death of relatives, dreams about death, and fears about death. Children's actual experiences with death were examined. These experiences included knowledge of someone who died, attendance at a funeral, and involvement with a serious physical illness of a relative or the child. Children's understanding of the finality of death was explored. An attempt was also made to elicit the child's affective orientation toward death, including judging whether the child considered death to be a pleasant, peaceful state or a horrible, frightening state.

Child I: Helen was a 9-year-old fourth grader who had no suicidal tendencies and no diagnosable psychopathology. She was the youngest of six children and the only girl in a middle-class Protestant family. Her family was a close group in which the maternal grandparents lived in the same building. Her parents rarely argued and have never been separated. One of Helen's brothers had a seizure disorder. Her paternal grandfather died of diabetes when Helen's father was 17 years old. Her paternal great-grandmother died in the last year, and her paternal stepgrandfather currently was being treated for cancer.

Helen knew that he was ill. There was no family history of severe depression, alcoholism, suicidal behavior, or psychiatric disorders. Helen's mother described Helen as "a wonderful girl," who had no problems and was always quick to learn. "She is like a little old lady who could chew your ear off in conversation and is a very good-natured person." The only time Helen was sad was when she was ill. She was sensitive to loss. This was most evident when her dog had to be given away and she cried intensely. She also cried when her 95-year-old great-grandmother died in the last year.

During the interview, Helen was very talkative. She stated: "I don't hit but when I get hit by my brother, that gets me real mad. If another person hits my brother, that gets me mad too and I will chase them but I will not hit. I'll say 'Don't hit my brother.' Once I was walking my dog and another child hit him and I said 'Don't you ever do that. Don't you ever hit him like that.' That scares me because I'm afraid someone will hit me too. I get scared and think about it before I go to bed. I think that there is a gang and I worry about them. Once I dreamt that this boy, Michael, was going to choke my brother and I got real scared and then I woke up. I never dream about me dying, only my brothers."

When asked about whether she knew of someone who died, she replied, "My great-grandmother, who was 94, she died in her sleep in January. It was very sad because we just got home from school and I was talking with my friend in the alley. I came inside and my father told me that my great-grandmother was dead. He was crying too. I cried for a whole hour. Sometimes I get real sad and cry about it."

When asked if she thought people can come back to life after they died she said, "I don't know." She said she never thought about it but she thinks "they cannot come back." Perhaps they "may go to a better place but if they did bad things they go to a terrible place. My grandmother had a terrible time in life so it was better she died." When asked if she worried about herself dying, she said, "Yes, when I walk in the street, I worry about getting stabbed. I worry that my mother and father may die too, but I don't think about this a lot."

Helen acknowledged that she did not feel sad often, but once, she said, "My brother got hit by a car while he was crossing the street. I got upset and I wished he didn't go in the middle of the street. I got very sad that he would be hurt."

She said, "I never felt like hurting myself," but she described some of her worries: "I have a whole bunch of friends. We play climbing games with the boys. The boys would jump down from a high wall. I'm afraid to do it because I may get hurt. I may slip. There are some things I don't want to do because I may get hurt. I'm scared of other things like running down a hill fast. I'm afraid I will hit a bump and fall. Once I fell and hit my head on a rock. I got dizzy for a minute and had a headache." Other worries were of getting lost. "Once I went to the supermarket with my brothers and they walked away. I got real scared." Other times she said, "I worry that things were my fault. Like once my father forgot his keys at home and I thought I made him do it."

This highly verbal child had a positive view of herself but described excessive anxiety about her aggressive feelings, guilt, and her fears of death. She showed a high degree of frustration tolerance with an inhibition of direct acting out of her aggressive feelings. Instead, these feelings were expressed verbally. She knew that death was final but that it may lead to a pleasant state, especially if one had been a good person. She viewed death as a relief from life's difficulties. She had a good feeling about self-preservation although she seemed to worry extensively especially about getting hurt.

Child II: Philip was an 8½-year-old boy who had no diagnosable psychopathology and no suicidal behavior. His parents described him as an independent child who liked to do things at his own pace.

Philip's parents had been married for 15 years, but they had a relationship beset with moderate degrees of conflict for which they sought family therapy. Philip's mother described herself as having episodes of depression with thoughts of wishing to kill herself. Philip's father tended to be reticent and not able to talk about his feelings.

During the interview, Philip denied having scary feelings, saying "I'm usually brave." However, he acknowledged having scary dreams about death and described one in which he almost got killed. "I was in an airplane and it fell down. It fell into sand or snow and there were people walking and they helped me get out."

Philip had no recollection of feeling sad except when "it's a very boring day and there is nothing to do." He denied wishes of wanting to die or wishes to kill himself. He understood that when people die, "they get put into coffins, are buried, and disintegrate. Sometimes I dream that someone could come back to life, like the bionic man who was in a plane crash and they put him back together. But people cannot come back to life after they die. When people die, they might go to a nice place, like paradise. Some could go to a terrible place. They call it the fire dungeon. I think it is a terrible thing when people die. I don't think about myself dying because I have a lot of years to live. An aunt died last year. She was my mother's sister. She was not old. She died because she smoked and had cancer."

This description illustrated the death preoccupations of a child with good impulse control. He clearly knew that death was final and that it was "a terrible thing." His dreams revealed that he was mildly preoccupied with death and he spoke of his thoughts about his aunt's terminal illness and her death.

Child III: Carla was an 11-year-old girl who had no suicidal tendencies. She worried about making friends and about being separated from her mother. Yet, Carla had several good friends whom she had known for many years. She rarely got into fights although she was often teased by her sisters. When angry, Carla frequently said to her younger, adopted sister, "We should never have adopted you."

Carla experienced several deaths when she was very young. Her paternal grandmother died from untreated diabetes. Her paternal grandfather died from a stroke 1 week after his wife died. These deaths occurred when Carla was 3 years old. Currently, Carla talked about worries that her dog, who was very old, would soon die.

Carla described "having a lot of problems" with her friends. "I was friendly with two girls, and another girl asked me to be her best friend but the others didn't like her. It makes me sad that my other friends are now angry with me for being with the other girl. I'm afraid that the other girls will be friends and I will be left out. Sometimes, when I think about it, I cry at night. Sometimes, I feel hopeless that it will not work out with them."

Carla described her angry feelings toward her sister: "I feel real mad if my sister does something and my mother and father blame me too. I get real mad when my sister does not admit to doing something wrong. She gets away with things a lot. She also argues with me a lot and that gets me real mad."

Carla spoke about scary things, especially dreams. "I have a lot of dreams that someone in my family has to be killed. I remember one scary dream that I should be killed and the others should be left, but then they kill everyone. This wakes me up at night. I have these dreams often but have a lot of nice dreams too. I dream that I am on a hunt and see if I can get the gold or I dream that I am someone on TV."

Carla knew her "father's grandfather, who died. I sometimes think that if I'll die I'll live afterwards and I will know how old my grandfather will be. I think that people could come back to life after they die, especially if they are good people. Bad people don't come back. I sometimes think that if someone dies they can go to a place where they can do whatever they want. But if they are bad they go to a bad place. Sometimes, I wish that I would die because it would be a better place. But I never think of killing myself. I also worry that something may happen to my mother and father."

This child was anxious, especially about her angry feelings. However, these feelings were contained, and she did not act on them impulsively. Carla feared death and had numerous repetitive dreams of dying. She conceptualized death as pleasant for good people and very unpleasant for bad people. Important conflicts were revealed regarding her relationship with her sister.

These examples vividly illustrate that normal, nonsuicidal children have preoccupations with death and are able to speak about them. These preoccupations were determined in large measure by the children's actual experiences. Death themes were evident in dreams and daily thoughts. Undoubtedly, additional research is needed to investigate the relationship between experiences with death and the quality of a child's psychological functioning. The next section explores an aspect of this issue in its discussion of the relationship between children's concepts of death and childhood suicidal behavior.

SUICIDAL CHILDREN'S CONCEPTS OF DEATH

It is evident that normal children are able to talk about their worries and fantasies about death. It should be emphasized that less is known about suicidal children's concerns about death. Pfeffer and associates (1979, 1980, 1982, 1984) have demonstrated in studies of child psychiatric outpatients, inpatients, and schoolchildren that suicidal children are preoccupied with fears of their own deaths, with family members' deaths, with dreams about people dying, and with fantasies about how people die. Many suicidal children believe that death is a temporary, pleasant state that will relieve all tensions.

Child IV: Ronald, age 10 years, illustrated death concepts and preoccupations noted in many suicidal psychiatric patients. He became increasingly depressed and angry for 1½ months before his suicide attempt. He had difficulty falling asleep and cried in bed, but once asleep he was awakened by nightmares of people dying and falling off cliffs. Before going to sleep, Ronald would "talk to God," saying "I want my mommy and daddy to be happy. If I die that may be the best thing." Ronald's increased distress could be attributed to his intense reactions to his father moving out of the house and his mother's boyfriend moving in. He reacted so angrily to this that his mother asked her boyfriend to leave. However, Ronald's symptoms persisted. He did not want the boyfriend to take his father's place, and he cried when he saw this man "hug and kiss" his mother. He felt that his mother did not care about him. He said, "Killing myself would end my crying and give me peace." He thought that he would "go to heaven," where he could watch over his mother and family. He seemed not to appreciate the finality of his death wishes but believed that in the future he could return home.

His suicide attempt, by taking 10 sleeping pills, occurred after his mother informed him that her boyfriend was returning to the house. Ronald screamed and cried, and his mother hit him with a belt. He became more agitated, and he said, "I felt as if the devil came into me and made me want to kill myself."

Many suicidal children show fluctuations in their understanding of death. Suicidal children may understand that death is final, but when stressed they begin to believe that death is temporary. Such ego regression has been described in Chapter 4 and is associated with the ego crises during the suicidal episode. The following example illustrates this:

Child V: Allen, age 7 years, attempted to kill himself as a way of relieving his confusion resulting from his desperate home situation. His grandfather, whom he loved dearly, had just died. Before the death, Allen understood that death was final. In addition, Allen believed that bad people were prone to die more readily than nice people, who, he believed, lived to an old age. After his grandfather died, however, Allen stated that death was not final and that his grandfather may someday return. Furthermore, he now talked about death being a pleasant place where good people go. Underlying Allen's suicidal attempt was an intense unconscious fantasy to reunite with his grandfather.

Allen provides a good illustration of fluctuations in children's ego functioning. As children mature, they begin to exhibit more complex cognitive capacities and better degrees of affect regulation and impulse control. However, transient states of regression in ego functioning can occur, especially when a child is undergoing stress. In most cases, suicidal children experience intense stress that invariably challenges the children's coping abilities and produces regressions in ego functioning. The example of Allen clearly shows that when this child was distraught by his grandfather's death, his concepts of death changed and he believed death was temporary. This transformation in his cognitive functioning, revealed in thoughts about death, was related primarily to his intense wishes to reunite with his grandfather. Suicidal children are excellent examples of how stress produces major changes in ego functioning.

Other investigators also have suggested that an idiosyncratic, distorted view of death is associated with suicidal tendencies in children. Orbach and Glaubman (1978, 1979) hypothesized that suicidal thinking evokes ego defenses that may result in distortion of the child's ideas of the meaning of death. This occurs when emotional pressure affects the child's still immature cognitive structure.

In an empirical study, Orbach and Glaubman (1978) explored suicidal children's concepts of personal death, that is, one's own death; and impersonal death, that is, the death of others. Twenty-one schoolchildren were interviewed: seven suicidal children, seven aggressive children, and seven normal children. All children were matched for age, socioeconomic status, and cultural background. The score on the Wechsler Intelligence Scales for Children (WISC) Similarities Subtest was used as a measure of each child's cognitive development. Their average score on the Similarities Subtest was 9.0. Questions asked about impersonal death included: How do things die? What happens to things when they die? and Can dead things come back to life? Questions about personal death included: How do you think you will die? What will happen to you when you die? and Can you come back to life after you die?

The suicidal children named suicide as a cause of their own death significantly more than the other children. The aggressive children gave significantly more frequent responses of brutality as the cause of their death. In addition, the suicidal children gave more aggressive causes of death than the normal children. Normal children thought that their death would be due to old age or illness. Normal children knew that death was final significantly more often than the suicidal or aggressive children. Suicidal children attributed life qualities to the state of death significantly more than the aggressive or normal children. However, this difference was significant only for responses about personal death, and not for responses about impersonal death. Furthermore, suicidal children gave significantly more responses about the possibility of returning to life after death for personal death than the other two groups of children. However, the suicidal children had an appropriate understanding of the finality of impersonal death.

The study concluded that death concepts are an integral part of each child's thinking and reflect life experiences and intrapsychic conflicts. The study suggested that there is a specific association between the qualities of a child's concepts about death and specific psychiatric symptomatology. Suicidal children seemed to demonstrate specific ideas about death. Since there were only a few children in each group, the results must be considered tentative. However, these findings are worthy of further exploration in studies that use a larger number of children.

Information about disturbed children's attitudes toward death and suicide was revealed in a study by Carlson and Orbach (1982) of 40 psychiatrically hospitalized children, who were 8 to 14 years old. A significantly greater number of children older than 11 years, in contrast to children less than 11 years old, volunteered that suicide would be a cause of their own death. However, there was no difference between the older and younger children in their belief that death was irreversible. Older children knew about someone who had shown suicidal behavior more than the younger children. When asked what could make a person want to die, the responses of most of the group of children focused on states of hopelessness and helplessness. Furthermore, children knew that it was necessary to use very lethal means in order to kill oneself. They considered methods such as stabbing, jumping, and hanging.

This study concluded that there was little difference between younger and older children regarding their attitudes and knowledge about death and suicide. However, the older children, in contrast to the younger children, cited suicide more frequently as a cause of their own death, and the older children more often knew about someone who exhibited suicidal behavior. Furthermore, 7 of the 17 suicidal youngsters felt that their own death was reversible while the death of others would be final. This finding concurred with previous studies of Orbach and Glaubman (1978, 1979). This study, among others, indicated that psychiatrically disturbed children are able to talk freely about themes of suicide.

SUICIDAL CHILDREN'S STATEMENTS ABOUT DEATH

The following are examples of verbatim statements about suicide of children who participated in my research. One child had a mother with suicidal tendencies and the other children exhibited suicidal tendencies themselves.

Child VI: James was an 11-year-old who had no diagnosable psychopathology and no suicidal tendencies. His parents had been divorced for 4 years and he rarely saw his father, who lived in a distant city. James lived with his mother and 13-year-old sister. During the time that his mother was having psychological and marital problems, James and his sister lived for a year with relatives.

James's mother described herself as severely depressed, requiring outpatient treatment. She thought of killing herself and made several suicide attempts by ingesting pills and cutting her wrists. However, she never was hospitalized because of this behavior. She recalled that the first time she attempted suicide was when she was a teenager. The most recent attempt was when she was divorced. A maternal aunt made several suicide attempts by drinking cleaning fluid. A maternal uncle was an alcoholic and the maternal grandfather required numerous psychiatric hospitalizations for treatment of recurrent severe depression and suicidal behavior. However, there was no history of psychiatric illness on the paternal side of the family.

James spoke about sad feelings. "I get sad if someone died. My grandmother died last year. I cried about her. Sometimes I think about her now. I think people can come back to life when they die and that they may go to a better place, but if they are rotten and don't show kindness to anyone they go to hell. If I die, I think it is better than being here. I think about my other grandmother dying, too. I worry that something will happen to my Mom, that she will get into an accident. If she died I wonder who I would live with. Sometimes I have scary dreams. I once dreamt that when we were with my father, I had to go to the bathroom. I felt like something was choking me and I was yelling and no one did anything. I don't have that many bad dreams though. I often daydream that all the kids on my block have BB guns and we go into school and take over the classes. Sometimes I think that I wish I were dead but I really don't mean it. This happens when I feel upset. I never think of killing myself though."

He talked about his parents' separation, noting that "there was a lot of yelling. Dad yelled at my sisters, too. I was very upset when they separated. I lived away from my sister and my mother. I didn't see my Mom or my Dad. I was really mad because my aunt had two daughters my age. They took me to the beach and to the zoo. But, I still missed my mother. I sometimes think about that. I still cry sometimes. Now, I don't see my father. He usually calls. I think about him but I haven't seen him. I don't think much about him, however."

This child experienced intense sadness and loneliness. It was not clear what he consciously knew of his mother's depression and suicidal behavior, but he was intensely preoccupied with her death and with the separation of his parents. He believed that death was reversible and possibly pleasant. He was able to clearly articulate these beliefs. Although he denied suicidal behavior, he acknowledged wishing that he were dead.

Child VII: Allen was a 10-year-old who exhibited suicidal ideas. He was creative and liked art but had trouble adjusting to his current grade. He did not do homework regularly and received poor grades. His teacher felt that he had the ability, but she felt infuriated by his lack of organization and preparation. He worried that he would fail in school, saying: "School is harder this year. I forget where I put things. I try to do my homework. I wish I did well. I'm afraid I will stay back. I need to get more organized. I need to keep my papers in one spot. I get sad about this but don't cry. My teacher tries to help me study. She looks at my assignment pad before I go home. Then at home my Mom and Dad check my assignments."

He spoke about feeling sad. "When my grandmother died I was sad but I did not cry. But I was sad." He spoke about his concepts that death is final and unpleasant. He mentioned, "Sometimes I wish I were dead." However, he did not speak about these thoughts at great length. He acknowledged that he thought that he wanted to kill himself, but said, "I have no idea of what I would do." He was very reticent to speak about these thoughts in detail but instead answered questions in short phrases.

This child illustrated the tensions of adjusting to a new school situation and his great worries of not being intelligent and of needing organization. He seemed very frightened of death and acknowledged that he thought of killing himself.

Child VIII: David was an 8-year-old son of immigrant working-class parents. He was very anxious and had suicidal ideas. He was intelligent and was interested in all subjects in school. He took karate lessons four times a week because he liked to do "men's type of things."

David worried a lot about being able to get his homework done and about whether he would advance in karate. He said, "What will I do if I do not do well when everyone is watching me?" His mother described him as being very hard on himself. He felt he had to learn everything and if he didn't, he was very angry at himself. He wanted to have the "best report card," and added, "I want to be the handsomest in school." If things don't go well for him, he "gets crazy," and he becomes angry at himself.

David's family was a close one. His parents were married for 11 years but if they argued, David worried that maybe he had done something bad. He worried that his parents would get divorced. David's paternal grandfather died last year at the age of 85. His paternal grandmother died when David was a young child. When a cousin died 1 year ago, David went to the funeral. There was no history of severe depression, suicidal behavior, violence, or alcoholism in the family.

David described receiving gifts from his father's friend, who died last year. "I was real sad and cried for days. Sometimes, now I think about him a lot. I had three dreams about him. In one dream, I saw him come back alive and I liked him. In my dream, he used to bring me things. The second dream was when he was alive and gave me 1000 comics. They were nice dreams."

David was not clear about what happened when someone died. "I don't know. I saw a paper on it which said two people, a lady and a little girl, died 20 years ago and they came back at Christmas. I hope my father's friend will come back. I don't know if animals come back either. I think people go to a nice place if they die, it's better than here because here people rob you. I hope they are having fun up there because I'm not having fun down here. I worry about robbers. Maybe when you die no bad things happen in that place. Some people can go to a terrible place if they are bad and God will send them down. If you curse, God may punish you. I try not to say things like that. It makes me upset and I get angry at myself.''

He described karate school, saying, ''Once I thought something was wrong with me. I could not punch the right way. I feel sad about it. Sometimes, I wish I would die. Once I was playing with my friend and he could play football better and I wished I were dead. I was going to jump over a railing and my friend said 'Don't do that.' My friend could catch better than me. I felt so bad about it. If I jumped I would have killed myself. I told my friend that I wanted to kill myself. That was the only time I felt like that. After that, I thought about it, and I did not want to end my life. I want to die at old age when I am supposed to. Sometimes, I get real upset with myself. Do other kids feel that way too?''

This child illustrated the stresses involving his perfectionistic aims. His family highly valued achievement. To be loved meant that he must be superior in school; therefore, he pressured himself to do exceptionally well. Recently, this pressure built up to such an extent that he thought about suicide and threatened to kill himself.

CHILDREN'S EXPERIENCES WITH DEATH

Pfeffer (1983) observed that a gradation exists in the intensity of children's death preoccupations. Suicidal children are most intensely preoccupied with death. Furthermore, nonsuicidal children who have experienced a recent death of an important person also repeatedly think about death. Finally, children who are not suicidal and have not experienced a recent death think least about death. Qualitative differences in children's death preoccupations exist, too. Children who are not suicidal but who experienced recent death talk logically and are not so emotionally invested in their preoccupations about death. Their death preoccupations are part of the normal process of recovery from the disturbing experiences of losing an important person through death. In contrast, suicidal children's death preoccupations have an extremely egocentric, morbid quality.

The following examples provide verbatim statements of children who had different death experiences.

Child IX: Teddy was a 9-year-old boy who was nonsuicidal and had no recent death experience. His maternal grandparents died 10 years ago, his paternal grandfather died 14 years ago, and two cousins died 4 years ago.

Teddy talked freely about his ideas about death: "I was sad when my cousins died. One choked in his sleep and one was found in the woods. Also, my aunt had a heart attack. I went to two funerals. I saw the bodies in the coffin. I was sad. I don't dream about death. I don't know what happens when someone dies. They don't come back to life again. Someone who is nice may go to a better place when he dies. Someone who is bad may go to a terrible place. I think it is bad when someone dies. I never think about others dying. I never wished I were dead and I never think of killing myself or hurting myself."

This child's remarks were decisive and clear. He experienced the deaths of emotionally important people, but he had emotional distance from these events. He was not burdened by excessive ruminations or fears of death. He had age-appropriate concepts about what happens when people die, as illustrated by his concrete notions that good people go to a good place and bad people go to a worse place after death.

Child X: Alice was an 8-year-old suicidal child. Her mother, too, had occasional suicidal thoughts. Her grandfather died when Alice was 4 years old.

Alice described her repeated thoughts of death vividly: "My grandpa is dead. I was there when he died. He was paralyzed. He passed out. He had a heart attack. I went to the hospital and they were taking blood out of him. I make believe he is rising from the dead. I wish he would come back. I make believe I was in the graveyard and he got out of the grave and rose from the dead. After a person dies, I don't like to talk about what happens. I don't think there is a devil. I think most people go to heaven. I don't know. When someone dies it is a bad thing. I always talk to my father about it. I ask him 'What does it mean about dying?' I wonder about it. He doesn't like me to ask about it. I know when you die, you go into a coffin and you are dead. I worry about dying. I worry I may die. I worry Mom or Dad may die. I will have to take care of my sister and will not know what to do.

"Once, I dreamed that Dad was looking at a skull. When he saw it he passed out. I didn't know what to do. I asked my mother and she saw it and passed out. I told my aunt that Mom and Dad went to the hospital and died. I have other dreams, too. I was in a graveyard and watched a spooky movie. I saw a big skeleton and it was chasing me. I fell on the ground. I was afraid of a spooky monster."

This child was extraordinarily preoccupied with death. She knew that death was final; but, although her grandfather died 4 years before, she vividly related the event as if it had just happened. Worries about death extended to all family members, and she intensely feared that she would be left entirely alone. Not only were her waking moments filled with these morbid preoccupations but her dreams actively focused on death. The pervasiveness of this child's death preoccupations was exceptional.

Child XI: Billy was a nonsuicidal 12-year-old whose brother had died 1 year ago. For at least 8 months after his brother's death, Billy's school work was poor. In addition during that time, he was irritable and argumentative, and had trouble concentrating.

Billy said: "I had a younger brother. He passed away. It was sad because we used to play around a lot. I used to take him for walks. It's sad that he's not around now. Now it's not the same. Things aren't the same as when he was here. We don't do things we used to do. We don't go to the same places. I think about dying. Sometimes, I think about it. I dream about what it would be like—what would happen when people die. When people die, other people will be sad. It would be hard to live alone. People don't come back after death but people can go to a better place if they were good here. Sometimes I dream I am dying. I picture myself just there and things are just blacking out. There would be good things about death, too. You would not have to put up with things. You don't have pain."

This child was very preoccupied with death when he was interviewed. He had recently experienced the death of his sibling and his thoughts about death focused on his dead brother. This child's death preoccupations appeared to be part of a normal response during the process of mourning.

It must be realized that sometimes it is difficult to differentiate children's expressions of death preoccupations that involve mourning an actual death from the more pathological death preoccupations that may be a sign of potential suicidal tendencies. It is recommended, therefore, that, regardless of the child's actual experience of death, excessive death preoccupations should be considered a signal of intrapsychic distress and a potential clue to suicidal tendencies. Evaluation of suicidal potential in such children is imperative.

SUMMARY

The development of death concepts is a slow process that is determined by the child's increasing cognitive capacities and personal experiences. Age alone does not determine how children will conceptualize death. Empirical studies have demonstrated that children may show variability in what they understand of the finality of death. Stress may affect the child's cognitive perceptions and alter concepts of death.

Empirical studies have demonstrated that suicidal children have intense preoccupations with death. Often suicidal children consider death to be reversible and pleasant. However, intense death preoccupations are also evident among children who experienced a recent death of an important person. These preoccupations are manifestations of normative mourning processes. It is recommended that excessive death preoccupations in any child, regardless of his or her actual experiences, should be considered a warning clue to the possibility of the child's suicidal tendencies.

CHAPTER EIGHT

FAMILIES OF SUICIDAL CHILDREN AND SUICIDAL PARENTS

> Then it was over and she was looking at Cassie again; not Cassie either. She had never been so still, so neat, so smooth, her little secrets always showing in her eyes; the smoothness and the neatness now kept well the secret of how she died. —Harriette Arnow, *The Dollmaker*

Morrison and Collier (1969) pointed out that childhood suicidal behavior is "a symptom not only of individual upheaval but of underlying family disruption" (p. 140). Among the risk factors for childhood suicidal behavior are certain family variables that may have a greater impact on childhood suicidal wish than for suicidal wish in older individuals. Recent studies have begun to investigate such variables in a systematic way. Two types of research designs have been used to understand family influences on suicidal behavior in children. One is to study suicidal children and evaluate the characteristics of their parents; the other is to study suicidal parents and evaluate the psychological and personality characteristics of their children.

Contained in this chapter is information about family factors derived from these two research designs. First, studies of family features associated with children known to be suicidal are described. Second, the results of studies are presented that utilized depressed and suicidal parents as a means of evaluating the relationship of these parental characteristics to childhood suicidal risk.

FAMILY FEATURES ASSOCIATED
WITH SUICIDAL CHILDREN

Suicide is often reacted to by family members with secretiveness, distortions about the cause of death, feelings of personal blame and guilt, and anger at the deceased child. Because of this, studies of families with a suicidal individual are hampered by the difficulty in obtaining objective information. Another compounding factor in enlisting cooperation of families to participate in studies is their realization that society also takes a critical view of families with a suicide victim. This point was illustrated by a study carried out by Calhoun, Selby, and Faulstick (1980). They examined the perceptions and attitudes of nonfamily members toward the surviving family when one member of the family committed suicide. They asked 119 adults in a large city to read one of two newspaper articles that described the deaths of 10-year-old children, one of whom died by hanging and the other from a viral illness. The participants were asked numerous questions about their impressions of the child's psychological state—that is, disturbance, and the parents' responses to their child's death. The results indicated that the parents of a child who commits suicide face specific psychological stresses that are greater than the stresses experienced by parents of a child who dies from natural causes. The parents of a child who commits suicide are less liked and are blamed more for the child's death. It could be expected that parents of a child suicide victim would be given less overt social support and that they would face greater negative social pressures. These factors inhibit many families from openly talking about their problems, and about the impact of family problems on the suicidal family member. The respondents in the study viewed the child suicide victim as more psychologically disturbed than a child who died from natural causes. The parents were blamed as contributing to the suicidal child's emotional turmoil. Thus, this study revealed that people outside the family firmly believe that parental factors strongly influence a child's propensity toward suicidal behavior.

Systematic investigations of families have shown that there are specific family factors that are significantly associated with risk for childhood suicidal behavior. Studies consistently have reported that families of suicidal children are disorganized by parental separations, divorce, and the stresses of living in a one-parent family (Garfinkel, Froese, & Hood, 1982; Murphy & Wetzel, 1982; Shaffer, 1974; Tishler, McKenry, & Morgan, 1981; Cohen-Sandler, Berman, & King, 1982a). For example, Morrison and Collier (1969) found that 76% of the 34 psychiatric outpatient children who were studied experienced a significant loss, separation, or anniversary of a loss within days or weeks before the child's suicide attempt. Furthermore, Cohen-Sandler and associates (1982), studying suicidal and nonsuicidal child psychiatric inpatients, noted that the suicidal children, in contrast to the nonsuicidal children, experienced greater amounts of such life stresses as losses and separation as they matured. These investigators studied 76 psychiatrically hospitalized children who were 5 to 14 years old and divided these children into three groups: 20 suicidal children, 21 depressed nonsuicidal children, and 35 nonsuicidal children with other psychiatric diagnoses. Using the Life Stress Inventory, life events were recorded during the child's infancy (birth to 1 year 5 months), preschool period (1 year 6 months to 4 years 5 months), early childhood (4 years 6 months, to 8 years 5 months), and later childhood/early adolescence (8 years 6 months, to 14 years 11 months). The findings revealed that the suicidal children had significantly more stress than the other children. By early childhood, the suicidal children more frequently experienced the birth of a sibling, parental divorce, and hospitalization of a parent than the nonsuicidal children. Furthermore, by the time the suicidal children reached later childhood/early adolescence they experienced, more than the other children, a variety of additional stresses such as death of a grandparent, remarriage of a parent, and the psychological trauma of actually witnessing the death of a grandparent. This study revealed that the suicidal children were distinguishable from depressed nonsuicidal children and children with other psychiatric diagnoses by the seriousness of family stresses. Losses were the predominant type of stress.

The following vignette elucidates these types of chronic family distress. This child experienced parental separation and divorce, paternal remarriage, and continued arguments between his parents.

Child I: Steven, age 10 years, was admitted to a children's psychiatric hospital because he set fire to paper towels at home, broke furniture, stole, and made statements to his mother that he wanted to kill himself. Steven acknowledged that he could not control himself and that he broke things and yelled in response to intense anger at his mother. Just before his hospitalization, he "tried to burn the house down." At other times he felt despondent, thought repeatedly about suicide, and developed a plan to take an overdose of his mother's tranquilizers.

Steven's mother believed that his problems began early: "I guess Steven was angry since he was born." After his first year of life, eating problems began. Steven's mother went out of her way to support his peculiar eating habits. His problems began to intensify when Steven was 4 years old and after his parents divorced. Steven's father kept up regular visits on weekends until he moved away, when Steven was 7 years old. Steven was intensely despondent about the loss of his father, who remarried when Steven was 8 years old.

During the year before Steven's hospitalization, his behavior worsened. Turmoil between Steven's mother and father escalated, especially around issues of visiting Steven. Steven's father felt that there was no way of being involved with Steven without being involved with his mother. He believed that most of Steven's problems stemmed from interactions between Steven and his mother.

The high degrees of parental inconsistency in providing a stable environment for Steven were the main sources of stress for this child. Not only could the parents not interact appropriately with each other to organize a consistent pattern of visits with Steven, but each parent had major problems relating to other people. Each parent was preoccupied with his or her own narcissistic concerns, and they were unaware of the impact they had on their son. The divorce and the remarriage of Steven's father intensified these difficulties because these events diminished chances of improved communication among the family members. Steven's problems were largely reactive to his life experiences. The central intrapsychic problem was regulation of his anger and depression. At times he felt so sad that he thought of suicide. These feelings usually occurred after confrontations with his mother.

The next child, Donald, is a vivid and extreme example of the sequellae of abandonment by parents. Although the previous child experienced the dissolution of his family, he was able to maintain contact with his parents so that he could express his feelings directly to them. Donald, age 9 years, in contrast, had this avenue of communication totally blocked. His feelings, therefore, were expressed in elaborate fantasies and preoccupations with death.

Child II: Donald was admitted to a children's psychiatric hospital unit because of increasing aggressive and self-destructive behaviors. He had been in foster care since the age of 3 years and had been in three new foster homes in the month prior to his hospitalization. At school, Donald hit, kicked, and bit other children. He refused to follow limits set on him at home. When confronted by his foster mother for disobedience, Donald threatened to jump out a window or try another way of killing himself. He had repeated thoughts of jumping out a window, hanging or stabbing himself, and of being put in a coffin.

Donald had a long history of behavioral and learning problems which became apparent soon after his first placement in foster care. At that time, he was rebellious and had difficulty following limits set by his foster parents. However, he was also so lovable, playful, and warm that his foster mother thought about adopting him. Donald remained in the home of his foster parents until shortly before his hospitalization. Eight months prior to the hospitalization, Donald's father, whom he had not seen for 5 years, attempted to contact him. His father said that he wanted to make a permanent home for his son. However, the father's visits continued to be inconsistent and little progress was made in the father's attempts to plan for Donald.

After his father's reappearance, Donald showed a severe exacerbation of behavior problems. At school, Donald exhibited increased aggressive behavior, appeared more infantile, and clung to teachers. He was intensely preoccupied with fantasies about the return of his father. He felt enraged that his father had abandoned him and was worried about losing his foster parents. At the foster home, Donald demanded money or other tangible assets. If his foster parents refused, Donald had a temper tantrum or ran out of the house.

Because of the intolerableness of his increased problems, the foster mother reluctantly but firmly requested his removal from the home about 1 month before his hospitalization. Thus, Donald's fantasies became a reality. He had lost the possibility of remaining in this foster home. Donald was sent to another foster home, where he was totally unmanageable. Two weeks before his hospitalization, the second foster mother requested that Donald be moved to another foster home. Donald was placed in a third foster home, where he became increasingly aggressive, hitting other children, and at the same time threatening to kill himself. After he threatened to jump out a window, he was referred to the hospital.

These more recent events were only some of the many traumatic experiences Donald endured. Little is known about his early history. He was placed in foster care at the age of 3 years because he was found in the early morning hours, accompanied by his father, who was intoxicated. Donald was clad only in urine-soaked pants and was cold, dirty, and hungry. When Donald was placed in foster care, his mother visited occasionally. Donald last saw his mother when he was 6 years old. Donald lost contact with his father at the time he was placed in foster care.

Donald's father's renewed involvement was the precipitant for Donald's extreme disturbances. It was difficult for him to appropriately assess reality and he retreated into a world of elaborate fantasies. He experienced auditory hallucinations of his mother's voice telling him to kill himself so that he could be with her. He was preoccupied with death and frequently asked "Would I die if . . . ?" He experienced suicide as a punishment, saying "I'm gonna kill myself because I'm bad"; or as a means of getting his way. He stated, "I hate being here in the hospital; if they make me stay I'm gonna jump out of the window."

This example is extreme and portrays some of the effects of parental abandonment. Donald, knowing that his parents were alive, realized that they had deserted him. The auditory hallucinations of his mother's voice helped him adapt to her loss. His preoccupations with killing himself resulted from his intense rage, his feelings that he was a bad person, and his intense wishes to be with his lost parents, with whom he fantasized he would reestablish an ideal life.

Other family factors that are commonly associated with suicidal behavior in children include parental violent and sexual abusive patterns. Green (1978) studied 60 physically abused children, 30 neglected children, and 30 normal children. All the children were 5 years to 12 years old and they were predominantly from low-income families. The forms of self-mutilation and self-destructive behaviors exhibited by the children were self-hitting, self-cutting, self-burning, hair pulling, head banging, and suicidal threats and attempts. Over 40% of the violently abused children, compared to 17% of neglected children and almost 7% of the normal children, were self-destructive. Five of the abused children made suicide attempts, two children made suicide threats, and

12 children were self-mutilators. In most cases, the self-destructive behaviors were precipitated by parental beating. Green hypothesized that the violently abused children's self-destructive behaviors had the protective function of enabling the child to escape from an intolerable situation. The violently abused child believes that he or she is to blame for family problems and, as a result, deserves punishment. As the child's self-hatred increases, and self-esteem diminishes, suicidal tendencies emerge and the child acts out the parental hostility and assaultiveness directed toward the child.

Adams-Tucker (1982) detailed the psychiatric findings on 28 children who were sexually abused out of 1037 children evaluated at a university child psychiatry clinic. The children were 2½ to 15½ years old, with a distribution of 22 girls and six boys. Fifty percent of the molesters were fathers or father surrogates, 19% were adult or teenage male relatives, 11% were male peers of the abused children, approximately 7% were mothers, and the remainder were not specified. Most of the children molested by their fathers were depressed. In general, the children molested at very young ages were not as disturbed as those who were molested as preadolescents or adolescents. The 28 sexually abused children had a variety of disturbances which were grouped into the following major areas, in decreasing order of severity: suicidal and self-destructive behaviors, aggressive behaviors and running away, school problems, anxiety, psychosomatic complaints, and sleep complaints. This study revealed that suicidal behavior was among the more common psychiatric disturbances in these sexually abused children. However, since there was no control group of sexually molested children who did not attend a psychiatric clinic, one does not know how frequent these symptoms and problems are in the general population of molested children. Only through a larger survey of this type would it be possible to identify the true incidence of suicidal behavior in sexually abused children.

The impact of violent abuse experiences as well as extreme family chaos is explicitly described in the following example.

Child III: Sally, age 11 years, was psychiatrically hospitalized after a suicide attempt by ingesting 17 aspirin tablets. Sally expressed suicidal ideas for 6 weeks preceding her suicide attempt. She stated that she intended to kill herself and "expected to be in the grave the next day."

Nine years before Sally's suicidal action, her aunt attempted suicide. Sally's brother, who left the family 2 years before Sally's hospitalization, also attempted to kill himself by an aspirin overdose. He has been in a psychiatric hospital since that event.

Sally's suicide attempt took place in the context of a very difficult year for the family. Sally's mother and stepfather separated after 9 years of marriage.

After the father moved out, he visited the family erratically. Four months after he moved out of the house, the mother's boyfriend moved into the house. The mother planned to divorce her husband and marry her boyfriend, who had become the major disciplinarian for the children; a fact that Sally intensely resented. Sally also complained of being "left out" in relation to the closeness she had with her mother. Another problem for Sally had been two school changes in the last 2 years which left Sally feeling friendless. In addition, she failed all her subjects in the last marking period.

Several weeks before her hospitalization, Sally learned of her brother's suicide attempt. Her brother attempted suicide after he met with their biological father, who had abandoned the family when Sally was a toddler. During the weeks preceding Sally's suicide attempt, she, too, met with her father but was greatly disappointed in him. She stated, "He turned out to be a nothing; just a drunk and a pot head." After the meeting, Sally became more irritable and depressed, had difficulty falling asleep, and woke up during the night. Sally became confused and preoccupied with the family developments. Her suicide attempt occurred in the context of an argument with her mother and younger brother.

Sally's earlier family history was as tumultuous as the recent events of her life. Sally's mother met and married the stepfather just 5 months after she separated from her first husband. At that time, Sally was approximately 2 years old. The relationship between the second husband and Sally's mother was very destructive and violent. He was physically and psychologically abusive to the children. He administered beatings with his belt. Protective services intervened when child abuse was suspected by Sally's nursery school teacher. In addition, Sally's mother was frequently absent from the home during Sally's early years because she needed to work to pay the bills. Sally was very upset by her mother's absence. Fortunately, her maternal grandmother was a consistent caretaker during this time. Sally often stated that she felt closer to her grandmother than to anyone else in the family. It was the grandmother who provided Sally with a feeling of stability. Another aspect of the increased stress for Sally had been her intensified worry about her grandmother's health.

This example is dramatic for its extreme degrees of family instability including several marriages, numerous separations, inconsistent caretaking, violent physical abuse by the adoptive father, suicidal behavior of close family members, and multiple school moves. It is impossible to point toward only one of these factors as being specifically associated with the child's suicidal behavior. Nevertheless, it was remarkable that Sally developed as well as she did and only recently resorted to suicidal acts.

A variety of other parent–child relationship problems occur because of the contribution of the parents' personality characteristics and psychological functioning. Shaffer's (1974) study of 30 children who committed suicide contained three children who had interactions with a psychotic parent that precipitated the child's suicide. One of these children left a note describing the problems of living at home with a "mad" parent. The child stated that he would rather die than carry on. In the two other cases, the suicides occurred on the day that a parent was released from a psychiatric hospital. Shaffer discovered that 55% of the families had one or more persons who had consulted a psychiatrist or had received treatment for emotional problems. In four cases, suicidal behavior of a parent or sibling was noted before the child's death.

Other features of parental psychopathology were revealed in a study by Tishler and McKenry (1982). They administered a questionnaire to parents of 46 adolescents who attempted suicide and 46 nonsuicidal adolescents matched for sex and social status with the suicidal adolescents. The fathers of suicide attempters had significantly lower self-esteem, more depression, and more alcoholism than the nonattempter fathers. Yet, there was no difference in suicidal ideation for the fathers of both groups. There was no difference in the self-esteem or depression of the mothers in both groups. Yet, the mothers of suicide attempters had higher suicide ideation scores and more alcoholism than the nonattempter mothers. These findings suggest valid trends that may also reflect psychopathology among suicidal preadolescents. In fact, investigators have found that family history of alcohol and drug abuse, depression, and suicidal behavior is common among preadolescents with suicidal behavior (Garfinkel et al., 1982; Carlson & Cantwell, 1982).

Finally, Pfeffer and associates (1979, 1980, 1984) and Myers, Burke, and McCauley (1985) discovered that there is a reliable association between childhood suicidal behavior and parental suicidal behavior. Their studies pointed out features in the parent–child relationship that lead to the child identifying with the parental suicidal behavior as a coping mechanism against stress. Thus, the children, like their parents, used suicidal behavior as a mechanism to diminish stress.

Systematic investigations support the possibility that there is a mechanism of genetic transmission of suicidal behavior. The studies of Kallmann and associates (Kallmann & Anastasio, 1947; Kallmann, DePorte, DePorte, & Feingold, 1949) were among the first to assess the genetic transmission of suicidal behavior. They noted that among 11 twin suicide cases, three suicides occurred in monozygotic twins and eight in dizygotic twins. This study, in contrast to more recent studies, concluded that there is no evidence that the tendency to commit suicide occurs in certain families as a result of a special hereditary trait. However, other more recent studies offer different conclusions that suggest that there are factors associated with suicidal behavior. Among some of these factors are psychiatric diagnoses such as severe affective disorders and schizophrenia. Research has shown that genetic factors play a significant role in the transmission of these psychiatric disorders. Tsuang (1977) noted that a number of studies of identical and fraternal twins indicate that there is a high prevalence of affective disorders and schizophrenia in certain families. He pointed out that for affective disorders, among 76.3% of identical twin cases, both twins had manic-depressive disorders, compared to 18.6% of cases of fraternal twins. He also showed that for schizophrenia, twin studies indicate that there are significantly higher coincidence rates (50%) in identical twins than in fraternal twins (17%). These relationships, however, do not suggest a specific genetic basis for these psychiatric disorders because these relationships may also be due to environmental factors. However, when studies analyze adopted and nonadopted subjects, the effects of environmental factors can be controlled and a primary genetic cause can be shown if the biological relatives of psychiatrically ill adoptees have a higher rate of illness. Such studies have shown that genetic factors are associated with schizophrenia, affective disorders, and alcoholism; these psychiatric disorders are significantly associated with suicidal behavior. There is a strong suggestion, therefore, that genetic factors may be responsible for increasing risk for certain mental disorders and suicidal behavior.

In summary, suicidal children often experience parental separation and divorce, parental violent and sexually abusive behaviors, and serious parental psychopathology. Many parents of suicidal children are depressed, suicidal, or alcoholic, and have poor self-esteem. The disturbances of some parents of suicidal children are so severe that the parents' psychopathology reaches psychotic proportions. Finally, there is a genetic factor in the transmission of certain mental disorders that are associated with high incidence of suicidal behavior. Therefore, in certain children, there may be a genetic predisposition to suicidal behavior.

CHILDREN OF DEPRESSED PARENTS

The previous section has discussed research that primarily used populations of suicidal children to evaluate parental characteristics. This section includes information derived from studies using populations of parents who were depressed and presents information about the suicidal status of the children.

Beardslee, Bemporad, Keller, and Klerman (1983) comprehensively reviewed all studies of children whose parents had an affective disorder. They noted that all studies show a high rate of psychological impairment among children of parents with affective disorder. However, there was no specific mention of suicidal status among these children.

Beardslee and his colleagues (1983) suggested that a variety of systematic studies that use adequate control groups, large numbers of children, standardized assessment instruments, adequate longitudinal follow-up, and assessment of the child's developmental level at the time of the parental illness are necessary to arrive at sound conclusions about the effects of parental affective illness in children. However most studies do not meet these suggested research design criteria. As a result, the information that currently exists must be considered to be preliminary. The findings do suggest that there are associations between parental affective disorders and childhood affective disorders.

For example, Cytryn, McKnew, Bartko, Lamour, and Hamovitt (1982) studied 19 children of 13 manic–depressive parents and 21 children of 13 normal parents. All the children were 5 to 15 years old. The children were evaluated for affective disorders using standardized DSM-III criteria. Each child was interviewed initially and at 4 months after the initial assessment. Although this study was limited by relatively small sample size, it revealed that of the 13 manic–depressive parents, nine families had at least one depressed child and four families had none. In the 13 normal families, three families had one depressed child and 10 families had none. Thus, there was a significant association between parental affective disorder and childhood affective disorder. There was no comment about suicidal propensities in the children. An interesting finding was that the frequency of affective disorders in the children was significantly higher if the child and the index parent were of the opposite sex. The investigators postulated that the incidence of depression in the children of families with affective disorders may be due to such factors as living with a parent with a chronic mental illness, separation from the parent who requires hospitalization, and genetic vulnerability.

Findings of a significant relationship between the presence of depressive disorder in parents and depressive disorder in offspring have been discussed by other investigators as well (Welner, Welner, McCrary, & Leonard, 1977; Greenhill, Shopsin, & Temple, 1980). Another finding noted by Orvaschel, Weissman, and Kidd (1980) was that children with a depressive parent were more likely to have some form of psychopathology than children of normal parents. Disturbances in the child include withdrawn, shy, and socially isolated behavior; school difficulties; inattentiveness; defiance; and somatic concerns. The acutely depressed mothers were less involved with their children and had impaired communication, increased friction, lack of affection, and greater guilt and resentment.

These investigators tested their observations in another study that interviewed 133 parents who had a major depressive disorder and 82 normal parents (Weissman, Prusoff, Gammon, Merikangas, Leckman,

& Kidd, 1984). Unfortunately, the study was limited by the fact that information about the children was obtained by family history from the parents rather than by direct interview or observation. There were 194 children, ages 6 to 18 years. The magnitude of risk for a psychiatric diagnosis was threefold greater for children of depressed parents than for children with normal parents. The most common DSM-III diagnoses of the children with depressed parents were major depression (7.2%), attention deficit disorder (6.2%), and separation anxiety (5.7%). The parental characteristics that increased risk of the children developing psychological problems were an earlier age of onset of depression in the parent, increased number of first-degree relatives who were depressed or had any psychiatric illness, and whether the parent was separated, divorced, or widowed. The study did not describe whether the children exhibited suicidal tendencies.

The following example illustrates a child's severe psychological dysfunction in a family with a depressed parent.

Child IV: Abby, age 11 years, was hospitalized after making two suicide attempts by cutting her wrists with a knife. She stated that she acted without understanding the reasons she was doing it or the consequences of her actions. Her suicidal actions took place several days apart. The first occurred after she woke up feeling angry and frustrated at herself. Her parents found out about it later that day and took her to a pediatric emergency room where she was considered "not suicidal" and sent home. Two days later, Abby cut herself on the wrist because she thought her mother was mad at her. Abby thought she was bad and deserved to die.

Abby had been unhappy most of her life but it was not until 1½ years before her hospitalization that it became clearly noticeable to her mother. Abby worried over minor things. She required her home to be perfectly ordered and neat. She constantly competed for her mother's attention and affection. She felt that no one cared about her. She thought of herself as demanding, easily irritable, and a bad girl. She believed that she was difficult to live with and saw no reason for being loved by her parents. She believed her parents yelled at her and did not understand her misery. Abby was jealous of her younger sister and could not understand why her sister was so well liked. Abby's parents described her as a demanding, stubborn child who did not listen to reason and insisted on having her own way most of the time. Often Abby seemed helpless and cried over minor incidents. She worried about her lack of friends. In school she constantly worried about failing although she was an excellent student.

Abby was the oldest of four children. Although the pregnancy and birth were normal, Abby's mother developed a postpartum depression after Abby's birth. Her mother had recurrent crying episodes, increased irritability, and difficulty feeling close to her child. The mother was extremely worried about being an adequate mother. She felt Abby was a very difficult child, who cried frequently and was cranky. Her mother was devastated when she discovered, 3 months after Abby was born, that she was pregnant again. This knowledge made it difficult to care for Abby. When the second child was born, Abby's mother felt totally overwhelmed and did not know how to handle her infant's demands. Abby's mother stated that she was just like Abby when she was a child and has essentially been depressed most of her life. Abby's maternal grandfather was described as a depressed, worried man. Two maternal siblings were described as depressed. A paternal uncle was repeatedly hospitalized throughout his life, and a cousin committed suicide when in his 40s. Abby's father described himself as a quiet person who left most of the child rearing to his wife. His main complaint about his wife was that she was too guilt ridden. He believed that Abby could snap out of her depressions if she tried harder.

This clinically depressed girl was negativistic and hostile, and felt unloved, misunderstood, and unfairly treated. She reacted to others in a demanding, attention-seeking way. She ensured that people disliked her and rejected her. Abby's mother was an extremely guilt-ridden, depressed woman who explained to her daughter what a bad mother she had been. The mother identified with Abby by recalling that she came from a very disturbed family background in which she had a very poor relationship with her own mother.

This example dramatically illustrates Philips's (1979) definition that "childhood depression does not refer to transitory moments of sadness or disappointment but rather to frank disorder that affects development and interferes with the fullest realization of innate potential" (p. 511). Philips remarked that depression in children may mirror or be responsive to similar affects in a parent. This was certainly the case for Abby. Philips also observed that childhood depression may take different forms according to the child's developmental level. For example, in infancy there may be a failure to thrive, withdrawal, apathy, and even death. In the preschool years, the child may show regressive reactions such as severe separation anxieties, hyperactivity, learning disorders, and somatizations. In the school-age period, the child may have symptoms of depression that are similar to symptoms of adult depression. These symptoms may mirror the depression of the caretaker. Abby's disturbances evolved during the course of her development and are demonstrative of Philips's hypotheses.

In summary, additional studies of children of depressed parents are needed, especially because of the shortcomings of research designs of currently published studies. Nevertheless, these studies have revealed that children of severely depressed parents are at high risk for such psychopathologies as major depressive, attention deficit, and separation anxiety disorders. They did not specifically present data on the prevalence of suicidal impulses among the children and among the severely depressed parents. It may be inferred, however, that such children are at greater risk for suicidal behavior because of their propensity to develop depressive disorders.

CHILDREN OF SUICIDAL PARENTS

Data from studies of suicidal parents and information about children's responses that include depression and suicidal behavior are presented in this section. These studies are limited, however, by the relatively small sample sizes of suicidal parents. In fact, many more studies are needed using this "high-risk" research methodology.

Although suicidal behavior elicits profound responses from those people who are emotionally close to the suicidal individual, little research has been carried out with regard to the interactions between a child and the suicidal parent. One issue that has received little research attention is the degree of influence of the presence of children in a family to either inhibit or promote parental suicidal impulses. Wenz (1979) attempted to study aspects of this issue by evaluating the child's potential role as a protection against the parent's expression of suicidal tendencies. However, the study was limited because it did not evaluate such factors as age and sex of the children and a variety of other stressors such as illness and separations of the parents. Nevertheless, this study is a beginning toward providing information about the impact of children on parental suicidal tendencies and about protective factors against suicidal tendencies.

Some 145 families consisting of at least one parent and one child under 18 years of age were selected for study. The families were chosen from all the attempted suicide cases seen by a medical emergency facility, physicians in private practice, a community crisis intervention center, and police records. To be included in the study, a parent either thought of or attempted suicide. The family size was determined by the number of children under 18 years old at the time of the parental suicide attempt. There were 243 parents and 392 children in the study. Parental suicidal status was shown to be related to family size and marital status. The suicide risk of married parents declined as the number of children increased in the family. It appeared that marriage and children provided an individual with a feeling of meaning and importance that may protect against expression of suicidal tendencies.

There are relatively few reports of how children respond to and are affected by their parents' suicidal tendencies. There is no doubt that parental suicidal behavior would be expected to have a serious impact on children. However, it is not known how parental suicidal behavior affects children's development and long-term outcome.

Such information about the effects on children of parental suicidal behavior may be obtained in many ways. One way was pursued by Pynoos, Gilmore, and Shapiro (1981), who focused on understanding children's acute responses to witnessing their parents' suicidal attempts. The subjects were 30 children whose parents were psychiatrically hospitalized after a first suicide attempt. There were 18 parents, and their children ranged in age from 3 to 17 years. All children and parents were interviewed during the parents' acute hospitalization. Interviews with the children consisted of eliciting a drawing and a story that told about the suicidal event. This study is the only study that has obtained information by direct interviews of both the children and their parents. Although there was a large age range of the children, the sample size was too small to be able to divide the children into age-related subgroups in order to make meaningful statistical comparisons with regard to developmental periods.

Many children drew pictures of the actual suicidal event they witnessed. However, other children did not depict the actual suicidal behavior in their fantasy stories, although they were able to recount the actual details of the suicidal event. For example, one 8-year-old boy, whose mother committed suicide by jumping out the hospital window, told the story of a woman in a building yelling for help. The building was on fire. Police and firemen came to save her. But while the rescuers were at the scene, an airplane crashed nearby, killing several people.

A second finding was that children of different ages elaborated specific types of themes in their descriptions of the suicidal episode. The fantasies of 3- to 5-year-olds included preoccupations with the unexpected separation from the parent. Almost all the 6- to 8-year-olds enacted in play or stories scenes of good and bad people, police themes, and punishment. The 9- to 12-year-olds used family romance themes of rescues and exiles. The adolescents depicted marital strife and portrayed the blame of one parent.

A third finding was that some children demonstrated imitation in play of parental suicidal behavior and spoke of feeling intensely unhappy. Some children spoke about their own suicidal ideas. Furthermore, many of the children sought to gain reassurances from the suicidal parent that the suicidal event would not happen again. Finally, many of the children fantasized about how they were expected to intervene and prevent another suicidal episode.

This study demonstrated that children respond intensely to their parents' suicidal actions and that the responses show specific trends. However, the study was greatly limited because when a trend was highlighted, the investigators gave no indication of how frequent the trend was with respect to the total sample of children studied. In addition, it is not known if children respond to parental suicidal death in ways similar to their responses to nonfatal suicidal actions of parents.

There have been no studies of interviews with children shortly after a parent committed suicide.

There is no doubt that the death of a parent has profound effects on a child. Children who experience a parent's death have to cope with the immediate events surrounding the death, experience a process of mourning, and continue to participate in life in an age-appropriate way. The study by Elizur and Kaffman (1982) of children bereaved by the death of their fathers during war will serve to illustrate the complex and long-term grief responses of normal children.

The investigation followed 25 normal kibbutz children, aged 1 to 10 years, during the period of 3½ years after the death of their fathers in war. Two children were under 2 years old, 15 were between 2 and 6 years of age, and eight children were between 6 and 10 years old when the father died. This study, therefore, illustrated both the effects of traumatic death other than suicide and the natural course of bereavement in normal children.

In the 2 to 6 months after the fathers' deaths, there were serious psychological disturbances in the children. The children immediately reacted to the loss with significant crying, moodiness, and expressions of longing. The children showed defensive measures that helped them gain distance from the acute trauma of the death. These defenses included repeated recollections of the deceased father and denial of the finality of his death. Within 1½ years after the death, the children achieved some understanding and acceptance of the loss, with a decrease in the defenses of denial of the finality of death. At the same time, there was a notable increase in the children's anxiety, especially about separation and fears of injury. The children's most common coping mechanisms were dependency and demandingness. These responses merged into increased aggressive behaviors and discipline problems.

As time passed into the third and fourth years after the death, the children showed a drastic decline in grief reactions, anxiety, and dependency. However, it was evident that in the 3½ years after the loss, 65% of the total clinical symptoms were rated as medium to severe. Severe impairments remained high at the 3½ year follow-up. Only a minority of children did not show serious signs of emotional impairment and were able to achieve a satisfactory adjustment. Therefore, the main conclusion of the study is that parental death created a crisis situation with long-term consequences. Extrapolating from these findings, it may be predicted that parental death by suicide may have a more profound effect on the child than death of a parent from natural causes.

There is some evidence about children's responses to parental suicidal death. However, most of the studies are limited by the small number of children studied, the ways information was obtained, and the varied lengths of time information was collected after the suicidal death.

One of the earliest reports was presented by Cain and Fast (1966). Their study used only children who were known to be psychiatrically disturbed. The 45 children studied were 4 to 14 years old and were patients in a psychiatric outpatient clinic. Because the information was obtained from the psychiatric clinic records, the findings must be considered limited since some essential information may not have been obtained during the usual clinic evaluation, or essential information may not have been recorded in the clinic record. Furthermore, the mean time period between the parental suicide and the psychiatric clinic evaluation was over 4 years. Therefore, this study did not evaluate the children's acute responses. Furthermore, any information about the child's acute perceptions of the parent's suicide was retrospective and probably distorted.

In one-quarter of the cases, the child witnessed the suicide. However, the surviving parent distorted the cause of death and insisted it was not a suicide but due to an illness or accident. For example, one child witnessed his father shooting himself but was told his father died of a heart attack. Another girl who discovered her father hanging in a closet was told that he had a car accident. Many children perceived that they should not know about the suicide and that they should not tell about it. Many children found these experiences vaguely unreal. They doubted what they were told or were uneasy about everyday certainties.

Furman (1974) also described the surviving parent's response of secrecy and distortion about the cause of the spouse's suicidal death. Her study was of 23 children's reactions to their parents' deaths. Among these children, she described three children whose parents committed suicide. One father threw himself under a train. The child's mother told the child that his father died of a sickness. In fact, she brought the child for therapy but then terminated the treatment when the therapy began to focus on the cause of the father's death. In another family, the father told the children that their mother's death from a suicidal leap from a building was caused by a "special illness." However, this family, too, could not allow the child to explore freely in therapy the cause of the mother's death. A third example was of a mother who could not talk with her son for months about the events of his father's suicidal death. These examples point out the intense impact of a parent's suicide on both the child and the surviving spouse. The responses of the surviving spouse are crucial in determining how the child will respond to the parental death.

The next example illustrates that a mother's responses to the suicide of her parent may provoke suicidal responses in her child. It illustrates the existence of suicidal behavior in several family generations and the association of parental suicidal tendencies with childhood suicidal behavior.

Child V: Nathan, age 6 years, was psychiatrically hospitalized because he had been very aggressive toward his 3-year-old brother and on one occasion threatened to stab him. One month before Nathan's hospitalization, Nathan said he would stab himself as he held a knife to his throat. In school Nathan seemed very sad, but at other times he was excessively angry. He had been increasingly disobedient with his mother. He broke windows at home and threw rocks at other children. Just before the hospitalization, Nathan preferred to stay home with his mother and not attend school.

His parents separated 3 years before Nathan's hospitalization and when Nathan's mother was pregnant with his younger brother. After her husband left the house, Nathan's mother made a suicide attempt by ingesting several sleeping pills. Months before his hospitalization, Nathan learned about this from his father and said, "I don't have to listen to Mommy because she is crazy. She took pills to kill herself."

Six months before Nathan was hospitalized, his maternal grandmother, a chronically disturbed woman, died from an overdose of her psychotropic medication. Nathan's mother went into a deep depression and was barely able to function at home. At school Nathan was described as initially sad, with proclivities for violent reactions. These episodes of violence intensified until Nathan's hospitalization. At home, lacking the inner strength to cope with Nathan, his mother became increasingly fearful of her son's safety.

Nathan's self-destructive and disobedient behaviors were related to his mother's feelings of despair and sadness over a difficult second pregnancy, separation from her husband, spouse brutality, and the subsequent suicide of her mother. Nathan strongly identified with his mother, whom he experienced as a suicidal parent from the time when he was very young. Just before his hospital admission, Nathan reexperienced a suicidal event; this time it was the suicide of his maternal grandmother. Nathan identified with his mother. As she grieved the loss of her mother, Nathan, who was so sensitive to her moods, acted out his identifications by suicidal tendencies.

Pfeffer (1980) interviewed child psychiatric inpatients within 2 years following the suicidal death of a parent. Although there were only five children in the study, the findings provided some additional insights that can be evaluated in more extensive investigations. Pfeffer concluded that these children experienced chronic family turmoil and were stressed by previous losses of the parents due to marital discord, separation, divorce, and parental hospitalization. As a result, these children were exquisitely sensitized to actual parental loss and deprivation of parenting at a time in their lives when they had not yet developed adequate adaptations to separation. Therefore, Pfeffer hypothesized that these children were especially vulnerable to the psychological effects of parental suicide because it stimulated previous memories and painful feelings of early losses and separations. She hypothesized that the parental suicide was a traumatic episode that produced profound influences on the child's character formation.

Pfeffer also proposed that the child developed problems if the surviving parent was unable to mourn. These parents became excessively dependent on the child. The surviving parent often projected his or her fantasies onto the child and identified qualities in the child with the dead parent. Pfeffer suggested that this heightened the child's attachment to the deceased parent at a time when it is necessary for the child to realistically experience the loss of the parent. Such children, who identify with and idealize the dead parent, have intense wishes to reunite with the deceased. This may be one mechanism that serves to deny the reality of the parent's death and promotes the suicidal action of the child.

The long-term outcome of children bereaved by the suicidal death of a parent requires additional systematic prospective research. These studies are difficult to conduct because of difficulty enlisting the cooperation of families initially. In fact, data about the long-term effects of parental death from natural causes have been derived for the most part from retrospective information obtained from adults. Some empirical studies conclude that parental death during childhood was significantly associated with increased risk for depressive and suicidal behavior in adulthood (Adam, Bouckoms, & Steiner, 1980; Greer, 1974; Lloyd, 1980; Roy, 1980).

Tenant, Bibbington, and Hurry (1980), however, argued that these studies are inconsistent in methodology and results. Therefore, they concluded that parental death in childhood has little impact on the risk of depressive illness in adult life. Crook and Raskin (1975) also suggested that early separation from or death of a parent does not predispose to future suicidal behavior. They hypothesized that a childhood experience of parental discord with parental separation may be more associated with attempted suicide in adult life than a childhood experience of a loss of a parent through death by natural causes. Their ideas imply that the quality of family interactions before and after the death is a significant factor influencing the long-term development and vulnerabilities of the child.

There is only one published long-term prospective study of children bereaved by a parental suicidal death. However, the methodology of the study was greatly limited by the fact that children were not directly interviewed. Instead, the surviving spouse provided information about the child. It may be assumed that such information may not be reliable due to unresolved conflicts of the parent about the marriage and the dead spouse. The study was limited also by the absence of comparison groups of children who experienced parental death from other causes. In this study, Shepherd and Barraclough (1976) evaluated 36 children who were 2 to 17 years old at the time of the parental suicide. This wide range in age of the children may have affected the conclusions of the study. Shepherd and Barraclough obtained information on these children 4 to 7 years later. The most unexpected follow-up result was a lack of specific effects of the parental suicide. This may have been due to the minimization of the child's psychological problems by the surviving parent. It may be due also to the wide age range of the children at the time of the parental suicide.

Fifteen children were reported to be functioning adequately, 16 were not functioning well, and the functioning of five children could not be determined. Only one child made suicidal threats, and no children committed suicide. The children who were functioning less well had parents who had separated, trouble with the police, and/or psychological problems. The researchers concluded that the most important determinant of the child's response to parental suicide was the quality of life experienced by the child before the death. Shepherd and Barraclough advocated that the suicide should not be seen as a sudden isolated disaster but as a major event in an unhappy, chaotic family situation that may bring grief but also the possibility of relief. These hypotheses are interesting but require extensive study that takes account of the child's stage of development at the time of the suicide as well as evaluating other factors associated with the specific family circumstances.

In summary, studies of suicidal parents and the effects on children of parental suicide have major methodological flaws. Hence, conclusions must be considered tentative. Nevertheless, these studies indicate that children respond intensively to their suicidal parents' behavior. The children often are confused and blame themselves for their parents' actions. The responses of the surviving parent are crucial to how the bereaved child will adjust to a parent's suicidal death. The long-term adjustments of children who have suicidal parents are not sufficiently known. The risk for suicidal behavior of the child has not been adequately evaluated. Well-planned, systematic studies are necessary to fill in the information gaps about the consequences of parental suicidal behavior for children.

SUMMARY

In the first part of this chapter family factors associated with suicidal tendencies in children have been described. Outstanding characteristics of these families were separation, divorce, parental alcoholism, parental abuse, parental depression, and parental suicidal behavior. It was evident that these suicidal children experienced major traumatic events in their families.

A second family view was obtained by selecting studies of depressed and suicidal parents, and noting the children's characteristics and responses. Children of severely depressed parents tended to have psychopathology marked by withdrawal, school-related problems, defiance, and/or somatic complaints. These studies have not commented specifically on the degree of suicidal tendencies in the children. Children whose parents were suicidal displayed guilt and bewilderment about the suicidal episode.

Studies have not been conclusive about the long-term effects of parental suicide on children, chiefly because of problems of research methodology. This is an area that requires systematic prospective study. Studies using parental suicide victims have not been able to clarify how parental suicide affects risk of suicide in their children. In contrast, studies of suicidal children indicate that there is a direct positive association between parental suicidal tendencies and childhood suicidal risk.

Another area that requires systematic study is the quality of family interactions in children at risk for suicidal behavior. These issues are addressed in the next chapter.

CHAPTER NINE

FAMILY INTERACTIONS OF SUICIDAL CHILDREN

"He puts on his best manners with you, Henry," said Aunty Rosa, "but I'm afraid, I'm very much afraid, that he is the Black Sheep of the family." —Rudyard Kipling, "Baa, Baa, Black Sheep"

The studies described in the previous chapter identified factors, such as parental depression and suicidal behavior, that adversely influence the quality of family interactions and child development. However, there have been relatively few systematic empirical investigations of suicidal children's families studied from the point of view of family psychodynamics. Clinical evidence about the families of suicidal children has been derived mostly from case reports. Since these reports have varied greatly in comprehensiveness in exploring family dynamics, a reasonably complete picture of how the family system affects suicidal risk for children is still to be rendered. This chapter contains a hypothesis about family interaction patterns of suicidal children. The hypothesis is based upon psychoanalytic theory and social system theory. The hypothesis was derived from my (Pfeffer, 1981a) clinical observations and impressions of a large number of suicidal and non-suicidal children's families.

The hypothesis proposed also must be considered to be only one possible explanation which requires extensive validation by means of systematic research. Nevertheless, as tentative as it is, it might be helpful to clinicians both for the evaluation of family psychodynamic factors that may affect risk for childhood suicidal behavior and for planning treatment.

INSIGHTS FROM CLINICAL REPORTS

Three reports are described in this section. They are examples that illustrate some of the insights gleaned from individual patient studies. These reports focus on family interactions that affect suicidal behavior in children. It should be noted that each of these reports tries to explain aspects of the child's suicidal behavior primarily in terms of problems in the parent–child relationship. As a result, these reports select out only one feature of the family that may be malfunctioning. These reports, therefore, do not depict other determinants of the family's psychodynamic equilibrium.

A case described by French and Steward (1975), of a 7-year-old boy who attempted suicide, pointed out the common observation that many families with a suicidal child appear to be healthy. However, an intensive psychiatric evaluation of this family uncovered subtle but important features of intrafamilial stress and problems. In this report, French and Steward revealed that the suicidal child perceived that his relationship with his father was distant and hostile, and that his relationship with his mother was warm and positive, but excessively overprotective. The child also sensed that there were significant family tensions and that, as a result, he felt helpless. This report, however, did not specify how the more global family tensions were manifest. For example, the report did not explicitly capture the essence of the spouses' interactions and how these interactions affected the parents' responses to other family members.

A second case report vividly depicted chronic difficulties in a mother–daughter relationship. The child, described by Aleksandrowicz (1975), was a 7-year-old girl who jumped out of her third-floor bedroom window. Aleksandrowicz assumed that a major aspect of the problem was the difference in temperament and personality style of the mother and child. The child's mother was a beautiful, soft-spoken woman who was compulsive and rigidly controlled her children's lives. When angry, or if there was too much noise in the house or too much movement, the mother withdrew to her bedroom with paralyzing headaches. In contrast to her mother, the child was socially extraverted and prone to temper outbursts and intense demands. In addition, the child was very sensitive and easily offended by the slightest remark, and her mood easily changed from happiness to intense sadness. She said that her anger was so intense that she could kill her mother. This was a striking example of a long-standing "mismatch" between the child's traits and the mother's personality. From the beginning of her life, the child failed to evoke good mothering and offered little gratification to her mother. However, the report did not consider other factors within the family that may have facilitated or inhibited the child's suicidal tendencies. For example, the contributions of other family members to the child's stress were not addressed in this report.

The third report, presented by Sabbath (1969), discussed a type of parent–child problem frequently observed in families with suicidal children. Although this type of parent–child difficulty is considered to be an important element of suicidal children's family dynamics, the report did not discuss the quality of other family members' interactions that may have an effect on how childhood suicidal behavior develops and persists. For example, the report did not focus on how the parents' relationship to each other affected the relationship they had with their children. In addition, personality attributes of individual family members that may have been potential facilitators of childhood suicidal behavior were not described.

Sabbath based his analysis on the assumption that the suicidal individual is designated as an "expendable child." He conceptualized a family interaction pattern that "presumes a parental wish, conscious or unconscious, spoken or unspoken, that the child interprets as their desire to be rid of him, for him to die. . . . the parent perceives the child as a threat to his well-being, and the child sees the parents as persecutors or oppressors" (p. 273).

The "expendable child" refers to one who is no longer tolerated or needed by the family. Sabbath observed that the roots of expendability may go back to the birth of the child or may begin when there seems to be a threat to the family stability. Sabbath recognized that disturbance in the parent–child relationship is only one factor that influences the expression of childhood suicidal tendencies. He proposed that often the parents identify their child with one of their own parents; thereby the child is used to "continue, in a repetitive, compulsive manner, this former frustrating relationship" (p. 275). Thus Sabbath believed that the essential psychodynamics of the family are that "all these children serve a specific need for the specific psychopathology of each parent, and help to maintain the precarious equilibrium within the family structure" (p. 282).

Sabbath's ideas, unlike other reported descriptions of family functioning which have a narrow focus on parent–child interactions, encompass the conscious and unconscious contributions of intergenerational influences. Sabbath noted that the parents' childhood experiences greatly influence the interactions with their children. This is an important factor in understanding the family functioning of suicidal children. However, Sabbath did not develop his concepts further to take account of features of interactions between other family members. He narrowed his focus to the interactions between the suicidal youngster and the parents.

These three reports depict some of the stresses that occur in family life of suicidal children. They depict one of the most crucial elements influencing the appearance of suicidal impulses in children; that is, extreme tensions and chronic conflicts in the parent–child relationship. The hypothesis discussed in the next section of this chapter presents a number of other features of family functioning. It takes account of the family as a system that includes a variety of interactions among family members, all of which affect the risk for suicidal behavior of the child. Therefore, this hypothesis attempts to understand multiple family components such as the parent–child relationship, the spouse relationships, and intergenerational factors.

A HYPOTHESIS ABOUT FAMILY ORGANIZATION

The hypothesis discussed in this section has been proposed by me (Pfeffer, 1981a) to include a holistic view of family functioning of suicidal children. This hypothesis includes elements of intergenerational influences, spouse interactions, parent–child relationship, and a consideration of the family system as a unit. This hypothesis proposed for children has features that are similar to hypotheses proposed for families of suicidal adults. For example, Richman (1981) observed that in families with a suicidal adult, some of the following elements exist: an inability to accept necessary changes; role conflicts of family members; a prohibition against intimacy outside the family; serious family depression, hopelessness, and aggression; and communication disturbances. These factors also seem apparent in families with a suicidal child. The most important feature is that the family is a system that includes subsets of interactions among family members.

Figure 9-1 shows the proposed family system of the suicidal child. Attention should first be drawn to the main components of the family system. First, the upper portion of Figure 9-1 depicts features of each parent's perceptions of his or her own parents and siblings. Second, the figure emphasizes the parents' interactions with each other. Third, the figure identifies qualities of the parent–child relationships. Fourth, the bottom of the figure portrays the intrapsychic processes and ego defenses of the suicidal child.

The hypothesis for the family system of suicidal children contains five elements that characterize the family organization. First, there is a lack of generational boundaries. There appears to be an insufficient individuation of the parents from their families of origin. What is often apparent in the child's parents are strongly felt and expressed hostility, feelings of deprivation, low self-esteem, and magnified attachments to the parents' families of origin.

Second, there is a severe, inflexible spouse relationship. There is marked ambivalence between them, and intense anger is expressed. The parental relationship centers on dependency, and the threat of separation is always present. One parent may be depressed or suicidal.

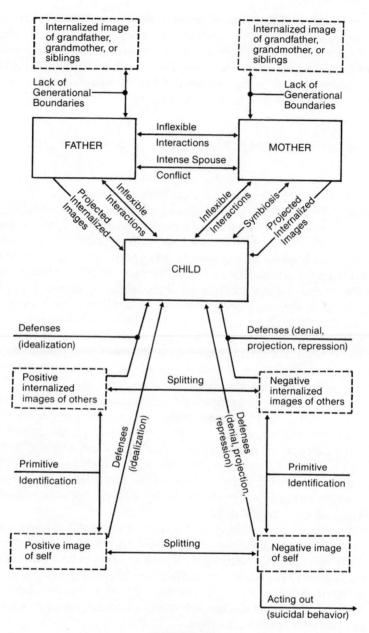

FIGURE 9-1
Family system of suicidal children.

Third, parental conscious and unconscious feelings are projected onto the child in such a way that there also exists an extreme inflexibility of the chronic parent–child conflicts. This is explicitly reflected by an inability of the parents to modify their interactions with the child in response to the child's temperament, feelings, and behavior.

Fourth, a symbiotic parent–child relationship persists. The symbiotic relationship seems to be most frequent between the child and the mother. Because of this quality of the parent–child involvement, the child may not be able to successfully develop autonomous functioning.

Fifth, these families may be characterized as having an inflexible family system. The family members relate in such a rigid way that any change is felt as a threat. Family changes produce intense anxiety. Secretiveness and lack of open communication occur. There are intense hostile interactions, with seemingly few expressions of empathy or support for other family members. Any achievement of personal goals or individuation is equated with separation, desertion, or death.

The effects of these five features of the family system on the suicidal child are illustrated in the bottom half of Figure 9-1. The pattern of family functioning produces pathological identifications in the child and deficiencies in the child's ability to personally achieve autonomous functioning. There is a lack of sufficient differentiation of the child from parental influences as well as an insufficient establishment of the child's stable and separate identity and positive self-esteem.

Figure 9-1 illustrates the assumed intrapsychic forces at play in producing a child's sense of self or identity. The child's sense of identity is based on a complex set of positive and negative internalized images of others. Ego defenses such as idealization of the parent preserve the child's positive nurturing image of the parent and enhance a positive sense of himself or herself. The child's hostile perceptions of the parent are introjected and felt by the child as self-hatred. As a result, a child may feel bad, worthless, and undesirable. The balance between these internalized positive and negative images is reflected in the child's sense of identity and self-esteem.

The family system described for suicidal children produces in the child a heightened negative self-image. As a result, ego defenses such as splitting, denial, projection, and repression are evoked to decrease overwhelming negative perceptions of self and others, and to enhance positive feelings about himself or herself and others. However, if the intense pain evoked by negative perceptions becomes unbearable, it may be hypothesized that the suicidal behavior of the child is an acted-out last-resort mechanism to remove from consciousness the child's negative self-perceptions.

CLINICAL EXAMPLES

The following three case examples illustrate these hypothetical elements of the family functioning of suicidal children. The first example is of a family with moderate degrees of family difficulty. The second is an example of extreme family chaos. The third illustrates, in a more specific way, the difficulties that arise from a symbiotic parent–child relationship.

Child I: Sara was a 10-year-old girl who was seen in a child psychiatric outpatient clinic because of increasing depression and suicidal wishes to ingest an overdose of pills. Sara's parents had just separated and Sara remained with her mother and younger brother. Sara's mother described her daughter as a difficult child who was impervious to discipline. Her mother blamed Sara for much of the marital difficulties and believed that a major reason that her husband left the family was because Sara could not be controlled.

Sara's parents were married after a long courtship. They described the early years of marriage as ideal, and they described themselves as being totally invested in each other. However, after Sara was born, the parents' relationship deteriorated. Sara's mother believed that her husband was envious of her relationship with Sara. However, Sara's father thought that his wife's overinvolvement with Sara was determined by the mother's deep fears of motherhood and its demands.

Sara's mother described her own unhappy childhood. She felt unwanted and unloved by her mother. She recalled feeling depressed during her adolescence and also after Sara was born. Her rage at Sara reflected her state of disappointment in not having a nurturing, supportive relationship with her own mother.

Sara's father recalled that his parents divorced when he was 9 years old. As a result, he saw his father infrequently. He felt sad about not being able to live with Sara and hoped that he could maintain a better relationship with her than the one he recalled having with his father.

This example depicts a family experience of intergenerational boundary difficulties, severe spouse conflicts, an intensely close but conflicted relationship between child and mother, inflexibility in the family interactions, and problematic parental feelings projected onto the child. Sara's mother was conflicted about her role as a mother, and this problem was related to her memories of her relationship with her own mother. Sara's mother blamed Sara for the marital problems and her own failings as a wife and mother. Sara felt unloved, worthless, and so desperate that she thought about committing suicide.

The following example illustrates, in a more extreme fashion, the hypothetical family mechanisms that have just been described.

Child II: Brian, 9 years old, was hospitalized because of serious suicidal episodes. "I am trying to kill myself. One more accident and that ought to do it," he openly stated. In the 3 months before hospitalization, Brian sustained many injuries. He hit his head twice and required stitches for the lacerations. On other occasions he broke both arms, hit his head with a shovel, acquired a laceration on the nose, and singed his hair while playing near the stove. Finally, he put a belt around his neck in an attempt to kill himself.

Brian's life was unusually traumatic. His father courted his mother when she was pregnant. A girl was born and given up for adoption. "Out of pity for her sadness from the loss of the girl, I decided to marry her," said Brian's father. When Brian's mother was pregnant with Brian, she was unstable and an alcoholic, and attempted an abortion and suicide. She divorced Brian's father after Brian's birth and later surrendered Brian to his father when Brian was 4 months old. Brian never saw his mother after his second birthday.

Brian had numerous caretakers when he was an infant. When Brian was 2½ years old, his father married a woman who was very reluctant to take care of Brian. Nevertheless, during this period, Brian had more stability. At the age of 5 years, when his stepsister was born, Brian developed behavior difficulties. Unfortunately for Brian, his sister was favored by his parents. When Brian was 7½ years old a stepbrother was born. At that time, Brian had to be psychiatrically hospitalized because of intolerable behavior, enuresis, and encopresis. After the hospitalization, Brian was placed in a long-term residential treatment center. However, after 1½ years of intensive work with Brian, the professional staff at the residential facility decided that Brian was not benefiting from the program. As a result, his parents were left with the dilemma of deciding to take Brian home or placing him for adoption. However, his parents definitely did not want him home, but they were indecisive about adoption. It was at this time that Brian became acutely suicidal.

Brian's catastrophies reflected the childhood conflicts of his parents. Brian's father was the youngest of three children. The father has been reared in an institution. This event had a major impact on Brian's father, who felt very guilty that Brian was in institutional care. The father remembered that his parents' marriage seemed unempathic and cold. They were divorced when the father was an adolescent. He described his mother as distant, hostile, and very disapproving of his girlfriends. In fact, she was argumentative with Brian's stepmother about how to care for Brian.

Brian's stepmother, much younger than Brian's father, married Brian's father against her family's wishes. Her parents had divorced when she was 5 years old because her father was an alcoholic. Brian's stepmother wished that her father would return home while at the same time she hated his unpredictability. She felt very guilty about not commiting herself to Brian's care. She liked Brian but resented her husband's previous marriage to an alcoholic.

In this example, the child's suicidal behavior resulted from his intense feelings of worthlessness. This example depicts all the elements proposed for the family system of suicidal children. The child was a repository of multiple unsolved parental conflicts. He was unwanted by his natural mother, rescued by his father, and ambivalently nurtured by his stepmother. He stood for every aspect of his parents' ambivalent fantasies that included a preponderance of badness, worthlessness, and rejection. Brian reminded his stepmother of her alcoholic, abandoning, but idealized father. His father, in turn, saw his cold, uncaring mother and hopeless, institutionalized father in Brian.

Brian's exclusion from the family and his simultaneous important involvement helped to maintain the family's specific type of unstable equilibrium. Brian was considered the reason that his parents related ambivalently to each other. Brian's father hopelessly longed for a kind, nurturing mother whom he never had and hoped that his wife would fulfill this role. However, by her rejection of Brian, the stepmother disappointed her husband. Furthermore, Brian's stepmother married an older man who was like her longed-for father. Her ambivalence and hostility toward her father was acted out in her relationship with her husband and in the rejection of her husband's son. Brian's uncontrollable behavior can be understood as a "protest" against all the rejection. Although a residential placement was a tolerable alternative for him, the parents' consideration of giving him up for adoption dashed his hopes of ever establishing a more acceptable role in the family.

Child III: Carol, 11 years old, was hospitalized after ingesting many of her mother's tranquilizers. She was angry about being reprimanded by her teacher and saddened by her father's drinking. Carol knew a girl who had overdosed and an aunt who was psychiatrically hospitalized after ingesting pills. In the months preceding Carol's hospitalization, she responded to her mother's crying spells by identical outbursts of crying and statements of wanting to die. Carol's mother talked of leaving the children and threatened to kill herself and her older daughter. The mother worried that her children were growing up and would abandon her. She was distraught over her husband's violence toward her but did not comprehend the effects that her own suicidal threats had upon her children. Carol's mother had been depressed for over a year and was in outpatient psychiatric treatment.

Of the five children, Carol was unusually close to her mother and was very sensitive to her mother's mood. Carol's mother said that Carol wanted to "feel the same things" that she did. Carol often clung to her mother and felt duty bound to protect her mother from her father.

Carol's mother was the second of five children, all born to different fathers. Her father left the family when she was born and she had not seen him since she was 7 years old. Carol's mother met Carol's father and immediately became pregnant. However, Carol's father left her mother when she was 6 months pregnant because he intended to marry another woman. However, he continued intermittent contact with Carol's mother. His visits were a major problem for the family, especially because he arrived drunk and ill-tempered. "I took the pills to get away from my father."

This example is striking in the overt expression of maternal suicidal and paternal homicidal tendencies. The constellation of maternal depression, hopelessness, and threats to kill or leave the children was a central force in the family dynamics. Carol's mother's inability to set limits and protect herself from her violent husband was related to a revival of her guilt over her angry feelings toward her unpredictable, rejecting father.

Carol maintained an unyieldingly close relationship with her mother in which she strongly identified with her mother's depression and suicidal tendencies. Although Carol would display hatred toward her father, the multiple threats of losing her mother interfered with Carol's expression of anger toward her mother. Instead, Carol's aggressive impulses were directed at harming herself.

SUMMARY

This chapter has included descriptions of the dynamic interactions among family members and a hypothesis about the family organization of suicidal children. Five components are considered important in characterizing the families of suicidal children: lack of generational boundaries, severely conflicted spouse relationships, parental feelings projected onto the child, a symbiotic parent–child relationship, and an inflexible family system. These factors interact to produce a family atmosphere that affects the child's personality development and identity. The child's suicidal tendencies arise from failure of the child's ego functioning to maintain a stable balance between forces promoting positive and negative perceptions of himself or herself and others. A more detailed description of ego mechanisms found in suicidal children is presented in the next chapter.

CHAPTER TEN

EGO FUNCTIONING OF
SUICIDAL CHILDREN

Moreover a piece of paper was found upon the floor, on which was written, in the boy's hand, with the bit of lead pencil that he carried: "Done because we are too menny." —Thomas Hardy, *Jude the Obscure*

In previous chapters, aspects of ego functioning have been discussed with regard to both the child's psychological state during the suicidal episode and his or her developmental history. This chapter contains more extensive information about certain qualities of ego functioning of suicidal children that include cognitive abilities, defense mechanisms, and motivations for suicidal behavior. The discussion is based on both psychoanalytic theory and data from empirical studies.

In the shorthand of psychoanalytic structural theory, the ego is the executive and adaptational instrument of the mind (Hartmann, Kris, & Loewenstein, 1946). It is the mediator of the conflicting demands of the id or the instinctual drives, the superego, and external reality. Actually, the ego consists of a large number of interrelated functions operating on conscious, preconscious, and unconscious levels. Among the "conflict-free" functions are perception, motility, speech, language, thinking, and other cognitive functions. These functions will develop normally, given an intact brain and body, and good-enough parenting and education.

Among the other ego functions are the defense mechanisms which are involved in conflict formation and resolution, symptom formation, and character development. The defense and other mechanisms operate subtly in the development of self and object representations, object relations, affect modulation, and impulse control. These functions determine how a child copes with stress; they will frequently determine whether the child will or will not make a suicidal attempt.

This chapter focuses on the ego functioning characteristic of suicidal children. Table 10-1 lists and defines the ego functions relevant to this discussion. These ego functions—cognition, impulse control or frustra-

TABLE 10-1
Definitions of ego functions

Reality testing: the capacity to differentiate between internal and external stimuli.

Affect expression: the quality, intensity, and timing of displays of such affects as joy, pleasure, anxiety, anger, sadness, and depression.

Intellectual and cognitive functions: a set of factors that interact to maintain one's comprehension of circumstances, memory of experiences, academic achievement, intellectual ability, and integration of perceptual and motor stimuli.

Frustration tolerance: the individual's tolerance for disappointment, capacity to delay action to a future time, ability to make decisions, and sense of planning for the future.

Interpersonal and object relations: a person's style of relating to others as well as his or her sense of identity.

---

tion tolerance, affect state, reality testing, and object relations—can be evaluated during interviews with the child by observing how the child comprehends, what themes he or she appears to be preoccupied with, and by noting behavior and interactions with others. In addition, psychological testing may provide specific information about such ego functioning as cognitive skills, reality testing, affect expression, and object relations.

Different manifestations of ego functioning have been associated with various stages of a child's normal development (A. Freud, 1952; Hartmann, 1952; Hoffer, 1952), deviations in development (Burlingham, 1965; Frankl, 1961), and childhood psychopathology (Hartmann *et al.*, 1946; Beres, 1956; Furman, 1956). This discussion addresses some qualities of ego functioning that are related to suicidal behavior in children.

EGO FUNCTIONS AND THE SPECTRUM
OF SUICIDAL BEHAVIOR

A spectrum of suicidal behavior has been defined that includes nonsuicidal behavior, suicidal ideas, suicidal threats, suicidal attempts, and suicide (Pfeffer *et al.*, 1979). Ackerly (1967) was one of the first clinicians to delineate differences and deviations in ego functioning in children with different degrees of suicidal tendencies. He proposed the hypothesis that children who threaten suicide express predominantly aggressive drives and a narcissistic orientation to life. In contrast, children who attempt suicide exhibit a major break with reality, a massive disruption of adaptive mechanisms, and an intense withdrawal of interests. In short, these children are psychotic.

The data from studies by Pfeffer and associates (1979, 1980, 1982) do not concur with Ackerly's (1967) proposition. Pfeffer and colleagues (1982) have shown in a population of 65 child psychiatric inpatients that childhood suicidal behavior is not associated specifically with psychotic disorders. Pfeffer and colleagues noted that there was no difference in most psychiatric diagnoses for children with suicidal ideas, suicidal threats, or suicidal attempts. However, children with either suicidal ideas or actions were more likely to have a major depressive disorder, an adjustment disorder, or a specific developmental disorder. Carlson and Cantwell (1982), in contrast to Pfeffer et al.'s observations, did find differences in children with suicidal ideas and attempts with respect to depressive disorders. In their study of 102 children and adolescents who were psychiatric inpatients and outpatients, they noted that there was an association between the degree of depression and severity of suicidal ideas. In contrast, there was no direct relation between degree of depression and suicidal attempts. Their findings suggest that there is a difference between children with suicidal ideas and children who attempt suicide.

With respect to preadolescents, there are no data from empirical research for a comparison of preadolescents who commit suicide and those who attempt suicide. Thus, Ackerly's (1967) proposal that that are differences among children with varying degrees of suicidal status requires additional systematic study using a variety of populations of suicidal children.

COGNITIVE FUNCTIONING OF SUICIDAL CHILDREN

Disturbances in cognitive functioning are beginning to be elucidated for depressed and suicidal children. How a child perceives and interprets situations, and how he or she is able to plan ways of coping with stress and conflict are important to the incidence of suicidal behavior. Therefore, if there are defects in cognitive functioning, the child may be hampered in his or her ability to adapt to stress. Such defects may increase risk of a child acting out suicidal impulses and fantasies. Because depression is most specifically associated with suicidal behavior, investigations evaluating cognitive functioning of depressed youngsters are also discussed in this section.

Chapman, Cullen, Boersma, and Maguire (1981) studied the relationship between self-concept, feelings, attitudes, motivation, task persistence, and academic functioning. They studied 376 children who were in grades three to six. Children who had positive perceptions of their abilities and expected high levels of success invested great effort in school. These children increased their levels of performance more than children who had negative perceptions of their abilities. Negative perceptions of abilities were more apparent among the depressed youngsters in the study.

Similar findings were noted by Berndt, Kaiser, and Van Aalst (1982) in a study of 248 gifted adolescents. There was a group of adolescents in the study who were not successful in carrying out goals. These youngsters were depressed and had symptoms of guilt, low self-esteem, helplessness, and cognitive difficulty. These studies pointed out that youngsters who are depressed do not function as well in academic and life tasks as other children. Such studies illustrate that if a child does not think well of himself or herself, he or she may be less motivated to achieve goals and to complete tasks. Such children may give up when they are faced with stress because they cannot think about alternative ways of managing the stress. Thus, such depressed children may be vulnerable to suicidal behavior because their helplessness in coping with stress is heightened and they begin to feel intensely hopeless about finding a solution.

Depression is associated with poor school performance in children who are intellectually competent. Colbert, Newman, Ney, and Young (1982) studied 282 children, ages 6 to 14 years, who were referred to a child and family psychiatric unit. Fifty-four percent of the children were diagnosed as having dysthymic or major depressive disorders. Seventy-one percent of the depressed children who were in regular classes at school were significantly underachieving. However, relatively few of these children had learning disabilities. When these children were treated with psychotherapy, many of these children improved in school achievement. These findings suggest that depression affects cognitive and school functioning in children. Furthermore, it may be hypothesized that diminished cognitive performance during periods of depression may hamper a child's abilities to adapt, so that a high-risk situation for the expression of suicidal behavior develops.

Child I: Andrea, an 8-year-old girl, vividly illustrates the effects of affective disorder upon cognitive functioning. Andrea was referred for psychiatric outpatient treatment because of severe withdrawal, preoccupations with death, and academic problems at school. Her initial school problems became evident when, in the second grade, she appeared to be very sad, refused to do homework, and performed erratically in school. Prior to this, she had been a good student and was highly motivated and quite sociable with peers. Psychological testing, at that time, revealed no organically based learning disabilities, but there were signs of depression. In the next grade Andrea showed increased classroom problems. She refused to do homework, arrived late to class, and occasionally wandered out of class. At times she wished she were dead and occasionally thought of killing herself. Psychotherapy and remedial tutoring were initiated. Within 2 months, Andrea's school participation improved, her depression diminished, and her preoccupations with death disappeared. She maintained appropriate grades and began to actively participate in class.

This child's case illustrated that the development of academic problems can develop at the time that a child experiences a depressive disorder. The decrease of depression by means of psychiatric intervention and the aid of special tutoring were factors that helped this child reach her previous higher level of academic performance.

Studies clearly show that there are cognitive deficits in individuals who are depressed or suicidal. Weingartner, Cohen, Murphy, Martello, and Gerdt (1981) observed in depressed adults that cognitive experience during episodes of clinical depression includes both qualitative and quantitative changes in how internal and external events are processed, interpreted, and stored in memory. Depressed patients use weak or incomplete strategies to organize and transform events, but deficits are less apparent if these individuals are helped to organize and process information. Similar trends were observed by Brumback, Staton, and Wilson (1980), who discovered that 58% of the 72 children referred for evaluation of learning and/or behavior problems met criteria for a depressive disorder. These investigators recommended that a diagnosis of depression should be considered when a child presents with learning problems and that remission of the depression must be achieved before the educational potential of a depressed child can be evaluated. These studies point out that problems with school are important features found in depressed children. Furthermore, Pfeffer and associates (1979) noted that suicidal children, more than nonsuicidal children, worry about doing poorly in school.

The relationship between suicidal behavior in children and intelligence requires additional study. Shaffer (1974), in his study of 30 children who committed suicide when they were 12 to 14 years old, observed that the majority of children had average to superior intelligence. Twenty children in that study had an IQ of 100 to 130. He inferred from these findings that children who commit suicide have high intellectual abilities. However, his findings must be considered to be preliminary because the sample of children was relatively small and there were no comparison groups of children who died from other causes.

Weiner and Pfeffer (1983) determined in a sample of 106 child psychiatric inpatients that intellectual functioning, measured by standard psychological test batteries that included the Wechsler Intelligence Scale for Children—Revised, Raven's Progressive Matrices, and the Illinois Test of Psycholinguistic Abilities, was not different for nonsuicidal children, children with suicidal ideas, and children with suicidal attempts. This study showed that there is no difference between suicidal and nonsuicidal psychiatric inpatients on IQ test performance.

Weiner and Pfeffer (1983) proposed that psychological tests may not be the best way to examine differences in cognition among suicidal and nonsuicidal children. These tests are complex and involve multiple cognitive operations. A number of factors besides those specific to a psychiatric symptom, such as suicidal behavior, could account for good or poor performance on psychological tests. Therefore, it may be necessary to employ tests that are restricted to measuring specific types of cognitive processes. Thus, perhaps there are specific cognitive deficits of suicidal children, such as poor attention or poor memory, that may be measured with other tests that are more specific to these cognitive functions. Furthermore, Weiner and Pfeffer (1983) suggested that studies of other populations of children such as psychiatric outpatients or nonpatient populations of children are required to assess whether the results of this study can be replicated.

The studies presented in this section suggested that there is a relation between depression and cognitive deficits in children. It was proposed that children who are hampered by cognitive deficits may not be able to assess a stressful situation in such a way that the child can work out alternative solutions to his or her problems. Therefore, such children may feel so helpless and hopeless that expression of suicidal tendencies may occur.

Levenson and Neuringer (1971) sought to see whether suicidal behavior was associated with decreased ability to seek alternative solutions to problems. Thirteen suicidal adolescents, 13 nonsuicidal adolescents who were psychiatric patients, and 13 normal adolescents were studied. The extent of problem-solving ability was tested by the Wechsler Adult Intelligence Scale (WAIS) Arithmetic Subtest and the Rokeach Map Reading Problems Test. The suicidal adolescents had significantly lower WAIS Arithmetic Subtest scores and failed the Rokeach Map Reading Problems Test more often than the psychiatric and normal groups. This indicated that suicidal adolescents had diminished problem-solving efficiency. The cognitive measures used in the study called for certain activities such as the ability to concentrate, to evaluate hierarchical relevances, and to reevaluate and recognize problem elements when there are changes in the problem situation. These tasks may be similar to the types of abilities needed when facing difficult situations in life. Thus, this study supports the hypothesis that decreased cognitive skills are related to diminished problem-solving abilities and that these deficits are related to suicidal tendencies in youngsters.

EGO DEFENSE MECHANISMS

Ego defenses are ego functions which prevent the eruption of unwanted impulses. Ego defenses work in such a way that the impulse can cease to be expressed or is expressed in a changed form. One of the issues that has received relatively little attention is whether suicidal children utilize specific ego defenses to cope with impulses that arise in response to intolerable perceived stress. Sandler and Joffe (1965) used psychoanalytic theory to explain how ego defenses affect expression of depression in children. Sandler and Joffe noted that depression could occur at any developmental stage and usually when the child faced a specific threat to his or her well-being. Depression could be described as a state of "helpless resignation in the face of pain, together with an inhibition both of drive discharge and ego functions" (p. 92). Their hypothesis was that depression arises when the ego becomes incapable of enduring painful affects or experiences. Sandler and Joffe believed that the ego defense of turning against the self was frequently operative in depressed children. They hypothesized that in depressed children, the ego defenses operate to direct anger against the self. Furthermore, if such self-directed anger becomes too intense, the child may exhibit suicidal behavior. Sandler and Joffe observed that other ego defenses, such as regression and intensification of fantasy, are also commonly observed in depressed children. Furthermore, they suggested that if a child cannot achieve a better state of well-being as a result of the operations of ego defenses, feelings of helplessness may occur. This state of helplessness may be a precipitant of suicidal behavior.

Sandler and Joffe's explanations were derived from clinical observations of depressed children, but there were no comparison groups of children in these studies. In fact, empirical studies of ego defenses in children are almost nonexistent. Among the few studies are those carried out by Pfeffer and associates (1979, 1980, 1982, 1984) to determine whether there is a relationship between children's suicidal behavior and ego mechanisms of defense. These studies utilized samples of children, age 6 to 12 years, who were evaluated in psychiatric inpatient and outpatient services as well as in nonpatient settings. Eleven ego defenses were specifically evaluated. The definitions of these ego defenses are listed in Table 10-2. Pfeffer and associates have shown that these defenses can be rated reliably by two independent clinicians who simultaneously observe the evaluation of a child.

Pfeffer and associates (1979, 1980, 1982, 1984) demonstrated in empirical studies that introjection, as an ego defense, was significantly more common among suicidal than nonsuicidal children. These researchers proposed that a pathological aspect of introjection is that it promotes and maintains poor psychological differentiation between

TABLE 10-2
Definitions of ego mechanisms of defense

Regression: the manifestation of an unconscious return to an earlier level of ego development.

Denial: includes unconscious mechanisms of isolation and splitting, and the tendency to deny painful sensations and facts.

Projection: occurs when emotions and wishes are unconsciously attributed to someone else.

Introjection: includes unconsciously taking in characteristics, ideas, and feelings of another person.

Repression: the unconscious purposeful forgetting or not becoming aware of internal impulses or external events.

Reaction formation: a manifestation of an unconscious reverse of the repressed instinctual impulses, for example, excessive cleanliness and covering up anal and sexual impulses.

Undoing: occurs when something is done or thought and is immediately unconsciously undone by an act or thought that negates it.

Displacement: the unconscious channeling of instinctual feelings, actions, and ideas into a new object or situation.

Intellectualization: occurs when a child unconsciously discusses ideas rather than expressing feelings in situations where feelings should be discussed.

Compensation: occurs when a child experiences inadequacy or inability and unconsciously overdevelops in another area.

Sublimation: evident when, under the influence of the ego, unacceptable feelings are changed unconsciously into a socially useful modality without blocking an adequate discharge.

---

parents and suicidal children. Pfeffer and colleagues observed that parents and suicidal children often show similar emotions and behaviors. Frequently, parents of suicidal children lack appreciation of their child's developmental needs, especially as a separate person. This is made evident by such parental statements as "My child is just like me." For example, one mother described her feelings toward her son: "John was the second child just like me. I had no friends, just like John. I always fought and was teased, just like John."

Pfeffer and associates (1979, 1980, 1982) observed that introjection enhances the relationship between suicidal individuals and emotionally important people in their lives. In this way, it serves two opposing functions. First, introjection may help prevent suicidal behavior that arises from feelings of loneliness and despair because it serves to enhance identifications among people. Second, because introjection helps intensify the parent–child bond, introjection may prevent a child from expressing autonomous feelings. The stress engendered in experiencing a decrease in autonomy may promote suicidal tendencies. Other investigators also described the relationship between intense dependency relationships and suicidal behavior in adults. Litman and Tabachnick (1968) and Richman (1978) observed that intense mutual sharing of experiences and perceptions is evident among suicidal adults who maintain very close or symbiotic relationships with other family members. These clinicians proposed that symbiotic relationships in a family constitute a major characteristic that is associated with suicidal behavior.

SUICIDAL MOTIVES

Fantasies form the unique aspects of human existence and arise out of the earliest perceptions of one's environment and physiological functions. Fantasies serve to synthesize and integrate stimuli and are coping mechanisms. Fantasies change as one matures; some fantasies acquire great degrees of complexity. In children, fantasies are obvious in play, verbalization, poetry, art, and music. Such avenues of fantasy expression help the child master new, frightening, or challenging experiences. Fantasies help a child turn passive feelings into activity which may decrease anxiety and helplessness. The elaboration of fantasy may be the first step in the child's ability to practice control over intense affects. Therefore, fantasy elaboration is an important ego mechanism for coping with stress. However, there are certain fantasies that are closely associated with suicidal behavior in children.

Suicidal fantasies can be defined as special ideas that provide the reason for suicidal actions. These fantasies are consciously expressed ideas that have unconscious derivatives. Types of suicidal fantasies are presented later in this section.

One function of suicidal fantasies is wish fulfillment. They are often action oriented, with the purpose of changing a child's passive perceptions into those of active mastery. Often, several suicidal fantasies coexist, or they may be expressed at different times by a given child. Another function of such fantasies is to help diminish painful states. However, when these fantasies fail in this function to decrease pain, suicidal fantasies paradoxically may foster expression of suicidal impulses.

Suicidal fantasies become catalysts for suicidal behavior only when a combination of ego functioning and stresses occurs that potentiates the possibility of acting out on wishes and impulses. This occurs when other ego mechanisms in conjunction with suicidal fantasies fail to decrease the child's state of painful helplessness. However, suicidal fantasies alone do not lead to suicidal behavior.

One of the most important theories about suicidal fantasies was offered by Karl Menninger (1933). He proposed that suicide involves the "wish to put oneself in a predicament from which one cannot except by suicide, escape" (p. 377). This mechanism "brings about an apparent justification in external reality for self-destruction" (p. 377). Menninger believed that unconscious wishes are more important in suicide than the observable external realities. Menninger pointed out three unconscious elements in suicidal fantasies: the wish to kill, the wish to be killed, and the wish to die. He considered that suicide "is a death in which are combined in one person the murderer and murdered" (p. 378). In any particular suicidal person, one of these three elements may be stronger than another. The mechanism associated with the wish to kill involves the displacement of aggression originally directed against a hated person onto oneself, who becomes unconsciously identified with the hated person. The wish to be killed results from intense guilt derived from one's murderous wishes that provoke a need for punishment. The processes leading to a wish to die seemed less clear to Menninger, but he believed they involved one's narcissistic gratification in having power to determine one's life or death.

Menninger's theories of suicidal behavior were based on his observations of adults; however, these ideas are equally applicable to children who express wishes to kill others as well as themselves. Suicidal children also have intense wishes to die.

Child II: Calvin, age 11 years, illustrates Menninger's three elements of suicide. Calvin lived with his parents and two younger brothers and had a hard time controlling his temper. He frequently hit or kicked his mother or siblings. He was disobedient at home and at school, where he fought with his classmates and provoked them to injure him. Just before his hospital admission, he became increasingly violent and threatened to jump out a second-story window. He intensely wished he were dead and wanted to kill himself. He felt that he hated himself and he seemed to reject anything good within himself. In addition, he threatened to harm his mother just before his hospitalization. He threw knives against the wall where she was standing. He wished he could kill her because she did not give him as much attention as his brothers.

This child's intense aggression was expressed at other people as well as at himself. He wished he were dead and his wish to kill himself arose from guilt generated by murderous wishes toward his younger siblings and mother. His murderous wishes were so intolerable that he had to be removed from his family. He wanted to die and waited for an appropriate moment to carry this out.

Another motive for suicidal behavior is a wish to be rescued, or "a cry for help" (Jensen & Petty, 1958). A cry for help is the child's desperate attempt to highlight dramatically the plight of helplessness resulting from overwhelming external stress. Often this phenomenon is associated with family chaos, physical illness, and school problems. The wish to be rescued is the fantasy that there is someone who is powerful and kind, and who will be able to decrease the stress perceived by the child. This fantasy is very common among suicidal children and may account for why many children orchestrate their suicidal episodes in such ways that help is immediately available. It may be the reason why suicidal episodes of children occur in the presence of others who can intervene.

The following example illustrates a suicidal child's unconscious wish to be rescued. This example is typical of how children involve another person in their suicidal episodes.

Child III: The girl, age 9 years, sat in the auditorium of her school planning to jump off the balcony. She was very despondent because her father had recently deserted the family. She felt guilty that she had driven him away, especially because she frequently argued with him. She waited in the auditorium until she heard a teacher arrive to see where she was. Immediately, she jumped out of her seat and ran to the balcony calling out, "I want to die. No one loves me." The teacher dashed to her rescue and held her as she approached the balcony.

This child, although deeply despondent over the loss of her father and guilty about possibly causing his departure, had sufficient hope that she might be helped with her feelings and loneliness. She staged her suicide attempt in such a way that someone would recognize her deep distress. Her rescuer unconsciously symbolized her father, who she believed would return and take care of her.

Bender and Schilder (1937) were among the first clinical investigators to describe the complex nature of suicidal motives in children. They noted that suicidal children were reacting to a perceived deprivation of parental love. In response, the children used aggressive actions to punish the parents. However, guilt over their own punitive and aggressive fantasies provoked the child's intense need to escape from an intolerable family situation. Suicide, therefore, was fantasized as a more peaceful state. Unconsciously, such a fantasized peaceful condition stood for a reunion with an idealized nurturing parent. Thus, Bender and Schilder showed that children's suicidal motives may include a variety of suicidal fantasies experienced simultaneously. They described the wish to punish the parents, the wish to escape from unbearable circumstances, the wish to achieve a pleasant state, and the wish to reunite with a kind parent.

Ackerly (1967) expanded upon this idea and proposed a specific type of suicidal fantasy that he called a "phoenix motif." This suicidal fantasy involved the child's wish to return to early childhood when he or she was ideally nurtured by an all-giving good mother. Ackerly interpreted suicidal behavior as a return to a state of primary narcissism or a oneness with an idealized mother. Such reunion fantasies are often observed in suicidal children who have lost a parent through death, divorce, or other types of separations.

Child IV: Allison, age 7 years, vividly illustrated this fantasy. Allison's father died when she was 4 years old. Allison had problems getting along with her depressed, alcoholic mother. Allison felt unloved and neglected. She longed for her father's return. One day, after an argument with her mother, Allison stayed in her room and swallowed 10 of her mother's tranquilizers. Allison lay on her bed thinking only about joining her father in heaven. She was found, an hour later, by her mother, who rushed Allison to the hospital.

The wish to be relieved of inner turmoil and psychic pain is often evident in extreme cases of confusion, panic, or psychosis. The inner suffering is so great that suicidal behavior is an attempt to remove this type of distress. It is another form of the "cry for help" phenomenon (Mattsson *et al.*, 1969). Death is a peaceful alternative and resolution to intense inner psychological suffering. This is illustrated by the next case example.

Child V: Sally, age 9 years, believed she had a small person inside her stomach. This evil person commanded her to "do bad things." Sally was terrified, especially at night, when she heard the voice of the small person telling her to kill her mother. Sally obtained a kitchen knife and cut her abdomen several times in the hopes of killing the small person. She was found by her father, who brought her to the hospital.

Finally, the act of revenge is based on the motivation to teach a hated parent a drastic lesson (Toolan, 1962). The child uses suicide as a means of gaining what he or she wishes. Often the desire to die is minimal. Although many of these suicidal children generate animosity from others and skepticism about genuine wishes to die, this form of suicidal fantasy must be taken very seriously, especially since the child may be quite able to succeed at harming himself or herself.

In summary, a number of fantasies have been associated with suicidal behavior in children. Often suicidal children express several simultaneous suicidal fantasies. Table 10-3 shows the types of suicidal

TABLE 10-3
Frequency of suicidal fantasies in children

Fantasy wishes	Degree of frequency
To die	Very common
To kill	Very common
To be rescued	Very common
To escape from intolerable situation	Very common
To be killed	Common
To punish others	Common
To achieve a peaceful state	Common
To reunite with a kind person	Common
To be relieved of inner turmoil	Less common
To gain revenge	Less common

fantasies and the degrees of frequency with which such fantasies occur in children. The most frequently expressed suicidal fantasies in children seem to be the wish to die, the wish to kill, the wish to be rescued, and the wish to escape from intolerable circumstances.

Empirical research on the fantasies of suicidal children is almost nonexistent. Santostefano, Rieder, and Beck (1984) studied the hypothesis that fantasy mediates between impulses and actions. They proposed that fantasy creates delay and is a way of rehearsing action in thought before these actions are performed in reality. They were interested in whether suicidal children construct and organize fantasies, as rehearsals of actions, in ways that are unique.

A scale was devised to evaluate motions depicted in images produced on the Rorschach Test. A study was made of 123 children, ages 8 to 16 years, hospitalized in a psychiatric facility. Each child was assigned to a suicidal group or a nonsuicidal group based on the existence or lack of existence of suicidal actions. In addition, 44 schoolchildren were studied as a nonhospitalized control group for the younger children. The results revealed that the suicidal children had difficulty conceptualizing future action. When a behavioral process required fantasy but not action, the suicidal children engaged in action rather than imagining. This suggested that fantasy was failing in interposing delay between impulses and action. Finally, the suicidal children's imagined motion was slower and less vigorous than the nonsuicidal children's fantasy motion. This is one of the first studies to show qualitative and quantitative differences in fantasies of suicidal children. It illustrates the important interactions between dynamic and cognitive variables in constructing fantasies among suicidal children. It also illustrates that when elaboration of fantasies fails to diminish painful affects and experiences, risk for suicidal behavior may increase.

PATHWAYS TO THE ONTOGENESIS OF
CHILDHOOD SUICIDAL BEHAVIOR

Utilizing the psychoanalytic propositions put forth about ego functioning, and my extensive observations of suicidal children, this section presents a hypothetical model of the pathways that lead to suicidal behavior in children. Suicidal behavior can be defined as a complex symptom that arises from multiple sources that include biochemical factors and interpersonal, sociological, and family derivatives. For a unified theory of suicidal behavior to exist, these factors must be integrated into the construction of a hypothesis about the interaction of intrapsychic functioning with the other classes of events.

Psychoanalytic theory proposes that a symptom results from attempts to resolve conflict via compromise formation. Figure 10-1 depicts the intrapsychic processes leading to the development of a symptom. S. Freud (1926) proposed that psychic conflict is generated when strong forces to achieve wish fulfillment are counteracted by strong forces of ego and superego mechanisms to restrain attainment of wish gratification. Psychic conflict arises from many sources including external stimuli and internally generated stimuli. The constellation of symptoms that arises from psychic conflict is determined by the organization and integration of the ego mechanisms of a given individual. Such ego mechanisms include fantasy elaboration, cognitive perceptions, reality testing, defense mechanisms, and expression of affects. Thus, some children, because of the specific nature of their intrapsychic functioning, may be more prone to suicidal behavior than other children.

Studies of suicidal children have shown that depression, death preoccupations, and hopelessness are specific risk factors for suicidal

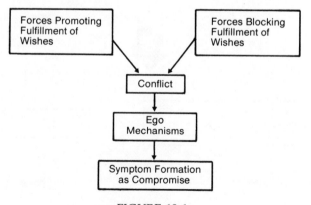

FIGURE 10-1
The processes of symptom development.

behavior. The association of depression, death preoccupations, hopelessness, and other ego states depends upon a complex process of change in ego functioning (Pfeffer, 1982). Figure 10-2 depicts a hypothesis of the intrapsychic processes leading to suicidal behavior in children. This figure shows the cumulative effects of stress that create the development of symptoms. The figure depicts four phases.

In Phase I a variety of forces attempt to promote and block gratification of wishes. This state leads to conflict; this is dealt with by the child's ego mechanisms, which produce symptoms as a compromise. This is the basic mechanism of symptom development. This process can occur among all children. The result of this process is the development of a variety of symptoms such as obsessions, compulsions, phobias, behavior problems, learning problems, or affective disturbances.

Phase II depicts the effects of added stress from physiological, developmental, and/or external factors that are superimposed upon the original stress. Some children, for whatever reason (e.g., genetic factors, early experience, poor physical environment, and temperament), may be highly vulnerable to stress. Two outcomes may occur and they depend upon the vulnerabilities of the child. In some cases, the child's personality, which is a reflection of the constellation of ego mechanisms that a child uses to manage stress, may promote the expression of additional symptoms. This is seen in the pathway for children with low

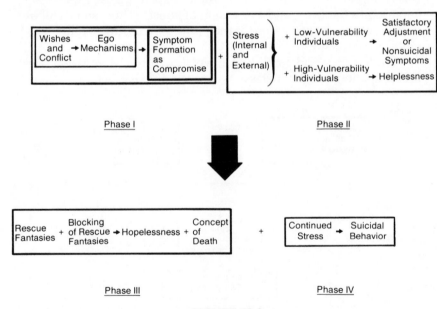

FIGURE 10-2
The intrapsychic processes leading to suicidal behavior in children.

vulnerability. In other children, with high vulnerability, the feeling of helplessness occurs. It must be noted that vulnerabilities are related to the types of ego mechanisms that developed in response to the effects of early childhood experiences. For example, suicidal children may be more prone to use such ego defenses as introjection, regression, and denial to manage stress while nonsuicidal children may use predominantly other ego defenses such as repression and intellectualization. This is a speculative point and there is not sufficient information to validate this hypothesis. However, some studies (Pfeffer *et al.*, 1979, 1980, 1982, 1984) have suggested that personality characteristics of suicidal children include the prominent use of introjection as a defense mechanism. In addition, such children characteristically have an intense attachment to a parent. Nevertheless, speculations about personality vulnerabilities in children require additional study.

Phase III shows the effects of helplessness and the conflict that develops between wishes to be rescued and forces that oppose gratification of rescue fantasies. Themes of rescue are aimed at encountering a powerful, kind, nurturing person who will be able to assist in diminishing the child's state of intense psychic helplessness. If there is not sufficient gratification of the wishes to be rescued, because there is a lack of a rescuer or the parent does not perceive that the child is in need of rescue, hopelessness occurs. Hopelessness subsequently becomes linked with the child's preoccupations with death. These include ideas that death is a pleasant state which will relieve the child of the pain of hopelessness and result in a peaceful resolution of his or her conflicts. Here death is conceptualized as the cessation of painful hopelessness.

Finally, as seen in Phase IV, if additional stress occurs, it will be the immediate stimulus for the expression of the child's suicidal behavior.

SUMMARY

Ego functioning is the cornerstone for psychological integration of internally perceived stimuli and external experiences. Some qualities of ego functioning that have been observed among suicidal children include deficits in cognitive functioning related to the way children think of themselves, make judgments about a situation, and arrive at a plan of action, and poor academic performance. Other qualities of ego functioning of suicidal children are the frequent use of such ego defenses as introjection and elaboration of intense conscious and unconscious fantasies. When these ego mechanisms fail to alleviate the child's psychological distress, suicidal impulses intensify.

ASSESSMENT OF SUICIDAL RISK

CHAPTER ELEVEN

THE EVALUATION OF CHILDHOOD SUICIDAL RISK BY CLINICAL INTERVIEW

Boris's suicide seems to me an indecency, for I was not expecting it.
—André Gide, *The Counterfeiters*

The assessment of suicidal risk in children includes evaluating the child's emotions, behaviors, and interpersonal relations. The previous chapters have outlined a variety of intrapsychic and psychosocial factors that increase risk for suicidal behavior in children. This chapter includes a clinical semistructured interview format that describes ways of assessing the various suicidal risk factors discussed in previous chapters. This clinical semistructured interview format can serve as a model for assessment, especially since every child who is evaluated psychiatrically should be assessed for suicidal risk.

In addition, common types of responses, reactions, and feelings elicited in the clinician during such an evaluation process are discussed in this chapter. These responses may serve to either enhance or inhibit the assessment procedure and, therefore, require specific attention from the clinician to his or her own reactions.

PRINCIPLES OF INTERVIEWING

Several principles are involved in the interview evaluation of suicidal risk in children. First, a clinician should have up-to-date information about the diagnosis, treatment, and natural course of suicidal behavior in children. Such knowledge is necessary so that the clinician is able to execute the necessary work with the suicidal child efficiently and effectively. Decisiveness in planning the care of a suicidal child is required so that appropriate intervention and prevention measures are offered rapidly.

Second, the clinician must be fully aware of his or her conscious feelings about death and suicide. This allows the clinician to have a more objective impression of the suicidal child's condition. It enhances the clinician's ability to make clear and appropriate recommendations and helps to diminish his or her fears about work with such children.

Third, the clinician must be able to evaluate his or her unconscious fantasies and emotions about these issues. This type of evaluation is complex and often requires assistance from colleagues and/or psychoanalysis or psychotherapy. By definition, unconscious fantasies and feelings are not observable by the individual. Therefore, discussions with colleagues or the clinician's own therapist will help elucidate the clinician's reactions that are influenced by his or her unconscious feelings and thoughts. By making such feelings and thoughts conscious, the clinician can more effectively monitor his or her responses to the suicidal patient.

Fourth, all suicidal ideas and actions of children should be taken seriously and evaluated thoroughly and repeatedly. The evaluation should include a detailed account from the child and the family of the child's suicidal tendencies and the factors that enhance risk for suicidal behavior.

Fifth, it is necessary to evaluate the degree of immediate or acute suicidal risk of the patient. Not only should a child's suicidal fantasies be assessed, but the actual potential that the child may take immediate action requires careful assessment. In addition, factors that should be evaluated include those that enhance protection of the child against harm.

Sixth, it is important to obtain a clear commitment from the child that he or she will work with the therapist and not attempt self-harm. Unless such an understanding is established, the child cannot be depended on to maintain his or her safety. In addition, it is essential, as part of the treatment plan, that other individuals will be available at all times to be with the child and to intervene to provide safety and emotional support for the child.

Seventh, it is essential to involve the family in the initial interviews. The interviews may be arranged in a flexible manner so that the parents can be interviewed as a couple, with the child and/or individually. This emphasizes to all members of the family the seriousness of the problem and stimulates appreciation that suicidal behavior reflects underlying problems within the family.

For example, the notion that a child's suicidal behavior is serious and is an indicator of a family problem was described by French and Steward (1975) in their case report of Tommy, a 7-year-old boy. Tommy was found by his mother "crimson-faced and struggling for air, having knotted a jumping rope around his neck and jerking it tight. She reported considerable difficulty in loosening the rope and, having done so, sought professional help immediately" (p. 32). During the evaluation, it appeared that Tommy perceived his situation as hopeless, especially because he was "caught between a distant, hostile, and threatening father on the one hand and a superficially warm and positive but destructively infantilizing mother on the other hand" (p. 33). The evaluation and treatment of the family helped the father decrease his tendency to scapegoat Tommy and the mother to feel less in need of protecting Tommy from his father's hostility. French and Steward's approach was similar to that recommended by Morrison and Collier (1969), who proposed that "the goal of the first interview with the family was to identify the external situation that had provoked the suicidal crisis and to clarify the family's internal susceptibility" (p. 150).

Another purpose for meeting with the family is to assess their understanding, their willingness, and their ability to make rapid changes that would ensure the safety of the child. This is accomplished by evaluating each person's influence upon the feelings and behavior of other family members.

Two examples from my research subjects point out contrasting degrees and qualities of family responses to a suicidal child.

Family I: This family could not make rapid changes to ensure the safety of a 9-year-old boy who thought of killing himself with a large butcher knife. The boy was intensely angry at his mother, who was chronically depressed and preoccupied with her college education. She was frequently not at home or tended to isolate herself so that she could study. The father, a competent and aggressive businessman, traveled extensively because of his work responsibilities. The child's suicidal ideas intensified 3 days before his father was to embark on a month-long business trip. During the initial interview with the parents and child, it was not possible to convince him to delay his trip and not possible to stimulate the mother to spend more time with her son. Because the parents could not be available to protect the child sufficiently from potential harm, this child was hospitalized on a child psychiatry inpatient unit for observation and evaluation of his suicidal impulses.

Family II: Jack's family was able to make rapid shifts in the family situation so that Jack's safety was assured. Jack's parents had separated 6 months before he thought of jumping out the classroom window. Jack, age 8 years, had increasing problems concentrating on his school work. He was referred because his teacher believed that "something was troubling Jack." Although he saw both parents regularly, he felt very anxious when he returned home after school because he felt that someone would enter the house to rob or harm him. He reported hearing voices telling him to hurt himself. Since his parents' separation, Jack's mother began to work. Jack was sad that his mother was not more available to him; he did not like to be alone after school. He wished his parents would be together again. During the initial evaluation, Jack's parents discussed ways they could provide someone to be with Jack after school. His father offered to support the cost of hiring someone to be at home when Jack returned from school. His mother spoke about how overwhelmed she had been feeling and said that perhaps she had not paid sufficient attention to Jack's feelings when she was with him. This family could acknowledge their wish to improve their circumstances and they were receptive to working on changes that would be beneficial.

Suicidal children have marked conscious and unconscious wishes to be taken care of by a kind, nuturing person. By gratifying these wishes during the initial phase of assessment, suicidal impulses may decrease because a sense of hopefulness is generated. Meeting with the family may serve to gratify the child's wishes by enlisting the parents to focus intensely on the child. The hope that the parents can respond to the child's needs is thereby increased. Having the parents present for discussion may create a renewed will for the child to live and to attempt to solve problems by other means. However, in situations where the parents are not insightful and resist working collaboratively with the therapist, the clinician must depend on other ways to ensure the safety of the child. Psychiatric hospitalization may be recommended in order to utilize additional staff and time to intensify the evaluation of the family and suicidal child.

An eighth principle is that a verbal mode should be the predominant format for evaluation. Talking about suicidal behavior with the child emphasizes the seriousness of the symptom. It gives the child a direct message that this is an extremely important and worrisome problem that must be dealt with by direct inquiry. Confronting the issues inherent in suicidal risk by verbal methods takes the diagnosis of risk out of the domain of inference and moves the evaluation into a reality-oriented approach. However, there are exceptions in using a primarily verbal mode of assessment, especially when working with young children or children who are not developmentally mature. In such situations, the use of play may enrich the evaluation. This is discussed in the next chapter.

The primary use of a verbal format provides language that will define a suicidal child's feelings, goals, hopes, behaviors, and worries. Katan (1961) put forth a valuable concept that is relevant also to the evaluation of suicidal risk in children. She worked with preschool children who had serious impulse disorders and emphasized the importance of verbalizing feelings and ideas to very young children. She concluded that

> verbalization of perceptions of the outer world precedes verbalization of feelings. Verbalization leads to an increase of the controlling function of

the ego over affects and drives. Verbalization increases for the ego the possibility of distinguishing between wishes and fantasies on the one hand, and reality on the other. In short, verbalization leads to the integrating process, which in turn results in reality testing and thus helps to establish the secondary process.

. . . if the child does not learn to name his feelings, a situation may arise in which there develops a discrepancy between the strength and complexity of his feelings on the one hand, and his modes of expression on the other. If the child could verbalize his feelings, he would learn to delay action. . . . (pp. 185–186)

Katan firmly believed that "verbalization of feelings leads to an increase of mastery by the ego. The young ego shows its strength by not acting upon its feelings immediately, but by delaying such action and expressing its feelings in words instead" (p. 186). She noted that she succeeded in helping children verbalize what they felt instead of acting on the feelings. In keeping with the premises of Katan's observations and hypotheses, deterrence of suicidal action can be promoted and processes of introspection and conflict resolution can occur when words are provided for feelings and behaviors.

Another reason to maximize dialogue between a child and therapist is that if a child can be helped to develop alternative ways of communicating his or her problems, suicidal risk may be diminished. The therapist can be a model to demonstrate that words are useful in settling disputes, in understanding confusing events, in overcoming intolerable situations, and in expressing intense emotions. Rather than acting out suicidal impulses, the child can develop ability to delay action, to cope with wishes for immediate gratification, and to understand motivations for behavior. Talking with the therapist can help the child realize that there is an interested person who is available to help the child develop life-enhancing ways of coping.

Finally, emphasizing language in the evaluation of suicidal tendencies in children must include an awareness of the child's developmental competence. The clinician must choose words, phrase ideas, or define terms in language that matches a child's ability to comprehend. Often concepts should be discussed in a number of different ways during the clinical interview. This process of repetition of concepts provides an opportunity for the child to reflect on the questions and elaborate upon his or her feelings and thoughts.

In summary, there are several basic principles that are essential to consider during the diagnostic assessment of suicidal risk in children. Eight basic principles have been described in this section, and these are listed in Table 11-1. Furthermore, these principles always should be adhered to during every evaluation of a suicidal child.

TABLE 11-1
Basic principles of assessing childhood suicidal risk

---

1. Clinician should be knowledgeable about diagnosis, treatment, and outcome of suicidal children.
2. Clinician must be aware of his or her conscious feelings about death and suicide.
3. Clinician must be able to evaluate his or her unconscious feelings about death and suicide.
4. All suicidal ideas and actions are serious and warrant extensive evaluation.
5. The degree of acute suicidal risk should be evaluated.
6. A commitment should be obtained from the child to work with the therapist and not attempt to harm himself or herself.
7. The family should be involved in the initial interviews.
8. A verbal mode should be the predominant format for evaluation.

A CLINICAL INTERVIEW FORMAT

Pfeffer and associates (1979, 1980, 1982, 1984) have shown that several factors specifically can influence risk of childhood suicidal behavior. These factors include the child's sadness or depression, the child's preoccupations with death, and depression and suicidal tendencies in family members. It is the combined effects of these variables that lead to expression of suicidal tendencies in children. The assessment of these factors requires that a clinician systematically focus on the components of these factors during the clinical interviews with the child and the family.

All children should be asked if they ever "thought of hurting themselves," if they ever "threatened or attempted to hurt themselves," if they ever "wished or tried to kill themselves," and/or if they "wanted to or threatened to commit suicide." Variations on these questions may be helpful to draw out more detailed responses of the child. Children generally have a good understanding of these questions. For example, an 8-year-old girl, when asked if she "felt so sad that she wanted to kill herself," responded "Many times I want to commit suicide but I am afraid to do it."

Clinicians often believe that young children are not able to talk about their suicidal impulses. However, this belief is unfounded. In fact, children are able to talk openly about suicidal tendencies, as the following cases illustrate. These examples were obtained from randomly selected school children who had no previous history of psychiatric symptoms.

Child I: Nina was a 7-year-old girl whose mother described her as "a normal child who needs a lot of time." Sometimes Nina said, "I wish I were dead" or "I wish I would hurt myself but I will not do it." Her mother once said to

Nina, "Why don't you do it and get it over with?" Nina's mother, too, acknowledged feeling depressed and said, "Sometimes I feel everything's falling apart and I think of killing myself, like ending it all."

In an interview with Nina, she stated: "Sometimes I want to kill myself. When my stomach hurts, I say, God I will kill myself because I feel so bad. This year I thought of it. On Halloween, I thought about killing myself because I did not feel well. My mother drives me crazy and I say to her that I will kill myself. One time I hurt myself and I was bleeding. I was so upset that I put my hand on an iron. I burnt my fingers. See, you can see it. But if I hurt myself, my mom will take care of me."

Child II: Martin was a 10-year-old boy whose mother described him as a child who loved to hug and kiss and was concerned about others. She noted that when Martin was mad he said "I wish I were dead" or "I want to kill myself." If his mother disciplined him, he might say "I wish I were dead. I will kill myself." His mother ignored him when he said this.

In an interview with Martin, he said: "Mom gets mad if I start fights with my brother. Sometimes she hits me with her belt. Not very hard. When this happens, sometimes I feel so sad that I want to kill myself. However, when she punishes me she is usually fair. I feel sad because I want to go out with my friends when she punishes me. Sometimes I cry and I feel real bad and I think that I wish I were dead."

Child III: Gregory, a 9½-year-old child, said the following: "Sometimes I get so mad that I want to kill myself. I had thoughts of wishing myself dead. Once I was outside with my cousin going shopping. When we were at the cash register my father got real mad at me for no reason. I wish I were not born and I wish I were dead. I thought about killing myself. My cousin and I went outside to play a game. We climbed into a tree and I slipped out onto the ground. My cousin ran down and picked me up. I had a scratch on my face. When I feel like killing myself, I feel it would not be good, however. Sometimes, I really get so mad that I want to hurt myself. I often wish I were dead. I think of hurting myself but also think it is not good because it is good to be alive. I want to hurt myself when my father is angry at me. I really want to die. However, it's hard to hurt yourself. It would hurt. I would then start to cry. My sister said that when you think about that you really don't mean it because it's good to have a good life in this world. My sister helps me."

Child IV: Sandy was a 12-year-old boy who said: "I want to hurt myself when I get upset. Once my grandmother found me with my head in the sink and I said that I was washing my face. However, I really was trying to drown myself. I wish I were dead. I have often thought of a variety of ways of killing myself such as the guillotine. I would go to France and have it done. It would be quick and painless. Guns are too painful. Stabbing is also too painful. If I feel my friends don't like me I feel very sad and sometimes I feel like crying. Then I wish I were dead.''

Child V: Debbie was a 12-year-old girl who stated: ''Recently I was so angry with my mother that I thought of going to my room and hanging myself. However, I really wouldn't be able to do it.''

Child VI: John was an 8½-year-old child who said: ''I get very sad when plans don't work out right. I often say that I would like to kill myself, but I wouldn't be able to do it and I don't mean it. I think that I would take a knife and stab myself or jump off the building. Sometimes I think I will stab myself in the head with a pencil.''

These children were very explicit in their statements and fantasies about suicide. Although these children had no previous history of psychiatric treatment, they must be considered at risk for suicidal behavior. That they had not been previously evaluated psychiatrically points out the dilemma of how to recognize children who are distressed and potentially suicidal before suicidal actions are expressed. In addition, these children's fantasies of the methods they would use to carry out suicidal actions were very similar to the suicidal methods contemplated and employed by child psychiatric inpatients and outpatients who were studied by Pfeffer and colleagues (1979, 1980, 1982).

Children use a wide variety of methods to carry out suicidal wishes. Jumping from heights, use of knives and drugs, running into traffic, hanging, drowning, and electrocution were among the most common methods. Assessment of the child's suicidal wishes and actions should include a very detailed account of what the child intended to have happen, what the child thought of the risk of death or serious injury if the action were carried out, and the specific circumstances in which the action was contemplated or implemented. Assessment of the circumstances should include what was happening before the suicidal impulse occurred. Was there an argument, frightening feelings generated by hallucinations or delusional thinking, or a feeling of rejection? The attempt of the child to involve others as potential rescuers must be evaluated. These questions will provide an objective appraisal of the child's suicidal intent and degree of lethality.

Historical information must be obtained from the child about harmful behavior and whether he or she thought about or attempted to commit suicide in the past. It is essential to elicit from the child whether the child knew about someone who thought about suicide, attempted suicide, or actually committed suicide. It is important to learn from the child what he or she knew about how the suicidal person carried out the action and when the action occurred. What the child believed were the reasons for it and what events were happening at the time of the suicidal behavior should be assessed. These questions will help a clinician know about the child's actual experiences with suicidal individuals, how the child perceives such people, and whether the child's suicidal tendencies are an identification with the behavior of other suicidal individuals.

One example will dramatically illustrate the relevance of these questions.

Child VII: Agatha was an 11-year-old girl whose father died from cancer when she was 6 years old. Her mother never recovered from the loss of her husband and became severely depressed after the husband's death. When Agatha was 10 years old, an aunt died of a sudden heart attack. Agatha's mother became deeply depressed over the loss of this sister; she spoke constantly about her dead husband and gradually developed auditory hallucinations of her husband's voice calling her name. One night when her mother could not sleep, she jumped out of her tenth-floor window and killed herself.

Agatha was in shock about her mother's death. She blamed herself for not staying up that night with her mother. Although she was given a good home with her uncle's family, Agatha remained deeply depressed. She began to think about killing herself so that she might join her parents. She told the psychiatrist who evaluated her, "I knew that it is not difficult to kill myself. My mother just jumped out a window and died." The tragic identification with her mother's suicidal action made it easier for Agatha to consider suicide as a way of coping with her despair.

Other important questions that should be asked involve the meaning and motivation of carrying out a specific method of suicidal action. Was the contemplated action meant to frighten a parent into gratifying the child's desires? Was it an act of revenge against a bad parent? Was it an attempt to be rescued by a benevolent parent? Was it a way of decreasing the despair of peer or family rejection? Was it a last effort to relieve internal pain and suffering from strong affective states, hopelessness, command hallucinations, or frightening delusions?

Child VIII: John, age 11 years, illustrated how suicidal behavior was meant to relieve him of his hopelessness and pain of his psychotic fantasies. He threatened to kill himself with a kitchen knife, which was pulled away from him by his father. John had been experiencing an acute psychotic breakdown. He could not concentrate in school, and he thought that people were laughing at him and that his mind was controlled. He wanted to rid himself of this painful state. He believed his condition was hopelessly incurable. He wanted to kill himself to relieve his misery and to gain peace.

Another concern in the clinical assessment of suicidal risk of children is that it is mandatory to determine the meaning of death for the child, what experiences the child had with death, the child's degree of preoccupation with death, and the child's affective and cognitive concepts of death. Discussion of these issues may provide the first warning signs of impending suicidal behavior.

Questioning children about death is not as formidable as some clinicians fear or believe. Unfortunately, many clinicians have little experience speaking with children about death and do not fully appreciate the importance of discussing these issues with children during the psychiatric assessment. Many clinicians fear that discussing this topic will cause children to withdraw and refuse to cooperate. As a result, some shy away from addressing this issue. For some, the fears about talking with children about death are determined by the clinician's memories of his or her own past experiences and perceptions regarding death.

Koocher (1974) was struck by the degree of anxiety of some clinicians, their inexperience, and misconceptions about interviewing children about death. Based on empirical studies with children about their ideas about death, Koocher made several suggestions for discussing death with children. He noted that there should be "no unspoken barriers to this topic of conversation" and that "children are capable of talking about death, and seem to want to do this. . . . they are pleased by the attention of understanding adults. Silence teaches that the subject is taboo" (p. 410). Speaking with suicidal children provides a necessary outlet of relief from disturbing preoccupations and beliefs.

A clinician should focus on issues pertaining to a child's experiences with death such as the death of relatives, pets, and friends. Fears of death from illness or accident, and self-inflicted death should be addressed. Children should be asked about dreams and preoccupations with death. A clinician should ask about issues pertaining to a child's own death. Questions should be asked such as "When do you think you will die? How will you die? What will happen when you die? Do you ever wish you will die? Do you think death is pleasant or unpleasant? Can someone return to life after they die? It must be realized that a child's preoccupations with death may be the first indications of thoughts of his or her own death by self-inflicted methods.

The next illustrations show that children can distinctly speak about death and that they have specific ideas about it. Since death preoccupations may be one of the first clues to suicidal behavior, a clinician should monitor the intensity of these preoccupations throughout the evaluation and treatment of child psychiatric patients. These examples are taken from statements of my research subjects who were not psychiatric patients.

Child IX: Tara was a 4-year-old whose older sibling, John, was hospitalized on a child psychiatric inpatient unit because he tried to hang himself. She was a gentle, sensitive, and intelligent girl who worried excessively about her family. She had no suicidal tendencies or psychopathology. She was preoccupied with death and described these concerns very vividly: "I have a dog named Charlie. He is a little dog. He is a poodle. He's 2. I don't have a cat. I had fish but they died. I thought about dying. When I sleep, I dream about it. John and me are dying. I dream that someone kills us. It scares me. I have a lot of dreams. I dream about death, that my mommy and daddy both die. My grandmother hit her elbow and went to the hospital. My mommy brought her cookies. People may come back to life after they die. Animals surely come back to life. Maybe people go to a better place after they die. I think that when you die, you first go to a hospital before you die. No one died in my family, yet. John is going to die, and me. So is my mommy. John and me are going to hold my dog when I die. John got sick. I just took out my tonsils. The doctor cut out my tonsils. He gave me a shot. It hurt. They put a bandage on where they gave me the shot. I don't want to kill myself. People die when they are sick."

Child X: Jacob was a 9-year-old boy who said: "I think about myself dying. I would not want to die because I don't know what it feels like. It is different than being here and you would not hear people. I worry about people in my family dying. I worry about what would happen to Mom. I worry that she might get killed by a car. I went to my grandfather's funeral. It was sad. I cried all night. He was dead. I saw the body. It looked like he was relaxed. He was dressed up. They put both hands over his chest, like this. I have dreams that I was killed. I was stepped on by King Kong. He was chasing me, stalking me and throwing things. I fell and landed in the garbage. I was bleeding and my mother came and put me in bed. Then I woke up."

Child XI: Jennifer, a 10-year-old girl, said: "When I see a movie about a ghost or someone coming out of the grave I get scared. My father said I could sleep with him. I was so scared I could not forget about it. I slept in the same room as my dad. I had a scary dream when I was at my mother's house. I often think about dying. Once my sister hit me in the head. I think about dying. I think I may lose my brain if I die. I ask my mother to do something to help me feel better. I worry that other people in my family may die. This happens especially if there's a storm, and me and my sister worry that my father may have a car accident."

Another issue in the assessment of suicidal risk of children is to evaluate the intensity, the frequency, and the type of predominant affects displayed by the children. Suicidal children often report feeling sad, hopeless, and worthless (Pfeffer *et al.*, 1979). However, it must be remembered that not all suicidal children appear depressed and that not all depressed children are suicidal. Nevertheless, criteria important to evaluate the degree of depression should be specifically addressed.

In children, factors that are associated with depression are similar to those factors noted in adults. These factors are elicited easily by asking children if they have difficulty sleeping, eating, concentrating in school, and participating in activities with friends. Children can acknowledge feeling sad, blue, and low, and enjoying things less. They can talk about feeling tired and worried about having intense guilt feelings. While it is still not clear whether parental reports about the child's depression will concur with the child's self-report of depression, it is wise to try to obtain the parents' report of observations of the child in addition to the child's statements. It is the role of the clinician to integrate all observational data and to make a preliminary diagnosis if there is uncertainty about the data. Such a task may be confusing, especially if the parents' and child's reports do not concur.

Discrepancy in parent–child reports is not an unusual happening. Kazdin, French, Unis, and Esveldt-Dawson (1983a) evaluated the correspondence of child and parental reports of children's depression in 104 children, ages 5 to 13 years, hospitalized on a psychiatric intensive care service. The parents, 101 mothers and 47 fathers, independently completed a variety of measures of the severity and duration of the children's depression. The child, the mother, and the father were consistent within their own ratings of the child's depression using different measures. However, the measures were not consistently correlated across children, mothers, and fathers. The mother–child and the father–child correlations tended to be low to moderate and not statistically significant. In contrast, the correlations between the mothers and fathers tended to be consistently significant and in the moderate range.

The investigators proposed several interpretations of why parent–child ratings did not concur. Perhaps children underestimate their symptomatology and severity of depression. The correspondence may vary as a function of the type of child psychopathology, of age, and of cognitive development; and as a function of parent psychopathology, which may influence the ability to report on the features of the child's difficulties. Therefore, during the assessment of childhood suicidal risk, it becomes the task of the clinician to evaluate all reports about a child's symptoms and then to draw conclusions that are relevant for each individual patient.

A final factor to be assessed when evaluating a child's risk for suicidal tendencies is the family's and the child's general environmental circumstances. Both the children and parents should be carefully interviewed about life experiences and the meanings of such events to the child. Always ask questions about academic problems at school, the child's expectations of parental punishment for doing poorly at school, expectations of ridicule from peers, changes in school, moves to a new home, changes in household composition, deaths, births, illness, and separations from parents. For example, Kalter and Plunkett (1984) indicated that children who experience parental divorce often perceive this as highly negative and the fault of the child. Such guilt feelings may be intense, to the extent that many suicidal children believe that they are the direct cause of the family discord. Family turmoil generated by separation, divorce, abuse, and violence has been documented as a factor experienced by suicidal children (Mattsson *et al.*, 1969; Paulson, Stone, & Sposto, 1978).

Depression and suicidal behavior among parents are specific risk factors for childhood suicidal behavior (Mattsson *et al.*, 1969; Paulson *et al.*, 1978; Pfeffer *et al.*, 1979, 1980, 1982, 1984). It is essential to inquire about the presence of these phenomena in family members. Frequently, such information may be difficult to obtain because of the guardedness of parents in discussing such information about themselves. One mother of a suicidal child waited 6 months before she talked about her elaborate fantasies about committing suicide. In another family of a suicidal youngster, the entire family kept secret the fact that the mother had attempted suicide on numerous occasions. Bowlby (1973b) pointed out that many children have trouble separating from their parents or refuse to go to school because the children are aware of parents' direct statements that a parent, usually the mother, will kill herself.

For all evaluations of suicidal risk of children, family sessions should be arranged. These should be scheduled so that the parents are seen as a couple and also so that the child can join them. The family alliances, the affective tone of the communication, the manifest content of the discussion, and hidden interactions and communications must be evaluated. Confusing statements, provocative communication, withdrawal, attacks, guilt feelings, and unpredictability are features observed in families of suicidal children. Many parents of suicidal children are very needy, immature, unaware of the developmental needs of their children, and are primitively identified with their distressed youngsters. One mother of a suicidal child kept her daughter home from school for half a semester so that the child could care for the mother's recurrent asthma condition. Often, the suicidal youngster is not able to differentiate from the enmeshed family. Such children seem perplexed, agitated, impulsive, and hopeless. A clinician must be able to evaluate the potential for resolution or therapeutic change that can be brought about and implemented by the family. If such change is not possible or very minimal, the risk of acute suicidal behavior might be great. However, if relief and ability to change are forthcoming, the suicidal risk of the child is less.

In summary, a format and a variety of questions that should be asked during the evaluation of suicidal risk in children have been outlined. The questions should be addressed to both the child and the parents. The questions should address the following key areas: suicidal fantasies or actions, concepts of what would happen, circumstances at the time of the child's suicidal behavior, previous experiences with suicidal behavior, motivations for suicidal behavior, experiences and concepts of death, depression and other affects, and the family and environmental situation. Table 11-2 lists a variety of sample questions that focus on these key issues. These questions can be used to guide the clinical interview process and are helpful in carrying out a comprehensive assessment of a child's suicidal tendencies.

CHILD SUICIDE POTENTIAL SCALES

Pfeffer and associates (1979, 1980, 1982, 1984) have devised a battery of scales that have been useful in studying suicidal behavior in children. These scales have been used as research tools for identifying factors associated with suicidal behavior in children. They are used during semistructured interviews with the child and the family. The child and parents are interviewed separately, and information gathered is used to complete the research scales. Some aspects of the reliability and validity properties of these scales have been reported (Pfeffer *et al.*, 1979, 1980, 1982, 1984), and continued investigation of their properties is in progress. These research instruments can be used for children who are 6 to 12 years old.

The Child Suicide Potential Scales consist of nine parts. Each part includes a variety of questions which elicit information relevant to the child's emotions, behaviors, family history, ego functioning, and concepts of death. Brief descriptions of the individual scales are given in Table 11-3.

These scales are provided in their entirety in the Appendix of this book. Questions that elicit the information about the variables contained in these scales can be asked at any time during the interview processes. However, the Concept of Death Scale, the Assessment of Current Ego Functions, and the Ego Defenses information is completed only after observation of the child. Information to complete all the other scales can be obtained from the child, the parents, and other relevant informants.

At present, the formal scoring properties of these scales are being determined. However, they also may be used clinically as a guide to the types of factors of suicidal risk to be evaluated. Thus, these scales

TABLE 11-2

Questions to ask in the evaluation of suicidal risk in children

---

1. *Suicidal fantasies or actions*:
    Have you ever thought of hurting yourself?
    Have you ever threatened or attempted to hurt yourself?
    Have you ever wished or tried to kill yourself?
    Have you ever wanted to or threatened to commit suicide?

2. *Concepts of what would happen*:
    What did you think would happen if you tried to hurt or kill yourself?
    What did you want to have happen?
    Did you think you would die?
    Did you think you would have severe injuries?

3. *Circumstances at the time of the child's suicidal behavior*:
    What was happening at the time you thought about killing yourself or tried to kill
        yourself?
    What was happening before you thought about killing yourself?
    Was anyone else with you or near you when you thought about suicide or tried
        to kill yourself?

4. *Previous experiences with suicidal behavior*:
    Have you ever thought about killing yourself or tried to kill yourself before?
    Do you know of anyone who either thought about, attempted, or committed sui-
        cide?
    How did this person carry out his suicidal ideas or action?
    When did this occur?
    Why do you think that this person wanted to kill himself?
    What was happening at the time this person thought about suicide or tried to kill
        himself?

5. *Motivations for suicidal behaviors*:
    Why do you want to kill yourself?
    Why did you try to kill yourself?
    Did you want to frighten someone?
    Did you want to get even with someone?
    Did you wish someone would rescue you before you tried to hurt yourself?
    Did you feel rejected by someone?
    Were you feeling hopeless?
    Did you hear voices telling you to kill yourself?
    Did you have very frightening thoughts?
    What else was a reason for your wish to kill yourself?

6. *Experiences and concepts of death*:
    What happens when people die?
    Can they come back again?
    Do they go to a better place?
    Do they go to a pleasant place?
    Do you often think about people dying?
    Do you often think about your own death?

(continued)

TABLE 11-2
(*Continued*)

Do you often dream about people or yourself dying?
Do you know anyone who has died?
What was the cause of this person's death?
When did this person die?
When do you think you will die?
What will happen when you die?

7. *Depression and other affects*:
   Do you ever feel sad, upset, angry, bad?
   Do you ever feel that no one cares about you?
   Do you ever feel that you are not a worthwhile person?
   Do you cry a lot?
   Do you get angry often?
   Do you often fight with other people?
   Do you have difficulty sleeping, eating, concentrating on school work?
   Do you have trouble getting along with friends?
   Do you prefer to stay by yourself?
   Do you often feel tired?
   Do you blame yourself for things that happen?
   Do you often feel guilty?

8. *Family and environmental situations*:
   Do you have difficulty in school?
   Do you worry about doing well in school?
   Do you worry that your parents will punish you for doing poorly in school?
   Do you get teased by other children?
   Have you started a new school?
   Did you move to a new home?
   Did anyone leave home?
   Did anyone die?
   Was anyone sick in your family?
   Have you been separated from your parents?
   Are your parents separated or divorced?
   Do you think that your parents treat you harshly?
   Do your parents fight a lot?
   Does anyone get hurt?
   Is anyone in your family sad, depressed, very upset? Who?
   Did anyone in your family talk about suicide or try to kill himself?

---

can be considered to be a basis upon which to focus the semistructured interview procedure. As a result, they may be helpful in decreasing a clinician's worries about approaching the interview process for a potentially suicidal child. These scales may help a clinician feel a sense of mastery in carrying out an appropriate comprehensive assessment of suicidal risk in children.

THE CLINICIAN'S RESPONSES TO SUICIDAL CHILDREN

Juxtaposition of the following two statements emphasizes the profound disparity between the clinician and the suicidal child. Koocher (1974) recalled his research observations that the "children seemed very interested in making their ideas about death known, and were quite willing to elaborate on them in great detail" (p. 406). The contrasting side of work with suicidal children was dramatically stated by Lowental (1976), a child psychoanalyst: "a child's vehement expression 'if I die they'll start loving me' makes me shudder, and I feel safe only after this phase has subsided" (p. 838). This disparity may greatly influence the clinician's ability to evaluate children for suicidal risk.

The child who clearly demonstrates suicidal propensities may be easier to interview than the child with no apparent suicidal tendencies.

TABLE 11-3
Description of the child suicide potential scales

---

1. *Spectrum of Suicidal Behavior*
   Classifies suicidal behavior along a 5-point spectrum of severity ranging from non-suicidal to serious attempts.
2. *Spectrum of Assaultive Behavior*
   Classifies assaultive behavior along a 6-point spectrum of severity ranging from non-assaultive to homicidal.
3. *Precipitating Events*
   Documents environmental stress during 6 months preceding the child's evaluation. Examples: school problems, household changes, quality of friendships, losses.
4. *General Psychopathology (Recent)*
   Documents emotional states and symptomatic behavior during 6 months preceding the child's evaluation. Examples: anxiety, sadness, hopelessness, temper tantrums, defiance, running away, fire setting.
5. *General Psychopathology (Past)*
   Similar to factors on General Psychopathology (Recent) except this documents the period before 6 months preceding the child's evaluation.
6. *Family Background*
   Documents family events and parental psychopathology. Examples: separations, death, severe discipline, parental depression, alcohol and drug abuse.
7. *Concept of Death Scale*
   Documents the child's preoccupations and experience with death and his or her view of death as pleasant, unpleasant, temporary, final.
8. *Assessment of Current Ego Function*
   Documents qualities of ego functioning. Examples: intelligence, affect regulation, impulse control, reality testing.
9. *Ego Defenses*
   Documents utilization of ego defenses. Examples: denial, reaction formation, repression.

This is due not so much to the accessibility or responsivity of the child but rather to the clinician's anxiety in introducing suicide into the discussion. There has been relatively little discussion in the literature of clinicians' responses to suicidal children although a few comprehensive reports highlight such conscious and unconscious reactions of therapists working with adult suicidal individuals. Tabachnick (1961) noted that a suicidal individual's desperation often goes unheeded by the helping profession. He pointed out that clinicians who work with suicidal individuals are vulnerable to countertransference crises which have to do with conflicts that involve the clinician's own hostile or sadistic responses. A clinician may resent the demandingness of suicidal adults and the circumstance of having no choice in the treatment of the patient. Unconscious hostile impulses of the physician are presented with temptations for expression because the provocations of a suicidal individual stress the clinician. As a result, the clinician may wish to reject the patient.

Maltsberger and Buie (1974) noted that when the countertransference becomes fully conscious, it can stimulate the therapist to redirect attention onto details of the patient's behavior and its meaning. However, when the clinician's responses remain unconscious, these unconscious responses may generate well-rationalized but destructive acting out by the therapist that may lead to abandonment of the patient, with the resultant possibility of precipitating the patient's suicidal behavior.

There are no reports discussing the conscious and unconscious reactions of clinicians working with suicidal children. An often voiced idea is amazement that children want to kill themselves. Therapists working with suicidal children often deny or minimize recognizing the severity of children's suicidal behavior because clinician's feel very anxious in work with such patients. Many clinicians resist talk about suicide because of fears that the interview may induce the child to act out ideas about hurting himself or herself. Some clinicians worry that asking the child about suicide will frighten the child and, as a result, make it difficult to establish a therapeutic alliance. This rationalization may be more related to a clinician's anxiety about how to handle the responses of the child who may express suicidal tendencies.

A clinician may worry about his or her ability to intervene upon realizing that the patient has suicidal impulses. Clinicians fear that questioning a child about suicidal behavior may open a Pandora's box of out-of-control reactions and urges. These worries stem from the clinician's own conscious and unconscious vulnerabilities to rejection, loss, sadness, and anger, fears of death, and helplessness. Other stresses that clinicians often feel are conflicts about omnipotence versus incompetence and initiating behavior versus guilt about activity. The more a clinician is in touch with, acknowledges, and understands these reactions, the better able the clinician will be in picking up clues to understanding the motives and dynamics of the suicidal child.

It is very rare that a child will act out suicidal behavior after a discussion with the therapist. However, a clinician's anxiety that a child may act out ideas discussed in the clinical interview may be a "signal" to make the clinician aware of the youngster's deficits in impulse control, frustration tolerance, concept of identity, and self-esteem, and poor capacity to differentiate reality. The clinician may be alerted by this "signal anxiety" to other vulnerabilities of the child such as diffusion of ego boundaries, narcissistic vulnerabilities, omnipotent fantasies, or withdrawal. These features may indicate that the child is not fully in touch with his or her relationships with others and cannot be depended upon to provide an accurate account of the state of distress. Thus, such children may be too unpredictable to maintain safety from their own self-destructive tendencies. Furthermore, a child who has no suicidal tendencies may be able to respond to questions about suicidal wishes in a definitive, logical manner, and with an appropriate affect. A clinician will be able to sense a feeling of relaxation engendered by the quality of the child's reciprocal interaction, appropriate affect, and ability to form a commitment to work with the therapist.

Finally, the clinician's anxiety about his or her ability to respond rapidly if the child is discovered to be suicidal may be a consciously derived feeling that is based on the worry about being able to implement the appropriate intervention. The clinician must be able to respond to the immediate needs of the child and have the capacity to maximize the safety of the child. Knowing that a variety of backup services such as a psychiatric hospital unit are available may diffuse a clinician's anxiety.

Another reality-based anxiety of clinicians arises from inexperience in talking with children about suicidal behavior. How to word questions or whether to explicitly use the word "suicide" are doubts expressed by clinicians. However, it is all right to use the word "suicide." Most children have an understanding of this term. Furthermore, a variety of questions should be asked, such as the ones listed in Table 11-2. In addition, the clinical skills of interviewing children about suicidal tendencies necessitate a focus on the age, the developmental level, and experiences of the child. Therefore, it is necessary to invoke a flexible interview style that approaches these issues directly but in a variety of ways. For example, to facilitate a natural flow of conversation, it is necessary to repeat and redirect questions at various points in the interview. An atmosphere of trust and respect must be created between the patient and therapist. This will foster a sense that the therapist is a reasonable person who cares about the child and believes that the child is a worthwhile person.

SUMMARY

The format for assessing suicidal risk in children should have both structured and unstructured elements. Specific questions should be asked but ample time should be allotted for the child to speak freely without the intrusions of specific questions. Several basic principles should be utilized during the assessment of suicidal risk. These principles include taking a child's suicidal impulses seriously, including the parents in the diagnostic process, and utilizing a primarily verbal format of assessment.

A variety of questions should be asked that focus on such issues as the child's suicidal fantasies and actions, affects, concepts of death, and family circumstance. Furthermore, research investigations have utilized special scales to measure factors associated with suicidal behavior in children. Finally, the clinician's conscious and unconscious reactions will greatly affect the assessment of suicidal risk in children.

CHAPTER TWELVE

OBSERVATIONS OF PLAY OF
SUICIDAL CHILDREN

He pictured himself lying sick unto death and his aunt bending over him beseeching one little forgiving word, but he would turn his face to the wall, and die with that word unsaid. Ah, how would she feel then? And he pictured himself brought home from the river, dead, with his curls all wet, and his sore heart at rest. How would she throw herself upon him, and how her tears would fall like rain, and her lips pray God to give her back her boy and she would never, never abuse him anymore! But he would lie there cold and white and make no sign—a poor little sufferer, whose griefs were at an end. —Mark Twain, *The Adventures of Tom Sawyer*

The previous chapter has presented a predominantly verbal format for evaluating suicidal risk in children. However, this format, alone, may not be as useful for young children or for children with language impairments. This chapter elaborates upon this premise and expands the dimensions of diagnosis of suicidal behavior in children in a discussion of features of play that may be useful warning clues to suicidal risk in children. The discussion includes theories of play in normal children and relates these ideas to the value of play analysis in the diagnosis of suicidal impulses in children. The hypotheses put forth in this chapter are based on psychoanalytic theory and my observations of suicidal and nonsuicidal children (Pfeffer, 1979a).

THEORY OF CHILDREN'S PLAY

The role of play in human development cannot be underestimated. "On the basis of play is built the whole of man's experiential existence" (Winnicott, 1971, p. 64). With these words, Winnicott defined play as a bridge between one's subjective and objective experiences. Based on these premises, it can be hypothesized that play of suicidal children will portray features of the children's emotions, actions, and experiences that relate to risk for suicidal behavior. Therefore, play may provide the first warning signs of suicidal behavior even before the child is able to acknowledge consciously having such tendencies.

The following example shows that play may provide the first warning signs of suicidal behavior.

Child I: Mark, age 8 years, repeatedly and intensively demonstrated jumping off tables and breaking objects. Several months after this play was observed, he said to his mother that he wanted to kill himself because he was angry at her, especially whenever she punished him. His play served to discharge his anger at his mother. It helped him overcome his vulnerability and helplessness, and was apparent before his suicidal ideas were stated.

S. Freud's ideas (1908) lend support to the hypotheses that play, which expresses the child's feelings, conflicts, and fantasy, is very important in the evaluation of a child. He said of play that

> the child's best loved and most intense occupation is with his play or games. Might we not say that every child at play behaves like a creative writer, in that he creates a world of his own, or rather, rearranges things of his world in a new way which pleases him? It would be wrong to think he does not take that world seriously; on the contrary, he takes his play very seriously and he expends large amounts of emotion on it. The opposite of play is not what is serious but what is real. In spite of all the emotion with which he perfects his world of play, the child distinguishes it quite well from reality; and he likes to link his imagined objects and situations to the tangible and visible things of the real world. (pp. 143–144)

Freud's ideas support the hypothesis that by observing a child's play, the diagnosis of suicidal risk may be facilitated and refined. Play has many functions that aid the child's interpretation of experiences through fantasies and emotions. As has been discussed in previous chapters, suicidal children experience stressful and often overwhelming environmental situations. In addition, suicidal children harbor intensely painful affects and fantasies. In play, a child may express aspects of stress, intense feelings, and fantasies that may provide early clues to suicidal risk.

Klein (1955) also recognized the diagnostic value of play by observing children's expression of fantasies and anxiety, and by inferring the unconscious meanings of play. She observed that one of the factors that make play so essential to children is that a great deal of relief from anxieties and guilt is experienced in play. For example, feelings of guilt may follow after a child has broken a play figure. The symbolic representation of the figure may have deep meaning to the child. The guilt may refer not only to the actual damage but also to what the toy stood for in the child's unconscious, such as a brother, a sister, or a parent. Therefore, it may be hypothesized that the symbolic aspects of play provide clues to suicidal risk in children.

The following example of a suicidal child illustrates the diagnostic value of play interviews. It depicts the child's traumatic experiences, his devices of coping with overwhelming feelings, and the fantasies he constructed.

Child II: Jordan, 7 years old, was admitted to a child psychiatry inpatient unit after attempting to jump from the fourth-floor window of his home. Fortunately, the attempt was aborted by his mother, who restrained him as he raced toward the window. Preceding this attempt, his mother refused to purchase a doll for him similar to one his older sister had received as a gift. Earlier that day, he had to be restrained by his mother when he tried to attack his sister with a knife as he shouted "I'll kill you."

During the year preceding his hospitalization, Jordan made two other attempts to jump out a window, both of which were averted by his mother. His mother, however, did not bring him for help until this last attempt. This kind of escalation and repetition of destructive behavior is a typical pattern in suicidal children. This kind of delay by the parent in seeking help is also quite typical.

Jordan was an unplanned child. His mother, severely depressed during the pregnancy, attempted an abortion by injecting quinine. Jordan's early development progressed normally. However, his schoolteacher found him to be stubborn, argumentative, and preoccupied with looking under skirts of girls in his class. Jordan's father, an alcoholic who had beaten his wife and children, disappeared after divorcing Jordan's mother, who subsequently became involved with another abusive man. When this relationship ended, Jordan's mother was admitted to a psychiatric hospital because she experienced auditory hallucinations and suicidal ideation. She remained in the hospital for an entire year. During this time, 5-year-old Jordan, confused about his mother's absence, was cared for by several adults, including his maternal grandmother. Upon discharge from the hospital, the mother established a relationship with a gentle man who was accepted by the children. Unfortunately, shortly before Jordan was hospitalized, this man left the family.

Jordan's self-destructive and aggressive behavior resulted from an identification with abusive and rejecting parental figures, the effects of constant threats of loss and abandonment, and the lack of consistent environmental structure. Sessions with his therapist revealed play scenes of ambivalence toward his mother, restitution of lost objects, and uncontrolled sexual and aggressive impulses. For example, in one of the main play scenes, he repeatedly threw dolls and furniture out of a doll house or held dolls precariously on the roof of the house before letting them tumble off. Over and over again, he placed dolls, which he identified as himself, in dangerous situations so that his therapist would come to the rescue. He was pleased when his therapist enacted this with him. In addition, he wanted the mother doll to catch the dolls that fell off a ledge. Similarly, he hid objects and joined the therapist in the search to find them. The pace of his play became exceedingly animated whenever he became noticeably anxious and angry. He growled harshly to the dolls, "You are stupid," as he pushed them off the roof of the house. He also directed his aggression at his therapist as well as at himself. On one occasion he hit and spit at his therapist, saying "I'll punch you in the mouth." On another occasion he hurt himself by swinging a lamp. Often he climbed on furniture and threatened to jump off. When firm limits were imposed, however, his dangerous behavior diminished. His intense rage toward his mother was demonstrated in a second main theme of play. A doll, depicting the mother, hit another doll depicting himself, until "he was dead." His doll recovered and strangled the mother doll.

In a third frequent theme, Jordan revealed his observations of parental intercourse, which he depicted vividly using a male and female doll. Jordan undressed the dolls and enacted the rhythm of intercourse. A baby doll, also undressed, alternated between hiding his eyes and excitedly looking.

The abuse, environmental disorganization, overstimulation, and many family losses overwhelmed Jordan with anxiety, rage, and hopelessness until he was no longer able to control his impulses. His complex and explicit play themes clearly revealed the dynamic issues underlying his desperate behavior. In play, he reversed the role of being a passive recipient of abuse and rejection to being the initiator of aggression. Scenes of rescue were repeated to master anxiety over loss of love, well-being, and security. His observations of his mother's sexual experiences were explicitly enacted in his attempt to assimilate the effects of these traumatic events. Jordan became the object of his own intense confusion, insecurity, and aggression as he directed aggression against himself.

Symptoms, such as suicidal behavior, may be directly observed in the action of a child's play. In fact, Bornstein proposed that

> every element of play has a meaning which is overdetermined. Every repetitive play contains unconscious conflict related to the child's symptoms. Repetitive play frequently contains symbolic expression either of masturbatory activity or of the fantasy connected with it. The content of repetitive play often reflects a particular traumatic experience. Repetitive play which contains more impulsive characteristics seems to indicate that a past reality experience (not just a fantasy) prior to the development of verbalization is being expressed. (cited in Feigelson, 1974, p. 22)

These notions about play suggest that some types of repetitive play associated with traumatic experiences may be clues to a child's suicidal behavior.

Other functions of play are relevant to suicidal children. S. Freud (1926) noted that children's play seems to diminish unpleasure even though the play may be derived from an unpleasant situation. Another function of play is to aid ego maturation. A. Freud (1963) outlined changes in play that coincided with a child's development. She noted that play begins in infancy and that it initially involves play with the infant's body and the mother. Eventually, as the child matures, more complex fantasies are expressed in the play. Play, therefore, is the symbolic representation of the child's experiences and fantasies, and is one of the most important activities of children.

Sarnoff (1976), too, realized that the ability to displace drive expression from real objects to representational objects of fantasy facilitates maturation and sublimations necessary for healthy character development. He believed that play and fantasy function as specific organizing structures, especially during the child's early development, to integrate the expression of emotions, perception of reality, and personal relationships with others.

Many other functions of play can be defined that are relevant to the emotional status of suicidal children. Waelder (1933) noted that play depicts the child's experiences, although the incident experienced in reality may be given a different arrangement in play. He noted that play results in the gratification of wishes and, in fact, often arises from real experiences which were devoid of pleasure. The memories of a real situation may be expressed in play for a time and then gradually abandoned. Furthermore, play provides functional pleasure that is experienced in the pure performance of the play without regard to the success of the activity. Play also represents the child's attempt to assimilate an experience by gaining active mastery of the situation. This is accomplished because play gradually assimilates those experiences too threatening to be assimilated instantly. In addition, play allows the child to gratify in fantasy wishes about real people that are prohibited in reality.

Peller (1954) classified play themes associated with specific phases of normal development. She pointed out that each developmental phase has focal anxieties and frustrations. For example, early in the child's life, there are frustrations and anxieties concerning the body. Later, frustrations focus on the child's relationship with the mother and certain frustrations related to guilt. Specific types of play are invoked to deny or lessen these frustrations or anxieties. For example, play that is based on the relationships to one's own body contains topics about the parts and functions of the body. Play involving the relationship to the mother focuses on the mother, who is a source of comfort as well as occasionally a source of fear. Furthermore, as the child matures, frustrations are depicted not only with the mother but with other peo-

ple. Eventually, during the phase of preadolescence, play involves individual and team sports with organized rules and formal structure.

In summary, the concepts discussed in this section about play of
normal children are relevant to understanding the role of play observation for the diagnosis of suicidal behavior. The next section describes
specific characteristics of play observed among suicidal children.

PLAY CHARACTERISTICS OF SUICIDAL CHILDREN

Four characteristics of play are commonly seen in children who have
expressed suicidal ideas, suicidal threats, and suicidal attempts. These
four characteristics of play also may be found in the play of nonsuicidal
children. For example, S. Freud (1917a), in his paper ''A Childhood
Recollection from *Dichtung und Wahrheit*,'' described a little boy's use
of toys to signify an unconscious wish to get rid of his sibling. The child
threw all the family dishes out onto the street and they were smashed
to pieces. Freud's understanding of this recollection was that ''the
throwing of crockery out of the window was a symbolic action, or, to
put it more correctly, a magical action, by which the child gave violent
expression to his wish to get rid of the disturbing intruder. . . . The
new baby must be got rid of'' (p. 152). This type of play of throwing
toys out of windows is commonly seen in suicidal children, too. However, the difference between suicidal and nonsuicidal children's play
is that these themes are repetitive in the play of suicidal children. In
addition, the intensity of affects is markedly greater in the play of
suicidal children.

Suicidal children are more out of touch with external reality than
normal children while engaging in play. It is more difficult to interrupt
or alter the play of suicidal children. This was illustrated by an anec-
dotal statement of one therapist who told of inability to interact with
a suicidal 10-year-old child during his play. The child intensely depicted, with the use of dolls, scenes of a child hitting his mother and
then running out into the street where he was hit by a car. The child
repetitively displayed this play. The therapist felt that no interpretative
statement made to the child altered the play. The child was unresponsive to any discussion about the meanings of this play. The play assessment of this suicidal child provided insights about understanding the
child's disturbed ego functioning. He had a symbiotic relationship with
his mother and felt engulfed by and totally identified with her. His
struggle to free himself from his mother was depicted in his play of killing her. However, his intense guilt about this was evident in the suicidal themes of his play.

Among the four characteristics of play of suicidal children, one reflects developmental issues regarding the process of separation and individuation from the parent. These play themes of suicidal children are remarkably similar to the content of play of younger children who are age-appropriately coping with these developmental issues. One example of play in a normal child depicting separation and individuation was described by Oremland (1973) as the "lap game." In this game, the mother holds the baby's hands, helps the baby to stand in her lap, and then lets the baby collapse in her lap, with delight and laughter. Then the mother often completely envelopes the baby in a hug. This game is repeated again and again. Another example of separation–individuation play is the peek-a-boo game described by Kleeman (1967). In this game, the infant covers and uncovers his or her face in an attempt at alternating between shutting out and viewing the parents.

Themes of loss and retrieval, jumping, throwing, and flying in the play of suicidal children serve defensive purposes to contain intense anxiety, aggression, and sadness about conflicts related to separation and individuation. A commonly seen action in suicidal children's play, namely jumping from heights, may be understood as a manifestation of a regression or a return to the elaboration of play often occurring in younger children who are mastering separation, loss, and development of personal autonomy. The following example illustrates play activities of jumping and being rescued in an 8-year-old suicidal girl.

Child III: The child attempted to jump off the balcony of the auditorium at school and repeated her suicidal behavior in play. Variations of jumping were repeated as she had dolls jump off roofs of houses, fall out of windows, and roll down hills. In most of her play sequences, she ensured that each doll would be caught by an adult who was fortuitously present at the moment of the doll's fearsome actions. This play dramatically reproduced the girl's actual suicidal episode in which she walked alone to the auditorium, waited in a seat until the teacher walked in to see what she was doing, and at that moment ran to the balcony edge screaming "I want to die, no one loves me." The quick-moving teacher who was with her raced to the girl and caught her as she was about to jump. Parallels can be drawn between the child's play and suicidal action. Her wish to be rescued by a benevolent adult was striking. However, her hope that she would be taken care of was left to chance. This play reflected her deep despair, her lack of trust in having a dependable and consistent environment, and her intense ambivalence in struggling with the fortunes of life. Her history indicated that at the age of 2 years she had been abandoned by her mother. She was raised by her alcoholic father until several months before her suicide attempt. At that time, he left her in the care of his mother so that he could seek employment in a distant town. The girl had not heard from him. Her rage about this loss stimulated other intense feelings of ambivalence toward her inconsistent, unreliable father.

A second play clue to suicidal behavior in children is the repetition of dangerous and reckless behaviors usually evidenced by children who use their own bodies as play objects. Such play may be attempts to relieve intense stress by direct motor discharge. For example, children may repeatedly jump off and onto furniture so impulsively that they put themselves in jeopardy of being hurt. Other children may dart in and out of traffic on busy streets or ride bicycles in dangerous areas.

A third feature of children's play that can warn of a potential for suicidal behavior involves the use of play objects. A. Freud (1967) discussed the processes affecting the quality of the child's use of play objects. She noted that

> children who are frustrated, dissatisfied, jealous, etc., but unable for internal or external reasons to react aggressively to their parents, may turn this same aggression toward material things and become destructive of their toys, their clothing, the furniture, etc. In a temper or rage, individuals of all ages may choose as their point of attack either their own bodies, or other people, or any objects within their reach. Children in separation distress may cling to any of these possessions which they invest for the time being, with cathexis displaced from their human objects. (p. 11)

Suicidal children often repeatedly abuse or misuse playthings. Such children may aggressively break toys, throw play objects around even if this is not the intended use of the toys, or discard or abandon toys.

Child IV: This 10-year-old boy came into the psychiatric hospital unit with a massive quantity of toys. The child had repeatedly attempted to hurt himself with a knife, to run into traffic, to cut himself, and to choke himself, and had threatened to leap out the window at home. Repeatedly, he was beaten by his father in a most severe fashion. The father verbally attacked the child with sadistic comments. On other occasions the father whipped the child with a belt, hit him with a stick, or locked him in his room. The child brought his most prized toys to this hospital, but within hours after admission he displayed his inappropriate handling of the toys by throwing toy soldiers at the nurses and at other children. He stated that he wanted others to catch the soldiers. However, he threw the soldiers with such force that they almost hurt others. When angry, the child went to his room and pounded his toys against the floor or the door. He pulled the limbs off some of the toy soldiers. At other times he gave his toys away to other children and subsequently demanded that they be returned to him. Frequently his toys would be found at different locations throughout the hospital unit. Forgetting where he left the toys made him feel so despondent that he spoke about wishing he were dead.

This demonstrative misuse of play objects captures the specific quality of ego functioning often seen in suicidal children; that is, poorly differentiated ego boundaries between themselves and others. As the pace, pitch, and content of the play intensify, suicidal children may lose the ability to discriminate between themselves and play objects. These children become so enmeshed in their play that the play objects take on a quality of animation that goes beyond symbolic representation. It is as if the play object actually is the child and vice versa. Therefore, a child who may repetitively throw toys out a window, may at times attempt to throw himself or herself out a window, too. The child just described was intensively reenacting, in the use of his toys, the abusive handling he received from his father. The toys stood for the child and they were subject to as severe treatment as the child himself. His toys were dismembered, abandoned, given away, and finally totally annihilated; all this representing the actual life experience of the child.

Another aspect of ego boundary diffusion of suicidal children is manifest when play ceases and becomes a form of personal acting out. The child who throws himself or herself out of the window after first throwing many toys away illustrates this feature of boundary diffusion. Since suicidal children frequently become captured by their play and eventually lose distinctions between themselves and play objects, history from a reliable observer is often needed to evaluate the quality of what may initially start out as play. These children, when questioned about their play, may not be aware of their inability to differentiate themselves from the toy.

A fourth warning clue in play of childhood suicidal behavior is the life-endangering acting out of omnipotent fantasies. This form of play has similarities to ego boundary blurring that are manifested by the way in which toys are handled. In this form of play the child explains that he or she is a "superhero" such as Superman, Wonder Woman, Batman, etc. Although most children like to pretend to be superheroes and in fact dress up in the costumes of the characters, this quality of play is different for suicidal children. Suicidal children repetitively play superhero themes using intensely sadistic or dangerous themes. Such children may depict fight scenes, but the plot becomes so intense that someone may actually be hurt. At other times, the child may attempt to enact death-defying maneuvers which may actually be dangerous to the child.

Child V: One suicidal child ran around his neighborhood wearing a Superman outfit. He jumped off cars and garbage cans, and at one time jumped from one fire escape to another. He was hospitalized after he attempted to jump out the window at school. He wanted to die because he felt so helpless about his mother, who was dying of cancer. Such fantasies of identifying with superheroes provide the defense of omnipotence that denies underlying, profound feelings of vulnerability. Such play, marked by feverish, rapidly evolving action that culminates in an ultimate sense of supreme omnipotent power, is a suicidal child's last means of containing intense and intolerable emotions and ideas.

Child VI: Another boy repeatedly played with Superman dolls and Batman dolls. In his play one superhero always got injured, kidnapped, or was beaten. The other superhero, his loyal friend, came to the rescue of the jeopardized superhero. This play captured elements of the child's life situation. The child had an extremely ambivalent relationship with his mother. He was intensely fond of her but also provoked strong rage episodes from her. During these fits of anger, his mother was verbally abusive to the child and unfairly disciplined him. His play depicted his sense of omnipotence and his sense of vulnerability. His wish to be rescued from the abusive punishment of his mother was displayed in play themes of being rescued by a loyal, omnipotent friend. The torture of one superhero depicted the child's vulnerability to the severe punishment of his mother.

APPLICATION OF PLAY FOR
DIAGNOSIS OF SUICIDAL POTENTIAL

Many children deny suicidal wishes when asked directly in conversation, either because language abilities may not be fully developed or because of serious ego deficits which may hamper the verbal description of feelings and actions. Therefore, a time period for play observation should be included in every diagnostic assessment of suicidal risk.

In addition to direct observation of a child's play, it is recommended that clinicians take a history of specific details of the child's play. Such history should be obtained from parents, siblings, and teachers, who may be more objective in commenting on the intensity, the themes, and the emotional tone of the child's play. Of course, history gathered directly from the child may provide an understanding of the meaning and motivation of the play. However, the child may be less objective about the dangerousness of his or her play. Often suicidal children deny that their play has inherent risk. They frequently may say that they were "in control," "knew what they were doing," or were "just having fun." Such comments, in fact, reflect the prime functions of play; that is, to gain mastery or control, to decrease anxiety, and to provide a pleasurable object. Therefore, while such behaviors are actually within the domain of play, the features of ignoring danger, simulation of intense affect, and repetition of the themes may alert a clinician to the implications of this type of play for diagnosing suicidal potential.

Finally, play may be the first sign of suicidal risk, but the characteristics of play associated with suicidal tendencies may persist even after the acute suicidal symptomatology has been resolved. Disappearance or persistence of play characteristics of suicidal impulses before, during, and after clinical signs of overt suicidal behavior is another characteristic of play; that is, the working through of conflicts, the mastery of instinctual and traumatic events, and the modulation and expression of affect. Therefore, during the treatment of a suicidal child, clues of suicidal behavior in play may emerge or persist, but this may not mean that suicidal behavior will necessarily occur. It implies that vulnerability exists and is being expressed as a function of play. It is essential to monitor changes in play that are evident in the intensity, repetitiveness, and themes of play which may signal either an increase or decrease of risk. Suicidal action may occur when ego functioning fails to sufficiently bind suicidal impulses. Under these circumstances, play may cease and suicidal action may occur. Moreover, throughout the treatment or evaluation process, a clinician should also monitor the child's degree of depression, preoccupations with death, and family interactions as indicators of increased or decreased suicidal risk. To repeat and emphasize: The clinician should periodically ask the child direct questions about wishes, plans, or actions to hurt himself or herself.

SUMMARY

This chapter has discussed the theory and characteristics of play of normal and suicidal children. It has described four characteristics of play associated with suicidal risk: responses to separation and autonomy, reckless and dangerous play, misuse of toys, and acting out of omnipotent fantasies. These play characteristics may be evident before and persist after acute suicidal ideas and actions are expressed. Used in conjunction with assessment of other risk factors of childhood suicidal behavior, the evaluation of these play characteristics may facilitate recognition of suicidal tendencies and behavior, and monitoring of change in the degree of severity of suicidal risk.

INTERVENTION FOR SUICIDAL BEHAVIOR

CHAPTER THIRTEEN

PLANNING TREATMENT FOR SUICIDAL CHILDREN

There was no one to help and no one to care, and the best way out of this business was death. —Rudyard Kipling, "Baa, Baa, Black Sheep"

Methods of treatment for childhood suicidal behavior are the least understood and least studied aspects of this childhood phenomenon. Case reports of therapy have been the major sources of information on treatment of suicidal children. Although these reports provide hypotheses about techniques of therapy, there have been almost no systematic investigations comparing the effectiveness of different treatment modalities for suicidal children. This may, in part, be due to the lack of appropriate research instruments and methods for measuring treatment effects.

The following four chapters on treatment of suicidal children rely on case reports, my own extensive observations of suicidal and nonsuicidal children, and research findings when available. This chapter covers the beginning phases of treatment; the chapters that follow focus on the longer-term processes involved in the variety of modalities of treatment for suicidal children.

GOALS OF TREATMENT

Treatment of suicidal children has a number of general goals, the attainment of which requires the use of several treatment modalities. The general goals of treatment of suicidal children are as follows:

1. Protect the child from harm.
2. Decrease acute suicidal tendencies.
3. Decrease suicidal risk factors.
4. Enhance factors that protect against suicidal tendencies.
5. Decrease vulnerability to repeated suicidal behavior.

Work toward achieving these goals begins during the initial stages of treatment planning and is continually reevaluated during the process of treatment.

COORDINATION OF TREATMENT SETTINGS

After a child is recognized to be suicidal, the initial stage of treatment planning often involves the coordinated efforts of a number of professionals who must make rapid assessments of the child's condition and make quick decisions about acute medical and psychological interventions. The complex interrelationships of professionals and treatment settings that are involved in the treatment planning phase for suicidal children are depicted in Figure 13-1.

Initially, a child may be discovered to have expressed suicidal ideas or actions by a parent, a school professional, a pediatrician, a friend, or any other person in his or her environment. Such a child should be referred for appropriate evaluation and emergency treatment. If a child has caused physical injuries, treatment in a medical hospital unit may be needed. If there are no physical sequellae, the child should be referred for psychiatric evaluation. Regardless of whether the child is evaluated in an acute medical hospital unit or an outpatient psychiatric center, decisions must be made about the most appropriate longer term treatment. Such treatment is carried out in a psychiatric outpatient or psychiatric inpatient service. Some children who show repeated suicidal tendencies and are unable to have a sufficient degree of environ-

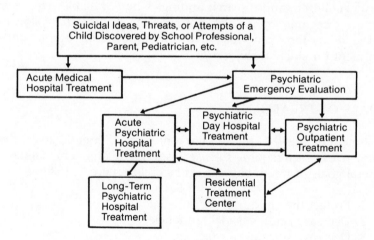

FIGURE 13-1
Treatment planning for suicidal children.

mental protection from harm may need repeated or prolonged psychiatric care.

It can be inferred from the schema presented in Figure 13-1 that a variety of professionals must work together during the process of treatment planning and long-term interventions for suicidal children. Doctors, nurses, and a variety of mental health professionals may be called upon to administer to the child's medical and psychiatric needs. Maximal degrees of communication and professional teamwork are required.

There are four aspects of treatment planning: (1) recognition of a suicidal child, (2) acute medical management, (3) involvement with therapists who have the necessary personal and professional characteristics for work with suicidal children, and (4) the decision process leading to psychiatric inpatient or outpatient treatment.

RECOGNIZING SUICIDAL CHILDREN

Pediatricians, family physicians, and teachers are among the professionals who may be most likely to discover the first signs of suicidal risk in children. Unfortunately, many of these professionals are not fully knowledgeable and skilled in recognizing this symptom and arranging for the beginning of intervention. For example, the following two studies have shown that pediatricians are not sufficiently aware of diagnostic indicators and the required forms of treatment for suicidal youngsters. Although systematic studies have not been done with school professionals, similar problems may exist for this group of professionals.

One study carried out by Hodgman and Roberts (1982) used a 1-page questionnaire which was sent to 55 practicing pediatricians in metropolitan Rochester and Syracuse, New York. Eighty-seven percent of the pediatricians answered the questionnaire, which revealed that pediatricians had limited experience with child and adolescent suicidal behavior. Many pediatricians asked their patients about suicide only if there was a previous history of this symptom while others commented that this question never came up in their practices.

The study by Cohen-Sandler and Berman (1980) indicated that there was more active involvement and awareness by pediatricians of suicidal children. Among 375 practicing pediatricians in Washington, D.C., who were contacted, 69 (27%) pediatricians responded to the questionnaire. Perhaps the differences in these two studies were due to the different percentages of pediatricians who responded to the questionnaires, discrepancies in local practice, differences in availability of psychiatric support services, and differences in the questionnaires themselves. The percentage of response to this questionnaire was relatively low; nevertheless, trends reported in this study provide insights that may be tested in other studies. Forty-five percent of the responding pediatricians reported knowing of suicide attempts among patients. Chemical ingestion as a suicide method was cited in 90% of children who made suicide attempts. This contrasted with reports in the psychiatric literature, where more active violent methods such as jumping from heights, running into traffic, stabbing, and hanging were reported as common suicidal methods among children.

Sixty-four percent of the respondents had at least one patient under 14 years old in treatment for depression with a mental health professional. However, there was a wide variation in the types of symptoms that pediatricians depended on to make a diagnosis of childhood depression. The least critical symptoms were somatic concerns and the most important indicators of depression were withdrawal and such family factors as parental divorce, a depressed parent, and physical or emotional abuse. Eighty-seven percent of the pediatricians considered the possibility of a child's self-destructive behavior after making a diagnosis of depression.

Pediatricians considered the most preferred mode of treatment for depression to be psychotherapy of the child and family. Medication was rarely used. However, if self-destructive behavior was evident, pediatricians were more likely to make referrals for inpatient treatment. Outpatient psychiatric treatment was the next most common treatment advised. Pharmacological treatment was used least. However, when medication was used, the drugs of choice were antidepressants (47%), anxiolytics (20%), neuroleptics (13%), antihistamine–sedatives (13%), and massive B vitamins (7%).

These two studies provide some insights into the varied attitudes and practices of pediatricians with suicidal children and adolescents. Depression and suicidal behavior seem to be underrecognized by pediatricians. Many suicidal children may not even be referred to mental health professionals or treatment centers. In view of these studies, it can be concluded that there is an urgent need to educate pediatricians and other professionals who work with children to be sensitive to the problem, to be able to recognize potentially suicidal children early, and to recommend psychiatric consultation for all children with suicidal ideas or actions.

One advance in helping professionals to screen potentially suicidal children more accurately was the development of a screening checklist for suicidal risk in children. Corder and Haizlip (1983) developed such a checklist. The Corder–Haizlip Child Suicide Checklist is shown in Table 13-1. The checklist has two parts: questions addressed to the parents and questions asked of the child. Unfortunately, this checklist

TABLE 13-1
The Corder–Haizlip Child Suicide Checklist

I. Questions addressed to parents:

1. Has your child seen a physician over a period of months for a series of physical complaints for which there was no recognizable physical basis?
2. Has your child been treated by a physician for a series of minor accidents or injuries?
3. Has any serious change occurred in your child's life during the past few months or year?
4. Has your child experienced a specific loss in the past months or year?
5. Has your child shown any significant difficulties or unexpected problems with school, sports, or other areas of achievement?
6. Has your child been very self-critical?
7. Has your child made any unusual statements about death or dying?
8. Do you as parents perceive your child as more adult-like, special, talented, sensitive, or intelligent than other children?
9. Do you as parents expect adult-type speech and behavior from your child?
10. Does your child have easy access to medication and firearms?
11. Has there been any noticeable change in your child's behavior or mood in the past few months?
12. Do you describe yourselves as being closer to each other than you perceive the average family?
13. Have there been any unusual changes in your family in the past few months?
14. Have members of your extended family been especially close and attentive to your child?
15. Have you been disappointed lately in your child's performance?
16. Have stresses of recent changes left you with less time to focus on your child?
17. Have there been friends or relatives who have attempted suicide?

II. Questions addressed to the child:

1. Have you had some sad and mad feelings that you have had trouble telling about or letting people know about?
2. Do you feel that things are going to get better or does it seem they will stay the same or get worse?
3. Do you ever think that things would be better if you were dead?
4. What do you think it would be like to be dead?
5. What do you think would happen with your mother and father if you were dead?
6. Have you thought about how you could make yourself die?

Note. Reprinted by permission from Billie F. Corder, EdD, and Thomas M. Haizlip, MD. A version of the checklist appeared in "Recognizing Suicidal Behavior in Children" by B. F. Corder and T. M. Haizlip (1983), *Resident and Staff Physician,* 29:18–23.

has not been standardized so that all responses can be scored, and there is no way to determine if specific scores indicate high risk for suicidal behavior. However, this checklist may be used to guide a screening assessment by professionals for suicidal risk of children. For example, if a child or a parent responds positively to questions involving loss, repeated injuries, somatic complaints, preoccupations with death, behavioral or mood changes, and depression, the child should be suspected to be at risk for severe depression and/or suicidal behavior. Such children should be referred for psychiatric assessment.

ACUTE MEDICAL MANAGEMENT

A number of suicidal children require immediate medical life-supporting measures. Such children may be directly referred to a pediatric or general medical hospital unit. Some guidelines for the acute medical treatment of suicidal children have been suggested in several reports (Lewis & Solnit, 1963; Editorial, 1981; College Report, 1982). There was high agreement among these reports in regard to basic principles of acute medical care. These principles are presented in Table 13-2.

These reports have all recommended that acute medical management of suicidal youngsters should include team efforts of pediatricians and child psychiatrists. Hospitalization has been consistently recommended to treat acute medical sequellae of suicidal actions and to begin the psychiatric diagnostic assessment that will lead to a long-range plan of care. In the next section, the nuances of planning psychiatric interventions are presented.

INITIAL PSYCHIATRIC INTERVENTIONS:
THERAPIST QUALITIES

The psychiatric evaluation and treatment of suicidal children is a complex process that is determined by the suicidal child's psychosocial status as well as the personal and professional characteristics of the

TABLE 13-2
Guidelines for acute medical treatment of suicidal children

1. Collaborative efforts should occur between pediatricians, child psychiatrists, nurses, and social workers.
2. Admission to a pediatric hospital unit is the safest treatment course to provide resuscitive and emergency care of a life-supporting nature.
3. Immediate prevention of repeated suicidal attempts is achieved by continuous observation of the child by nurses, aides, and selected relatives.
4. Psychiatric evaluations by means of frequent meetings with the child and family should commence immediately upon hospital admission.
5. Involvement of the parents and other family members is essential.
6. A definitive plan for sustained treatment should be made before the patient leaves the hospital.

therapist. It is the interrelationship between these factors that affects the intervention outcome. Many reports discussing therapy of suicidal individuals comment on specific therapist characteristics that create a successful treatment outcome. This section includes ideas about therapist qualities that are essential in work with suicidal children.

Glaser (1981) and Stone (1980) stated that the therapist must be available to the suicidal patient without delay and at all hours. The more a therapist demonstrates a high degree of availability, the less anxious the patient will feel. Stone (1980) said that therapists "should not undertake the treatment of suicidal patients on behalf of whom they would not feel like extending themselves quite far should the situation require it" (p. 69).

Schechter (1957) realized that one of the most important aspects of the treatment of suicidal children is to strengthen interpersonal relationships. He stated: "Not only is there a need to make a quick and firm relationship with the therapist, who must be most giving, but also, [it is necessary] as soon as possible, to give interpretations so that the child can understand his motivations" (p. 140). In addition, Ackerly (1967) believed that the therapeutic aim is to modify the child's perception of himself or herself in order to increase self-esteem. The principles suggested by Schechter (1957) and Ackerly (1967) are of major importance because, all too often, the suicidal child views the world as pessimistic and hopeless. Because of these pessimistic and hopeless feelings, the therapist must be able to be honest with the suicidal patient, be consistent in actions and statements, and be able to provide an atmosphere of trust so that the child is made aware that the therapist has the child's best interests in mind.

Lesse (1975) realized that the therapist must be "thoroughly acquainted with the range of treatment procedures that are available and must be trained in the appropriate application of the proper type of therapy or types of therapies for a given patient at a given time" (p. 310). The range of therapies required for suicidal children is discussed in subsequent chapters. Extending the principle put forth by Lesse (1975), Toolan (1980) stated that only highly experienced and adequately trained therapists should work with suicidal and depressed children. In agreement with Toolan's beliefs and because of the complex nature of suicidal behavior in children and the variety of potential medical and psychosocial interventions required, it can be advocated that only very experienced and highly trained child psychiatrists and child mental health professionals be involved with the initial diagnostic evaluation of suicidal children and the formulation of appropriate treatment plans, which may subsequently include the services of other therapists who have expertise in a particular aspect of the treatment.

Stone (1980) said:

> It is most important that the therapist not become engulfed in the suicidal patient's protestations about the hopelessness of the situation, lest the therapist come to agree with him. No matter how elegant the patient's logic, he must be helped to see the irrationality of it; he must be helped to see the many alternatives to which he has remained blind. The therapist who cannot extricate himself from the patient's despondent outlook, is morally obliged to excuse himself from the case and to provide a new therapist whose attitude towards the patient is one of genuine hopefulness. (p. 58)

This is even truer for children because it is very easy for a therapist to identify with the hopelessness of the child.

Toolan (1980) noted that the therapist working with suicidal children may become overly frightened by the child's suicidal propensities or may "believe that he can omnipotently handle any problem and thus not protect the youngster adequately. Many therapists find it difficult to work with both youngsters and their parents together" (p. 593). Because of dependency needs inherent in normal development of children, it is essential for a therapist to be able to work with the family and the suicidal child, especially in the initial phases of intervention. Finally, the therapist must be very verbal and actively stimulate discussion with patient and family because suicidal children are often quite reticent, hopeless, and helpless. Lesse (1975) emphasized this point: "The therapist must have a positive feeling with regard to the value of life. There should be no confusion between the act of saving the person's life and the long-term psychotherapeutic re-education of a severely depressed patient. The therapist must have the capacity to psychically transfuse the severely depressed patient during the initial phases of treatment" (p. 311). This principle must be even more emphasized in work with suicidal children, who require active intervention to bolster self-esteem, hope, and a sense of mastery.

CHOICES AND DECISIONS ABOUT INITIAL PSYCHIATRIC INTERVENTIONS

The previous section has focused on qualities of the therapist that can affect the treatment process of suicidal children. In contrast, this section encompasses facets of the child's psychosocial state that affect what decisions need to be made about planning psychiatric intervention.

Since suicidal behavior is a multidetermined, very complex symptom that arises from the interaction of intrapsychic, environmental, and biological factors, treatment will require multiple modalities that combine psychodynamic, cognitive, pharmacological, and family approaches. The clinician must carry out interventions aimed at specific goals. During the initial phases the most important goals are to protect the child from self-inflicted harm and to determine treatment modalities that would enhance the child's age-appropriate development. Eisenberg (1980) noted that one of the initial decisions the clinician must make is whether or not to hospitalize a suicidal youngster.

The following two examples illustrate the symptomatic factors that influence the decision for treatment on an outpatient or inpatient basis.

Child I: Sandra was an 11-year-old girl who left a note on her bedroom desk saying, "To die, to die . . . I want to die." One day Sandra's mother saw this message while she was cleaning Sandra's room. She was alarmed and fearful. That evening Sandra's parents told her that they wanted to "speak about something very important." Sandra's mother said: "Today, while I was cleaning your room, I saw a note on your desk saying that you want to die. When I saw it, I was very frightened and I immediately wanted to talk with you. I am very concerned about how you are feeling." Sandra became tearful upon hearing her mother talk this way. She looked up at her father, who was intently looking at her. Sandra continued to cry and told her parents that she wanted to die because she felt "all alone": "No one at school likes me. They all think I am a snob and am self-centered. The other kids talk about me, behind my back. They say things about me that are not nice." Sandra's parents told her that they would call her pediatrician because they were worried about her sadness. They told her, "We want to help you feel better and we need to know how to do this." Sandra agreed that she would like to feel better but did not think anything could be done about her problems.

The pediatrician referred Sandra's parents to a psychiatrist, who immediately arranged a meeting with Sandra and her parents. Sandra told her therapist that she wanted to die and had considered taking her mother's tranquilizers. She was upset about not having many friends but was even more frightened about her parents' arguments about money. Sandra thought about killing herself so that she would not be a burden on her parents. She believed that without her at home there would be no need for more money. Sandra appreciated her therapist's suggestion that "perhaps we could think of other ways to deal with these difficulties rather than by thinking of killing yourself." Sandra said that she was "not sure if that would be possible" but was willing to talk with the therapist again. She did not think that she would hurt herself now but said that she did "think about it a lot."

After meeting with Sandra, the therapist met with her parents, who were very worried but did not realize how upset Sandra felt. They agreed that they wanted to do whatever was necessary to help her. They were intelligent and very verbal, and recognized that they were having difficulties in their marriage. Sandra's mother was very lonely and angry that her husband traveled so much because of his work. Sandra's father felt that he was under pressure at work and that his wife did not understand. He felt relieved to be away from home so that he could avoid these arguments. He felt that his wife was too dependent on him and made too many demands when he was home. They both realized that their own marital difficulties precluded realizing how distressed Sandra had been. They were willing to work together on helping their daughter and welcomed the opportunity to understand the entire family's problems.

In the last part of the meeting, the therapist talked with Sandra and her parents together. He told them that there were so many things happening in their lives all at one time and that they needed to understand what the problems were. Her parents agreed to watch Sandra at home so that she could be safe. They told her that they wanted her to feel better and that they wanted to decrease the many family tensions. They agreed to see the therapist the next day. Sandra looked relieved as she left the office.

During this first therapeutic meeting, a clinical decision was made not to hospitalize Sandra because she was interested in working on understanding her problems. She responded to the therapist's statement that there was hope that she could feel better and that the upsetting problems could be diminished. This ray of hope, her agreement to see the therapist the next day, her positive feelings that her parents wanted her to feel well and wanted to help her, and their wish to work on changing their problematic situation were all signs that a positive therapeutic process was in operation. Sandra and her parents had sufficient impulse control to prevent them from carrying out any adverse actions while the therapeutic process began. Finally, Sandra's parents genuinely wanted her to remain alive and did not want harm for anyone in the family. The predominant communication in the family was a wish to live which was stronger than any death-seeking tendencies.

Child II: Roger was a 7-year-old boy who was hyperactive, had a very poor attention span in school, and became uncontrollably angry with children in his class. He tried to stab himself with a knife during a fight with his mother. Roger's parents were divorced when he was 4 years old and his father disappeared when Roger was 5. Roger's mother struggled with intense bouts of depression and left Roger with babysitters during her depressions.

Roger threatened to stab himself because his mother reprimanded him for being suspended from school. His mother told him that she no longer could tolerate his bad behavior and that she had no way of helping him. Upon hearing this, he ran to the kitchen where the knives were kept and waved a knife at her, saying that he would kill himself. Roger's mother grabbed the knife from him and spanked him. Roger was frightened and tearful, and became more cooperative. However, his mother was totally overwhelmed by this experience. She brought him to the pediatric emergency room and told the doctor that she could not take care of Roger at home. She felt exhausted and helpless at the thought of living alone with Roger. She worried that he might again threaten to kill himself.

Roger was referred for psychiatric hospitalization with the purpose of ensuring that he would be more protected from self-destructive impulses. In addition, his mother was relieved of the worrisome burden of constantly watching him. Psychiatric hospitalization could provide a structured protective setting for Roger while extensive psychiatric evaluation of him and his family situation could be undertaken.

These examples illustrate that the decision to hospitalize a suicidal child is dependent on a number of factors.

Eisenberg (1980) proposed that one factor important in the decision to hospitalize a child is the psychosocial resources of the patient's family. Eisenberg stated the following belief:

> If the parents show understanding and concern, counselling on an outpatient basis is feasible. On the other hand, if the parents are indifferent and worse, if they are angry, show no understanding of the stress represented by the attempt, and cannot be supportive, then hospitalization will be necessary. Failure of the gesture to bring about an affirmation of genuine concern may serve to confirm the patient's worst fears of being unloved; the parent who belittles the youngster as a failure may make it necessary for the youngster to try again to preserve face. (p. 319)

Eisenberg emphasized that "what is crucial is a therapeutic context that permits the rebuilding of hope and the re-establishment of healthy ties among family members. Because the patient feels unloved and unworthy of love, the task of treatment is to convey a sense of caring and to restore faith in the possibility of a satisfying future" (p. 319). Eisenberg believes that "suicide is the ultimate expression of alienation. It is best conceptualized as a deficiency disease, a deficiency of social connections. The aim of treatment is to restore to the patient the sources of emotional sustenance which all of us depend on for our survival" (p. 319). Treatment of suicidal children must always include interventions that are geared to fostering a supportive environmental network of people. Assessment of the strengths and weaknesses of this network will be a guide to treatment planning.

During the initial interview with a suicidal child, many other parameters must be assessed in order to decide whether to hospitalize the child or whether continuing in the home environment is feasible. Carlson and Cantwell (1982), in their study of 102 children and adolescents, noted that for these youngsters, who were psychiatrically hospitalized, "it was probably the suicide attempt in an apparently depressed youngster that prompted psychiatric hospitalization" (p. 366). Similar findings were noted by Weiner and Pfeffer (1983) for 100 consecutively admitted child psychiatric inpatients in which the diagnosis that specifically distinguished the suicidal children from the nonsuicidal children was major affective disorder among the suicidal children.

Therefore, it is recommended that a child with a major affective disorder and suicidal behavior should be hospitalized for more extensive evaluation and treatment planning.

Other parameters that help in deciding whether to hospitalize a child were highlighted by Pfeffer and Plutchik (1982) in a study of 103 children, ages 6 to 12 years, who were evaluated in a psychiatric outpatient clinic and an inpatient unit of a large municipal hospital. The results of this study identified specific factors distinguishing psychiatric inpatients and outpatients. These are listed in Table 13-3.

This study suggested that the psychiatrically hospitalized children, compared to the outpatient children, had more severe and complex problems that included difficulties with affects, tendencies toward suicidal and assaultive behaviors, marked family turmoil, and severe parental psychopathology, especially among the mothers. The chronicity of the symptoms was greater for inpatient children. The inpatients had multiple deficits in ego functioning that included lower intellectual functioning, poor school achievement, and impaired assessment of reality. Indicators of pregnancy, birth, and neonatal problems were more evident among inpatient children. The parameters highlighted in this study provide guidelines of factors that should be evaluated during the first meeting with a suicidal child. In fact, the study showed that the combination of factors that best predicted the need for psychiatric hospitalization was: (1) the degree of the child's assaultive behavior, (2) seriousness of suicidal behavior, (3) antisocial behavior, (4) poor reality testing, (5) parental pregnancy complications, and (6) parental separation. A suicidal child should be considered for psychiatric

TABLE 13-3
Differences between child psychiatric inpatients and outpatients

Factor	Inpatients	Outpatients
Suicidal behavior	Severe	Mild to moderate
Assaultive behavior	Severe	Mild
Depression	Severe	Mild to moderate
Anxiety	Severe	Mild to moderate
Antisocial behavior	Moderate	Mild
Reality testing	Poor	Good
Parental separation	Frequent	Occasional
Pregnancy and neonatal complications	Frequent	Occasional
Parental suicidal behavior	Serious	Minor
Parental depression	Severe	Mild to moderate
Parental assaultive behavior	Severe	Mild
Parental psychiatric hospitalization	Occasional	Rare

hospitalization if he or she has characteristics similar to the inpatient children in this study.

Another parameter that must be carefully determined during the initial therapeutic session is the quality of communication among family members. Stone (1980) noted that the risk for suicidal behavior will be higher in a family with a humiliating, rejecting atmosphere, especially since suicidal individuals experience life in either/or terms. The suicidal person feels compelled to take his or her life after a minor provocation. This is especially pertinent for children, who may perceive statements in a concrete way. For example, a parent's statement to "drop dead" may be taken by the child as a specific command to kill himself or herself. Therefore, in the therapeutic process with suicidal children, it is mandatory to involve the parents.

Toolan (1980), too, advocated involving the parents in the therapy of suicidal children. He pointed out that often parents minimize the seriousness of their child's suicidal communications. In fact, some parents insist that it was a mistake and that "the child did not know what he was doing." Toolan noted that it was not unusual to find the parents very angry at the child. They may think, "How could she have done this to me?"

Ackerly (1967) noted that an immediate intervention goal is to facilitate treatment of the mother and father to modify their perceptions of their child, especially their own aggressive feelings and death wishes. In keeping with these ideas, a very malignant type of parent–child relationship is described by Sabbath (1969) as the "expendable child" concept. Sabbath contended that suicide represents a failure in communication between the individual and other meaningful family members, together with an inability to cope with the stresses of life. He noted that one youngster admitted that her mother loved her but said it was "because I am her daughter, not because I am me." This youngster also stated: "My parents wanted to make me perfect; they failed, and therefore they want to get rid of me." Sabbath proposed that one factor important in suicidal behavior is a parental conscious or unconscious wish to be rid of the child that the child perceives after years of verbal and nonverbal communications. Thus, the child is faced with psychological abandonment and anticipates physical abandonment as well. The "expendable child" is one who is no longer tolerated or needed by the family: "He ceases to be useful either as an object of affection or as the vicarious fulfiller of the needs of his parents" (p. 282).

Sabbath (1969) dramatized the child's plight by saying:

The roots of expendability go back at times to birth or even before conception. The child may be unwanted and unplanned for, or, if there is planning, this may quickly give way to a disappointment in the product. With this beginning, there is little chance for an early confident mother–child relationship to develop. The consequences are interferences with the healthy development of the ego and its functions. Meanwhile, the parents themselves may have their own special problems and adjustments which may either contribute to or at times ameliorate their difficulties in relating to the child . . . the parents are as much victims of their own past as they are the contributors to their children's current predicament. (p. 283)

Therefore, during the initial intervention stage, family perceptions of the child must be evaluated.

In addition, other factors suggested by Pfeffer (1981a) and described in Chapter 9, such as intergenerational boundary problems, spouse conflict, inflexible family interactions, parental feelings projected onto the child, and symbiotic ties between parent and child should be assessed. These five family factors preclude the satisfaction of the needy parents and the child's attainment of autonomy. The intergenerational boundary problems of the parents reflect the parents' inabilities to become independent from the influence of their own parents. The symbiotic ties between the parent and suicidal child and unrealistic parental feelings toward the child make it unlikely that the child will be able to escape from the intense aggression-laden relationship with the parent. Furthermore, the severe spouse conflicts create an atmosphere of tension, anger, fear, and desperation among the family members. Finally, the entire family is locked into rigid and set patterns of relating so that a sense of inflexibility of family interactions is apparent. If these conditions exist in the family, the risk of the child's suicidal behavior may be too great for the child to remain in the home. In such a case, psychiatric hospitalization is warranted.

SUMMARY

This chapter has been devoted to the initial stages of intervention that has as its main goal planning for continued treatment. If there are medical sequellae to the suicidal behavior, hospitalization on a pediatric unit is recommended. Simultaneously, a psychiatric assessment should be started. If there are no medical injuries, the initial psychiatric assessment has as its main goal the determination of how to protect the child while treatment begins. Psychiatric hospitalization may be the intervention of choice although outpatient treatment may be feasible also in certain cases. Parameters that may be useful in making this clinical decision have been discussed. Finally, an analysis has been made of specific personal and professional qualities of the therapist that influence the outcome of therapeutic work with suicidal children.

CHAPTER FOURTEEN

OUTPATIENT PSYCHOTHERAPY WITH SUICIDAL CHILDREN

> A log raft in the river invited him, and he seated himself on its outer edge and contemplated the dreary vastness of the stream, wishing, the while, that he could only be drowned, all at once and unconsciously, without undergoing the uncomfortable routine devised by nature —Mark Twain, *The Adventures of Tom Sawyer*

Individual psychotherapy is the core of the treatment of suicidal children. It enables the therapist to monitor closely the degree of the child's suicidal tendencies and to work intensively with the child's underlying conflicts. Because there is a complex interaction of factors associated with suicidal behavior in children, other interventions such as use of medication and family interventions must be incorporated into the schema of therapeutic work with suicidal children. Some of these other interventions are described in Chapter 16.

Unfortunately, there are no systematic studies evaluating the efficacy of psychotherapy with suicidal children. Most information about psychotherapy with suicidal children is derived from case reports which generate theoretical insights that can be empirically investigated.

This chapter presents numerous hypotheses about the treatment of suicidal children that are based on my therapeutic work with suicidal children and other clinicians' case reports of suicidal children. The psychotherapeutic strategies discussed here are based on psychoanalytic theory.

STRUCTURE OF THE SESSIONS OF OUTPATIENT PSYCHOTHERAPY

In most cases, suicidal children require long-term psychotherapy that focuses on all of the factors underlying suicidal risk. However, the goals of treatment for some suicidal children may be accomplished in a psychotherapeutic process that requires less time. A short-term psychotherapy process may be utilized if a child develops acute suicidal behavior in response to a new situational disturbance. For example, a child with a learning disability who is transferred to a new school that does not have a remedial program suited to the child's specific needs may feel so stressed that the child entertains suicidal ideation. Brief psychotherapy in conjunction with special educational assistance may decrease the school stress and increase the child's sense of self-worth and confidence. In contrast, a child with a chronic depressive disorder and recurrent suicidal threats may require long-term psychotherapy and possibly additional interventions in order to counteract depressive and suicidal symptomatology and resolve the intrapsychic conflicts.

In all circumstances, follow-up contacts with the therapist at defined time periods are advised after the ongoing psychotherapy has terminated. These follow-up contacts, either by telephone or in person, create a method of recognizing or monitoring the expression of suicidal tendencies in the child. Therefore, the treatment of suicidal children is essentially a long-term process. However, the individual psychotherapy may vary in actual duration.

The structure of the sessions of individual psychotherapy is defined by the number and length of time of meetings with the therapist. Although there is no uniform structure that can be prescribed for treatment for suicidal children, one principle that should be followed is that a carefully planned but flexible approach must be established. The number of sessions and their length should be organized to ensure that the child's suicidal impulses can be monitored closely and that the child is protected from self-destructive actions. For example, when a child is acutely suicidal, he or she may need to be seen *daily* for at least a full therapy session. The purpose of such intensive treatment is optimal monitoring of the degree of suicidal risk while working toward diminishing the risk. Such an approach is feasible if the child can make a commitment to the therapist to not act upon suicidal impulses and if the family is able to closely supervise the child while also working to make sufficient family changes that will lead to a reduction of the child's suicidal behavior. If these criteria are not met, however, psychiatric hospitalization may be indicated.

As the acute suicidal crisis resolves, a gradual decrease of number and length of psychotherapy sessions can be arranged and a constant schedule can be established. The number of psychotherapy sessions can range from one to three per week. If acute suicidal symptomatology reappears, a more intensive schedule may be resumed.

PHASES, GOALS, AND SOME INTERVENTIONS OF OUTPATIENT PSYCHOTHERAPY

Phases of outpatient psychotherapy can be conceptualized as including a beginning, a middle, and an end phase. Specific goals are accomplished in each phase of the treatment. The specific goals and some treatment techniques during the phases of outpatient psychotherapy of suicidal children are listed in Table 14-1.

THE BEGINNING PHASE

During the beginning phase, the primary goal is to establish a therapeutic alliance. This is one of the most fundamental components that allows treatment to continue. The therapeutic alliance consists of both the child's acknowledgment and sense of trust that the therapist wishes to help the child and the child's commitment to continue the work of treatment. Essentially, the therapeutic alliance is based on a commitment that allows the child and therapist to work together regardless of the degree of stress experienced in the therapeutic process.

The therapist should always be aware of the need to evaluate the status of the therapeutic alliance. In addition, the therapist should try to foster and promote the therapeutic alliance by making repeated comments that refer to such issues as the child's need for help and the purpose of the work of treatment; that is, to help the child develop a better understanding of his or her difficulties and ways to cope with them. Such comments also enhance a feeling of hopefulness about the outcome of treatment.

In part, as a result of the establishment of a therapeutic alliance, the child may be able to agree either not to resort to suicidal behavior or to inform the therapist if he or she has suicidal inclinations. This process is an important way to ensure the protection of a child. Another issue that helps to protect the child from harm is the child's realization that suicidal behavior has harmful and not beneficial consequences. The therapist should emphasize the detrimental aspects of suicidal behavior by frankly emphasizing that suicidal behavior is not an effective way of handling problems and distressing feelings. There are much better ways of resolving problems and relieving painful feelings. These concepts also help define, as one of the main goals of treatment, the eventual abolishment of the child's suicidal tendencies.

THE MIDDLE PHASE

Transference reactions can be defined as the child's reactions to the therapist that reflect the child's unconscious tendencies to equate the therapist with other emotionally important persons in the child's life. Transference is the most crucially important aspect of the child's psychotherapy and is most intensively seen during the middle phase of therapy.

By making inferences about transference reactions, the therapist can develop hypotheses about how the child perceives and relates to other significant people. These hypotheses can be used for interpreta-

TABLE 14-1

Goals and some interventions during the phases of outpatient psychotherapy of suicidal children

---

Beginning phase

Goal I: Develop therapeutic alliance
Interventions:
  1. State that treatment can help
  2. State that therapist and child work together to solve problems

Goal II: Protect child from harm
Interventions:
  1. Emphasize dangerousness of suicidal behavior
  2. Urge the child to inform therapist of the child's suicidal urges
  3. Emphasize that suicidal behavior is a poor alternative in dealing with problems

---

Middle phase

Goal I: Decrease suicidal tendencies
Interventions:
  1. Discuss alternative solutions to problems
  2. Discuss child's unfulfilled wishes and outline acceptable compromise gratifications

Goal II: Decrease depression
Interventions:
  1. Talk with the child about positive elements of the situation
  2. Discuss how the child can form new supportive relationships to replace lost ones
  3. Suggest ways to structure day so child eats and sleeps appropriately

---

(continued)

tive interventions that may ameliorate the child's intense conflicts and suicidal tendencies. For example, many suicidal children feel alienated from relationships with others and devoid of love from their parents. These feelings often are observed in the transference when the child withdraws from interacting with the therapist. The therapist may tell the child that it seems that the child does not feel that the therapist cares about him or her. The therapist may also interpret to the child that it appears that the child feels that he or she does not desire the therapist's attention. These comments may stimulate discussion about how the child can establish satisfying relationships with others.

An important aspect of the transference is that the child's suicidal tendencies can take on different meanings at different times within the treatment process. Kernberg (1974) suggested that many suicidal dynamics can be found in a single patient and that treatment permits the exploration of the variety of meanings of the patient's suicidal tenden-

TABLE 14-1
(*Continued*)

Goal III: Enhance self-esteem
  Interventions:
  1. Compliment child's accomplishments, skills, and appropriate independent behaviors
  2. Suggest ways the child can behave independently and successfully
  3. Support child's attempts to develop friendships
  4. Help the child to accept shortcomings and disabilities

Goal IV: Modify aggressive responses
  Interventions:
  1. Outline alternative ways of responding to frustrations
  2. Help child accept disappointment by outlining other ways of obtaining satisfaction
  3. Remind child that it is unacceptable in life for anyone to be injured by the child's anger

---

End phase

Goal: Cope with feelings involving separation and loss
  Interventions:
  1. Discuss feelings of loneliness, sadness, anger, joy, and relief about ending treatment
  2. Discuss ways to develop new relationships
  3. Discuss specific warning signs of suicidal tendencies
  4. Make agreement that child will reenter treatment if clues of suicidal tendencies develop

---

cies. For example, expression of suicidal tendencies may reflect the child's wishes to control the responses of the therapist. Thus, the child's suicidal tendencies may express the unconscious wish "If you don't respond to what I want, I will kill myself." Furthermore, a child's suicidal tendencies may reflect rage at not feeling loved. The suicidal behavior may include the child's response: "If you don't love me now, you will be sorry if I die." The way the therapist makes a judgment or inference about the meaning of a particular pattern of behavior is a general problem for psychoanalytic theory. The inference is a complex judgment which is based upon observation of a patient's behavior over a period of time, specific verbalizations of the child, special events that precede the appearance of suicidal ideas or acts, and the expected consequences of the act. Thus, by understanding the various transference responses, the therapist may begin to focus on why the child feels that he or she cannot achieve gratification of his or her wishes and how the child can develop a sense of fulfillment from compromise solutions.

The discussion may focus on helping the child develop alternative ways of solving problems.

The therapist must always be attentive to the child's conscious communications and transference reactions. By understanding the communications of the child, it is possible to achieve the goals of therapy such as decreasing suicidal tendencies and depression, enhancing self-esteem, and modifying aggressive responses. A variety of interventions to achieve these goals are enumerated in Table 14-1. For example, a child may be angry at the therapist just after describing how he or she lost a friendship as a result of an argument. The therapist–child relationship can be used to point out alternative ways of settling disagreements and reaching compromise solutions in order to develop better peer friendships and to avoid intense arguments. Thus, all interventions are aimed at improving the child's cognitive and emotional understanding of his or her conflicts and reactions.

THE END PHASE

The end phase of treatment occurs at the time that lasting treatment effects are evident. Important achievements of treatment are observable when the child shows self-assurance, self-respect, an appropriate autonomous functioning to make compromises, ability to decide on alternative solutions to problems, and an increase in the quality and scope of personal relations.

An essential task of the end phase is to help the child accept the termination of treatment and separation from the therapist. It is important to determine how the child will feel about not having the therapist to speak with regularly. The discussion about the child's feelings in regard to stopping treatment or in not seeing the therapist can help clarify how the child views being on his or her own.

One of the indications that the child has entered the final phase of treatment is evidence that the child is able to recognize the early warning signs of suicidal impulses. It is like the development of a radar system in which the child can recognize the imminent presence of dangerous impulses when they are still relatively distant and can still be put under his or her control. The therapist reinforces the idea that the child should seek help when these early warning signs are identified. It should be made clear to the child that the therapist or a colleague will be available to the child even after treatment has terminated if such warning signs arise. *Pari passu*, the parents are helped along the same lines, so that, if necessary, treatment can be resumed as promptly as possible.

INTERVENTION STRATEGIES FOR SUICIDAL CHILDREN

There are specific types of psychodynamic features that are commonly evident among suicidal children. Suicidal children are in a deep state
of withdrawal and alienation. They perceive themselves as being denied or not deserving of any type of supportive interpersonal relationship. Many of these children feel that they have lost their sense of identity, self-esteem, and purpose in life. In the extreme agonizing form,
the child feels that he or she does not have, and does not deserve, a
place in this world. The strategies of intervention must be actively utilized as a way of counteracting the child's feelings of loss and hopelessness.

Depression and its component parts of helplessness, hopelessness,
and loss are commonly experienced by suicidal children. Toolan (1978)
hypothesized that depression is a reaction to loss that can be either a
loss of an object or a loss of a state of well-being which leads to diminished self-esteem. Children who experience loss at an early age may
show signs of developmental deviations in their ability to form interpersonal relationships and to identify with significant individuals in their
lives.

Many suicidal depressed children use a variety of defense mechanisms such as repression, denial, projection, and somatization to ward
off the painful feelings associated with loss. Thus, one of the most important tasks of psychotherapy with depressed suicidal children is to
observe and analyze these features as they unfold within the treatment
transference. The work of treatment is to help alter the defenses against
feelings of loss by actively trying to promote a close relationship with
the child. In this way, the child can be helped to express anger, disappointments, and sadness about his or her actual and fantasized losses
while simultaneously experiencing a new and important relationship
with the therapist.

The following brief examples point out the responses of children
who experienced a loss early in life. Their responses were intensely
manifest in the relationship with their therapists.

Child I: Simon, age 9 years, exhibited intense mistrust and accused his therapist
of being uncaring. Simon insisted that his therapist did not care about him and
was furious whenever his therapist started a session 1 minute late. Simon felt
deeply deprived and spoke with anger about the loss of his father, which
resulted from his parents' divorce 4 years ago.

Child II: Katherine, age 8 years, had intensely ambivalent feelings about her
therapist. She both liked and hated her therapist and felt intensely ashamed

of exposing her thoughts to her therapist. Katherine felt so ashamed of herself that she sat in her therapist's office with her head down and insisted that she did not want to be there. Yet, when asked if she would prefer seeing a different therapist, Katherine quickly insisted that she would see no one else. Katherine was struggling with her painful feelings about the death of her mother when Katherine was 5 years old. Katherine felt so bad about herself that she felt unloved, rejected, and unworthy of anyone's attention.

Child III: Sandra, age 11 years, repeatedly confessed her guilty feelings about creating family problems. Her parents separated when Sandra was 6 years old, after several years of a tumultuous, argument-filled marriage. Sandra believed that she was the sole cause of her family's problems. She felt that she was evil and deserved extreme punishment. Her suicidal ideas intensified whenever she was engaged in an argument with her therapist.

Child IV: Jacob, age 12 years, was preoccupied with a sense of failure, worthlessness, and hopelessness. His parents divorced when he was 9 years old, and he felt so overwhelmed by intense sadness that he gave up trying to succeed at school and to maintain friendships. Jacob believed that he was not as good looking or athletic as other boys in his class. He repeatedly told his therapist that he did not deserve the therapist's time and attention. As a result, any interpretation offered by the therapist was responded to by Jacob with a negation and a sense of hopelessness. Jacob thought that the best thing that could happen to him was for him to disappear or die so that no one would have to be concerned about him.

These examples illustrate how somewhat similar types of loss experiences may be expressed in quite different ways in different children. These differences undoubtedly relate to such things as the personality of the child; the nature of the ongoing relationships with the parents before the loss occurred; the degree of congruity of the parents in handling the children; and the presence of siblings, friends, and extended family members as support networks; as well as the temperament of the child. Very few hard data exist on these issues, but they certainly form important hypotheses for future research.

In work with such children, the therapist usually experiences intense feelings of anger and rejection by the child, who is recapitulating memories about his or her conflicted relationship with the lost person. The therapist should actively interpret how the child's behavior toward the therapist is largely determined by the child's feelings about losing someone who was special to him or her; it must be shown to the child that the therapist is very worried and frightened that something may happen in their relationship that will create another experience of loss. As a result of this fear the child behaves in such a way as to ward off the possibility of experiencing closeness and dependent feelings toward the therapist. The therapist should clearly define the therapeutic relationship as different from any previously experienced relationship, as one in which the therapist and child can work together to understand the painful feelings being experienced by the child. The aim of treatment is to help the child develop an understanding of previous experiences of actual and/or fantasied losses.

Most suicidal depressed children experience serious problems with maintaining a sense of self-esteem. Sandler and Joffe (1965) proposed a mechanism that explains the relationship between loss, depression, and self-esteem. They hypothesized that a common feature of depressed children was a specific type of threat to their well-being which manifested itself as the feeling of having a loss or of being unable to obtain something which was essential to the child's narcissistic integrity. The pain of experiencing loss resulted in a state of helplessness, inhibition of expression of feelings, and activation of a variety of ego defenses. They concluded that the child has fantasies about how he or she would like to be but is unable to achieve this idealized state. As a result, the child experiences a sense of low self-esteem and sense of failure. Many suicidal depressed children need the actual presence of a loved person in order for the child to experience a state of satisfactory self-esteem. Therefore, the loss of such a loved person will produce mental pain, low self-esteem, and depression.

During this process of treatment, the therapist can try to clarify to the child what the therapist understands of the child's wishes and self-expectations, and how the child views his or her abilities to achieve them. The treatment, therefore, focuses on what the child can do to try to achieve desires, when it may be necessary to accept compromises, and how to cope with feelings of disappointment and frustration. The therapist assumes the role of the loved person who is essential to foster the child's sense of self-esteem. Developing positive identifications with the therapist can be helpful in enhancing the child's self-esteem. The child may identify with how the therapist solves problems and how the therapist assesses his or her own interactions with others. This becomes an important way of strengthening the child's personal relationships and fostering an inner sense of strength.

It must be realized that while it is essential to analyze the psychodynamics of suicidal children's depressive propensities that include aspects related to loss, hopelessness, worthlessness, and helplessness, it is also essential to monitor the signs and symptoms that indicate the intensity of the depression. This is mandatory because the psychodynamics of children with mild depression may be exactly the same as those of children with severe depression. Therefore, the psychodynamic features will not provide clear indications of the severity of depression. It is essential to monitor the severity of depression because it has been shown that risk for suicidal behavior increases as the severity of depression increases. Among those parameters that indicate the degree of intensity of depression are signs of sadness, sleep and appetite disturbance, psychomotor activity, lack of ability to concentrate, guilt, hopelessness, worthlessness, and helplessness. A more detailed discussion of how to make this assessment has been presented in Chapter 6.

Finally, treatment strategies should be geared to specific types of suicidal children. Pfeffer, Plutchik, and Mizruchi (1983) defined at least two types of suicidal children. One type is the predominantly depressed child with relatively good reality testing, severe depression, suicidal parents, and a stressful family environment. The second type is the depressed suicidal child who shows extreme rage episodes, aggressive behavior, deficits in reality testing, and parental violence and suicidal behavior. This second type of suicidal child often requires psychiatric hospitalization in order to provide an environment that can monitor and intervene when the youngster experiences intense affects, poor reality testing, and suicidal tendencies.

Glaser (1981) also recommended that special interventions be used in the psychotherapy of aggressive suicidal youngsters. He proposed that the suicidal behavior of these youngsters is the result of extreme rage arising from prolonged experiences of frustration. He warned that if the therapist's responses do not address the intense neediness of these youngsters, they will feel immediately rejected and may express acute suicidal behavior. It is important for the therapist to acknowledge that the child is enraged and upset, and to point out that there are other ways of achieving what he or she wishes than by suicidal behavior. It is important for the therapist to reinforce the child's efforts to try to decrease feelings of frustration. The therapist should tell the child that resorting to suicidal threats or attempts is not a way that will help accomplish his or her goals. The therapist should tell the child that he or she will not respond to the child's suicidal behavior by gratifying demands but will instead respond by trying to protect the child from harm. Glaser acknowledged that these youngsters often require psychiatric hospitalization, which can provide a highly structured environment that maintains controls against precipitous suicidal and/or aggressive behaviors.

ILLUSTRATIONS OF OUTPATIENT PSYCHOTHERAPY

The following two examples point out specific psychodynamic features in outpatient psychotherapy of suicidal children. These include the multiple conscious and unconscious meanings associated with suicidal tendencies and the interrelated cognitive and affective states of the child. The first child was in my study of children evaluated and treated in a child psychiatric outpatient clinic.

Child V: Samuel was 7 years old when he jumped out his first-floor bedroom window. Outpatient treatment was feasible because Samuel showed great willingness to meet with the therapist. In his initial session with the therapist, he denied wishes to kill himself, but at the time he jumped out the window he voiced an intent to die. He had been preoccupied with death for approximately 2 years. In play, he demonstrated suicidal behavior. He wrapped belts around dolls necks and had them say to other dolls: "You will be sorry when I die. You treat me like shit and I will kill myself." Samuel was considered a special child in the family. He was bright and attractive, and tended to cling to his mother, who was chronically depressed and had suicidal ideas. At the time Samuel jumped out the window, he was doing poorly in school and had an argument with his mother about his homework.

Samuel developed a strong emotional attachment to his therapist as soon as treatment began. He liked to be with his therapist and expressed the wish to live with his therapist. These wishes represented Samuel's hopes that he could have an all-giving mother. In contrast to the positive feelings toward his therapist, Samuel's play demonstrated intense fantasy with themes of violence and monsters. Furthermore, dolls were depicted as traveling back and forth in a time machine. These play fantasies and responses to his therapist revealed Samuel's perceptions of his relationship to his unstable and depressed mother. Drawings of himself showed a boy smiling, but he said: It's not really me, it's a monster; you can tell by the hole in the head. Monster heads are special." Samuel wished for a kind mother with whom he could have a very close nuturing relationship, and he felt angry at her for being withdrawn, inconsistent, and depressed. In addition, Samuel's anger at his mother was experienced as a bad feeling within himself; therefore, he was a monster.

Samuel perceived his mother as a dangerous person who disregarded his needs. However, he constantly longed to be with her. These themes were experienced in his reactions to his therapist. Treatment centered around his great neediness. For example, he searched through his therapist's desk and personal belongings. He asked the therapist if he could live at home with the therapist. When his therapist replied that it was not possible, Samuel withdrew, felt rejected, and only wanted to play with blocks. Samuel was especially enraged when his therapist went on vacation. He felt so angry about this loss that he jumped out the first-floor window of his apartment just before his therapist's vacation. This behavior was reminiscent of his first suicide attempt after an argument with his mother. Samuel's therapist spoke with him about how angry he was over his therapist's vacation. The therapist told Samuel that it appeared that Samuel felt rejected, as he often felt when his mother was not available to him. Samuel understood these remarks and told his therapist that it felt like the therapist would never return. However, Samuel recognized that when his therapist returned, they would be able to continue the work.

During the second year of treatment, Samuel's mood improved. There were no suicide attempts except for some ideas before the therapist's vacation. Themes of giving his therapist presents emerged. Samuel felt very close to his therapist. He played with his therapist in a noncompetitive way. Their play focused on themes of two people engaged in joint endeavors. For example, he and his therapist threw airplanes together. Samuel had a special drawer in the therapist's desk where he left his possessions. In contrast to the caring interactions between Samuel and his therapist, his play still contained themes of violence. Toy soldiers had indiscriminate fights with no one fighting anyone in particular. The war seemed chaotic and repetitive. Thus, Samuel's underlying rage continued to emerge in play fantasy. A new feature of the treatment became evident. Instead of expressing anger only in play, Samuel was able to express these feelings to his therapist directly.

However, Samuel did not want to be asked questions. Any question or clarification interpretation was met with denunciation and anger. He accused his therapist of wrecking his life and making incorrect statements. It was inferred by the therapist that these accusations represented transference reactions related to Samuel's anger and frustration with his depressed mother. Because they were expressed toward his therapist, these reactions could be discussed openly in treatment. Samuel experienced any interpretation as a deprivation; in response to this, the therapist made fewer interpretations.

In time, Samuel told his therapist that his grades had improved and that he liked attending school. Samuel regularly completed his homework and rarely had arguments with his mother about school. Samuel felt better about himself. He believed he could cope with separations from his therapist during vacation period. Samuel's play still exhibited themes of violence. It seemed that within the sphere of play, Samuel expressed his most aggressive tendencies. Furthermore, suicidal tendencies disappeared. Finally, by the end of the year Samuel decided to stop treatment. His therapist agreed and they parted with Samuel having a good sense of mastery and control over his actions.

This example summarizes a 2-year process of treatment that provided an atmosphere of trust and support, and a special relationship with the therapist. Cooperative joint play adventures characterized the patient–therapist relationship. A main dynamic was Samuel's instant emotional attachment to his therapist, which was followed by disappointment in not being able to be with the therapist constantly. This transference reaction reflected the conflicted mother–child interactions. It may be presumed that it was the supportive, consistent, and nonthreatening relationship with his therapist that allowed Samuel to develop better feelings about himself.

The next example, reported by Alarron (1982), illustrates details of play that became the major focus for the treatment of a 7-year-old boy who showed serious suicidal behavior.

Child VI: This child threatened to put a knife through his stomach, to walk in front of cars, and to strangle himself. His history was characterized by extreme chaos in the home. When he was 2 years old, two older siblings were taken out of the home because of child abuse. His parents divorced when the child was 5 years old, and he remained with his mother. At age 6 years he was placed in foster care because of child abuse and was then transferred to a residential facility, where he became uncooperative, mute, and suicidal. Eventually he was returned home. It was at this time that he attempted to run into traffic and to suffocate himself.

The child, when first seen, was sad, angry, and negativistic. He thought he was a bad boy and that the separations from his mother were punishment for his bad behavior. The initial phases of therapy were spent in building a trusting relationship with his therapist. Because the child never responded to questions and never produced fantasy, most sessions consisted of the therapist and child working together to build models and repair a doll house. The therapist pointed out that together they could mend and build things. The child agreed with these interpretations.

Gradually, the child demonstrated fantasy in play. He developed a positive feeling toward his therapist. The doll house, which they had repaired together, became filled with animals, which he controlled by building fences. The therapist pointed out that the wild, angry animals in the house were like the child's angry feelings, so that they could be controlled by keeping them inside the doll house instead of letting them run out and kill other animals. In time, the doll house became inhabited by statues that had no feelings and were not alive. These statues, the child said, preferred to be without feelings rather than suffer from painful feelings.

The therapist said to the child that he preferred to be a statue with no feelings rather than himself with fears and anger. A change occurred when the doll house became a ghost house filled with scary feelings. The child told stories of different ghost families who had scary feelings. He began to elaborate detailed themes that portrayed how he felt in the different homes in which he had lived. Sometimes he got out of control and appeared to be out of touch with reality. The therapist introduced the Superman ghost that came to the rescue. The child and therapist constructed weapons so that they could master the situations. However, this mechanism sometimes failed, and then the therapist needed to comfort the child directly.

Remarkably, the child began to talk about his anger and fear of his mother. He spoke about how much he missed his brothers and said that he often searched for them in the street. He talked about being afraid that he could be abandoned by his mother. Soon he began to do better in school and showed greater self-confidence. No suicidal ideas or actions occurred. The treatment lasted 2 years, and then the child was placed in a therapeutic boarding school. Both the child and mother were prepared to accept this separation from each other.

Self-esteem, affect regulation, and responses to separation from the mother were the essential issues dealt with in this treatment. Outpatient treatment was possible in this case because the child and his mother formed a positive alliance with the therapist and quickly responded by ensuring the safety of the child. The therapist's goal was to provide a structure in which the child could gradually express his feelings without fear and guilt over destroying himself or someone else. This helped the child master his feelings and resulted in bolstering self-esteem.

This example also illustrates specific issues during the three phases of treatment. Initially, the therapeutic task consisted of forming a relationship with the child and making him feel worthwhile. The next phase of treatment focused on developing insight into the child's problems. For example, the therapist spoke with the child about his fears, his angry feelings, and being out of control, and interpreted these as being directed toward his mother. Play became more and more elaborate and included animals and people rather than only a barren house. The final phase was spent discussing the child's fears of abandonment. This allowed the child to master the termination of therapy and to accept the transfer to a residential school where his treatment could continue.

SUMMARY

This is the first of two chapters that focus on the psychotherapeutic processes used with suicidal children. The most important features of psychotherapy with the suicidal child are the development of a positive therapeutic alliance and the development of a close relationship with the therapist. The therapeutic alliance allows the child to recognize that the therapist wishes to help the child. The relationship with the therapist allows a variety of conscious and unconscious feelings and conflicts to be expressed and understood. As a result of understanding the nature of the therapeutic relationship, the suicidal child's conflicts can be diminished and the child's abilities to cope in nonsuicidal ways can be improved.

Modifications in the psychotherapeutic process are made when a child is psychiatrically hospitalized. These issues are discussed in the next chapter.

CHAPTER FIFTEEN

PSYCHIATRIC HOSPITAL TREATMENT OF SUICIDAL CHILDREN

The child's tired-looking, unhappy face troubled her. All the doubts and wonders that had at times tormented her since she'd done away with Callie Lou more than a week ago came over her now, though her reason told her that a little thing like a mother's scolding wouldn't make a child lose her appetite and be restless in her sleep. —Harriette Arnow, *The Dollmaker*

The psychiatric hospital, compared to psychiatric outpatient, pediatric inpatient, and pediatric outpatient settings, is the treatment setting for the largest number of suicidal patients (Pfeffer *et al.*, 1979, 1980, 1982). Acute psychiatric hospitalization is one of the most important modalities of treatment available for suicidal children.

Many of the ideas discussed in this chapter about the treatment of suicidal children can be applied to psychiatric hospital treatment of children in general. The concepts discussed in this chapter are based primarily on my experiences directing child psychiatric hospital units for many years in both private and municipal hospitals. Essentially, the discussion focuses on the tasks and the phases of hospital treatment. Clinical examples illustrate these concepts.

REFERRAL SOURCES FOR PSYCHIATRIC HOSPITALIZATION

Acute psychiatric hospital treatment is an important link in the chain of treatments utilized for suicidal children. Children are referred to the hospital from many sources and discharged from the hospital to a variety of settings. Some of the psychiatric hospital referral sources for admission and discharge are listed in Table 15-1. Although the admission referral facilities widely vary, discharged child psychiatric inpatients should be referred to practitioners or programs that offer long-term psychiatric treatment for the child and the family. In fact, it is the discontinuation of psychiatric treatment after psychiatric hospitaliza-

TABLE 15-1
Referral resources for psychiatric hospital treatment of suicidal children

Admission referral sources:
1. Family
2. School
3. Pediatrician
4. Private psychiatrist, psychologist, or social worker; other mental health professionals
5. Psychiatric clinic and emergency room
6. Psychiatric day hospital
7. Residential treatment setting
8. Camp
9. Pediatric outpatient clinic and hospital unit; emergency room
10. Police and community social agencies

Discharge referral resources:
1. Psychiatric outpatient treatment
2. Psychiatric day hospital
3. Long-term psychiatric hospitalization
4. Residential treatment center
5. Special education classes
6. Boarding school

tion or the continuation of previous interpersonal turmoil that accounts for a large number of repeated episodes of suicidal behavior and rehospitalization. Other factors associated with recurrence of suicidal behavior among discharged suicidal child psychiatric inpatients require systematic study.

One follow-up study, carried out by Cohen-Sandler and colleagues (1982b), provided valuable information about the posthospitalization course of child psychiatric inpatients. Their study followed 76 children who were originally admitted to a child psychiatric inpatient unit in a large metropolitan area. The children, when hospitalized, were categorized into three groups: 20 suicidal children, 21 nonsuicidal children, and 35 nonsuicidal nondepressed children. The follow-up was conducted 3 months to 3 years after discharge. The average time for follow-up was 18 months after discharge. Follow-up information was obtained for 72 of the original children. Of the children not followed up, two could not be located, one family refused to cooperate, and one 14-year-old boy drowned in a boating accident.

One consequence of a child's suicidal behavior and psychiatric hospitalization was a long-term removal from the home. Eighty-five percent of the 20 suicidal children lived with one parent at the time of admission, but only 44% of these children were living home at the time of follow-up. In contrast, a significantly greater proportion of nonsuicidal children (70%) who were living with a parent at the time of admission remained with this parent at follow-up. Another finding was that after discharge the suicidal children experienced significantly more psychosocial stress, such as separations from family members and hospitalization of a parent, than the nonsuicidal children. However, the suicidal children participated in aftercare treatment to the same extent as the nonsuicidal children. Only one suicidal child was rehospitalized because of a subsequent suicide attempt. Furthermore, only 4 of the 20 suicidal children acknowledged thoughts of suicide after discharge. In contrast, none of the nonsuicidal children revealed suicidal tendencies after discharge. Among the children initially known to be suicidal, the children who exhibited subsequent suicidal behavior were found to be older than the children without subsequent suicidal behavior. In addition, the initial suicidal behaviors of the children who exhibited subsequent suicidal behavior were more serious than the initial suicidal behaviors of the children with no subsequent suicidal behavior. Furthermore, the suicidal repeaters suffered significantly more psychosocial stress after discharge than the suicidal nonrepeaters.

Psychiatrically hospitalized suicidal children required long-term intensive treatment in settings away from home more frequently than nonsuicidal child psychiatric inpatients. The suicidal children were more vulnerable to repeating their suicidal behavior when environmental stress continued to be extreme. Thus, it is clear that one of the most important roles of psychiatric hospital treatment of suicidal children is to carefully develop a long-term plan for the child that can be carried out in a setting that minimizes the degree of psychosocial stress on the child. In addition, the more serious the initial suicidal behavior, the more likely it is that repeated suicidal behavior will occur, especially as these youngsters enter adolescence. Finally, further study is necessary to delineate those factors that protect suicidal children from repeated suicidal behavior after hospital discharge.

CHARACTERISTICS OF SUICIDAL CHILD PSYCHIATRIC INPATIENTS

Pfeffer and colleagues (1980, 1982) documented that suicidal child psychiatric inpatients display more dangerous suicidal behavior than suicidal psychiatric outpatients. Their studies indicated that approximately 20% of 39 child psychiatric outpatients (1980) expressed suicidal threats and attempts, in comparison to 52.3% of 65 child psychiatric inpatients (1982). As documented by these studies, suicidal children who require admission to a psychiatric hospital suffer from more extensive ego deficits and psychosocial stresses than suicidal children who can be managed in an outpatient setting. These children exhibit such associated symptoms as severe assaultive behavior, intense aggressive feelings, severe depression, stealing, lying, truancy, and severe cognitive and reality testing deficits. In addition, there exist serious environmental stresses from parental depression, other forms of parental psychopathology, and severe overt conflict. In fact, the serious degree of family turmoil and parental psychopathology makes it necessary for the psychiatric hospital treatment of suicidal children to focus on intensive work with the parents and family environment as well. In summary, suicidal children who require psychiatric hospital treatment are multiproblem children who are in need of coordinated interventions.

TASKS OF PSYCHIATRIC HOSPITAL TREATMENT

Psychiatric inpatient treatment incorporates a multimodality approach for the multiproblem suicidal child. Subsumed in psychiatric hospital treatment are a variety of interventions that include individual, group, and family psychotherapy; psychopharmacotherapy; recreational, art, music, and nursing interventions; and educational programs. Psychiatric inpatient treatment includes diagnostic assessments, interventions, and aftercare planning. These features of psychiatric hospital care are standard for suicidal and nonsuicidal children.

The tasks of psychiatric hospitalization for suicidal children are outlined in Table 15-2.

The initial and specific task of acute psychiatric hospital care for suicidal children is to protect the child from acting out his or her suicidal impulses. Although there have been no reports of preadolescents committing suicide in the psychiatric hospital, suicidal threats and attempts do occur. Therefore, all staff must be on the alert at all times for any signs of suicidal tendencies. In the hospital, an acutely suicidal child

TABLE 15-2
Tasks of psychiatric hospital treatment of suicidal children

1. Protect the child from suicidal behavior
2. Remove the child from environmental stresses
3. Coordinate observations of a variety of therapists
4. Offer multimodality diagnostic assessments
5. Effect an immediate change in the family equilibrium
6. Stimulate the child to maintain appropriate activities of daily living
7. Support ego strengths and remediate ego deficits by a multimodality approach administered on a 24-hour basis
8. Decrease the child's isolation by involvement with peers, school, and recreational activities
9. Monitor treatment effects
10. Plan discharge treatments

is maintained on constant observation by assigning a nursing staff member to be with the child at all times. As a result, the child is never left alone. Eating, sleeping, and toileting patterns are observed. School and unit activities are constantly monitored. The child is not able to leave the unit while still acutely suicidal.

The constant monitoring of the child fulfills two important purposes. First, a staff member is immediately available to intervene if the child threatens or attempts to express suicidal impulses. Second, in the hospital, every staff member carries out a therapeutic role. If the child is feeling tense, sad, angry, and hopeless, and suicidal ideas escalate, a staff member can intervene and discuss these reactions with the child. This permits the child to speak about feelings and ideas at any moment. Staff are available to the child on a 24-hour basis in order to help the child evaluate and understand the meanings of his or her emotional reactions and develop more appropriate adaptive skills. The approach of constant monitoring is a supportive measure that provides auxiliary ego control to the child at a time when the child is in a most desperate suicidal state.

A unique feature of psychiatric hospital treatment is that the child is removed from his or her environmentally stressful situation and provided with a supportive therapeutic setting. But, the hospital admission creates a sudden change in the family constellation and in the dynamic equilibrium of the family. A new family crisis is thereby generated which often mobilizes the family to become involved in the therapeutic process of understanding its contributions to the suicidal child's problems.

One of the first tasks of psychiatric hospital treatment of suicidal children is to foster a therapeutic alliance with the parents. This can be effected by explicitly interpreting the serious problems of the child and by directly stating that psychiatric hospitalization will be helpful to the child and to them. It is essential to evaluate the unique therapeutic needs of the parents and to offer assistance so that such treatment needs can be carried out. Many of the suicidal child inpatients experienced extremely conflicted family interactions, with physically and sexually abusive parents, depressed and suicidal parents, and psychotic parents. Because of these parental problems, many of the parents do not appreciate the stresses that overwhelmed their child and do not comprehend the child's needs for hospital treatment. Therefore, very active intervention with the parents is required in order to facilitate a therapeutic alliance with the child and parents. In fact, it is often necessary to conduct individual and/or couple treatment of the parents in order to ensure optimal treatment of the child.

In most situations, the anxiety of being away from the child provokes family participation in the child's treatment. Intensive work with the child's parents is indicated immediately to help them cope with the loss of the child from the home environment. In some cases, the separation distress is so great that the family cannot tolerate the child's hospitalization. Such parents are not able to develop a therapeutic alliance and insist on taking their child out of the hospital. This problem does not occur often, but when it does, and the child is acutely suicidal, legal commitment is indicated. In such circumstances, a court hearing is requested by the hospital psychiatrist. A judge hears the evidence for the child's need to be kept in the hospital. In addition, the parents present their reasons why the child should be discharged. Based on this evidence, the judge decides upon the hospital status of the child. In many states, preadolescents, too, have the right to request their discharge from the hospital. The process of requesting involuntary hospitalization by the hospital psychiatrist is the same in these cases as when parents request discharge of their child.

Child I: Benjamin, age 11 years, is an example of how an involuntary commitment helped to ensure his proper treatment. He was brought to the hospital by his school guidance counselor after Benjamin threatened to jump out a window in the corridor of the school. Benjamin's mother joined him in the hospital admitting office and reluctantly signed for his admission. She did not believe her son wanted to kill himself but was too frightened to refuse hospitalization. However, a week after the admission, she wanted to remove her son from the hospital.

While in the hospital, Benjamin acknowledged extensive thoughts about suicide, preoccupations with death, and intense depression. He had difficulty sleeping and concentrating, and withdrew from activities. He was afraid whenever his parents argued. Benjamin's father drank heavily, had recently lost his job, and stayed home all day. Benjamin's mother worked in order to provide the family with a stable income. Benjamin dated the onset of his sad feelings and suicidal preoccupations to the time his father lost his job.

Because of the intense family turmoil and Benjamin's serious depression and suicidal proclivity, the hospital psychiatrist considered it mandatory to retain Benjamin in the hospital on an involuntary basis. After hearing the history from the psychiatrist and the parents, and interviewing Benjamin, the judge decreed that Benjamin remain in the hospital.

One benefit of involuntary hospitalization is that it emphasizes to the child and the family that the child's suicidal behavior is a very serious condition and that the hospital staff is trying to protect the child from harm. This strategy demonstrates, in a concrete way, that the hospital can provide a structure in which intense fears, painful emotions, and life-threatening behaviors can be managed.

One of the major assets of psychiatric hospital treatment of suicidal children is that the hospital is a self-contained setting that allows the child to participate in organized activities of daily life. School, dining, recreation, and sleeping take place within the therapeutic milieu. The setting, therefore, provides a structure that supports adaptive behaviors and intervenes against maladaptive reactions. The hospital environment facilitates intensive observation of the child's responses in a variety of individual and group activities. Thus, the hospital is an excellent mileau in which to clarify diagnostic impressions and to monitor the effects of interventions. The diagnostic and therapeutic expertise of a number of professionals can be coordinated in the hospital setting. For example, in addition to the psychotherapist, the efforts of the clinical psychologist, neurologist, pediatric nurses, social workers, and recreational staff are some of the special services offered within the hospital setting.

Finally, the psychiatric hospital facilitates the detailed and repeated assessments of the child that are essential in planning long-term psychiatric care. Suggestions about the child's needs, living situation, and psychiatric treatment can be formulated on the basis of the psychiatric hospital diagnostic assessments and treatment responses of the child.

In summary, the specific tasks of psychiatric hospital treatment for suicidal children are to provide protection from and monitoring of the child's acute suicidal impulses. Other tasks of psychiatric inpatient treatment are utilized similarly for nonsuicidal children and suicidal children. These tasks focus on strengthening adaptive skills and diminishing maladaptive behaviors so that stability can be achieved to permit the child to function in a less intensive psychiatric treatment setting.

THE PSYCHIATRIC HOSPITAL THERAPISTS

Psychiatric hospital treatment requires that a team of professionals work together to coordinate a variety of treatment efforts. All professionals working with the child are therapists. Thus, a child may have a number of therapists with varied treatment responsibilities. Table 15-3 outlines the therapeutic functions of the different psychiatric inpatient unit therapists, who are from diverse professional disciplines.

The primary psychotherapist may be a child psychiatrist, a psychologist, or a social worker whose main tasks are to work psychotherapeutically with the child and family. If the primary psychotherapist is the child psychiatrist, medication, if indicated, is prescribed and monitored by this therapist. However, if a nonphysician is the primary psychotherapist, a child psychiatrist is included to recommend, prescribe, and monitor medication. Another role of the primary psychotherapist is to gather observational information from other staff members about the behaviors of the child. Exchange of information is effected

TABLE 15-3
Therapeutic functions of psychiatric hospital therapists

I. *Primary psychotherapist* (may be psychiatrist, psychologist, or social worker)
    1. Evaluate acute suicidal status
    2. Administer individual and family psychotherapy
    3. Synthesize observations of other hospital therapists
    4. Coordinate work of other hospital therapists
    5. Coordinate discharge planning
II. *Child psychiatrist*
    1. Evaluate acute suicidal status
    2. Prescribe and monitor medication
    3. Diagnose and treat acute medical problems
III. *Nurse*
    1. Monitor acute suicidal status
    2. Plan and foster the child's participation in activities of daily life
    3. Available for child's emotional crises
IV. *School personnel*
    1. Diagnose and treat academic problems
    2. Provide age-appropriate educational program
V. *Psychologist*
    1. Provide information about suicidal status
    2. Diagnose cognitive and emotional problems
VI. *Social worker*
    1. Help with family intervention
    2. Recommend discharge programs
VII. *Art, music, recreational therapists*
    1. Provide basis for expression of physical and creative activities

---

in multidisciplinary staff meetings. The synthesis of these observations determines planning for subsequent interventions.

Of primary concern is the suicidal status of the child. The child psychotherapist discusses suicidal tendencies and evaluates associated risk factors of the patient. Monitoring the intensity of depression, preoccupations with death, and family interactions is an essential additional task of the psychotherapist.

Other staff members carry out diagnostic and treatment goals that are associated with their respective professional disciplines. Thus, the schoolteachers plan and implement an educational program for the child. The nurses organize the child's daily activities of eating, sleeping, peer interactions, and community life. The psychologist administers a battery of psychological tests, particularly cognitive tests that are helpful in augmenting the diagnostic assessment of and treatment planning for the child. The art, music, and recreational professionals provide modalities for the child to express emotions and behaviors in personally creative ways.

All hospital staff are therapists who work intensively with every child. Psychiatric hospital care allows for a greater range of intervention modalities and more systematic observations of the child than outpatient treatment. It provides a hospital milieu with its large and diverse compliment of hospital staff. The staff, and especially the nurses, carry out interventions 24 hours a day. These therapists help regulate, structure, and normalize the child's life on the unit. Milieu treatment augments the individual, family, and group treatment.

PHASES OF PSYCHIATRIC HOSPITAL TREATMENT

Pfeffer (1977, 1979b) conceptualized a model of psychiatric hospital treatment for suicidal children that includes three phases: Of these, the working-through phase and the termination phase of inpatient treatment are conceptually similar to the same phases of psychiatric outpatient treatment; the initial phase is different. The goals of the phases of psychiatric hospital treatment are enumerated in Table 15-4, along with some interventions used.

THE INITIAL PHASE

The major differences between hospital treatment and outpatient treatment are that the suicidal child is separated from the home situation and that more extensive and intensive observations are possible in the hospital. During the initial phase of hospital treatment, attention must be given to the abilities of the child and family to separate from each other and to the ways in which the child adjusts to the hospital routine. Since many suicidal children require constant supervision when admitted to the hospital, the person who is always with the child can also help orient the child to the hospital setting. Concrete explanations of when and where activities take place and personal introductions to staff and patients help the child adjust to the hospital unit. Discussion with the child and parents about separating from each other is essential to easing the process of adjustment to the hospital unit.

Many suicidal children accept the need for hospital treatment easily, so that a therapeutic alliance can be readily established. However, for some children the therapeutic alliance develops only when the child becomes more adjusted to the hospital unit. Some children resist forming a therapeutic alliance when they sense that their parents are ambivalent about the hospital admission. Therefore, it is always essential to try to form a therapeutic alliance with the parents. In contrast, some children form a therapeutic alliance even if the parents are uncooperative with the hospital treatment.

The therapeutic alliance can be facilitated by conveying several significant ideas to the child and parents. Emphasis is placed on the

TABLE 15-4

Goals and some interventions of psychiatric hospital treatment of suicidal children

---

Initial phase

Goal I: Adjust to hospital routine
  Interventions:
  1. Discuss child's and parent's responses to separation from each other.
  2. Explain hospital program to child and parents
  3. Introduce child to peers and staff

Goal II: Develop therapeutic alliance
  Interventions:
  1. Interpret helping role of the hospital
  2. State that the therapist, the child, and the parents will work together to solve problems

Goal III: Protect the child from harm
  Interventions:
  1. Emphasize the seriousness of the child's suicidal tendencies
  2. Establish an agreement with the child to inform staff of suicidal urges or assaultive impulses
  3. Emphasize that suicidal behavior is a poor way of coping with problems; discuss alternatives
  4. Observe the child's behavior at all times

Working-through phase

Goal I: Decrease suicidal tendencies and underlying conflict
  Interventions:
  1. Discuss alternative solutions to problems
  2. Discuss child's unfulfilled wishes and outline acceptable compromise satisfactions

Goal II: Decrease depression
  Interventions:
  1. Talk with the child about many of the positive aspects of his or her situation
  2. Discuss how the child can develop new supportive relationships to replace lost ones
  3. Suggest ways to organize the day so that the child eats and sleeps regularly
  4. Encourage the child to participate in hospital activities.

Goal III: Enhance self-esteem
  Interventions:
  1. Compliment and reward child's accomplishments, skills, and appropriate autonomous behaviors
  2. Suggest ways in which the child can behave independently and successfully
  3. Support child's attempts to develop friendships
  4. Help the child to accept his or her limitations or handicaps

---

(continued)

TABLE 15-4
(*Continued*)

Goal IV: Modify aggressive responses
Interventions:
1. Define alternative ways of responding to frustrations
2. Talk with child about being able to accept disappointment and to plan other ways of obtaining satisfaction
3. Remind child that it is unacceptable for anyone to be injured by the child and vice versa
4. Isolate the child during episodes of uncontrollable anger and allow a quiet period for the child to calm himself or herself
5. Provide rewards when the child can control angry feelings
6. Discipline child for uncontrollable aggressive behaviors

Goal V: Enhance peer relationships
Interventions:
1. Support the child's participation in therapeutic group activities
2. Suggest ways to make friends and how to maintain friendships

Goal VI: Enhance school achievement
Interventions:
1. Reward appropriate classroom participation and academic success
2. Reward child's attempts to remediate learning problems
3. Provide school assignments that are of interest to the child
4. Provide help for the child to carry out independently chosen assignments
5. Use special education methods to decrease learning problems

Goal VII: Diagnose and treat neurophysiological disorder
Interventions:
1. Examine child, observe behavior, do an EEG
2. Use appropriate indicated medication

Goal VIII: Monitor responses to medication
Interventions:
1. Observe that child takes medication as indicated.
2. Observe child for signs of medication-induced decrease in symptoms
3. Observe child for adverse medication side effects

Termination phase

Goal I: Ameliorate child's suicidal tendencies
Interventions:
1. Talk with child about presence of suicidal feelings
2. Talk with the child about death preoccupations and depression
3. Teach child to be able to recognize early signs of sadness, thoughts about death, and suicide
4. Talk with child about telling someone if suicidal tendencies occur

---

(*continued*)

TABLE 15-4
(*Continued*)

Goal II: Evaluate responses to discharge from the hospital
  Interventions:
  1. Talk to the child about leaving the hospital, loss of hospital friends, and memories of hospitalization
  2. Talk to the child about going to a new living arrangement, whether it be return to home or a setting away from home
  3. Talk with child about need for continued treatment

---

seriousness of the child's suicidal behavior. Statements are made that the hospital staff can help the child and family gain relief from their problems. In addition, it is pointed out that suicidal symptoms of children are an indication of family distress. Discussion of the multiple contributions of stresses upon the child and family permits more direct communication and subsequent insight which will facilitate therapeutic changes. Furthermore, all initial attempts of the child and parents to participate in treatment are recognized and supported.

The initial phase of treatment is a critical time with regard to the child's acute suicidal symptomatology. By means of intensive observation and intervention by the nursing staff, individual work with the psychotherapist, participation in unit activities, and removal of the child from his or her stressful environmental situation, many of the child's suicidal symptoms disappear or diminish during this phase of treatment. Hospitalized suicidal children rapidly respond to the supportive hospital atmosphere. The hospital setting instills a message of hopefulness that many of the child's problems can be diminished or resolved.

Specific statements are made by the staff in their efforts to protect the child from self-inflicted injuries. The serious nature of suicidal behavior is discussed with the child. Emphasis is placed upon the idea that although suicidal behavior may be the child's way of coping with problems, it is a very poor method of decreasing problems and stress. The staff discuss with the child specific alternative methods to deal with the child's wishes and frustrations. Among the ways this can be accomplished is for the child and staff to develop a list of concrete ways that the child can handle stressful situations. In addition, an agreement can be established with the child so that he or she immediately informs the staff about any suicidal urges.

THE WORKING-THROUGH PHASE

During the working-through phase, the child increasingly demonstrates his or her characteristic behavioral and ego defensive styles. Because of the extensive capacity to coordinate observations on the inpatient unit, repetitive patterns of behavior can be observed and analyzed with the child. By means of discussion and immediate intervention within the milieu of the hospital unit, the child can be helped to decrease suicidal impulses. Staff discuss with the child ways of coping with stress in nonsuicidal ways. In addition, extensive discussions about the child's wishes and disappointments can help elucidate approaches that can be implemented to achieve compromise gratifications. For example, one 10-year-old girl was excessively frustrated that two other girls on the unit did not want to include her in some games. The girl told another child that she wanted to kill herself because she felt that other people thought she was a bad person. Staff intervened and spoke with the girl about developing other friendships and involving herself in activities with other children on the unit. In addition, the staff helped the girl to understand that she could not always be appreciated by everyone and that perhaps the other girls would include her in their activities at a future time.

Associated symptomatology of depression, low self-esteem, and aggressive feelings can be monitored and treated in the hospital setting. Because of the highly structured hospital environment, with the constant availability of staff, highly focused treatment approaches can be implemented to treat these problems.

Some specific interventions can be aimed to lessen a child's depressive state, allowing enough time fully to express his or her depressed and other feelings. Repeated discussion can occur about positive and optimistic aspects of the child's situation. For example, the child can be told that the family is very concerned about the child's well-being, if this is true. The child's achievements in school, with peers, and in activities can be recognized with appreciation. Areas of progress can be defined and hope generated that, with continued work, the child can improve his or her situation and the parents can improve their attitudes. The child's eating and sleeping patterns can be monitored and reorganized to decrease problems. Often depressed children feel the pressure of loss of important people in their lives and as a result, they feel hopeless and alone. Ample people are involved in the child's care in the hospital to help the child understand how he or she relates to others and how newly supportive relationships can be developed. These newly formed hospital relationships can serve as models to help the child overcome feelings of isolation and loss, and develop a more optimistic outlook on his or her abilities to develop new relationships.

One of the most important attributes of child psychiatric inpatient treatment is the potential to help children gain a better sense of self-esteem. Because all activities take place under the supervision of trained staff, the child's accomplishments, skills, and autonomous functioning can be observed and rewarded. The program can be organized to augment the child's strengths while also aiming to improve his or her weaknesses. For example, if a given activity is too difficult for a child, the activity program can be adjusted to include activities the child can participate in successfully. In addition, the hospital unit is an especially good setting to help a child develop more adequate peer relationships. Staff can be available to mediate interactions and to suggest ways a child can promote positive peer interactions. Furthermore, in the hospital, a child's inadequacies and deficits can be evaluated and interventions can be offered to help a child accept limitations and develop new or alternate ways of coping. Alternate routes of achieving success can be defined, and the child, with the assistance of the hospital staff, can practice carrying them out.

The psychiatric hospital unit is uniquely suited to help a child modify aggressive responses. Often uncontrolled aggressive behaviors occur in response to disappointments and frustrations which can be defined. Discussion with the child can focus on planning alternative ways of coping with these issues. Rewards can be offered whenever a child can control inappropriate aggressive responses. In addition, discipline can be carried out if a child shows uncontrollable aggressive behaviors. Finally, a child can be isolated from others during periods when aggressive responses are uncontrollable. This "time out" will provide the child with a chance to gain control of his or her behavior.

Because the milieu atmosphere fosters peer involvement, isolation experienced by many suicidal children can be diminished. Participation in small and large groups is available to the suicidal child. Discussion of peer problems such as aggressive interactions, shyness, and fears can be conducted within the context of group psychotherapy meetings as well as individual psychotherapy sessions. By means of these interventions, the suicidal child can be helped to develop a better sense of self-esteem and perception of his or her abilities to function autonomously with age mates.

Most child psychiatric inpatients have school problems that affect their abilities to learn easily. In the hospital, classroom participation and the child's efforts to decrease problems in learning are rewarded. Opportunities are provided to allow the child to choose class assignments that are of specific interest to the child. Special remedial education techniques are used to help a child compensate for specific learning problems.

In addition to the psychotherapeutic work carried out by the various therapists on the unit, diagnosis of neurophysiological disorders such as seizures can be made and appropriate interventions offered. Furthermore, by means of direct observation on the inpatient unit, treatment effects can be measured.

The capacity to coordinate psychopharmacological and psychotherapeutic interventions makes psychiatric hospital treatment the choice setting to evaluate children's complex symptomatology. For example, specific symptoms of depression can be observed, and change in these symptoms can be monitored during the course of psychotherapeutic and drug treatment. Furthermore, if medication is indicated, the child's cooperation in taking the medication can be evaluated and maintained. Problematic side effects can be documented and immediately treated. Therefore, when complex and multiple interventions are required, the psychiatric hospital setting can provide a place for maximal precision in treatment coordination.

In summary, during the working-through phase of psychiatric hospital treatment, the most intensive treatment occurs. Problems are diagnosed and specific interventions carried out. The working-through phase comes to an end when the goals of this phase are accomplished. However, acute psychiatric hospital care can accomplish only relatively limited goals. For example, during the working-through phase, the child's functioning is stabilized sufficiently so that acute suicidal behavior is not likely to occur. However, longer-term treatment is almost always needed to modify other symptoms and to strengthen ego functioning. This is done by providing social supports, affection, reinforcement of all desirable behaviors, and guidance for developing alternative methods of coping with stress.

THE TERMINATION PHASE

The termination phase begins once a plan for a long-term treatment is discussed. The child may express intense feelings of loss, abandonment, rejection, anger, and depression during this phase, in response to the impending plans for discharge from the hospital. Anxiety about the discharge and recurrence of many of the initial suicidal symptoms may be evident as regressive trends. Therefore, during this phase, careful clinical assessment of the child's suicidal status must be made by specifically asking the child about thoughts of wanting to hurt or kill himself or herself. Assessment of death preoccupations and degree of depression is necessary during this phase. If a child shows intense suicidal tendencies, extreme death preoccupations, or severe depression, discharge may have to be delayed until these problems are ameliorated. The possibility of long-term psychiatric hospitalization must be considered in such cases.

During the termination phase, the therapeutic work also focuses on discussion of posthospitalization treatment plans. The child's anxieties are discussed. Visits to the new treatment setting are arranged for the child and family. Discussions with the child focus on the hope that continued treatment will improve the child's situation. Furthermore, as a way of demonstrating to the child that while in the hospital, he or she formed meaningful relationships with staff and peers, the staff explicitly point out that they will miss the child. In addition, they help the child remember a variety of events that took place while hospitalized. In this way, memories are utilized to help the child overcome fears of losing the people that he or she befriended in the hospital.

Finally, feelings about returning home are explored with those children who can live with their families. In addition, discussion is encouraged about not returning to the family if a child requires long-term psychiatric hospitalization or residential treatment. These discussions are critical to aid a good initial adjustment in the next treatment setting.

CLINICAL EXAMPLES

The following examples illustrate the treatment process, the variety of behaviors, and the depth of pathology associated with suicidal behavior in psychiatrically hospitalized children.

Child II: Judy age 10 years, was severely depressed. Her family was available and involved with her. She was admitted after ingesting 16 of her mother's phenobarbital tablets. In the months before admission she had become increasingly depressed over the separation from her maternal grandmother, who had raised her since her birth. One month before admission, Judy threatened to jump out the window. She was living with her father, an elderly man, and her mother, who had a seizure disorder.

Judy was a verbal, very depressed girl who wanted to be admitted so that she could be protected from her father, who had been beating her with a belt when she refused to cooperate at home. She said she took the pills because she felt hopeless about returning to her grandmother. She wanted her parents to know how sad she felt. She was angry at her mother for not protecting her. Hospitalization was indicated to protect her from self-inflicted and parental injury.

Her parents were very worried but surprised about her suicidal actions. They felt helpless in handling Judy's argumentative, defiant behavior. As an early attempt to foster a therapeutic alliance, it was pointed out to the parents that children who attempt to harm themselves are asking for help and that the parents, too, need assistance with their current worries. Her therapist emphasized that Judy and her parents could be helped. Judy's parents agreed to meet once a week with her therapist.

During the initial phase of hospitalization, Judy showed dissatisfaction with whatever was done for her. She cried a lot and wanted to leave the hospital. She argued in an attempt to have her way. She spoke about her sad parents, who could not live without her at home to make them happy. Her therapist reminded Judy that she could be helped in the hospital and that her parents wanted her to feel better. However, her father appeared several days after admission, demanding Judy's release from the hospital. Judy's mother had refused to come to the hospital because she was depressed and unable to sleep, and had an increased number of seizures since Judy was away from home. Judy realized that her parents were distressed by the separation from them.

Her father was told that he could not take Judy out of the hospital because she was very depressed and might harm herself, and that the hospital would take court actions to keep her if necessary. Her father agreed to allow her to stay. He spoke about his guilt for severely beating and punishing her as he acknowledged being unable to cope with Judy's anger and impulsive behavior. He was overwhelmed by the responsibility of caring for both Judy and her mother and appreciated the staff's desire to help his family. He agreed with the suggestion that he and his wife meet with the therapist regularly.

Judy continued to cry and demand release. She wanted to take care of her mother because she worried that her mother would have a seizure. Although Judy expressed an intense desire to go home, she told the story of a girl who was raped and beaten by a father. Memories of her father's severe discipline were discussed. Judy was told that her father was adequately taking care of her mother. Soon, Judy calmed down and became more involved in her treatment.

During the working-through phase of hospitalization, Judy continued to provoke and disobey the staff. She stated, for example, that they were not her mother so they could not tell her what to do. These responses reflected Judy's intense conflicts with her mother. In order to intensify positive feelings toward her therapist and staff, she was told that the staff welcomed her and enjoyed the contributions she made to the unit. However, there were unit rules which had to be obeyed. It became evident that Judy looked forward to her therapy sessions, and she brought gifts to her therapist of pictures she had drawn. However, when frustrated by lack of immediate verbal response from her therapist, Judy became enraged. This reaction was similar to her behavior at home. Suicidal ideas were rarely expressed, although she sometimes talked about people dying in an accident.

At this point in the treatment, when Judy made demands to leave the hospital, her parents supported the staff's plan for further hospitalization. Concrete ways of coping with Judy's demands were discussed with her parents. They were advised to set limits and to carry them out. Her father realized that beating her was detrimental. Furthermore, since Judy missed her grandmother, the family initiated letters to the grandmother, who then began to correspond with Judy. Soon Judy acknowledged feeling better and more hopeful. She identified with her therapist and frequently liked to hold her therapist's pocketbook and tell other children that it was hers. She spoke about how angry she felt that her mother could not take care of her and she spoke about worries that her grandmother would die. Her needs for a nurturing adult were quite apparent in the relationship with her therapist.

During the termination phase of treatment, discharge plans were arranged. Since her family could recognize the seriousness of Judy's distress and understood many of the causes of her suicidal behavior, a sense of hope developed. Her parents understood that Judy's frustrations arose from loneliness and loss of her grandmother. They appreciated Judy's intense wishes to be nurtured. Her father realized that beating Judy only increased her difficulties. Her parents acknowledged the need for help, and Judy's father felt confident about arranging continued psychotherapy. Discharge was planned, with a woman therapist seeing Judy at the outpatient clinic.

Judy showed increased defiance and demands on the ward as time for discharge neared. She felt sad about leaving and arranged to write to the staff and her therapist. She promised to visit occasionally. She was happy she could return to her family and was overjoyed to hear that her grandmother would visit in the summer. All staff supported her desire to maintain contact with them, emphasizing that they would be available at any time. They told her that they would miss her and that they would always remember her.

Child III: Martin, age 7 years, had diagnoses of a severe conduct disorder and a specific developmental disorder. His family was minimally involved in his treatment. He threatened to jump off the roof at school just before his hospital admission. Threats to run away and to kill himself began several months before admission and at the time his brother was born. Martin had a severe learning disability, which made him frustrated, angry, and humiliated. His parents ignored this and punished him harshly for his difficulties at school. He felt no one loved him and no one wanted to protect him from the anxiety and humiliation of school. As a result, he often thought that he would jump off the roof.

Martin lived with his mother, stepfather, and two younger siblings. His stepfather, who was rarely home, often provoked arguments with his mother. Martin's mother was a quiet, depressed, and passive person. She denied the severity of her son's problems as well as her own family problems. Martin was frightened of punishment from his stepfather.

During the initial phase, Martin was verbal and bright, and complained that children at home did not like him and that his teacher in his school was mean to him. He told the story of a boy he knew who died by jumping off a roof because his mother would not buy him anything. In the hospital, Martin stayed by himself, appeared depressed, and was frightened of other children. When angered, Martin withdrew and seldom spoke to others. He was delighted to see his therapist and felt comforted in having a friendly adult who listened to him. Discussion focused on why he felt so bad about himself and how he could work on improving peer interactions. His therapy sessions had a positive effect on his interactions in the unit. Martin became more verbal and animated, and he even initiated fights with other children whom he felt did not like him. However, at times, he told his therapist that he wanted to go home because the other children did not like him. When he said this he also warned of his past threat to jump off the roof. His wishes to leave the hospital were interpreted as resulting from his fears not only of developing close relationships but of losing these relationships.

During the working-through phase, he spoke openly about feelings of being a victim of other children and of being frightened. He talked about killing himself whenever he did not get his way. It was upsetting to him that his mother came to see his therapist. Interpretations were made to him that his sense of victimization, anger, and suicidal ideas were related to his frustrations that his mother was not intensely involved in his care. He missed her but felt enraged that she did not want to be with him.

As his relationship to his therapist intensified, he asked her to help him learn to read. As a result, his sessions were spent reading to each other. Unlike Martin's mother, his therapist showed great interest in Martin's academic progress. Soon his schoolwork improved and he became competitive academically with other children. Fights with other children decreased. Eventually, plans for discharge home were considered, but he reminded his therapist about the roof. Confirmation of his fears about returning home were obtained by his allusions in his play to secrets and family problems that he could not openly talk about. The staff felt that he needed a comprehensive day program with intensive psychotherapy and a special education class for his learning disabilities. Although his mother showed increased awareness of his needs, his family could not be relied on to be sufficiently sensitive to his anxieties. It was necessary to provide a network of concerned adults who would respond immediately if his suicidal thinking returned. A day treatment program at the nearby state children's hospital accepted him.

During the termination phase, Martin was happy about leaving the hospital, although he was anxious about having a new therapist. He was afraid that a new therapist would not understand his feelings and needs. This response was related to his frustrations with his mother. Talking about this with the staff helped him realize that he would be protected and have other staff who would appreciate him. His transition to the day treatment program was aided by his knowledge that some of his hospital friends were also attending that program. At this time, no suicidal ideas were expressed, and he was hopeful about the future. His family was pleased that he would return home.

Child IV: Allen was an 11-year-old schizophrenic boy with an unavailable family. He was referred to the hospital by his psychiatric clinic therapist because of auditory and visual hallucinations, and delusions about a man who intended to kill Allen. Allen expressed a desire to join a dead friend in heaven so that he would no longer be frightened. Several months before hospitalization, Allen began to hear voices after seeing his friend die by falling off a roof. The voices commanded Allen to kill himself with a knife, with poison, or by jumping through a window. He reported visual hallucinations of the dead boy and of a man in a black coat sharpening a knife.

Allen lived with his mother and three siblings. His mother was a depressed, isolated woman, who had little insight into Allen's distress. She was separated from her husband, who was a violent alcoholic man. Allen's father left the house after he slashed the mother's arms with a knife. Allen feared that his father might also attempt to kill him. It was obvious that his family did not have the capacity to understand and protect Allen from suicide attempts.

Allen was a husky boy who exhibited slow movement and infrequent eye contact. At the time of his admission, he cooperated with the ward staff but became tearful at the moment of separation from his mother. His mother, although cooperative, denied Allen's serious condition. She was surprised that he needed hospitalization.

Allen quickly adjusted to the ward. He felt comfortable in the presence of helping adults, and soon he denied having hallucinations. However, he spoke of his intent to kill himself when he returned home. His therapist explained to his mother that Allen needed the hospital for his safety since he heard the voices and he had difficulty in not obeying their commands. His mother was told that until the hallucinations could be diminished, Allen was a high risk for suicide. Since his mother did not understand the seriousness of her son's difficulties, her cooperation in his treatment was marginal. She missed therapy appointments and often came late to visit Allen.

During the working-through phase Allen became more aggressive with his peers, threatened to harm them, and initiated fights. His behavior was closely monitored and he was removed from situations when his anger became too intense. He told the nurses that there were three of him: the double who caused him to fight, the angel who helped him to cooperate, and himself, who was good at mealtime. He appreciated the limits that were set for him by the staff. He was started on chlorpromazine to treat his threatening delusions and hallucinations, and poor impulse control.

Allen remarked to his therapist that he liked to beat up little children but did not know why. His therapist spoke with him about other ways of handling his aggressive feelings. Allen believed that he might be killed, especially by the man in the black coat. His fear was associated with his guilt about his own aggressive behavior. Though his interactions with staff and children provided some pleasure and comfort, he was filled with terror; yet being alone was equally frightening, and he became tormented by images of people who sought to kill him. Therefore, staff made efforts to be with him and not leave him alone. He spoke of killing himself if he had to eat alone. His meals were closely monitored and a staff member was available to speak with him while he ate. It was observed that he maintained contact by his aggressive behavior, which protected him from feelings of isolation. He looked forward to meeting with his therapist and was able to establish a trusting relationship. He liked to draw and tell stories that revealed his terror of aggressive impulses. His play depicted animals killing each other and dead animals being eaten. By allowing Allen to express his feelings, Allen's therapist helped Allen realize that ways of solving problems could be developed.

A turning point occurred with his mother when she began to express concern about his hallucinations. She inquired about them instead of denying them. Allen appreciated his mother's concern. Soon he reported relief from the disturbing voices. He began to feel very relaxed and self-confident. In addition, he was able to delay eruptions of anger. The frequency of fights on the unit decreased. His mother worried appropriately that she could not protect him sufficiently at home because he might harm himself. Since it was apparent that Allen needed a continued protective hospital environment, plans for long-term hospitalization were considered.

During the termination phase, Allen became anxious and bothered by a man's voice telling him to kill himself. Plans were arranged for him to attend a nearby long-term hospital. He was afraid of leaving the protection of the hospital and meeting strangers in another hospital. Allen initiated fights with other children and attempted to run away from the unit. As a result, he had to be observed constantly. The staff spoke with him about his worries about going to a new hospital and about his sadness at leaving his friends here. His mother, too, worried about the other hospital. One day she brought "magic water" to spray Allen with so he would get better. Upon transfer to the state hospital, Allen was tearful but reacted warmly to the acceptance and affection expressed by the staff and other children.

The final example provides a longitudinal view of a child who was chronically suicidal. This example illustrates the involvement of the child with outpatient therapy, the use of acute psychiatric hospitalization, and the demonstrated need for long-term residential treatment. It also illustrates the principle that it is essential to work with the parents.

Child V: Alex, a 10-year-old, was admitted to the psychiatric hospital unit because of intermittent suicidal ideas over a 2-year period; acute suicidal threats; increased feelings of sadness, hopelessness, and social isolation; irritability; and temper tantrums. The exacerbation of his chronic difficulties began after return from camp, where he experienced severe homesickness. Once home, Alex was argumentative with his mother. Alex hurled objects around the home and threw the contents of his closets onto the floor. His adjustment to a new junior high school was problematic. He complained that his teachers did not like him and that children teased him and provoked physical fights with him. Six weeks before admission to the hospital, Alex complained that he wanted to die and thought of jumping off the building or of stabbing himself. Three weeks before admission, he took a large, sharp kitchen knife and expressed the intent to plunge it into his chest, but instead he stabbed a sofa pillow. During the 6 weeks before admission, he repeatedly banged his head against the wall and on more than one occasion stood at a window several stories above the ground and threatened to jump.

His parents were divorced when Alex was 4 years old, and his father stopped having contact with him when he was 7. When Alex was 8, he spoke about wishing to die and once attempted to walk in front of a moving car when with his mother. He told his mother, who had successfully restrained him, that he intended to kill himself. His mother immediately arranged an emergency psychiatric consultation, which revealed that Alex had an intensely dependent relationship with his mother. He had difficulty tolerating frustration and believed that he had to protect himself from an excessively dangerous world. He experienced intense guilt and bad feelings about himself.

Outpatient psychiatric treatment included six group sessions with children whose parents were divorced. It was believed that Alex could gain a better perspective about children's problems when their parents divorce. His mother was seen individually also. The aim of his mother's treatment was to encourage her to develop a social life and to help Alex to be more independent. Attempts were made to reintroduce Alex's father to him but his father could not be found. When the group treatment terminated, Alex's functioning had improved. He began to attend Cub Scouts and formed a good relationship with the leader of the Scout troup. In addition, Alex's mother had become more confident in her role as a mother.

Nine months later Alex returned to therapy because of increased anxiety and sadness. He was admitted to the clinic for individual psychotherapy. He held the belief that he was adopted and that his mother lied about his real parents. Discussion focused on conflicts with his mother and his intense wishes to have a better home life. Within 3 months some of his difficulties with peers, sadness, and suicidal ideation diminished. Allen liked his therapist. However, treatment was interrupted when he started summer camp. During the summer, Alex continued to feel sad and was teased by peers at camp. He called home nightly and begged his mother to take him home. He wanted to see his therapist again. When he returned home from camp, Alex felt angry at his mother for abandoning him at camp. He was very sad and preoccupied with gloomy aspects about life. He complained that he had no friends and often woke up with bad dreams. He wanted to die. He returned to his therapist, who made a diagnosis of major depressive disorder and a recommendation for psychiatric hospitalization.

On admission to the hospital, Alex said that he wanted to come to the hospital so that he "could feel better and have less problems with classmates." He was sad, worried, and tearful, and picked at his clothes and hands. He felt it would be better if he died because he had little hope of his future improvement. He thought his mother was very demanding. He said that he shared many worries with his mother such as a fear that he would be kidnapped if he walked alone to his friend's house. When asked about being teased by peers, he became anxious and refused to discuss this.

The separation imposed during hospitalization was initially difficult for Alex and his mother. Alex worried that his mother would not be able to handle things on her own and that she might have a nervous breakdown. He felt he was in prison and virtually described fantasies of breaking out only to be pursued by the hospital guards, who would kill and dismember him. When he described these fantasies, he appeared emotionally detached from his therapist. While describing violent fantasies, he often ignored the verbal interventions made by his therapist.

Following the initial few sessions, he became increasingly reluctant to describe his thoughts and stated that they were too personal and that they were no one's business. He vehemently stated that he would never inform the staff of suicidal thoughts because his passes home would be canceled. However, he reminded his therapist: "I really do think about dying just about all the time."

In the hospital unit, he quickly became scapegoated by peers. He was particularly bullied and teased by older, more aggressive children on the unit. However, he related in a very provocative manner and insulted other children.

He was teased because he related in a childish way. When angered, Alex had difficulty controlling his temper and acted out by throwing property or striking other people. As a result, Alex was often removed from peer activities, and lengthy discussions with staff were organized. In addition, he was started on medication. Imipramine was used to treat his severe depression.

During individual psychotherapy sessions, violent play themes were expressed. When Alex felt stressed he had difficulty maintaining control. He showed regressive behavior by speaking in a whining voice or by throwing toys. He avoided conversation with his therapist but conveyed worries through play with puppets. His therapist respected the distance Alex created and did not intrude on his play. For example, he told the story of the son who disemboweled his mother and other adults. The son felt guilty and then committed suicide by running in front of a speeding truck. He elaborated upon how cruel the mother was to the son. Thus, by means of play, Alex was able to reveal the intense conflicts he had with his mother.

Alex's behavior on the unit showed improvement after 2 months. His peer relationships were less turbulent, although when anxious he provoked others into bullying or teasing him. He continued to be a suicidal risk especially when he was angry. Alex required long-term residential treatment to protect him and to help him develop better ego controls. Alex was very anxious about the anticipated plan of transfer to a residential treatment center and expressed wishes to remain in the hospital forever. He even expressed the desire not to grow up and to be taken care of forever.

Another theme that emerged in his therapy was his disappointment that his father had abandoned him. Alex spoke about his mistrust of men. He stated that it would be better if he were a girl. He thought women were stronger and more powerful than men. After seeing the movie *Tootsie* he asked his therapist if people would like him better if he wore women's clothing. Alex continued to have suicidal ideas. He spoke about hopeless feelings and expressed fears that he would always be in a mental hospital. The suicidal ideas coincided with periods of emotional stress, especially in relation to passes with his mother or confrontations with children on the unit. However, he made no suicidal threats or attempts on the unit.

Alex's mother met with Alex's therapist and spoke of a significant conflict she had between a wish to remain very close to her son versus a desire to gain distance from him. She acknowledged feeling dependent on her son. Her close relationship with him gave her a feeling of safety and fulfillment. As a result of her regular meetings with Alex's therapist, his mother decided to enter her own outpatient psychotherapy.

During his fourth month in the hospital, Alex was accepted for residential treatment. He felt anxious about leaving the unit and demonstrated variable interactions with others. At times he was appropriate, while at other times he was more regressed. However, by this time there was no evidence of suicidal behavior or ideas. Alex realized that he had been helped in the hospital and that he needed more treatment. He began to understand his difficulties with peers and to realize that he provoked problems. At the time of his discharge, Alex looked forward to beginning at the new residential treatment center. He wished to remain in contact with the hospital staff and promised to call or write to them. He no longer was suicidal but acknowledged that he often felt sad.

SUMMARY

The phases, goals, and interventions of psychiatric hospital treatment of suicidal children have been discussed in this chapter. These treatment phases and goals are similar to those of psychiatric outpatient treatment of suicidal children. During the initial phase, a critical goal is to protect the child from suicidal tendencies and to help the child adapt to separation from the family. The main task of the working-through phase is to analyze the child's conscious and unconscious reactions. A variety of treatments that include individual, family, and group psychotherapy; medication; and educational approaches are provided during this phase. The termination phase includes an extensive reassessment of the child's suicidal tendencies and discussion about leaving the hospital and entering a new treatment setting. Throughout all phases of treatment, the child's suicidal tendencies are carefully monitored while his or her underlying problems are thoroughly investigated and treated.

The goals of psychiatric hospitalization are based on elimination or reduction of the child's suicidal tendencies and are attained by a variety of simultaneous treatment modalities. In addition, hospitalization results in the removal of the child from the previously stressful environmental situation; another important factor in decreasing the child's suicidal tendencies. Finally, several clinical examples have illustrated the variety of psychopathologies of suicidal child psychiatric inpatients and the interventions utilized.

CHAPTER SIXTEEN

ADJUNCTIVE TREATMENT MODALITIES FOR SUICIDAL CHILDREN

"I think that whenever children be born that are not wanted they should be killed directly before their souls come to 'em, and not allowed to grow big and walk about!" —Thomas Hardy, *Jude the Obscure*

The treatment modalities discussed in this chapter are considered adjunctive treatment modalities because they should be used in combination with individual psychotherapy of the child. These adjunctive treatment modalities are used to bolster the child's intrapsychic functioning by providing a variety of additional therapeutic influences.

As described in previous chapters, the factors that enhance risk for childhood suicidal behavior are numerous. They include variables associated with the family and the neurophysiological, intrapsychic, and environmental spheres of the child's life. Because of the complex interrelationships of these variables, the treatment of suicidal children requires a variety of intervention modalities that are utilized simultaneously and at different intervals during the period of time the child requires treatment.

Individual psychotherapy, on either an outpatient or inpatient basis, should be considered the core of treatment of the suicidal child. The principles of such treatment have been discussed in the previous two chapters.

Figure 16-1 depicts the variety of treatment modalities that are often necessary for suicidal children. Figure 16-1 depicts the individual psychotherapy of the child as the central form of treatment. The adjunctive treatments are used to support the work of the child's psychotherapy by modifying the child's perceptions of, and actual experiences within, his or her social sphere. Therefore, modifications in the child's school and family atmosphere may be fostered by specifically focused measures. The child's perceptions of and responses to his or her environmental experiences may be modified by cognitive therapy techniques, psychopharmacotherapy, and group therapy. Characteristic

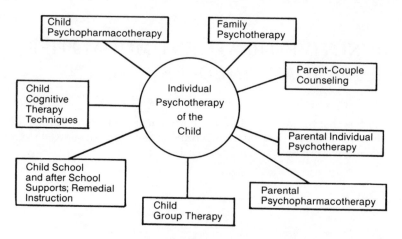

FIGURE 16-1
Treatment modalities for suicidal children.

features of these modalities of treatment are outlined in this chapter.

There are two principal groupings of adjunctive treatment modalities. First are those adjunctive treatments that are aimed primarily at the child's environmental support system and at the child's perceptions of himself or herself and others. Second are those adjunctive measures that effect change in the child's physiological functioning. These two groupings of adjunctive treatment modalities are shown in Table 16-1.

Some of the adjunctive treatments have several key aims. For example, family psychotherapy and group therapy may serve not only to enhance family and peer functioning as an environmental support system but also to clarify the child's perceptions of other people and the child's relationships with them. In some cases, all of these interventions are applied simultaneously. In other cases, several of these ad-

TABLE 16-1
Groupings of adjunctive treatments of suicidal children

Environmental support system and self-perception	Physiological therapy
1. Family psychotherapy	1. Child psychopharmacotherapy
2. Parent–couple counseling	2. Medical treatments for physical disorders (e.g., nutritional and orthopedic; toxic effects of drug ingestion)
3. Parental individual psychotherapy	
4. Parental psychopharmacotherapy	
5. School supports	
6. Child group therapy	
7. Child cognitive therapy	

junctive treatments may be involved during certain phases of the child's treatment. For example, family conflicts may be so great that family psychotherapy is used along with individual psychotherapy of the child. In addition, it may be necessary specifically to work with the parents in couple counseling sessions to clarify and resolve spouse conflicts. Furthermore, a parent may be so distressed that individual psychotherapy and/or psychopharmacological intervention may be essential from the start of the child's treatment.

Adjunctive treatments of the child may be used simultaneously also. For example, a schizophrenic suicidal child may require medication as well as special school instruction. These types of adjunctive treatment address the child's specific deficits in ego functioning.

It must be kept in mind that systematic research regarding the use of specific types of treatment modalities and the results of treatment of suicidal children has been meager. Hence, much of what is discussed here was derived from my observations and treatment efforts with suicidal and nonsuicidal children. The ideas put forth can be considered to be hypotheses that can be used to develop systematic studies of treatment of suicidal children. Whenever possible, this chapter presents information from systematic studies of treatment.

ENVIRONMENTAL SUPPORT

The suicidal child reacts to environmental stress with self-negating feelings. The slightest admonition, failure in performance, or social challenge may precipitate a devastating emotional reaction that could result in suicidal behavior. Prevention of such responses must be built into the treatment of every suicidal child. One means of decreasing a child's suicidal tendencies is to define a group of supportive people who are available to the child in every sphere of his or her activities. A therapeutic team should be created to include school personnel, family members, peers, and other emotionally important people. These people can carry out a number of tasks that will help to support the child emotionally, and thus decrease suicidal risk. Table 16-2 presents the functions of the environmental support team.

Among the most important tasks of the therapeutic team is the recognition of signs of impending suicidal behavior. In addition, the members of the team should have direct access to the child's therapist, who can advise on the indicated interventions. Finally, the team constitutes a network of concerned individuals with whom the child can interact. Thus, childhood suicidal behavior is an important issue for a large group of people.

TABLE 16-2
Functions of the environmental support team

1. Recognize suicidal tendencies in children.
2. Refer suicidal children to mental health professionals: mental health clinics, private therapists, psychiatric and pediatric emergency rooms.
3. Augment the treatment of suicidal children by providing people to interact with the suicidal child in the setting of daily activities.
4. Discuss with the child's therapist the child's behavior, emotions, and interactions with other people.
5. Carry out the therapist's suggestions about how to interact with the suicidal child.
6. Communicate with the child's parents about how the child is functioning in activities.

FAMILY THERAPY

In previous chapters many family factors that increase childhood suicidal risk have been discussed. Among these are the interactions within the entire family system, parent–child interactions, and parental psychopathology. Adjunctive family therapy focuses primarily on reducing family conflict and stress so that the family atmosphere becomes more conducive to the appropriate development of the child. This is essential for the child's successful coping with suicidal proclivities and the underlying conflicts. The goals of adjunctive family interventions are delineated in Table 16-3.

The primary therapeutic tasks of adjunctive family therapy are to guide the parents toward working together in their role as parents. In their role as parents, they must come to appreciate the seriousness of the child's suicidal tendencies and the need for effective interventions. The parents can learn how to handle their conflicts so as not to interfere

TABLE 16-3
Goals for family adjunctive treatments

1. Establish empathic relationships between family members.
2. Open avenues for communication between parent and child.
3. Plan alternative ways of dealing with disagreements between parent and child.
4. Develop awareness of feelings, ideas, and needs of others.
5. Achieve a tolerance for change while maintaining a consistently stable family atmosphere.
6. Promote individual autonomous functioning.
7. Decrease tendencies for impulsive and severely aggressive behaviors in both parents and child.
8. Diminish fears of separation between parents and child.

with their work in helping their child overcome his or her state of despair and hopelessness.

Another task of adjunctive family therapy is to define and remediate marital conflicts that may detract from the parents' ability to carry out adequate parenting responsibilities. A third goal of adjunctive family intervention is to reduce inappropriate parental behaviors and to treat severe parental psychiatric disturbances that may affect the child's suicidal proclivities.

A variety of adjunctive family treatments may be enlisted to accomplish these tasks, which may ultimately achieve the goals of reorienting the entire family atmosphere. Family psychotherapy includes all family members who are intimately involved with the child. Grandparents, aunts, uncles, cousins, and siblings may be helpful for defining problems and introducing approaches that can achieve resolution of conflicts in nonsuicidal ways. All of these family members should attend family sessions during the initial family evaluation and treatment planning. If the problems of a given family member are too severe or if the marital conflicts are too overwhelming, individual psychotherapy, psychopharmacotherapy, and/or parental–couple counseling may need to be added. These additional treatments make it possible to focus more exclusively on certain problem areas that are not easily approached within the context of the family psychotherapy. For example, a seriously depressed parent may require individual psychotherapy and antidepressant medication in order to function appropriately in his or her role as a parent, a spouse, and a family member. By providing specific therapy for this family member, his or her functioning within the context of the family system can be improved. The beneficial effects of such interventions for the suicidal child may be to free the child of the burden of taking care of the emotionally impaired parent. It may also strengthen the parent's ability to nurture the child appropriately. Thus, certain types of family stress, once defined, may be alleviated by specific interventions.

THE SCHOOL PROFESSIONAL

Other supports for the child may be provided within the school setting. Educational programs geared to teach children how to recognize signs of impending suicidal behavior may be helpful in preventing suicidal behavior. Educating children to inform teachers, guidance counselors, principals, school psychologists, or other people working in the school about their suicidal tendencies may help diffuse a child's suicidal crisis. Educating children to recognize distressing and depressive reactions of their peers and seek help from appropriate adults may help prevent suicidal behavior.

It is important to educate school personnel about recognizing and working with suicidal children. Hickler (Mack & Hickler, 1981), a teacher who is experienced in working with suicidal children and who is involved in suicide prevention programs in schools, provided a teacher's perspective on this issue. She noted:

> Teachers have their limitations. They may be frightened of emotional crisis. They may mistake what they are hearing. They may lack the personal insight and training that illuminate for psychologists, not only the meaning of confidences young people offer, but, perhaps even more important, their own blind spots and denials. Teachers are not professional psychologists. They need to know when to turn to experts. There is a distinct line between what the counseling profession offers and what educators can do to prevent suicide. (p. 255)

Therefore, the support system that includes school personnel must be encouraged to form active relationships with mental health professionals. The liaison system between school personnel and mental health professionals may be useful in defining the abilities and limitations of school professionals in their therapeutic work with suicidal children.

Another contribution of the person working in the school is his or her immediate availability within the school setting to talk with a youngster who may be distressed and suicidal. In this way, an external support for the child is provided within the school setting. In addition, the school personnel may be among the first observers to recognize signs and symptoms of depression and suicidal tendencies in children. As a result, persons working in the school may constitute the most important referral source for suicidal children for psychiatric evaluation and treatment. In this role, school personnel have to work closely with parents in order to help them obtain the appropriate help for their child.

A summary of the complex functions of school personnel in work regarding suicidal tendencies of children is provided in Table 16-4. This list of functions for school personnel may also be applied to functions of other people within the community who are involved in work with children. Therefore, this list of functions may also apply to recreational therapists, policemen, clergymen, pediatricians, and camp counselors. The most important function is to recognize potentially suicidal children and refer them to appropriate mental health professionals for comprehensive assessment of psychiatric disorder and suicidal risk.

GROUP PSYCHOTHERAPY

Another form of environmental support for suicidal children is that obtained from peer interactions. One vehicle for developing peer interactions is group psychotherapy. However, there are no reports of group

TABLE 16-4
Functions of school personnel who work with suicidal children

---

1. Recognize signs and symptoms of depression and suicidal risk in children. Requires teamwork between teachers, school psychologist, guidance counselor, principal, and others working in the school.
2. Refer suicidal children for comprehensive psychiatric evaluation as promptly as possible.
3. Help parents follow through in obtaining psychiatric intervention for their suicidal child.
4. Maintain therapeutic liaison work with mental health professionals regarding suicidal children who may be attending the school.
5. Provide a support system within the school that allows children to speak about distressing feelings and suicidal tendencies.
6. Educate children to recognize suicidal tendencies in themselves and peers.
7. Educate parents to recognize childhood suicidal risk and to appreciate the need for psychiatric intervention.
8. Educate children about alternative methods of coping with stress.
9. Educate children about treatment opportunities for their feelings of sadness, hopelessness, and worthlessness, and their suicidal impulses.

---

psychotherapy of suicidal children. Nevertheless, group psychotherapy participation may have some unique attributes that are not provided by other modalities of treatment. Some of these attributes are listed in Table 16-5.

Essentially, group psychotherapy is a structured format that brings peers together to discuss problems, interact, and experience the presence of agemates. During group psychotherapy the main focus is on analyzing the conscious and unconscious feelings, personality characteristics, and behaviors of the participants. Therefore, a major task of group psychotherapy is to help a child apply the insights gained in the group to development of healthy relationships with peers in the child's community. As a result, group psychotherapy may decrease a child's feelings of loneliness and isolation. It functions as an adjunctive treatment modality to enhance the child's social support system and to develop more appropriate understanding of himself or herself and others.

PSYCHOPHARMACOLOGICAL INTERVENTIONS

A variety of medical interventions may be needed with suicidal children. Such interventions may include the acute treatment of injuries sustained because of suicidal behavior. Another may be the treatment of associated physical illness that may diminish a child's capacity to cope with stress. Such interventions are not the focus of discussion in

TABLE 16-5
Tasks of group therapy of suicidal children

---

1. Decrease loneliness and isolation.
2. Understand how peers perceive the suicidal child.
3. Express perceptions of self to peers.
4. Explore one's perceptions of peers.
5. Discuss with peers age-appropriate values and methods of coping with stress and conflict.
6. Provide a forum for sharing common experiences.
7. Enhance relationships with peers in the community who are not members of the psychotherapy group.

---

this section. However, they must be kept in mind as possible adjunctive treatments of suicidal children, when indicated.

A variety of psychotropic medications may be indicated to treat suicidal children. The choice of medication depends upon the symptoms and psychiatric diagnosis of the child. For example, a suicidal child with an attention deficit disorder may require a stimulant drug, a suicidal schizophrenic child may need a major tranquilizer, and a suicidal child with a major depressive disorder may require antidepressant medication. In the treatment of suicidal children, medication utilized in conjunction with appropriate psychotherapy has the most beneficial results.

Since depression is a specific risk factor for suicidal behavior in children, this section focuses primarily on treatment utilizing antidepressant medication. For more than a decade there have been many studies evaluating the efficacy of imipramine for depression in children (Frommer, 1968; Kuhn & Kuhn, 1972; Puig-Antich, Blau, Marx, Greenhill, & Chambers, 1978; Puig-Antich & Weston, 1983). Before this, imipramine had its widest use in children for the control of enuresis, school refusal, and attention deficit disorder. Early studies of imipramine for childhood depression could not be considered conclusive because of a variety of research methodological deficits such as lack of adequate controls, lack of systematic techniques to establish the child's diagnosis, lack of specificity of the symptoms targeted for treatment, and variability of dose and duration of the medication. However, in recent years, more precise methodological studies have been developed.

One of the most important studies of imipramine for the treatment of childhood depression has been conducted by Puig-Antich and his colleagues. Two simultaneous studies have recently been completed on the same sample of children (Puig-Antich & Weston, 1983). One of these studies utilized 30 depressed children who participated in a 5-week double-blind, placebo-controlled study of imipramine used in doses up to 5 mg/kg/day. Imipramine was given in daily doses that were increased every third day from 0 to 1.5 to 3.0 to 4.0 to 5.0 mg/kg/ day. Drug side effects noted in electrocardiograms and blood pressure readings were evaluated before each dose increase. The drug was either not increased or was slightly decreased if side effects occurred. Limits for safety determined by the electrocardiagram readings included a resting heart rate greater than 130 beats per minute, a PR interval no greater than 0.18 sec, or a QRS no greater than 130% of baseline. Systolic blood pressure greater than 145 mm Hg and diastolic blood pressure greater than 95 mm Hg were upper-range levels of safety.

The results of this double-blind study showed a 60% response rate for the children receiving placebo and a 60% response rate for the children on imipramine. Thus, it appeared that imipramine was not more efficacious than placebo in treating severely depressed children. However, the results of the second study provided important additional insights for understanding the beneficial effects of imipramine and the need to monitor the steady-state plasma levels of medication in depressed children.

This second study evaluated the relationship between levels of imipramine and its metabolite, desmethylimipramine, and the clinical response in depressed children. The data revealed that among the 30 depressed children studied, the drug responders had significantly higher plasma levels of imipramine and desmethylimipramine than the nonresponders. In addition, maintenance plasma levels over 155 ng/ml of imipramine and desmethylimipramine were associated with a clinical response. Furthermore, children who exhibited depressive hallucinations required higher plasma levels to obtain adequate clinical response. In addition, when the children receiving imipramine were subdivided according to steady-state plasma level above and below 155 ng/ml, the response rate in the high plasma level subgroup was 100%, but in the subgroup with low plasma levels of the medication it was only 33%. Therefore, this study demonstrated that plasma level of the medication was a key variable in determining clinical response in depressed children. It indicated that children with a drug plasma level at or above 155 ng/ml had a 100% decrease of depression.

Another study, carried out by Preskorn, Weller, and Weller (1982), provided more extensive information about the role of plasma levels of imipramine for adequate clinical response. Twenty psychiatrically hospitalized children, ages 7 to 12 years, were studied. The study design included 2 weeks of hospital observation and counseling without medication; 3 weeks of treatment with a fixed oral dose of 75 mg of imipramine at bedtime for children whose depression did not remit after the initial 2 weeks in the hospital; and 3 weeks of additional treatment with imipramine at an altered dose for those children who did not respond to the 75-mg dose. During this third phase, the dose was increased to a maximum of 5 mg/kg/day if there were no previous side effects and no clinical response.

The results indicated that after treatment with 75 mg of imipramine, 4 of the 20 children experienced a remission of depression. Their steady-state tricyclic plasma concentrations ranged from 125 to 225 ng/ml. One other child within this plasma range showed no remission. None of the 15 children either above or below the 125- to 225-ng/ml range remitted or showed improvement. Therefore, there was an 80% remission rate in 3 weeks on medication for the five children in the 125- to 225-ng/ml range and no remissions for those outside of this range.

Another 3-week trial of medication was instituted for the remaining nonresponders, with changes in dose ranging to a maximum of 5 mg/kg/day. At the end of this period, 12 of the 16 children achieved a steady-state antidepressant plasma concentration of 125 to 225 ng/ml, and 11 of these children fully remitted. This was a response rate of 92%.

This study showed that childhood depression that was unresponsive to outpatient counseling and brief hospitalization was responsive to antidepressant treatment. In addition, there was a relation between plasma drug concentration and clinical response. The clinical response was determined primarily by the plasma concentration of the antidepressant medication.

The potential side effects associated with imipramine administration must be constantly monitored during drug administration. These side effects should be carefully explained to the child and the parents before beginning drug treatment. Among the side effects are dry mouth, drowsiness, dizziness, lethargy, tremors, sweating, insomnia, nausea, constipation, appetite disturbance, and cardiac conduction changes. The latter effect must be monitored closely with serial electrocardiograms before any change in medication dose.

Other side effects that have been studied are withdrawal symptoms after gradual cessation of imipramine in children (Law, Petti, & Kazdin, 1981; Petti & Law, 1981). The hospital charts of 22 children receiving imipramine in doses ranging from 3.4 to 5.5 mg/kg/day were reviewed. There was a documented gradual tapering of medication in these cases. The total number of days on imipramine for the 22 children ranged from 27 to 106 days. The range of days needed to taper the drug was 3 to 10 days. The withdrawal symptoms observed included gastrointestinal complaints, drowsiness, decreased appetite, tearfulness, apathy or withdrawal, headaches, agitation, irritability or moodiness, and insomnia. However, the particular combination of withdrawal symptoms in each of the 22 children was variable. Therefore, careful monitoring of withdrawal symptoms in children during the period when the drug is being tapered should be carried out.

Many issues are still to be determined about the use of antidepressant medication in the treatment of depressed, suicidal children. For example, the optimal length of medication administration has not been determined. The relationship between drug efficacy and other diagnostic entities in which symptoms of depression are also present has not been systematically studied. The effects of antidepressant medication used in conjunction with other psychotropic medication have not been studied. Finally, the efficacy of other types of antidepressants such as desipramine, amitriptyline, and trazodone that have been used to treat depressed adults requires inquiry and study.

Nevertheless, it appears that the antidepressant medication imipramine should be considered to be a valuable adjunctive treatment for severely depressed suicidal children. In summary, Table 16-6 outlines factors to consider in the administration of imipramine to severely depressed suicidal children.

COGNITIVE INTERVENTIONS

Beck (1967) and Rush and Beck (1978) formulated a cognitive theory of depression which provides the basis for cognitive therapy of depression in adults. The cognitive theory of depression postulates three ideas: cognitive triad, schemas, and cognitive errors. One component of the cognitive triad involves the individual's negative view of the self.

TABLE 16-6
Imipramine treatment of depressed suicidal children

---

1. *Dose*:
   Gradually increase dose to no more than 5 mg/kg/day. (This dose is for research purposes and should be used only on an inpatient treatment basis.)
2. *Plasma imipramine–desmethylimipramine levels*:
   Ranges from 125 to 225 ng/ml.
3. *Monitor side effects*:
   a. Dry mouth, drowsiness, dizziness, lethargy, tremors, sweating, insomnia, nausea, constipation, appetite disturbances.
   b. Cardiac conduction changes. Safety limits for EKG:
      • Resting heart rate no greater than 130 beats per minute.
      • PR interval no greater than 0.18 sec.
      • QRS no greater than 130% baseline.
   c. Blood pressure safety limits:
      • Systolic blood pressure no greater than 145 mm Hg.
      • Diastolic blood pressure no greater than 95 mm Hg.
4. *Monitor target symptoms of depression*:
   Dysphoric mood, appetite, weight, sleep, psychomotor status, loss of interest, fatigue, worthlessness, guilt, inability to concentrate, suicidal fantasies and behavior.

The depressed individual believes he or she is defective, inadequate, or unworthy. A second component of the cognitive triad involves the individual's interpretation of experiences in a negative way. A third component is the negative view of the future. Therefore, the individual who expects a negative outcome may not endeavor to attain a goal. Suicidal tendencies are understood as the extreme expression of the desire to escape from what appear to be insoluble problems or unbearable situations.

The idea of schemas attempts to explain why a depressed person will hold on to painful attitudes despite objective evidence of positive factors in his or her life. This may be due to the selective attention an individual gives to various stimuli in a situation and how the person combines them into a pattern of perception. The schema forms the basis for molding information into cognitions. The depressed person's conceptualizations of situations are distorted to fit his or her individual schemas. As depression intensifies, the individual's thinking may be increasingly dominated by negative ideas.

The concept of cognitive errors includes a variety of thinking patterns. The depressed person makes a conclusion in the absence of evidence to support the conclusion. He or she focuses on details that are taken out of context. The depressed person draws a general conclusion on the basis of a single incident or distorts perceptions of a given situation. The depressed person relates external events to himself or herself when there is no basis for making such a connection.

Cognitive therapy consists of specific techniques for treating depressed patients. It is a short-term, time-limited psychotherapy. The therapist actively directs the discussion to focus on selected problem areas presented by the patient and to explore inner contradictions and flaws in logical thinking. Therefore, the patient's thoughts are treated as if they were hypotheses requiring validation. The patient and therapist are collaborators who work together to identify basic attitudes, beliefs, and assumptions that shape the patient's thinking.

There has been very little investigative work on the cognitive styles of cognitive therapy or its application to depressed and suicidal children. One recent study is discussed to illustrate some approaches in understanding cognitive styles of and interventions with suicidal children.

Cohen-Sandler and Berman (1982) evaluated a method to train suicidal children to solve problems in nonsuicidal ways. This study focused on developing a cognitive therapy approach to suicidal children. The study was designed to remedy deficient problem-solving styles by training suicidal children to resolve interpersonal problems. Thirty psychiatrically hospitalized children, 8 to 13 years old, were studied. They were classified as 20 nonsuicidal children and 10 suicidal children who had engaged in overt self-destructive behavior or verbalized a wish to harm or kill themselves. The 20 nonsuicidal children were divided into two groups. One group received the problem-solving training and the other did not receive this training. Instruments that assessed the children's coping skills were administered before and after the children received the training. The problem-solving training program consisted of seven 45-minute individual sessions on consecutive days and included presentations, visual materials, modeling, role playing, and discussions to teach basic social and empathy skills and specific cognitive problem solving.

Prior to problem-solving training, the suicidal and nonsuicidal hospitalized children were comparable in their problem-solving skills as measured by the research instruments. However, these children scored below a standardized sample of children who were not psychiatric patients. After treatment, the suicidal children improved more than the nonsuicidal hospitalized children who also received the problem-solving training. The treatment increased the suicidal children's forethought, social knowledge, appreciation for the consequences of behavior, and ability to generate more solutions to conflicts. This study pointed out that this type of treatment was valuable in identifying and remediating specific cognitive errors among suicidal children. This study showed that a cognitive therapy approach can alter a child's perceptions and methods of solving problems into more effective ways. The cognitive format may prove to be an excellent adjunctive treatment for suicidal children. Systematic studies are needed to compare cognitive therapy with the effects of more traditional individual psychotherapy of suicidal children.

SUMMARY

This chapter has focused on intervention techniques that can be combined with individual psychotherapy of suicidal children. The therapies discussed in this chapter are considered adjunctive treatments and have been suggested as additional methods of improving the child's environmental support system, psychophysiological status, and perceptions of the child's self and his or her experiences.

In every treatment of suicidal children, interventions must include a family focus. Such interventions should guide the parents to respond more appropriately to their children and help the parents understand their own individual conflicts. This approach provides a greater degree of support for suicidal children as they endeavor to separate from and develop within the family system.

Psychopharmacological treatment of suicidal children must be tailored to ameliorate the symptoms associated with specific diagnostic entities. Studies have shown that antidepressant medication enhances remission of major depressive disorders in children. Dose, plasma drug concentration, side effects, and target symptoms must be carefully evaluated during this type of psychopharmacological treatment.

While cognitive therapy has been shown to be effective in the treatment of adult depression, little research has focused on cognitive styles of suicidal children. Some studies indicate that attention should be devoted to incorporating a cognitive therapeutic approach in intervention strategies with suicidal children.

Finally, it is strongly suggested that systematic studies be developed to compare and evaluate the effectiveness of the variety of treatments available for suicidal children.

EPILOGUE

Ten-year-old Justin wrote the following note to his parents:

> Dear Mom and Dad,
>   I love you. Please tell my teacher that I cannot take it anymore. I quit.
> Please don't take me to school anymore. Please help me. I will run away
> so don't stop me. I will kill myself. So don't look for me because I will be
> dead. I love you. I will always love you. Remember me.
>   Help me.
>
> Love Justin

Although suicide notes are rare in preadolescents, suicidal ideation, threats, and attempts are common. The sentiments expressed by Justin are usual among suicidal preadolescents. Justin's parents were shocked by his explicit statements. They immediately responded to his "cry for help" by speaking with him and bringing him to a child psychiatrist. He was fortunate because his signal of distress was taken very seriously and responded to without delay. Thus, Justin's case illustrated a principle that should always be followed: *Any suicidal communication by a child should be taken very seriously and responded to immediately.*

The principles involving recognition of, intervention in, and prevention of suicidal behavior in such children are the main themes of this book. The book includes a comprehensive review of current psychiatric literature on facts and theory about childhood suicidal behavior; a difficult and painful subject to think about. Attention has been focused on the fact that suicidal behavior in preadolescents is a real problem; it does exist. Such behavior should be taken very seriously. On the positive side, the book demonstrates that *the condition can be successfully treated and prevented,* notably via the early recognition of depressive symptoms and family problems. Furthermore, since children are relatively resilient and labile, they are likely to respond favorably to kind and thoughtful interventions. Many interventions are possible. A range of interventions can be utilized, from the least intrusive into the child's daily life to the most extensive approaches that dramatically alter the child's environment. For example, the least intrusive intervention with the child may be aimed at treating the parents. The most intrusive includes removing the child from the family for psychiatric hospitalization or long-term residential treatment.

Repeated statements have been made in this book that the signs and symptoms of risk for suicidal behavior should be recognized early and interventions offered immediately. In general, the basis for assessment, prevention, and treatment is the application of practical measures to decrease the risk. Attention should focus on such risk factors as the child's intensity of depression, preoccupations with death, and parental depression and suicidal behavior. An important feature of treatment is the involvement of a network of people. The network should be a system that offers constant observation of the child, protection from self-harm, and an opportunity for the child to communicate about his or her worries. The people in this network should have clearly defined goals: first, to keep the child alive; then, to provide the environment and stimulation needed for optimal development.

Another major issue discussed is the need to educate both the public and professional people to recognize the signs of suicidal risk early, and take appropriate steps to provide treatment. It is essential to refer such children to well-trained mental health professionals who can administer specialized treatments as indicated. Among the many treatments that are involved are individual, family, and group therapy, and medication.

Finally, this work has focused primarily on what is currently known about preadolescent suicidal behavior: its classification, epidemiology, risk factors, diagnostic assessment methods, and prevention and interventions. It is, I hope, the beginning of a major focus in the study and treatment of suicidal behavior in the young. Many features of childhood suicidal behavior are similar to those of adolescents and adults, thereby illustrating a continuity of expression of this symptom throughout the life cycle.

There are many gaps in our knowledge. It is, therefore, evident that more research is necessary to deal with many of the issues and hypotheses that have been discussed in this volume. For example, this book has pointed out that subgroups of suicidal children exist that have distinct symptoms and diagnostic characteristics. This suggests that future research and clinical work should be devoted to learning more about these characteristics and whether different approaches to evaluation, treatment, and prevention are required for specific subgroups of suicidal children. Finally, it must be remembered that every suicidal child is a unique individual who has become vulnerable to life-threatening behavior because a combination of factors have become operative simultaneously to create a high suicidal risk. Therefore the clinician's skill involves applying his or her knowledge of general principles about suicidal children to the individual suicidal child who requires a uniquely conceptualized plan for assessment, prevention, and treatment of his or her life-threatening behavior.

CHILD SUICIDE POTENTIAL SCALES

Name of child _____ Sex _____
Age _____ Date of birth _____ Race/ethnicity _____ Religion _____
Sample population: Hospital _____ Outpatient _____ Comparison _____
Date of admission _____
Address _____ Phone _____ Business phone _____
Mother's name _____ Race/ethnicity _____ Religion _____
Occupation _____ Highest school grade completed _____
Date of birth _____
Father's name _____ Race/ethnicity _____ Religion _____
Occupation _____ Highest school grade completed _____
Date of birth _____
Siblings or others at home:

	Name	Relationship	Date of birth
1.	_____	_____	_____
2.	_____	_____	_____
3.	_____	_____	_____
4.	_____	_____	_____
5.	_____	_____	_____

Siblings not home:

	Name	Relationship	Date of birth
1.	_____	_____	_____
2.	_____	_____	_____
3.	_____	_____	_____
4.	_____	_____	_____
5.	_____	_____	_____

SPECTRUM OF SUICIDAL BEHAVIOR

Listed below are definitions and some examples of the suicidal behavior spectrum. Please consider them when rating the severity of this child's suicidal behavior during the past 6 months.

1. *Nonsuicidal*—No evidence of any self-destructive or suicidal thoughts or actions.

2. *Suicidal ideation*—Thoughts or verbalization of suicidal intention.
   Examples:
   a. "I want to kill myself."
   b. Auditory hallucination to commit suicide.

3. *Suicidal threat*—Verbalization of impending suicidal action and/or a precursor action which, if fully carried out, could have led to harm.
   Examples:
   a. "I am going to run in front of a car."
   b. Child puts a knife under his or her pillow.
   c. Child stands near an open window and threatens to jump out.

4. *Mild attempt*—Actual self-destructive action which realistically would not have endangered life and did not necessitate intensive medical attention.
   Example:
   a. Ingestion of a few nonlethal pills; child's stomach pumped.

5. *Serious attempt*—Actual self-destructive action which realistically could have led to the child's death and may have necessitated intensive medical care.
   Example:
   a. Child jumped out of fourth-floor window.

Describe suicidal ideas or acts: _____

_____

SPECTRUM OF ASSAULTIVE BEHAVIOR

Listed below are definitions and some examples of the assaultive behavior spectrum. Please consider them when rating the severity of the child's assaultive behavior. Circle as many types of behavior as are appropriate.

During the last 6 months, which forms of assaultive behavior were most applicable?

1. *Nonassaultive behavior*—No evidence of assaultive ideas and/or behavior which could have injured someone.

2. *Assaultive ideation*—Thoughts of wanting to harm or kill someone.
   Examples:
   a. "I wish you were dead." "Drop dead."
   b. Hallucinations commanding to hurt or kill someone.

3. *Assaultive threats*—Ideas and/or a precursor assaultive act toward someone.
   Examples:
   a. Child holds knife, planning to hurt or kill someone.
   b. Child tells someone he or she will hurt or kill someone.

4. *Mild assaultive action*—Assaultive actions which may have injured someone but would not have resulted in injury requiring extensive medical care. Examples:
   a. Hitting, pushing, burning, kicking, throwing objects at someone.
   b. Child scratches another but no stitches required.

5. *Serious assaultive action*—Assaultive actions toward others which may have resulted in serious injury requiring extensive medical care. Examples:
   a. Child pushes mother downstairs.
   b. Child burns another.
   c. Child cuts another with a knife.
   d. Child set fires.
   e. Child rapes or sexually molests someone.

6. *Homicide*—An action which caused the death of a victim. Examples:
   a. Child beat infant sibling until dead.
   b. Child drowned another.
   c. Child pushed another out window.

Describe specific type of assaultive behavior: _____
_____

PRECIPITATING EVENTS

During the last 6 months, have any of the following things happened?

	Yes	No
1. Has the child expected to do poorly at school?	___	___
2. Has the child expressed fears of being punished for doing poorly at school?	___	___
3. Did the child do poorly at school?	___	___
4. Was the child punished for doing poorly at school?	___	___
5. Has the child changed schools?	___	___
6. Did the child tend to stay by himself or herself?	___	___
7. Did the child have no friends to play with outside of school?	___	___
8. Has the child been worried about losing a good friend?	___	___
9. Did the child break up with a good friend?	___	___
10. Did the child tend to be bullied or teased?	___	___
11. Has the child had many physical illnesses?	___	___
12. Has the child had a serious illness?	___	___
13. Has the child been hospitalized?	___	___
14. Has the child been punished more than usual?	___	___
15. Has the child moved to a new home?	___	___

	Yes	No
16. Has someone joined the household?	___	___
17. Has someone left the household?	___	___
18. Did the child blame himself or herself as the cause of family problems?	___	___
19. Has the child lost a pet?	___	___
20. Has the child been separated from mother for more than 1 week?	___	___
21. Has the child been separated from father for more than 1 week?	___	___
22. Has someone emotionally important to the child been seriously ill?	___	___
23. Has someone emotionally important to the child been hospitalized?	___	___
24. Has someone emotionally important to the child died?	___	___
25. Has a child been born into the family?	___	___

GENERAL PSYCHOPATHOLOGY (RECENT)

During the last 6 months, have any of the following things happened?

	Yes	No
1. Has the child become more nervous or anxious?	___	___
2. Has the child become more fearful?	___	___
3. Has the child become more quiet?	___	___
4. Has the child become more withdrawn?	___	___
5. Does the child seem more sad or depressed?	___	___
6. Has the child cried more frequently?	___	___
7. Has the child expressed feelings of hopelessness?	___	___
8. Has the child expressed feelings of being worthless?	___	___
9. Does the child blame himself or herself for bad things that have happened?	___	___
10. Does the child never seem proud of the things he or she does?	___	___
11. Has the child said that he or she wanted to die?	___	___
12. Has the child exhibited more nail biting?	___	___
13. Has the child changed eating pattern?	___	___
14. Has the child complained more about aches and pains?	___	___
15. Has the child had more difficulty sleeping?	___	___
16. Has the child shown an increase in nighttime bed wetting?	___	___
17. Has the child shown an increase in his or her tendency to ignore danger?	___	___
18. Has the child become more irritable or belligerent?	___	___
19. Has the child become more defiant?	___	___
20. Has the child become more argumentative?	___	___

	Yes	No
21. Has the child had more fights?	___	___
22. Has the child had more temper tantrums?	___	___
23. Has the child shown more restless, hyperactive movements?	___	___
24. Has the child been more easily frustrated?	___	___
25. Has the child been more destructive of objects?	___	___
26. Has the child more often tried to hurt other children?	___	___
27. Has the child shown evidence of stealing?	___	___
28. Has the child set fires?	___	___
29. Has the child shown an increase in truancy?	___	___
30. Has the child run away?	___	___
31. Has the child ingested any harmful materials?	___	___
32. Has the child had any accidents requiring a physician's attention?	___	___
33. Has the child shown greater difficulty in learning?	___	___

GENERAL PSYCHOPATHOLOGY (PAST)

Prior to the last 6 months, did any of the following things happen?

	Yes	No
1. Was the child nervous or anxious?	___	___
2. Was the child fearful?	___	___
3. Was the child quiet?	___	___
4. Was the child withdrawn?	___	___
5. Was the child depressed?	___	___
6. Did the child cry frequently?	___	___
7. Did the child express feelings of hopelessness?	___	___
8. Did the child express feelings of being worthless?	___	___
9. Did the child blame himself or herself for bad things that had happened?	___	___
10. Was the child never proud of the things he or she did?	___	___
11. Did the child exhibit nail biting?	___	___
12. Did the child say he or she wanted to die?	___	___
13. Did the child expect to do poorly at school?	___	___
14. Did the child express fears of being punished for doing poorly at school?	___	___
15. Did the child tend to be bullied or teased?	___	___
16. Did the child blame himself or herself as the cause of family problems?	___	___
17. Has the child had more difficulty sleeping?	___	___
18. Did the child have problems eating?	___	___
19. Has the child shown an increase in nighttime bed wetting?	___	___
20. Has the child been irritable or belligerent?	___	___

	Yes	No
21. Was the child defiant?	——	——
22. Was the child argumentative?	——	——
23. Did the child get into fights?	——	——
24. Did the child show restlessness, hyperactive movements?	——	——
25. Was the child easily frustrated?	——	——
26. Was the child destructive of objects?	——	——
27. Did the child try to hurt other children?	——	——
28. Was the child a head banger?	——	——
29. Did the child have temper tantrums?	——	——
30. Has the child been frequently punished?	——	——
31. Has the child shown evidence of stealing?	——	——
32. Has the child set fires?	——	——
33. Has the child shown an increase in truancy?	——	——
34. Has the child run away?	——	——
35. Has the child shown an increase in his or her tendency to ignore danger?	——	——
36. Was the child's speech delayed?	——	——
37. Did the child have poor coordination?	——	——
38. Did the child ingest harmful materials?	——	——
39. Did the child have accidents requiring a physician's attention?	——	——
40. Did the child show difficulty in learning?	——	——
41. Did the child do poorly at school?	——	——
42. Did the child have serious physical illnesses?	——	——

FAMILY BACKGROUND

Note: The word "mother" refers to the child's natural mother or to a surrogate. The same applies to the word "father."

	Yes	No
1. Are the child's parents currently separated?	——	——
2. Were the child's parents ever separated?	——	——
If "yes," how old was the child at first separation? ___		
3. Are the child's parents divorced?	——	——
If "yes," how old was the child at divorce? ___		
4. Have there been several parental separations?	——	——
5. Has a father figure always been absent in the child's household?	——	——
6. Has the child had multiple father figures?	——	——
7. Has the child had multiple mother figures?	——	——
8. Is the child's mother dead?	——	——
If "yes," how old was the child at her death? ___		
If "no," go to Item #9.		

	Yes	No
a. Did the mother's death result from an accident?	___	___
b. Did the mother's death result from illness?	___	___
c. Did the mother's death result from suicide?	___	___
d. Did the mother's death result from homicide?	___	___

9. Is the child's father dead? ___ ___
   If "yes," how old was the child at his death? ___
   If "no," go to Item #10.

	Yes	No
a. Did the father's death result from an accident?	___	___
b. Did the father's death result from illness?	___	___
c. Did the father's death result from suicide?	___	___
d. Did the father's death result from homicide?	___	___

10. Has any other person who lived in the child's household died? ___ ___
    If "no," go to Item #11.

	Yes	No
a. Did this person's death result from an accident?	___	___
b. Did this person's death result from illness?	___	___
c. Did this person's death result from suicide?	___	___
d. Did this person's death result from homicide?	___	___

11. Does the mother hit or beat the child frequently? ___ ___
12. Does the father hit or beat the child frequently? ___ ___
13. Has the child witnessed frequent arguments or violence between his or her parents? ___ ___
14. Is the child frequently blamed for family problems? ___ ___
15. Does the child frequently hear parental arguments about the child? ___ ___
16. Is the child frequently picked on by siblings? ___ ___
17. Do the child's parents frequently not speak with each other? ___ ___

For the following items, please place a checkmark where applicable.

	Mother	Father	Other family member
18. Chronic medical illness?	___	___	___
19. Severe depression?	___	___	___
20. Hospitalization for psychiatric illness?	___	___	___
21. Problems with alcohol and/or drug abuse?	___	___	___
22. Extensive use of over-the-counter medications?	___	___	___
23. Suicide attempt(s)?	___	___	___
24. Verbal expression of suicidal thoughts?	___	___	___
25. Assaultive ideation (thoughts of wanting to harm or kill someone)?	___	___	___
26. Assaultive threats (ideas and/or a precursor assaultive act toward someone)?	___	___	___

	Mother	Father	Other family member
27. Mild assaultive attempt (assaultive action that may have injured someone but did not result in injury requiring extensive medical care)?	——	——	——
28. Serious assaultive attempt (assaultive action toward others that may have resulted in serious injury requiring medical care)?	——	——	——
29. Homicide (an action that caused the death of a victim)?	——	——	——

CONCEPT OF DEATH SCALE

Please ask the child the following:

	Never	Sometimes	Often
1. Have you ever thought about dying?	——	——	——
2. Have you ever thought about people in your family dying?	——	——	——
3. Do you ever dream about people dying?	——	——	——
4. Do you dream that you are dying?	——	——	——
5. Do you dream about dead relatives?	——	——	——
6. Have you ever thought about the death of someone you liked a lot?	——	——	——

	Yes	No
7. Have you ever seen a dead person?	——	——
8. Have you ever been to a funeral home?	——	——
9. Have you ever been to a funeral?	——	——
10. Do you think people come back to life after they die?	——	——
11. Do you think animals come back to life after they die?	——	——
12. Do you think a person goes to a better place after death?	——	——
13. Do you think a person goes to a terrible place after death?	——	——

Interviewer's rating of child's concept of death

(Please circle appropriate number.)

Does the child think of death as pleasant or unpleasant?   Unpleasant 1 2 3 4 5 Pleasant

Does the child think of death as final or
    temporary?   Final 1 2 3 4 5 Temporary

ASSESSMENT OF CURRENT EGO FUNCTIONS

1. *IQ*
    If tested: Verbal _____ Performance _____ Full scale _____
    If not tested: Dull normal _____ Normal _____ Above normal _____

2. *Achievement*
    Reading score _____ at or above grade level _____ below grade level _____
    Spelling score _____ at or above grade level _____ below grade level _____
    Math score _____ at or above grade level _____ below grade level _____

3. *Affects*	Never	Sometimes	Often	All the time
How frequently does the child show these affects?				
a. Irritability, aggression, anger	_____	_____	_____	_____
b. Depression, sadness, crying	_____	_____	_____	_____
c. Anxiety, fearfulness	_____	_____	_____	_____
d. Passivity, dependency, timidity	_____	_____	_____	_____
e. Cheerfulness, humor	_____	_____	_____	_____

How often does the child shift affects?
    Seldom_____ Sometimes_____ Often_____
Is the child's affect appropriate to the situations that arise?
    Seldom_____ Sometimes_____ Often_____

4. *Impulse control*	Low	Average	High
a. Degree of frustration tolerance	_____	_____	_____
b. Ability to delay actions	_____	_____	_____
c. Ability to plan for future events	_____	_____	_____
d. Ability to tolerate deprivations	_____	_____	_____
e. Ability to handle restlessness resulting from restrictions	_____	_____	_____
f. Ability to make a decision when faced with alternatives	_____	_____	_____
g. Tendency to retreat into fantasy in face of a choice problem	_____	_____	_____
h. Persistent tendency to daydream	_____	_____	_____

5. *Reality testing*
    a. Knowledge of present place
       Yes_____ No_____

b. Knowledge of time
   Yes____ No____
c. Knowledge of identity
   Yes____ No____
d. Child answers questions logically
   Never____ Sometimes____ Often____ All the time____
e. Child perceives situations appropriately
   Never____ Sometimes____ Often____ All the time____
f. Child appears to understand the consequences of his or her behavior
   Never____ Sometimes____ Often____ All the time____

6. *Object relations*
   a. Does the child relate to the interviewer in an appropriate way?
      Seldom____ Sometimes____ Often____
   b. Does the child relate to other people in an appropriate way?
      Seldom____ Sometimes____ Often____

EGO DEFENSES

To what extent does the child use each of the defense mechanisms defined
below?

	Never	Sometimes	Often
1. *Regression* (manifestation of a return to an earlier level of ego development) Examples: Biting, sucking fingers and objects, autistic behavior, smearing and dirtying, use of baby talk or more primitive language, refusal of child to do tasks when he or she is capable of them	____	____	____
2. *Denial* (will include mechanisms of isolation and splitting, the tendency to deny painful sensations and facts) Examples: a. Child's parent deserted the family, and the child believes parent will return soon. b. Child says he or she has many friends, but has none. c. Child's parents are severely punishing, and child says that this does not happen. d. Child tells a frightening story in a calm way without manifestation of frightened feelings (isolation).			

	Never	Sometimes	Often

e. Child shows love to one person
   and to another person only hate
   (splitting).   ____   ____   ____

3. *Projection* (emotions and ideas which the
   ego tried to ward off are attributed to
   someone else)
   Examples:
   a. Child whose anger is intense
      believes that others are angry at the
      child.
   b. Child who has difficulty controlling
      his or her impulses thinks that
      others will harm the child.
   c. "All teachers are stupid."   ____   ____   ____

4. *Introjection* (taking in of characteristics,
   ideas, and feelings of another person)
   Examples:
   a. Child's aggressive behavior is an
      identification of a parent's aggres-
      sive behavior.
   b. Child's mother or father is de-
      pressed, and child becomes de-
      pressed.
   c. Parent is punitive, and child acts
      similarly to peers.   ____   ____   ____

5. *Reaction formation* (manifestation of a reverse of the repressed instinctual impulses)
   Examples:
   a. Child cannot tolerate dirt or messy
      things.
   b. Child feels disgusted by certain
      foods.
   c. Child too intensely dislikes show-
      ing off.   ____   ____   ____

6. *Undoing* (something is done or thought
   and is immediately undone by an act or
   thought that negates it)
   Examples:
   a. Child buys toys and usually
      changes his or her mind and
      returns them.
   b. Child is friendly and then im-
      mediately becomes angry.   ____   ____   ____

	Never	Sometimes	Often

7. *Displacement* (channelling instinctual feelings, actions, and ideas into a new object or situation)
Examples:
   a. Child afraid of parent and becomes afraid of dogs.
   b. Child scapegoats other children.
   c. Child kicks pet when angry.   ____   ____   ____

8. *Intellectualization* (child discusses ideas rather than expressing feelings in situation where feelings should be discussed)
Examples:
   a. Child reads, in contrast to playing with others.
   b. Child says little about his or her feelings but becomes enthusiastic when discussing intellectual ideas.   ____   ____   ____

9. *Compensation* (child experiences inadequacy or inability and overdevelops in another area)
Example:
   a. Child tries to be group clown.
   b. Child tries to be superstrong.
   c. Child is a risk taker.   ____   ____   ____

10. *Sublimation* (under the influence of the ego, unacceptable feelings are changed into a socially useful modality without blocking an adequate discharge)
Examples:
   a. Child enjoys hobbies.
   b. Child has strong aggressive feelings and collects soldiers.
   c. Child likes to paint.
   d. Child likes to model clay.   ____   ____   ____

11. *Repression* (unconsciously purposefully forgetting or not becoming aware of internal impulses or external events)
Examples:
   a. Child has difficulty describing events of childhood, and child says he or she does not remember.

	Never	Sometimes	Often
b. Child does not remember feelings when first entered school.			
c. Child does not remember feelings when siblings were born.			
d. Child does not remember dreams.	____	____	____

DIAGNOSTIC IMPRESSION(S)

Check all that apply.

1. Mental retardation _____
2. Attention deficit disorder _____
   a. With hyperactivity _____
3. Conduct disorder _____
   a. Undersocialized, aggressive _____
   b. Undersocialized, nonaggressive _____
   c. Socialized, aggressive _____
   d. Socialized, nonaggressive _____
4. Anxiety disorder _____
   a. Separation anxiety disorder _____
   b. Avoidant disorder _____
   c. Overanxious disorder _____
5. Other disorders of childhood _____
   a. Oppositional disorder _____
   b. Identity disorder _____
6. Eating disorders _____
7. Stereotyped movement disorders _____
8. Other disorders with physical manifestations (stuttering, functional enuresis, functional encopresis, sleep walking, sleep terror) _____
9. Pervasive developmental disorders (infantile autism, childhood onset, atypical, etc.) _____
10. Specific developmental disorder _____
    a. Developmental language disorder _____
11. Organic brain syndrome (delirium, dementia, amnesic syndrome, organic delusional, etc.) _____
12. Epilepsy _____
13. Schizophrenic disorder _____
14. Psychotic disorders, other (schizophreniform, brief reactive, psychosis, schizoaffective, atypical) _____
15. Neurotic disorders _____
16. Affective disorders _____
    a. Major depression _____
    b. Dysthymic disorder _____
    c. Cyclothymic disorder _____

17. Adjustment disorder   ———
18. Personality disorder   ———
    a. Borderline personality   ———
    b. Schizotypal   ———
    c. Other (specify) _____   ———
19. No psychopathology   ———

REFERENCES

Ackerly, W. C. (1967). Latency-age children who threaten or attempt to kill themselves. *Journal of the American Academy of Child Psychiatry*, 6:242–261.

Adam, K. S., Bouckoms, A., & Steiner, D. (1980). Parental loss and family stability in attempted suicide. *Archives of General Psychiatry*, 39:1081–1085.

Adams-Tucker, C. (1982). Proximate effects of sexual abuse in childhood: A report in 28 children. *American Journal of Psychiatry*, 139:1252–1256.

Agren, H. (1980). Symptom patterns in unipolar and bipolar depression correlating with monoamine metabolites in the cerebrospinal fluid: II. Suicide. *Psychiatry Research*, 3:225–236.

Alarron, O. (1982). Outpatient treatment of a suicidal seven year old child. In *Suicide and the Life Cycle: Proceedings of the 15th Annual Meeting of the American Association of Suicidology*, Eds. C. Pfeffer & J. Richman. New York.

Aleksandrowicz, M. K. (1975). The biological strangers: An attempted suicide of a seven-and-a-half-year-old girl. *Bulletin of the Menninger Clinic*, 39:163–176.

Amir, A. (1973). Suicide among minors in Israel. *Israel Annals of Psychiatry and Related Disciplines*, 11:219–269.

Anthony, E. J. (1975). Childhood depression. In *Depression and Human Existence*, Eds. E. J. Anthony & T. Benedek. Little, Brown, Boston.

Anthony, S. (1940). *The Child's Discovery of Death*. Harcourt Brace, New York.

Arana, G. W., Barreira, P. J., Cohen, B. M., Lipinski, J. F., & Fogelson, D. (1983). The dexamethasone suppression test in psychotic disorders. *American Journal of Psychiatry*, 140:1521–1523.

Arnow, H. (1954). *The Dollmaker*. Avon Books, New York.

Asberg, M., Traskman, L., & Thoren, P. (1976). 5-HIAA in the cerebrospinal fluid: A biochemical suicide predictor? *Archives of General Psychiatry*, 33:1193–1197.

Baer, A. (1901). *Der Selbstmord in kindlichen Lesbensalter*. Leipzig.

Beardslee, W. R., Bemporad, J., Keller, M. B., & Klerman, G. L. (1983). Children of parents with an affective disorder: A review. *American Journal of Psychiatry*, 140:825–832.

Beck, A. T. (1967). *Depression: Clinical, Experimental, and Theoretical Aspects*. Harper & Row, New York.

Beck, A. T., Beck, R., & Kovacs, M. (1975). Classification of suicidal behaviors: I. Quantifying intent and medical lethality. *American Journal of Psychiatry*, 132:285–287.

Beck, A. T., Steer, R. A., Kovacs, M., & Garrison, B. (1985). Hopelessness and eventual suicide: A 10-year prospective study of patients hospitalized with suicidal ideation. *American Journal of Psychiatry*, 142:559–563.

Beck, A. T., Weissman, A., Lester, D., & Trexler, L. (1974). The measurement of pessimism: The hopelessness scale. *Journal of Consulting and Clinical Psychology*, 42:861–865.

Beck, A. T., Weissman, A., Lester, D., & Trexler, L. (1976). Classification of suicidal behavior: II. Dimensions of suicidal intent. *Archives of General Psychiatry*, 33:835–837.

Bender, L., & Schilder, P. (1937). Suicidal preoccupations and attempts in children. *American Journal of Orthopsychiatry*, 7:225–235.

Beres, D. (1956). Ego deviation and the concept of schizophrenia. *Psychoanalytic Study of the Child*, 11:164–235.

Berndt, D. J., Kaiser, C. F., & Van Aalst, F. (1982). Depression and self-actualization in gifted adolescents. *Journal of Clinical Psychology*, 38:142–150.

Bowlby, J. (1973a). *Separation: Anxiety and Anger*. Basic Books, New York.

Bowlby, J. (1973b). *Separation: Attachment and Loss*. Basic Books, New York.

Brent, S. B. (1977). Puns, metaphors, and misunderstandings in a two-year-old's conception of death. *Omega*, 8:285–293.

Brown, G. L., Ebert, M. H., Goyer, P. F., Jimerson, D. C., Klein, W. J., Bunney, W. E., & Goodwin, F. K. (1982). Aggression, suicide, and serotonin: Relationship to CSF amine metabolites. *American Journal of Psychiatry*, 139:741–746.

Brumback, R. A., Staton, R. D., & Wilson, H. (1980). Neuropsychological study of children during and after remission of endogenous depressive episodes. *Perceptual and Motor Skills*, 50:1163–1167.

Burlingham, D. (1965). Some problems of ego development in blind children. *Psychoanalytic Study of the Child*, 20:194–208.

Cain, A. C., & Fast, I. (1966). Children's disturbed reactions to parent suicide. *American Journal of Orthopsychiatry*, 36:873–880.

Calhoun, L. G., Selby, J. W., & Faulstich, M. E. (1980). Reactions to the parents of the child suicide: A study of social impressions. *Journal of Consulting and Clinical Psychology*, 48:535–536.

Caprio, F. S. (1950). A study of some psychological reactions during prepubescence to the idea of death. *Psychiatric Quarterly*, 24:495–505.

Carlson, G. A., & Cantwell, D. P. (1980). A survey of depressive symptoms, syndrome, and disorder in a child psychiatric population. *Journal of Child Psychology and Psychiatry*, 21:19–25.

Carlson, G. A., & Cantwell, D. P. (1982). Suicidal behavior and depression in children and adolescents. *Journal of the American Academy of Child Psychiatry*, 21:361–368.

Carlson, G., & Orbach, I. (1982). *Depression and Children's Attitudes toward Death*. Paper presented at the 29th Annual Meeting of the American Academy of Child Psychiatry, Washington, D.C.

Carroll, B. J., Feinberg, M., Greden, J. F., Tarika, J., Albala, A. A., Haskett, R. F., James, N., McI., Kronfol, Z., Lohr, N., Steiner, M., deVigne, J. P., & Young, E. (1981). A specific laboratory test for the diagnosis of melancholia. *Archives of General Psychiatry*, 38:15–22.

Chadwick, M. (1929). Notes upon the fear of death. *International Journal of Psycho-Analysis*, 10:321–334.

Chambers, W., Puig-Antich, J., & Tabrizi, M. A. (1978). *The Ongoing Development of the Kiddie-SADS (Schedule for Affective Disorders and Schizophrenia for School-Age Children)*. Paper presented at the Annual Meeting of the American Academy of Child Psychiatry, San Diego.

Chambers, W. J., Puig-Antich, J., Tabrizi, M. A., & Davies, M. (1982). Psychotic symptoms in prepubertal major depressive disorder. *Archives of General Psychiatry*, 39:921–927.

Chapman, J. W., Cullen, J. L., Boersma, F. J., & Maguire, T. O. (1981). Affective variables and school achievement: A study of possible causal influences. *Canadian Journal of Behavioral Science*, 13:181–192.

Chess, S., Thomas, A., & Hassibi, M. (1983). Depression in childhood and adolescence: A prospective study of six cases. *Journal of Nervous and Mental Disease*, 171:411–420.

Cohen-Sandler, R., & Berman, A. L. (1980). Diagnosis and treatment of childhood depression and self-destructive behavior. *Journal of Family Practice*, 11:51–58.

Cohen-Sandler, R., & Berman, A. (1982). Training suicidal children to problem-solve in nonsuicidal ways. In *Suicide and the Life Cycle: Proceedings of the 15th Annual Meeting of the American Association of Suicidology*, Eds. C. Pfeffer & J. Richman. New York.

Cohen-Sandler, R., Berman, A. L., & King, R. A. (1982a): Life stress and symptomatology: Determinants of suicidal behavior in children,. *Journal of the American Academy of Child Psychiatry*, 21:178–186.

Cohen-Sandler, R., Berman, A. L., & King, R. A. (1982b). A follow-up study of hospitalized suicidal children. *Journal of the American Academy of Child Psychiatry*, 21:398–403.

Colbert, P., Newman, B., Ney, P., & Young, J. (1982). Learning disabilities as a symptom of depression in children. *Journal of Learning Disabilities*, 15:333–336.

College Report, The (1982). The management of parasuicide in young people under sixteen. *British Journal of Psychiatry*, 7:182–185.

Corder, B. F., & Haizlip, T. M. (1983). Recognizing suicidal behavior in children. *Resident and Staff Physician*, 29:18–23.

Corder, B. F., & Haizlip, T. M. (1984). Environmental and personality similarities in case histories of suicide and self-poisoning by children under ten. *Suicide and Life-Threatening Behavior*, 14(1):59–66.

Coryell, W., & Schlesser, M. A. (1981). Suicide and the dexamethasone suppression test in unipolar depression. *American Journal of Psychiatry*, 138:1120–1121.

Crook, T., & Raskin, A. (1975). Association of childhood parental loss with attempted suicide and depression. *Journal of Consulting and Clinical Psychology*, 43:277.

Cytryn, L., & McKnew, D. H. (1972). Proposed classification of childhood depression. *American Journal of Psychiatry*, 129:149–155.

Cytryn, L., McKnew, D. H., Bartko, J. J., Lamour, M., & Hamovitt, J. (1982). Offspring of patients with affective disorders: II. *Journal of the American Academy of Child Psychiatry*, 21:389–391.

Cytryn, L., Mcknew, D. H., & Bunney, W. E. (1980). Diagnosis of depression in children: A reassessment. *American Journal of Psychiatry*, 137:22–25.

Cytryn, C., McKnew, D. H., Logue, M., & Desai, R. B. (1974). Biochemical correlates of affective disorders in children. *Archives of General Psychiatry*, 31:659–661.

Diagnostic and Statistical Manual of Mental Disorders (3rd ed.). (1980). American Psychiatric Association, Washington, D.C.

Dorpat, T. L., & Ripley, H. B. (1960). A study of suicide in the Seattle area. *Comprehensive Psychiatry*, 1:349–359.

Dorpat, T. L., & Ripley, H. S. (1967). The relationship between attempted suicide and committed suicide. *Comprehensive Psychiatry*, 8:74–79.

Durand-Fardel, M. (1885). Etude sur le suicide chez les enfants. *Annals of Medical Psychology*, p. 61.

Editorial. (1981). Children and parasuicide. *British Medical Journal*, 283:337–338.

Eisenberg, L. (1980). Adolescent suicide: On taking arms against a sea of troubles. *Pediatrics*, 65:315–320.

Elizur, E., & Kaffman, M. (1982). Children's bereavement reactions following death of the father: II. *Journal of the American Academy of Child Psychiatry*, 21:474–480.

Emminghaus, H. (1887). *Die psychischen Störungen des Kindesalters*. Verlag der Laupp'schen Buchhandlung, Tübingen.

Eth, S., Pynoos, R. S., & Carlson, G. A. (1984). An unusual case of self-inflicted death in childhood. *Suicide and Life-Threatening Behavior*, 14(3):157–165.

Feigelson, C. I. (1974). Play in child analysis. *Psychoanalytic Study of the Child*, 29:21–27.

Feighner, J. P., Robins, E., Guze, S. B., Woodruff, R. A., Jr., Winokur, G., & Muñoz, R. (1972). Diagnostic research for use in psychiatric research. *Archives of General Psychiatry*, 26:57–63.

Frankl, L. (1961). Some observations on the development and disturbances of integration in childhood. *Psychoanalytic Study of the Child*, 16:146–163.

Fredrick, C. J. (1978). Current trends in suicidal behavior in the United States. *American Journal of Psychotherapy*, 32:172–200.

Freeman, L. N., Poznanski, E. O., Grossman, J. A., Buchsbaum, Y. Y., & Banegas, M. E. (1985). Psychotic and depressed children: A new entity. *Journal of the American Academy of Child Psychiatry*, 24:95–102.

French, A. P., & Steward, M. S. (1975). Family dynamics, childhood depression, and attempted suicide in a 7 year old boy. *Suicide*, 5:29–37.

Freud, A. (1936). *The Ego and the Mechanisms of Defense*. Hogarth Press, London.

Freud, A. (1952). The mutual influences in the development of ego and id: Introduction to the discussion. *Psychoanalytic Study of the Child*, 7:42–50.

Freud, A. (1963). The concept of developmental lines. *Psychoanalytic Study of the Child*, 18:245–265.

Freud, A. (1967). About losing and being lost. *Psychoanalytic Study of the Child*, 22:9–19.

Freud, S. (1901). The psychopathology of everyday life. In *The Standard Edition of the Complete Psychological Works of Sigmund Freud*, 6. Hogarth Press, London.

Freud, S. (1908). Creative writers and day-dreaming. In *The Standard Edition of the Complete Psychological Works of Sigmund Freud*, 9. Hogarth Press, London.

Freud, S. (1914). Remembering, repeating and working through (Further recommendations on the technique of psycho-analysis: II). In *The Standard Edition of the Complete Psychological Works of Sigmund Freud*, 12. Hogarth Press, London.

Freud, S. (1917a). A childhood recollection from *Dictung and Wahrheit*. In *The Standard Edition of the Complete Psychological Works of Sigmund Freud*, 17. Hogarth Press, London.

Freud, S. (1917b). Mourning and Melancholia. In *The Standard Edition of the Complete Psychological Works of Sigmund Freud*, 14. Hogarth Press, London.

Freud, S. (1926). Inhibitions, symptoms, and anxiety. In *The Standard Edition of the Complete Psychological Works of Sigmund Freud*, 20. Hogarth Press, London.

Frommer, E. (1968). Depression disorders in childhood. *British Journal of Psychiatry*, 2:117–136.

Furman, E. (1956). An ego disturbance in a young child. *Psychoanalytic Study of the Child*, 11:312–335.

Furman, E. (1974). *A Child's Parent Dies*. Yale University Press, New Haven.

Garfinkel, B. D., Froese, A., & Hood, J. (1982). Suicide attempts in children and adolescents. *American Journal of Psychiatry*, 139:1257–1261.

Geller, B., Chestnut, E. C., Miller, M. D., Price, D. T., & Yates, E. (1985). Preliminary data on DSM-III associated features of major depressive disorder in children and adolescents. *American Journal of Psychiatry*, 142:643–644.

Geller, B., Rogol, A. D., & Knitter, E. F. (1983). Preliminary data in the dexamethasone suppression test in children with major depressive disorder. *American Journal of Psychiatry*, 140:620–622.

Gide, A. (1973). *The Counterfeiters*, Trans. D. Bussy. Vintage Books, New York.

Glaser, K. (1967). Masked depression in children and adolescents. *American Journal of Psychotherapy*, 21:565–574.

Glaser, K. (1981). Psychopathic patterns in depressed adolescents. *American Journal of Psychotherapy*, 35:368–382.

Goldney, R. D., & Katsikitis, M. (1983). Cohort analysis of suicidal rates in Australia. *Archives of General Psychiatry*, 40:71–74.

Green, A. H. (1978). Self-destructive behavior in battered children. *American Journal of Psychiatry*, 135:579–582.

Greenhill, L. L., Shopsin, B., & Temple, H. (1980). Children of affectively ill parents: Psychiatric status determined by structured interview. *Psychopharmacology Bulletin*, 16:23–24.

Greer, S. (1974). The relationship between parental loss and attempted suicide: A control study. *British Journal of Psychiatry*, 110:698–705.

Grimm, The Brothers. (1952). The poor boy in the grave. In *Tales of Grimm and Andersen*. The Modern Library—Random House, New York.

Guze, S. B., & Robins, E. (1970). Suicide and primary affective disorder. *British Journal of Psychiatry*, 117:437–438.

Hardy, T. (1961). *Jude the Obscure*. New American Library, New York.

Hartmann, H. (1952). The mutual influences in the development of ego and id. *Psychoanalytic Study of the Child*, 7:9–30.

Hartmann, H., Kris, E., & Loewenstein, R. M. (1946). Comments on the formation of psychic structure. *Psychoanalytic Study of the Child*, 2:11–38.

Hellon, C. P., & Solomon, M. I. (1980). Suicide and age in Alberta, Canada, 1951–1977: The changing profile. *Archives of General Psychiatry*, 37:505–510.

Herjanic, B., & Campbell, W. (1977). Differentiating psychiatrically disturbed children on the basis of a structured interview. *Journal of Abnormal Child Psychology*, 5: 127–134.

Herjanic, B., Herjanic, M., Brown, F., & Wheatt, T. (1975). Are children reliable reporters? *Journal of Abnormal Child Psychology*, 3:41–48.

Herjanic, B., & Reich, W. (1982). Development of a structured psychiatric interview for children: Agreement between child and parent on individual symptoms. *Journal of Abnormal Child Psychology*, 10:307–324.

Hodgman, C. H., & Roberts, F. N. (1982). Adolescent suicide and the pediatrician. *Journal of Pediatrics*, 101:113–123.

Hoffer, W. (1952). The mutual influences in the development of ego and id: earliest stages. *Psychoanalytic Study of the Child*, 7:31–40.

Holinger, P. C. (1978). Adolescent suicide: An epidemiological study of recent trends. *American Journal of Psychiatry*, 135:754–756.

Holinger, P. C., & Offer, D. (1982). Prediction of adolescent suicide: A population model. *American Journal of Psychiatry*, 139:302–307.

Insel, T. R., & Goodwin, F. K. (1983). The dexamethasone suppression test: Promises and problems of diagnostic laboratory tests in psychiatry. *Hospital and Community Psychiatry*, 34:1131–1138.

Jacobziner, H. (1960). Attempted suicides in children. *Journal of Pediatrics*, 56:519–525.

Jacobziner, H. (1965). Attempted suicides in adolescence. *Journal of the American Medical Association*, 191:101–105.

Jan-Tausch, J. (1964). *Suicide of Children 1960–63*. Trenton, N.J., Public Schools, Department of Education.

Jensen, V. W., & Petty, T. A. (1958). The fantasy of being rescued. *Psychoanalytic Quarterly*, 27:327–339.

Kallmann, F. J., & Anastasio, M. M. (1947). Twin studies on the psychopathology of suicide. *Journal of Nervous and Mental Disease*, 105:40–55.

Kallmann, F. J., DePorte, J., DePorte, E., & Feingold, L. (1949). Suicide in twins and only children. *American Journal of Human Genetics*, 1:113–126.

Kalter, N., & Plunkett, J. W. (1984). Children's perceptions of the causes and consequences of divorce. *Journal of the American Academy of Child Psychiatry*, 23:326–334.

Kashani, J. H., Barbero, G. J., & Bolander, F. D. (1981a). Depression in hospitalized pediatric patients. *Journal of the American Academy of Child Psychiatry*, 20:123–134.

Kashani, J. H., Cantwell, D. P., Shekim, W. O., & Reid, J. C. (1982). Major depressive disorder in children admitted to an inpatient community mental health center. *American Journal of Psychiatry*, 139:671–672.

Kashani, J., & Hakami, N. (1982). Depression in children and adolescents with malignancy. *Canadian Journal of Psychiatry*, 27:474–477.

Kashani, J. H., Husain, A., Shekim, W. O., Hodges, K. K., Cytryn, L., & McKnew, D. H. (1981b). Current perspectives in childhood depression: An overview. *American Journal of Psychiatry*, 138:143–153.

Kashani, J. H., McGee, R. O., Clarkson, S. E., Anderson, J. C., Walton, L. A., Williams, S., Silva, P. A., Robins, A. J., Cytryn, L., & McKnew, D. H. (1983). Depression in a sample of 9 year old children. *Archives of General Psychiatry*, 40:1217–1223.

Kashani, J., & Simonds, J. F. (1979). The incidence of depression in children. *American Journal of Psychiatry*, 136:1203–1205.

Kashani, J. H., Venzke, R., & Millar, E. A. (1981c). Depression in children admitted to hospital for orthopedic procedures. *British Journal of Psychiatry*, 138:21–25.

Katan, A., (1961). Some thoughts about the role of verbalization in early childhood. *Psychoanalytic Study of the Child*, 16:184–188.

Kazdin, A. E. (1981). Assessment techniques for childhood depression. *Journal of the American Academy of Child Psychiatry*, 20:358–375.

Kazdin, A. E., French, N. H., Unis, A. S., & Esveldt-Dawson, K. (1983a). Assessment of childhood depression: Correspondence of child and parent ratings. *Journal of the American Academy of Child Psychiatry*, 22:157–164.

Kazdin, A. E., French, N. H., Unis, A. S., Esveldt-Dawson, K., & Sherick, R. B. (1983b). Hopelessness, depression, and suicidal intent among psychiatrically disturbed inpatient children. *Journal of Consulting and Clinical Psychology*, 51:504–510.

Kernberg, P. F. (1974). The analysis of a 15 and a half year old girl with suicidal tendencies. In *The Analyst and the Adolescent at Work*, Ed. M. Harley. Quadrangle, New York Times Book Company, New York.

Khantzian, E. J., & Mack, J. E. (1983). Self-preservation and the care of the self: Ego instincts reconsidered. *Psychoanalytic Study of the Child*, 38:209–232.

Kipling, R. (1950). Baa, baa, black sheep. In *Wee Willie Winkie*. Grosset & Dunlap, New York.

Klee, S. H., & Garfinkel, B. D. (1984). Identification of depression in children and adolescents: The role of the dexamethasone suppression test. *Journal of the American Academy of Child Psychiatry*, 23:410–415.

Kleeman, J. A. (1967). The peek-a-boo game: Part I. Its origins, meanings, and related phenomena in the first year. *Psychoanalytic Study of the Child*, 22:239–273.

Klein, M. (1948). A contribution to the psychogenesis of manic–depressive states. In *Contributions to Psycho-analysis*. Hogarth Press, London.

Klein, M. (1955). The psychoanalytic play technique. *American Journal of Orthopsychiatry*, 25:223–237.

Koocher, G. P. (1973). Childhood, death, and cognitive development. *Developmental Psychology*, 9:369–375.

Koocher, G. P. (1974). Talking with children about death. *American Journal of Orthopsychiatry*, 44:404–411.

Kovacs, M. (1983). The Children's Depression Inventory: A Self-Rated Depression Scale for School-Age Youngsters. Unpublished paper.

Kovacs, M., & Beck, A. T. (1977). An empirical clinical approach towards a definition of childhood depression. In *Depression in Children*. Eds. J. G. Schulterbrandt & A. Raskin. Raven Press, New York.

Kovacs, M., Feinberg, T. L., Crouse-Novak, M. A., Paulauskas, S. L., & Finkelstein, R. (1984). Depressive disorders in childhood. *Archives of General Psychiatry*, 41:229–237; 41:643–649.

Kuhn, B., & Kuhn, R. (1972). Drug therapy for depression in children. In *Depressive States in Childhood and Adolescence*, Ed. A. C. Annel. Wiley, New York.

Kuperman, S., & Stewart, M. A. (1979). The diagnosis of depression in children. *Journal of Affective Disorders*, 1:213–217.

Law, W., III, Petti, T. A., & Kazdin, A. E. (1981). Withdrawal symptoms after graduated cessation of imipramine in children. *American Journal of Psychiatry,* 138:647–650.

Lesse, S. (1975). The range of therapies in the treatment of severely depressed suicidal patients. *American Journal of Psychotherapy,* 29:308–326.

Lester, D., & Beck, A. T. (1977). Suicidal wishes and depression in suicidal indicators: A comparison with attempted suicides. *Journal of Clinical Psychology,* 33:92–94.

Levenson, M., & Neuringer, C. (1971). Problem-solving behavior in suicidal adolescents. *Journal of Consulting and Clinical Psychology,* 37:433–436.

Lewis, M., & Solnit, A. J. (1963). The adolescent in a suicidal crisis: Collaborative care on a pediatric ward. *Modern Perspectives in Child Development,* Eds. A. Solnit & S. Provence. International Universities Press, New York.

Litman, R. E., & Tabachnick, N. D. (1968). Psychoanalytic theories of suicide. In *Suicidal Behaviors, Diagnosis, and Management,* Ed. H. L. P. Resnick. Little, Brown, Boston.

Lloyd, C. (1980). Life events and depressive disorder reviewed. *Archives of General Psychiatry,* 37:541–548.

Lowental, U. (1976). Suicide—The other side. *Archives of General Psychiatry,* 33:838–842.

Lukens, E., Puig-Antich, J., Behn, J., Goetz, R., Tabrizi, M. A., & Davies, M. (1983). Reliability of the psychosocial schedule for school-age children. *Journal of the American Academy of Child Psychiatry,* 22:29–39.

Lukianowicz, N. (1968). Attempted suicide in children. *Acta Psychiatrica Scandinavica,* 44:415–435.

Mack, J. E., & Hickler, H. (1981). *Vivienne: The Life and Suicide of an Adolescent Girl.* Little, Brown, Boston.

Malmquist, C. P. (1971). Depressions in childhood and adolescence. *New England Journal of Medicine,* 284:887–893.

Maltsberger, J. T., & Buie, D. H. (1974). Countertransference hate in the treatment of suicidal patients. *Archives of General Psychiatry,* 30:625–633.

Mattsson, A., Seese, L. R., & Hawkins, J. W. (1969). Suicidal behavior as a child psychiatric emergency. *Archives of General Psychiatry,* 20:100–109.

McIntire, M. S., & Angle, C. R. (1970). The taxonomy of suicide as seen in poison control centers. *Pediatric Clinics of North America,* 17:697–706.

McKnew, D. H., & Cytryn, L. (1979) Urinary metabolites in chronically depressed children. *Journal of the American Academy of Child Psychiatry,* 18:608–615.

McKnew, D. H., Jr., Cytryn, L., Efron, A. M., Gershon, E. S., & Bunney, W. E., Jr. (1979). Offspring of patients with affective disorders. *British Journal of Psychiatry,* 134: 148–152.

Melear, J. D. (1973). Children's conceptions of death. *Journal of Genetic Psychology,* 123: 359–360.

Menninger, K. (1933). Psychoanalytic aspects of suicide. *International Journal of Psycho-Analysis,* 14:376–390.

Millay, E. St. V. (1956). From a very little sphinx. In *Collected Poems by Edna St. Vincent Millay.* Harper & Row, New York. p. 264.

Morrison, G. C., & Collier, J. G. (1969). Family treatment approaches to suicidal children and adolescents. *Journal of the American Academy of Child Psychiatry,* 8:140–153.

Morselli, H., (1881). *Der Selbstmord.* International Bibliothek, Leipzig, p. 210.

Murphy, G. E., & Wetzel, R. D. (1980). Suicide risk by birth cohort in the United States, 1949–1974. *Archives of General Psychiatry,* 37:510–523.

Murphy, G. E., & Wetzel, R. D. (1982). Family history of suicidal behavior among suicide attempters. *Journal of Nervous and Mental Disease,* 170:86–90.

Myers, K. M., Burke, P., & McCauley, E. (1985). Suicidal behavior by hospitalized preadolescent children on a psychiatric unit. *Journal of the American Academy of Child Psychiatry,* 24:474–480.

Nagy, M. (1948). The child's theories concerning death. *Journal of Genetic Psychology*, 73:3–27.

Ninan, P. T., Van Kammen, D. P., Scheinin, M., Linnoila, M., Bunney, W. E., & Goodwin, F. K. (1984). CSF 5-hydroxyindoleacetic acid levels in suicidal schizophrenic patients. *American Journal of Psychiatry*, 141:566–569.

Oppenheim, D. E. (1910). A report on Dr. Baer's publication *Suicide in Childhood. Minutes of the Vienna Psychoanalytic Society*, 2:479–497.

Orbach, I., & Glaubman, H. (1978). Suicidal, aggressive and normal children's perception of personal and impersonal death. *Journal of Clinical Psychology*, 34:850–857.

Orbach, I., & Glaubman, H. (1979). The concept of death and suicidal behavior in young children: Three case studies. *Journal of the American Academy of Child Psychiatry*, 18:668–678.

Oremland, J. D. (1973). The jinx game. *Psychoanalytic Study of the Child*, 28:419–432.

Orvaschel, H., Puig-Antich, J., Chambers, W., Tabrizi, M. A., & Johnson, R. L. (1982). Retrospective assessment of prepubertal major depression with the Kiddie-SADS-E. *Journal of the American Academy of Child Psychiatry*, 21:392–397.

Orvaschel, H., Weissman, M. M., & Kidd, K. K. (1980). Children and depression. *Journal of Affective Disorders*, 2:1–16.

Paulson, M. J., Stone, D., & Sposto, R. (1978). Suicide potential and behavior in children ages 4 to 12. *Suicide and Life-Threatening Behavior*, 8:225–242.

Paykel, E. S., Myers, J. H., Lindenthal, J. J., & Tanner, J. (1974). Suicidal feelings in the general population: A prevalence study. *British Journal of Psychiatry*, 124:460–469.

Peller, L. E. (1954). Libidinal phases, ego development, and play. *Psychoanalytic Study of the Child*, 9:179–198.

Persier, E. (1899). Le suicide chez l'enfant et l'adolescent. *Annales de Médecine et de l'Enfant*, p. 821.

Petti, T. A., & Law, W., III (1981). Abrupt cessation of high dose imipramine treatment in children. *Journal of the American Medical Association*, 246:768–769.

Petty, L. K., Asarnow, J. R., Carlson, G. A., & Lesser, L. (1985). The dexamethasone suppression test in depressed, dysthymic, and non-depressed children. *American Journal of Psychiatry*, 142:631–633.

Pfeffer, C. R. (1977). Psychiatric hospital treatment of suicidal children. *Suicide and Life-Threatening Behavior*, 8:150–160.

Pfeffer, C. R. (1979a). Clinical observations of play of hospitalized suicidal children. *Suicide and Life-Threatening Behavior*, 9:235–244.

Pfeffer, C. R. (1979b). A model for acute psychiatric inpatient treatment of latency-age children. *Hospital and Community Psychiatry*, 30:547–551.

Pfeffer, C. R. (1980). Parental suicide: An organizing event in the development of latency age children. *Suicide and Life-Threatening Behavior*, 11:43–50.

Pfeffer, C. R. (1981a). The family system of suicidal children. *American Journal of Psychotherapy*, 35:330–341.

Pfeffer, C. R. (1981b). Suicidal behavior of children: A review with implications for research and practice. *American Journal of Psychiatry*, 138:154–159.

Pfeffer, C. R. (1982). Clinical observations of suicidal behavior in a neurotic, a borderline, and a psychotic child: Common processes of symptom formation. *Child Psychiatry and Human Development*, 13:120–124.

Pfeffer, C. R. (1983). *Preoccupations with Death in "Normal" Children: The Relationship to Suicidal Behavior*. Paper presented at the symposium "The Child's Concept of Death," The Foundation of Thanatology, New York.

Pfeffer, C. R., Conte, H. R., Plutchik, R., & Jerrett, I. (1979). Suicidal behavior in latency-age children: An empirical study. *Journal of the American Academy of Child Psychiatry*, 18:679–692.

Pfeffer, C. R., Conte, H. R., Plutchik, R., & Jerrett, I. (1980). Suicidal behavior in latency-age children: An empirical study: An outpatient population. *Journal of the American Academy of Child Psychiatry*, 19:703–710.

Pfeffer, C. R., & Plutchik, R. (1982). Psychopathology of latency-age children: Relation to treatment planning. *Journal of Nervous and Mental Disease*, 17:193–197.

Pfeffer, C. R., Plutchik, R., & Mizruchi, M. S. (1983). Suicidal and assaultive behavior in children: Classification, measurement, and interrelations. *American Journal of Psychiatry*, 140:154–157.

Pfeffer, C. R., Plutchik, R., Mizruchi, M.S., & Lipkins, R. (1986). Suicidal behavior in child psychiatric inpatients and outpatients and in nonpatients. *American Journal of Psychiatry*, 143: 733-788.

Pfeffer, C. R., Solomon, G., Plutchik, R., Mizruchi, M. S., & Weiner, A. (1982). Suicidal behavior in latency-age psychiatric inpatients: A replication and cross-validation. *Journal of the American Academy of Child Psychiatry*, 21:564–569.

Pfeffer, C. R., Zuckerman, S., Plutchik, R., & Mizruchi, M. S. (1984). Suicidal behavior in normal school children: A comparison with child psychiatric inpatients. *Journal of the American Academy of Child Psychiatry*, 23:416–423.

Philips, I. (1979). Childhood depression: Interpersonal interactions and depressive phenomena. *American Journal of Psychiatry*, 136:511–515.

Picker, M., Poling, A., & Parker, A. (1979). A review of children's self-injurious behavior. *Psychological Record*, 29:435–452.

Pierce, D. W. (1977). Suicidal intent in self-injury. *British Journal of Psychiatry*, 130:377–385.

Poznanski, E. O., Carroll, B. J., Banegas, M. C., Cook, S. C., & Grossman, J. A. (1982). The dexamethasone suppression test in prepubertal depressed children. *American Journal of Psychiatry*, 139:321–324.

Poznanski, E. O., Cook, S. C., & Carroll, B. J. (1979). A depression rating scale for children. *Pediatrics*, 64:442–450.

Poznanski, E. D., Grossman, J. A., Buchsbaum, Y., Banegas, M., Freeman, L., & Gibbons, R. (1984). Preliminary studies of the reliability and validity of the Children's Depression Rating Scale. *Journal of the American Academy of Child Psychiatry*, 23:191–197.

Poznanski, E. O., Krahenbuhl, V., & Zrull, J. P. (1976). Childhood depression: A longitudinal perspective. *Journal of the American Academy of Child Psychiatry*, 15:491–501.

Poznanski, E. P., & Zrull, J. P. (1970). Childhood depression: Clinical characteristics of overtly depressed children. *Archives of General Psychiatry*, 23:8–15.

Preskorn, S. H., Weller, E. B., & Weller, R. (1982). Depression in children: Relationship between plasma imipramine levels and response. *Journal of Clinical Psychiatry*, 43:450–453.

Puig-Antich, J. (1980). Affective disorders in childhood: A review and perspective. *Psychiatric Clinics of North America*, 3:403–424.

Puig-Antich, J. (1982). Major depressive and conduct disorder in prepuberty. *Journal of the American Academy of Child Psychiatry*, 21:118–128.

Puig-Antich, J., Blau, S., Marx, N., Greenhill, L., & Chambers, W. (1978). Prepubertal major depressive disorder: A pilot study. *Journal of the American Academy of Child Psychiatry*, 17:695–707.

Puig-Antich, J., Goetz, R., Hanlon, C., Davies, M., Thompson, J., Chambers, W. J., Tabrizi, M. A., & Weitzman, E. D. (1982). Sleep architecture and REM sleep measures in prepubertal children with major depression. *Archives of General Psychiatry*, 39:932–939.

Puig-Antich, J., Goetz, R., Hanlon, C., Tabrizi, M. A., Davis, M., & Weitzman, E. D. (1983). Sleep architecture and REM sleep measures in prepubertal major depressives. *Archives of General Psychiatry*, 40:187–192.

Puig-Antich, J., Lukens, E., Davies, M., Goetz, D., Brennan-Quattrock, J., & Todak, G. (1985a). Psychosocial functioning in prepubertal major depressive disorders: Interpersonal relationships during the depressive episode. *Archives of General Psychiatry*, 42:500–507.

Puig-Antich, J., Lukens, E., Davies, M., Goetz, D., Brennan-Quattrock, J., & Todak, G. (1985b). Psychosocial functioning in prepubertal major depressive disorders: II. Interpersonal relationships after sustained recovery from affective episode. *Archives of General Psychiatry*, 42:511–517.

Puig-Antich, J., Novacenko, H., Goetz, R., Corser, J., Davies, M., & Ryan, N. (1984). Cortisol and prolactin responses to insulin-induced hypoglycemia in prepubertal major depressives during episode and recovery. *Journal of the American Academy of Child Psychiatry*, 13:49–57.

Puig-Antich, J., & Weston, B. (1983). The diagnosis and treatment of major depressive disorder in childhood. *Annual Review of Medicine*, 34:231–245.

Pynoos, R., Gilmore, K., & Shapiro, T. (1981). *The Response of Children to Parental Suicidal Acts*. Paper presented at the 28th Annual Meeting of the American Academy of Child Psychiatry, Dallas.

Richman, J. (1978). Symbiosis, empathy, suicidal behavior, and the family. *Suicide and Life-Threatening Behavior*, 8:139–149.

Richman, J. (1981). Suicide and the family: Affective disturbances and their implications for understanding, diagnosis, and treatment. In *Family Therapy and Major Psychopathology*, Ed. M. R. Lansky. Grune & Stratton, New York.

Rie, H. E. (1966). Depression in childhood: A survey of some pertinent contributors. *Journal of the American Academy of Child Psychiatry*, 5:653–685.

Robbins, D. R., & Alessi, N. E. (1985a). Depressive symptoms and suicidal behavior in adolescents. *American Journal of Psychiatry*, 142:588–592.

Robbins, D. R., & Alessi, N. E. (1985b). Suicide and the dexamethasone suppression test in adolescence. *Biological Psychiatry*, 20:107–110.

Robins, E., Murphy, G. E., Wilkinson, R. H., Jr., Gassner, S., & Kayes, J. (1959). Some clinical considerations in the prevention of suicide based on a study of 134 successful suicides. *American Journal of Public Health*, 49:888–899.

Rochlin, G. (1965). *Griefs and Discontents*. Little, Brown, Boston.

Rockwell, D. A., Winget, C. M., Rosenblatt, L. S., Higgins, E. A., & Hetherington, N. W. (1978). Biological aspects of suicide. *Journal of Nervous and Mental Disease*, 166:851–858.

Rosenthal, P. A., & Rosenthal, S. (1984). Suicidal behavior by preschool children. *American Journal of Psychiatry*, 141:520–525.

Roy, A. (1980). Early parental loss in depressive neurosis compared with other neurosis. *Canadian Journal of Psychiatry*, 25:503–505.

Rush, A. J., & Beck, A. T. (1978). Cognitive therapy of depression and suicide. *American Journal of Psychotherapy*, 32:201–219.

Sabbath, J. C. (1969). The suicidal adolescent—The expendable child. *Journal of the American Academy of Child Psychiatry*, 8:272–289.

Safier, G. (1964). A study in relationships between the life and death concepts in children. *Journal of Genetic Psychology*, 105:283–294.

Sandler, J., & Joffe, W. G. (1965). Notes on childhood depression. *International Journal of Psycho-Analysis*, 46:88–96.

Santostefano, S., Rieder, C., & Beck, S. A. (1984). The structure of fantasied movement in suicidal children and adolescents. *Suicide and Life-Threatening Behavior*, 14(1):3–16.

Sarnoff, C. (1976). *Latency*. Aronson, New York.

Sathyavathi, K. (1975). Suicide among children in Bangalore. *Indian Journal of Pediatrics*, 42:149–157.

Schecter, M. D. (1957). The recognition and treatment of suicide in children. In *Clues to Suicide*, Eds. E. Shneidman & N. Farberow. Blakiston, New York.

Shaffer, D. (1974). Suicide in childhood and early adolescence. *Journal of Child Psychology and Psychiatry*, 15:275–291.

Shaffer, D., & Fisher, P. (1981). The epidemiology of suicide in children and young adolescents. *Journal of the American Academy of Child Psychiatry*, 20:545–565.

Shafii, M., Carrigan, S., Whittinghill, J. R., & Derrick, A. (1985). Psychological autopsy of completed suicide in children and adolescents. *American Journal of Psychiatry*, 142:1061–1064.

Shepherd, D. M., & Barraclough, B. M. (1976). The aftermath of parental suicide for children. *British Journal of Psychiatry*, 129:267–276.

Shintoub, S. A., & Soulairac, A. (1961). L'enfant auto-mutilateur. *Psychiatry Enfant*, 3:119.

Shneidman, E. S. (1975). Suicide. In *Comprehensive Textbook of Psychiatry II*, Eds. H. Kaplan & B. Sadock. Williams & Wilkins, Baltimore.

Shneidman, E. S. (1980). *Voices of Death*. Harper & Row, New York.

Shneidman, E. S. (1985). *Definition of Suicide*. Wiley, New York.

Siegert, G. (1893). *Das Problem der Kinderselbstmude*. Leipzig.

Silver, M. A., Bohnert, M., Beck, A. T., & Marcus, D. (1971). Relation of depression of attempted suicide and seriousness of intent. *Archives of General Psychiatry*, 25: 573–576.

Solomon, M. E., & Hellon, C. P. (1980). Suicide and age in Alberta, Canada 1951–1977: A cohort analysis. *Archives of General Psychiatry*, 37:511–513.

Spitz, R. (1945). Hospitalism: An inquiry into the genesis of psychiatric conditions in early childhood. *Psychoanalytic Study of the Child*, 1:53–75.

Spitz, R. (1946). Anaclitic depression. *Psychoanalytic Study of the Child*, 2:313–342.

Spitzer, R. L., & Endicott, J. (1977). *Schedule for Affective Disorders and Schizophrenia (SADS)* (3rd ed.). New York State Psychiatric Institute, New York.

Stallone, F., Dunner, D. L., Ahearn, J., & Fieve, R. R. (1980). Statistical predictors of suicide in depressives. *Comprehensive Psychiatry*, 21:381–387.

Stanley, M., Virgilio, J., & Gershin, S. (1982). Tritiated imipramine binding sites are decreased in the frontal cortex of suicides. *Science*, 216:1337–1339.

Stengel, E. (1962). Recent research into suicide and attempted suicide. *American Journal of Psychiatry*, 118:725–727.

Sterba, E. (1951). The schoolboy suicide in André Gide's novel *The Counterfeiters*. *American Imago*, 8:307–320.

Stone, M. (1980). The suicidal patient: Points concerning diagnosis and intensive treatment. *Psychiatric Quarterly*, 52:52–70.

Tabachnick, N. (1961). Countertransference crisis in suicidal attempts. *Archives of General Psychiatry*, 4:572–578.

Tabachnick, N., Litman, R. E., Osman, M., Jones, W. L., Cohn, J., Kasper, A., & Moffat, J. (1966). Comparative psychiatric study of accidental and suicide death. *Archives of General Psychiatry*, 14:60–68.

Targum, S. D. (1981). Dexamethasone suppression test in prepubertal conduct disorder. *Psychiatry Research*, 5:107–108.

Tenant, C., Bibbington, P., & Hurry, J. (1980). Parental death in childhood and risk of adult depression disorders: A review. *Psychological Medicine*, 10:289–299.

Tishler, C. L., & McKenry, P. C. (1982). Parental negative self and adolescent suicide attempts. *Journal of the American Academy of Child Psychiatry*, 21:404–408.

Tishler, C. L., McKenry, P. C., & Morgan, K. C. (1981). Adolescent suicide attempts: Some significant factors. *Suicide and Life-Threatening Behavior*, 11:86–92.

Toolan, J. M. (1962). Depression in children and adolescents. *American Journal of Orthopsychiatry*, 32:404–414.

Toolan, J. M. (1978). Therapy of depressed and suicidal children. *American Journal of Psychotherapy*, 32:243–251.

Toolan, J. M. (1980). Depression and suicidal behavior. In *Treatment of Emotional Disorders in Children and Adolescents*, Ed. P. Sholevar. Spectrum, New York.

Traskman, L., Asberg, M., Bertilsson, L., & Sjostrand, L. (1981). Monoamine metabolites in CSF and suicidal behavior. *Archives of General Psychiatry*, 38:631–636.

Tsuang, M. T. (1977). Genetic factors in suicide. *Diseases of the Nervous System*, 38:498–501.

Tsuang, M. T. (1978). Suicide in schizophrenics, manics, depressives, and surgical controls. *Archives of General Psychiatry*, 35:153–155.

Twain, M. (1980). *The Adventures of Tom Sawyer*. New American Library, New York.

United States Monthly Vital Statistics. (1979). Unpublished.

United States Monthly Vital Statistics. (1980). Unpublished.

United States Monthly Vital Statistics. (1982). Vol. 31.

United States Monthly Vital Statistics. (1984). Vol. 33.

Von Hug-Hellmuth, H. (1965). The child's concept of death. *Psychoanalytic Quarterly*, 34:499–516.

Waelder, R. (1933). The psychoanalytic theory of play. *Psychoanalytic Quarterly*, 2:208–224.

Wass, H. & Scott, M. (1978). Middle school students' death concepts and concerns. *Middle School Journal*, 9:10–12.

Weinberg, W. A., Rutman, J., Sullivan, L., Penick, E. C., & Dietz, S. G. (1973). Depression in children referred to an educational diagnostic center: Diagnosis and treatment. *Journal of Pediatrics*, 83:1065–1072.

Weiner, A., & Pfeffer, C. R. (1983). *Cognition, Depression, and Suicidal Behavior in Child Psychiatric Inpatients*. Paper presented at the Annual Meeting of the American Orthopsychiatric Association, Boston.

Weingartner, H., Cohen, R. M., Murphy, D. L., Martello, J., & Gerdt, C. (1981). Cognitive processes in depression. *Archives of General Psychiatry*, 38:42–47.

Weissman, M. (1974). The epidemiology of suicide attempts, 1960 to 1971. *Archives of General Psychiatry*, 30:737–746.

Weissman, M. M., Prusoff, B. A., Gammon, G. D., Merikangas, K. R., Leckman, J., & Kidd, K. K. (1984). Psychopathology in the children (ages 6–18) of depressed and normal parents. *Journal of the American Academy of Child Psychiatry*, 23:78–84.

Weller, E. B., Weller, R. A., Fristad, M. A., & Preskorn, S. H. (1984). The dexamethasone suppression test in hospitalized prepubertal depressed children. *American Journal of Psychiatry*, 141:290–291.

Welner, Z., Welner, A., McCrary, D., & Leonard, M. A. (1977). Psychopathology in children of inpatients with depression: A controlled study. *Journal of Nervous and Mental Disease*, 164:408–413.

Wenz, F. V. (1979). Family constellation factors, depression, and parent suicide potential. *American Journal of Orthopsychiatry*, 49:164–167.

Wetzel, R. D. (1976). Hopelessness, depression, and suicide intent. *Archives of General Psychiatry*, 33:1069–1073.

Winnicott, D. W. (1944). Ocular psychoneurosis of childhood. In *Collected Papers*. Tavistock, London.

Winnicott, D. W. (1971). *Playing and Reality*. Basic Books, New York.

Zilboorg, G. (1936). Suicide among civilized and primitive races. *American Journal of Psychiatry*, 92:1348–1369.

Zilboorg, G. (1937). Considerations on suicide, with particular reference to that of the young. *American Journal of Orthopsychiatry*, 7:15–31.

Zung, W. W. K. (1965). A self-rating depression scale. *Archives of General Psychiatry*, 12:63–70.

AUTHOR INDEX

Ackerly, W. C., 155, 156, 165, 213, 219, 291n.
Adam, K. S., 141, 291n.
Adams-Tucker, C., 129, 291n.
Agren, H., 76, 291n.
Ahearn, J., 67, 301n.
Alarron, O., 232, 291n.
Albala, A. A., 73, 292n.
Aleksandrowicz, M. K., 145, 291n.
Alessi, N. E., 69, 75, 300n.
Amir, A., 27, 291n.
Anastasio, M. M., 131, 295n.
Anderson, J. C., 104, 296n.
Angle, C. R., 18, 297n.
Anthony, E. J., 85, 291n.
Anthony, S., 109, 291n.
Arana, G. W., 73, 291n.
Arnow, H., 291n.
Asarnow, J. R., 75, 298n.
Asberg, M., 4, 76, 291n., 302n.

Baer, A., 4, 76, 291n.
Banegas, M. E., 90, 294n.
Barbero, G. L., 104, 295n.
Barraclough, B. M., 142, 301n.
Barreira, P. J., 73, 291n.
Bartko, J. J., 133, 293n.
Beardslee, W. R., 132, 133, 291n.
Beck, A. T., 60, 61, 65, 67, 87, 269, 291n., 296n., 297n., 300n., 301n.
Beck, R., 61, 291n.
Beck, S. A., 197, 300n.
Behn, J., 106, 297n.
Bemporard, J., 132, 133, 291n.
Bender, L., 8, 33, 49, 164, 292n.
Benegas, M., 74, 93, 299n.
Beres, D., 155, 292n.
Berman, A. L., 35, 70, 125, 209,

236, 270, 292n., 293n.
Berndt, D. J., 157, 292n.
Bertilsson, L., 76, 302n.
Bibbington, P., 141, 301n.
Blau, S., 266, 299n.
Boersma, F. J., 156, 292n.
Bohnert, M., 60, 65, 301n.
Bolander, F. D., 104, 295n.
Bonney, W. E., 76, 292n.
Bouckoms, A., 141, 291n.
Bowlby, J., 83, 185, 292n.
Brennan-Quattrack, J., 106, 300n.
Brent, S. B., 109, 292n.
Brown, F., 91, 295n.
Brown, G. L., 76, 292n.
Brumback, R. A., 158, 292n.
Buchsbaum, Y., 90, 93, 294n., 299n.
Buil, D. H., 190, 297n.
Bunney, W. E., 84, 93, 293n., 297n., 298n.
Burke, P., 131, 297n.
Burlingham, D., 155, 292n.

Cain, A. C., 139, 292n.
Calhoun, L. G., 125, 292n.
Campbell, W., 91, 295n.
Cantwell, D. P., 69, 80, 104, 131, 156, 217, 292n., 295n.
Caprio, F. S., 109, 292n.
Carlson, G. A., 16, 69, 75, 80, 104, 117, 131, 156, 217, 292n., 293n., 298n.
Carrigan, S., 28, 301n.
Carroll, B. J., 73, 74, 93, 292n., 299n.
Chadwick, M., 109, 292n.
Chambers, W., 78, 88, 89, 90, 266, 292n., 298n., 299n.

303

SUBJECT INDEX